PEARSON   ALWAYS LEARNING

Henry M. Sayre

The Humanities: Culture, Continuity and Change
Second Edition

Custom Edition for Waubonsee Community College:
The Global Village, Volume I

Taken from:
The Humanities: Culture Continuity & Change, Second Edition
Volume I: Prehistory to 1600
by Henry M. Sayre

Cover Art: Courtesy of Photodisc, Stockbyte, Digital Vision, Purestock/Getty Images.

Taken from:

The Humanities: Culture, Continuity & Change, Second Edition
Volume I: Prehistory to 1600
by Henry M. Sayre
Copyright © 2012, 2008 by Pearson Education, Inc.
Published by Prentice Hall
Upper Saddle River, New Jersey 07458

This special edition published in cooperation with Pearson Learning Solutions.

All trademarks, service marks, registered trademarks, and registered service marks are the property of their respective owners and are used herein for identification purposes only.

Pearson Learning Solutions, 501 Boylston Street, Suite 900, Boston, MA 02116
A Pearson Education Company
www.pearsoned.com

Printed in the United States of America

10 V0ZN 16 15 14

000200010270766096

CT

ISBN 10: 1-256-35844-4
ISBN 13: 978-1-256-35844-2

SERIES CONTENTS

CONTENTS

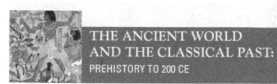

7 Other Empires
URBAN LIFE AND IMPERIAL MAJESTY IN CHINA AND INDIA 213

9 The Rise and Spread of Islam
A NEW RELIGION 285

DEAR READER,

You might be asking yourself, why should I be interested in the Humanities? Why do I care about ancient Egypt, medieval France, or the Qing Dynasty of China?

I asked myself the same question when I was a sophomore in college. I was required to take a year long survey of the Humanities, and I soon realized that I was beginning an extraordinary journey. That course taught me where it was that I stood in the world, and why and how I had come to find myself there. My goal in this book is to help you take the same journey of discovery. Exploring the humanities will help you develop your abilities to look, listen, and read closely; and to analyze, connect, and question. In the end, this will help you navigate your world and come to a better understanding of your place in it.

What we see reflected in different cultures is something of ourselves, the objects of beauty and delight, the weapons and wars, the melodies and harmonies, the sometimes troubling but always penetrating thought from which we spring. To explore the humanities is to explore ourselves, to understand how and why we have changed over time, even as we have, in so many ways, remained the same.

I've come to think of this second edition in something of the same terms. What I've tried to do is explore new paths of inquiry even as I've tried to keep the book recognizably the same. My model, I think, has been Bob Dylan. Over the years, I've heard the man perform more times than I can really recall, and I just saw him again in concert this past summer. He has been performing "Highway 61" and "Just Like a Woman" for nearly fifty years, but here they were again, in new arrangements that were totally fresh—recognizably the same, but reenergized and new. That should be the goal of any new edition of a book, I think, and I hope I've succeeded in that here.

ABOUT THE AUTHOR

Henry M. Sayre is Distinguished Professor of Art History at Oregon State University–Cascades Campus in Bend, Oregon. He earned his Ph.D. in American Literature from the University of Washington. He is producer and creator of the 10-part television series, *A World of Art: Works in Progress*, aired on PBS in the Fall of 1997; and author of seven books, including *A World of Art*, *The Visual Text of William Carlos Williams*, *The Object of Performance: The American Avant-Garde since 1970*; and an art history book for children, *Cave Paintings to Picasso*.

The Humanities: Culture, Continuity & Change helps students see context and make connections across the humanities by tying together the entire cultural experience through a narrative storytelling approach. Written around Henry Sayre's belief that students learn best by remembering stories rather than memorizing facts, it captures the voices that have shaped and influenced human thinking and creativity throughout our history.

With a stronger focus on engaging students in the critical thinking process, this new edition encourages students to deepen their understanding of how cultures influence one another, how ideas are exchanged and evolve over time, and how this collective process has led us to where we stand today. With several new features, this second edition helps students to understand context and make connections across time, place, and culture.

To prepare the second edition, we partnered with our current users to hear what was successful and what needed to be improved. The feedback we received through focus groups, online surveys, and reviews helped shape and inform this new edition. For instance, to help students make stronger global connections, the organization of the text and the Table of Contents have been modified. As an example, reflections of this key goal can be seen in Chapters 6 and 7, which are now aligned to show parallels more easily in the developments of urban culture and imperial authority between Rome, China, and India.

Through this dialogue, we also learned how humanities courses are constantly evolving. We learned that more courses are being taught online and that instructors are exploring new ways to help their students engage with course material. We developed MyArtsLab with these needs in mind. With powerful online learning tools integrated into the book, the online and textbook experience is more seamless than ever before. In addition, there are wonderful interactive resources that you, as the instructor, can bring directly into your classroom.

All of these changes can be seen through the new, expanded, or improved features shown here.

SEE CONTEXT AND MAKE CONNECTIONS . . .

NEW
THINKING AHEAD

These questions open each chapter and represent its major sections, leading students to think critically and focus on important issues.

NEW
THINKING BACK

These end-of-chapter reviews follow up on the **Thinking Ahead** questions, helping students further engage with the material they've just read and stimulate thought and discussion.

NEW
CLOSER LOOK

Previously called "Focus" in the first edition, these highly visual features offer an in-depth look at a particular work from one of the disciplines of the humanities. The annotated discussions give students a personal tour of the work–with informative captions and labels–to help students understand its meaning. A new critical thinking question, *Something to Think About*, prompts students to make connections and further apply this detailed knowledge of the work.

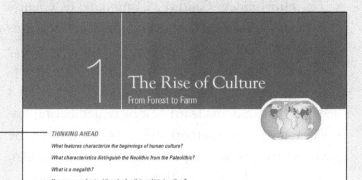

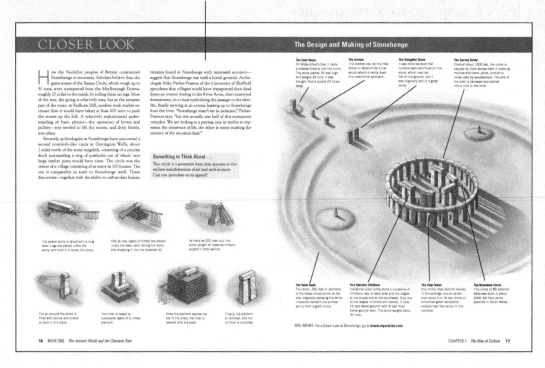

CONTINUITY & CHANGE ESSAYS

These full-page essays at the end of each chapter illustrate the influence of one cultural period upon another and show cultural changes over time.

CONTINUITY & CHANGE ICONS

These in-text references provide a window into the past. The eye-catching icons enable students to refer to material in other chapters that is relevant to the topic at hand.

CONTINUITY & CHANGE

The Pyramids of Menkaure, **p. 74**

CONTEXT

These boxes summarize important background information in an easy-to-read format.

MATERIALS AND TECHNIQUES

These features explain and illustrate the methods artists and architects use to produce their work.

CONTINUITY & CHANGE

Representing the Power of the Animal World

The two images shown here in some sense bracket the six volumes of *The Humanities*. The first (Fig. 1.24), from the Chauvet Cave, is one of the earliest known drawings of a horse. The second (Fig. 1.25), a drawing by contemporary American painter Susan Rothenberg (b. 1945), also represents a horse, though in many ways less realistically than the cave drawing. The body of Rothenberg's horse seems to have disappeared and, eyeless, as if blinded, it leans forward, its mouth open, choking or gagging or gasping for air.

In his catalog essay for a 1993 retrospective exhibition of Rothenberg's painting, Michael Auping, chief curator at the Albright-Knox Museum in Buffalo, New York, described Rothenberg's kind of drawing: "Relatively spontaneous, the drawings are Rothenberg's psychic energy made imminent . . . . [They] uncover realms of the psyche that are perhaps not yet fully explicable." The same could be said of the cave drawing executed by a nameless hunter-gatherer more than 20,000 years ago. That artist's work must have seemed just as strange as Rothenberg's, lit by flickering firelight in the dark recesses of the cave, its body disappearing, too, into the darkness that surrounded it.

It seems certain that in some measure both drawings were the expression of a psychic need on the part of the artist—whether derived from the energy of the hunt or of nature itself—to fix upon a surface an image of the power and vulnerability of the animal world. That drive, which we will see in the art of the Bronze Age of the Middle East in the next chapter—for instance, in the haunting image of a dying lion in the palace complex of an Assyrian king at Nineveh—remains constant from the beginnings of art to the present day. It is the compulsion to express the inexpressible, to visualize the mind as well as the world. ∎

Fig. 1.24 Horse. Detail from Chauvet Cave, Vallon-Pont-d'Arc, Ardèche gorge, France (Fig. 1.1). ca. 30,000 BCE. Note the realistic shading that defines the volume of the horse's head. It is a realism that artists throughout history have sometimes sought to achieve, and sometimes ignored, in their efforts to express for the forces that drive them.

Fig. 1.25 Susan Rothenberg. Untitled. 1978. Acrylic, flashe, and pencil on paper, 20″ × 20″. Collection Walker Art Center, Minneapolis. Art Center Acquisition Fund, 1979. © 2008 Susan Rothenberg/Artists Rights Society (ARS), NY. Part of the eeriness of this image comes from Rothenberg's use of flashe, a French vinyl-based color that is clear and so creates a misty, ghostlike surface.

CHAPTER 1 *The Rise of Culture* 27

PRIMARY SOURCES

Each chapter of *The Humanities* includes Primary Source Readings in two formats. Brief readings from important works are included within the body of the text. Longer readings located at the end of each chapter allow for a more in-depth study of particular works. The organization offers great flexibility in teaching the course.

Materials & Techniques

Methods of Carving

Carving is the act of cutting or incising stone, bone, wood, or another material into a desired form. Surviving artifacts of the Paleolithic era were carved from stone or bone. The artist probably held a sharp instrument, such as a stone knife or a chisel, in one hand and drove it into the stone or bone with another stone held in the other hand to remove excess material and realize the figure. Finer details could be scratched into the material with a pointed stone instrument. Artists can carve into any material softer than the instrument they are using. Harder varieties of stone can cut into softer stone as well as bone. The work was probably painstakingly slow.

There are basically two types of sculpture: sculpture in the round and relief sculpture. **Sculpture in the round** is fully three-dimensional; it occupies 360 degrees of space. The Willendorf statuette (see Fig. 1.3) was carved from stone and is an example of sculpture in the round. **Relief sculpture** is carved out of a flat background surface; it has a distinct front and no back. Not all relief sculptures are

alike. In *high relief* sculpture, the figure extends more than 180 degrees from the background surface. *Woman Holding an Animal Horn,* found at Laussel, in the Dordogne region of France, is carved in high relief and is one of the earliest relief sculptures known. This sculpture was originally part of a great stone block that stood in front of a Paleolithic rock shelter. In *low or bas relief,* the figure extends less than 180 degrees from the surface. In *sunken relief,* the image is carved, or incised, into the surface, so that the image recedes below it. When a light falls on relief sculptures at an angle, the relief casts a shadow. The higher the relief, the larger the shadows and the greater the sense of the figure's three-dimensionality.

Woman Holding an Animal Horn, Laussel (Dordogne), France. ca. 30,000–15,000 BCE. Limestone, height 17 ⅓″ Musée des Antiquites Nationales, St. Germain-en-Laye, France.

EXPLORE MORE To see a studio video about carving, go to **www.myartslab.com**

(for example, "the land shattered like a pot").

Perhaps most important, the epic illuminates the development of a nation or race. It is a national poem, describing a people's common heritage and celebrating its cultural identity. It is hardly surprising, then, that Ashurbanipal preserved the *Epic of Gilgamesh.* Just as Sargon II depicted himself at the gates of Khorsabad in the traditional horned crown of Akkad and the beard of Sumer, containing within himself all Mesopotamian history, the *Epic of Gilgamesh* preserves the historical lineage of all Mesopotamian kings—Sumerian, Akkadian, Assyrian, and Babylonian. The tale embodies their own heroic grandeur, and thus the grandeur of their peoples.

The poem opens with a narrator guiding a visitor (the reader) around Uruk. The narrator explains that the epic was written by Gilgamesh himself and was deposited in the city's walls, where visitors can read it for themselves. Then the narrator introduces Gilgamesh as an epic hero, two parts god and one part human. The style of the following list of his deeds is the same as in hymns to the gods (Reading 2.3a):

READING 2.3a
from the *Epic of Gilgamesh,* Tablet I
(ca. 1200 BCE)

Supreme over other kings, lordly in appearance, he is the hero, born of Uruk, the goring wild bull. He walks out in front, the leader, and walks at the rear, trusted by his companions. Mighty net, protector of his people, raging flood-wave who destroys even walls of stone! It was he who opened the mountain passes, who dug wells on the flank of the mountain.

READINGS

READING 2.3

from the *Epic of Gilgamesh,* Tablet I (ca. 1200 BCE) (translated by Maureen Gallery Kovacs)
The Epic of Gilgamesh describes the exploits of the Sumerian ruler Gilgamesh and his friend Enkidu. The following passage, from the first of the epic's 12 tablets, recounts how Enkidu, the primal men raised beyond the reach of civilization and fully at home with wild animals, loses his animal powers, and with them his innocence, when a trapper, tired of Enkidu freeing animals from his traps, arranges for a harlot from Uruk to seduce him. The story resonates in interesting ways with the biblical tale of Adam and Eve and their loss of innocence in the Garden of Eden.

TABLET I

THE HARLOT
The trapper went, bringing the harlot, Shamhat, with him, they set off on the journey, making direct way. On the third day they arrived at the appointed place, and the trapper and the harlot sat down at their posts(?). A first day and a second they sat opposite the watering hole. The animals arrived and drank at the watering hole, the wild beasts arrived and slaked their thirst with water. Then he, Enkidu, offspring of the mountains, who eats grasses with the gazelles, came to drink at the watering hole with the animals, with the wild beasts he slaked his thirst with water. Then Shamhat saw him—a primitive, a savage fellow from the depths of the wilderness!
"That is he, Shamhat! Release your clenched arms, expose your sex so he can take in your voluptuousness.

Shamhat unclutched her bosom, exposed her sex, and he took in her voluptuousness.
She was not restrained, but took his energy.
She spread out her robe and he lay upon her, she performed for the primitive the task of womankind.
His lust groaned over her; for six days and seven nights Enkidu stayed aroused, and had intercourse with the harlot until he was sated with her charms.
But when he turned his attention to his animals, the gazelles saw Enkidu and darted off, the wild animals distanced themselves from his body. Enkidu . . . his utterly depleted (?) body, his knees that wanted to go off with his animals went rigid; Enkidu was diminished, his running was not as before. But then he drew himself up, for his understanding had broadened.

---

which Enkidu manages to interpret in a positive light. As the friends approach the forest, the god Shamash informs Gilgamesh that Humbaba is wearing only one of his seven coats of armor and is thus extremely vulnerable. When Gilgamesh and Enkidu enter the forest and begin cutting down trees, Humbaba comes roaring up to warn them off. An epic battle ensues, and Shamash intervenes to help the two heroes defeat the great guardian. Just before Gilgamesh cuts off Humbaba's head, Humbaba curses Enkidu, promising that he will find no peace in the world and will die before his friend Gilgamesh. In a gesture that clearly evokes the triumph of civilization over nature, Gilgamesh and Enkidu

SEE CONTEXT AND MAKE CONNECTIONS . . .

MORE CONNECTIONS
TO MyArtsLab

The text is keyed to the dynamic resources on MyArtsLab, allowing instructors and students online access to additional information, music, videos, and interactive features.

The **'SEE MORE'** icon correlates to the Closer Look features in the text, directing students to MyArtsLab to view interactive **Closer Look** tours online. These features enable students to zoom in to see detail they could not otherwise see on the printed page or even in person. **'SEE MORE'** icons also indicate when students can view works of architecture in full 360-degree panoramas.

No trace of the city's famous Hanging Gardens survives, once considered among the Seven Wonders of the World, and only the base and parts of the lower stairs of the Marduk ziggurat still remain. But in the fifth century BCE, the Greek historian Herodotus [he-ROD-uh-tus] (ca. 484–430/420 BCE) described the ziggurat as follows:

There was a tower of solid masonry, a furlong in length and breadth, on which was raised a second tower, and on that a third, and so on up to eight. The ascent to the top is on the outside, by a path which winds round all the towers. . . . On the topmost tower, there is a spacious temple, and inside the temple stands a couch of unusual size, richly adorned with a golden table by its side. . . . They also declare that the god comes down in person into this chamber, and sleeps on the couch, but I do not believe it.

Although the ziggurat has disappeared, we can glean some sense of the city's magnificence from the Ishtar Gate (Fig. 2.18), named after the Babylonian goddess of fertility.

Fig. 2.18 **Ishtar Gate (restored), from Babylon, ca. 575 BCE.** Glazed brick. Staedliche Museen, Berlin. The dark blue bricks are glazed—that is, covered with a film of glaze—and they would have shown brilliantly in the sun.

SEE MORE To view a Closer Look feature about the Ishtar Gate, go to **www.myartslab.com**

CHAPTER 2 *Mesopotamia* 55

Fig. 9.13 **Great Mosque of Córdoba. Begun 785, extensions 832, 950, 961–76, and 987.** The caliphs of Spain intended their mosque to rival those in Jerusalem, Damascus, and Iraq. The forest-like expanse of the interior is a result of these aspirations. Even though only 80 of the original 1,200 columns survive, the space appears infinite, like some giant hall of mirrors.

LEARN MORE View an architectural simulation of Islamic arches at **www.myartslab.com**

by the Umayyads in Toledo [toh-LEH-doh] soon was responsible for spreading the nearly forgotten texts throughout the West. Muslim mathematicians in Spain invented algebra and introduced the concept of zero to the West, and soon their Arabic numerals replaced the unwieldy Roman system. By the time of Abd ar-Rahman III (r. 912–61), Córdoba was renowned for its medicine, science, literature, and commercial wealth, and it became the most important center of learning in Europe. The elegance of Abd ar-Rahman III's court was unmatched, and his tolerance and benevolence extended to all, as Muslim students from across the Mediterranean soon found their way to the mosque-affiliated madrasa that he founded—the

earliest example of an institution of higher learning in the Western world.

Outside of Córdoba, Abd ar-Rahman III built a huge palace complex, Madinat al-Zahra, to honor his wife. (Its extensive remains are still being excavated.) Its staff included 13,750 male servants along with another 3,500 pages, slaves, and eunuchs. Its roof required the support of 4,300 columns, and elaborate gardens surrounded the site. As many as 1,200 loaves of bread were required daily just to feed the fish in the garden ponds.

The decorative arts of the era are equally impressive. A famous example is a pyxis, a small, cylindrical box with a lid, made for Prince al-Mughira, Abd ar-Rahman III's

CHAPTER 9 *The Rise and Spread of Islam* 301

The **'HEAR MORE'** icons indicate where musical performances can be listened to in streaming audio on www.myartslab.com. Online audio also includes **'Voices'**– vivid first-person accounts of the experiences of ordinary people during the period covered in the chapter.

The **'LEARN MORE'** icons lead students online for additional primary source readings or to watch architectural simulations.

The **'EXPLORE MORE'** icons direct students to videos of artists at work in their studios, allowing them to see and understand a wide variety of materials and techniques used by artists throughout time.

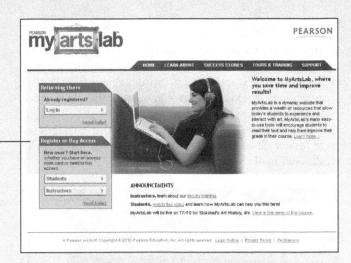

Designed to save instructors time and to improve students' results, MyArtsLab, is keyed specifically to the chapters of Sayre's *The Humanities*, second edition. In addition, MyArtsLab's many features will encourage students to experience and interact with works of art. Here are some of those key features:

• A complete **Pearson eText** of the book, enriched with multimedia, including: a unique human-scale figure by all works of fine art, an audio version of the text, primary source documents, video demonstrations, and much more. Students can highlight, make notes, and bookmark pages.

• 360-degree **Architectural Panoramas** for major monuments in the book help students understand buildings from the inside and out.

• **Closer Look Tours** These interactive walk-throughs offer an in-depth look at key works of art, enabling students to zoom in to see detail they could not otherwise see on the printed page or even in person. Enhanced with expert audio, they help students understand the meaning and message behind the work of art.

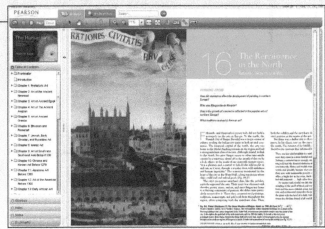

• Robust **Quizzing** and **Grading Functionality** is included in MyArtsLab. Students receive immediate feedback from the assessment questions that populate the instructor's gradebook. The gradebook reports give an in-depth look at the progress of individual students or the class as a whole.

• MyArtsLab is your one stop for instructor material. Instructors can access the Instructor's Manual, Test Item File, PowerPoint images, and the Pearson MyTest assessment-generation program.

MyArtsLab with eText is available for no additional cost when packaged with *The Humanities*, second edition. The program may also be used as a stand-alone item, which costs less than a used text.

To register for your MyArtsLab account, contact your local Pearson representative or visit the instructor registration page located on the homepage of www.myartslab.com.

FLEXIBLE FORMATS

CourseSmart eTextbooks offer the same content as the printed text in a convenient online format—with highlighting, online search, and printing capabilities. With a CourseSmart eText, student can search the text, make notes online, print out reading assignments that incorporate lecture notes, and bookmark important passages for later review. *Students save 60% over the list price of the traditional book.* www.coursesmart.com.

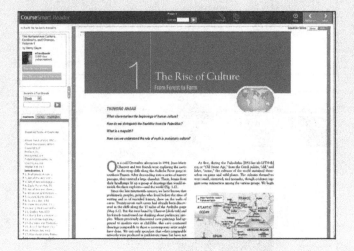

Books à la Carte editions feature the exact same text in a convenient, three-hole-punched, loose-leaf version at a discounted price—allowing students to take only what they need to class. Books à la Carte editions are available both with and without access to MyArtsLab. *Students save 35% over the net price of the traditional book.*

Custom Publishing Opportunities

The Humanities is available in a custom version specifically tailored to meet your needs. You may select the content that you would like to include or add your own original material. See you local publisher's representative for further information. www.pearsoncustom.com

INSTRUCTOR RESOURCES

Classroom Response System (CRS) In-Class Questions
Get instant, class-wide responses to beautifully illustrated chapter-specific questions during a lecture to gauge students' comprehension—and keep them engaged. Available for download under the "For Instructors" tab within your MyArtsLab account–www.myartslab.com.

Instructor's Manual and Test Item File
This is an invaluable professional resource and reference for new and experienced faculty. Each chapter contains the following sections: Chapter Overview, Chapter Objectives, Key Terms, Lecture and Discussion Topics, Resources, and Writing Assignments and Projects. The test bank includes multiple-choice, true/false, short-answer, and essay questions. Available for download from the instructor support section at www.myartslab.com.

ClassPrep

Instructors who adopt Sayre's *The Humanities* will receive access to ClassPrep, an online site designed to make lecture preparation simpler and less time-consuming. The site includes the images from the text in both high-resolution JPGs, and ready-made PowerPoint slides for your lectures. ClassPrep can be accessed through your MyArtsLab instructor account.

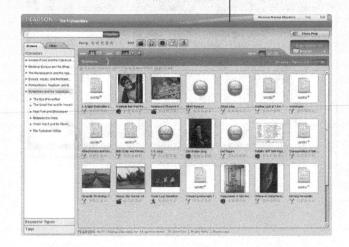

MyTest

This flexible, online test-generating software includes all questions found in the printed Test Item File. Instructors can quickly and easily create customized tests with MyTest. **www.pearsonmytest.com**

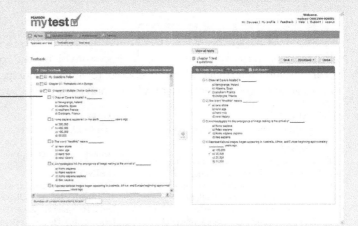

ADDITIONAL PACKAGING OPTIONS

Penguin Custom Editions: The Western World lets you choose from an archive of more than 1,800 readings excerpted from the Penguin Classics™, the most comprehensive paperback library of Western history, literature, culture, and philosophy available. You'll have the freedom to craft a reader for your humanities course that matches your teaching approach exactly! Using our online book-building system, you get to select the readings you need, in the sequence you want, at the price you want your students to pay. **www.pearsoncustom.com** keyword: penguin

 Titles from the renowned Penguin Classics series can be bundles with *The Humanities* for a nominal charge. Please contact your Pearson Arts and Sciences sales representative for details.

 The Prentice Hall Atlas of World History, second edition includes over 100 full-color maps in world history, drawn by Dorling Kindersley, one of the world's most respected cartographic publishers. Copies of the Atlas can be bundled with *The Humanities* for a nominal charge. Please contact your Pearson Arts and Sciences sales representative for details.

 Connections: Key Themes in World History. Series Editor Alfred J. Andrea. Concise and tightly focused, the titles in the popular Connections Series are designed to place the latest research on selected topics of global significance, such as disease, trade, slavery, exploration, and modernization, into an accessible format for students. Available for a 50% discount when bundled with *The Humanities*. For more information, please visit **www.pearsonhighered.com.**

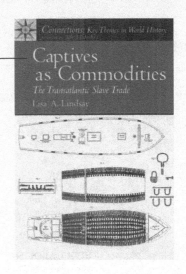

THE HUMANITIES: *CULTURE, CONTINUITY & CHANGE*

is the result of an extensive development process involving the contributions of over one hundred instructors and their students. We are grateful to all who participated in shaping the content, clarity, and design of this text. Manuscript reviewers and focus group participants include:

ALABAMA
Cynthia Kristan-Graham, Auburn University

CALIFORNIA
Collette Chattopadhyay, Saddleback College
Laurel Corona, San Diego City College
Cynthia D. Gobatie, Riverside Community College
John Hoskins, San Diego Mesa College
Gwenyth Mapes, Grossmont College
Bradley Nystrom, California State University-Sacramento
Joseph Pak, Saddleback College
John Provost, Monterey Peninsula College
Chad Redwing, Modesto Junior College
Stephanie Robinson, San Diego City College
Alice Taylor, West Los Angeles College
Denise Waszkowski, San Diego Mesa College

COLORADO
Renee Bragg, Arapahoe Community College
Marilyn Smith, Red Rocks Community College

CONNECTICUT
Abdellatif Hissouf, Central Connecticut State University

FLORIDA
Wesley Borucki, Palm Beach Atlantic University
Amber Brock, Tallahassee Community College
Connie Dearmin, Brevard Community College
Kimberly Felos, St. Petersburg College
Katherine Harrell, South Florida Community College
Ira Holmes, College of Central Florida
Dale Hoover, Edison State College
Theresa James, South Florida Community College
Jane Jones, State College of Florida, Manatee-Sarasota
Jennifer Keefe, Valencia Community College
Mansoor Khan, Brevard Community College
Connie LaMarca-Frankel, Pasco-Hernando Community College
Sandi Landis, St. Johns River Community College-Orange Park
Joe Loccisano, State College of Florida
David Luther, Edison College
James Meier, Central Florida Community College
Brandon Montgomery, State College of Florida
Pamela Wood Payne, Palm Beach Atlantic University
Gary Poe, Palm Beach Atlantic University
Frederick Smith, Florida Gateway College
Kate Myers de Vega, Palm Beach Atlantic University
Bill Waters, Pensacola State College

GEORGIA
Leslie Harrelson, Dalton State College
Lawrence Hetrick, Georgia Perimeter College
Priscilla Hollingsworth, Augusta State University
Kelley Mahoney, Dalton State College
Andrea Scott Morgan, Georgia Perimeter College

IDAHO
Jennifer Black, Boise State University
Rick Davis, Brigham Young University-Idaho
Derek Jensen, Brigham Young University-Idaho

ILLINOIS
Thomas Christensen, University of Chicago
Timothy J. Clifford, College of DuPage
Leslie Huntress Hopkins, College of Lake County
Judy Kaplow, Harper College
Terry McIntyre, Harper College
Victoria Neubeck O'Connor, Moraine Valley Community College
Sharon Quarcini, Moraine Valley Community College
Paul Van Heuklom, Lincoln Land Community College

INDIANA
Josephina Kiteou, University of Southern Indiana

KENTUCKY
Jonathan Austad, Eastern Kentucky University
Beth Cahaney, Elizabethtown Community and Technical College
Jeremy Killian, University of Louisville
Lynda Mercer, University of Louisville
Sara Northerner, University of Louisville
Elijah Pritchett, University of Louisville

MASSACHUSETTS
Peter R. Kalb, Brandeis University

MICHIGAN
Martha Petry, Jackson Community College
Robert Quist, Ferris State University

MINNESOTA
Mary Johnston, Minnesota State University

NEBRASKA
Michael Hoff, University of Nebraska

NEVADA
Chris Bauer, Sierra College

NEW JERSEY
Jay Braverman, Montclair State University
Sara E. Gil-Ramos, New Jersey City University

NEW MEXICO
Sarah Egelman, Central New Mexico Community College

NEW YORK
Eva Diaz, Pratt Institute
Mary Guzzy, Corning Community College
Thelma Ithier Sterling, Hostos Community College
Elizabeth C. Mansfield, New York University
Clemente Marconi, New York University

NORTH CAROLINA
Melodie Galloway, University of North Carolina at Asheville
Jeanne McGlinn, University of North Carolina at Asheville
Sophie Mills, University of North Carolina at Asheville
Constance Schrader, University of North Carolina at Asheville
Ronald Sousa, University of North Carolina at Asheville
Samer Traboulsi, University of North Carolina at Asheville

NORTH DAKOTA
Robert Kibler, Minot State University

OHIO
Darlene Alberts, Columbus State Community College
Tim Davis, Columbus State Community College
Michael Mangus, The Ohio State University at Newark
Keith Pepperell, Columbus State Community College
Patrice Ross, Columbus State Community College

OKLAHOMA
Amanda H. Blackman, Tulsa Community College-Northeast Campus
Diane Boze, Northeastern State University
Jacklan J. Renee Cox, Rogers State University
Jim Ford, Rogers State University
Diana Lurz, Rogers State University
James W. Mock, University of Central Oklahoma
Gregory Thompson, Rogers State University

PENNSYLVANIA
Elizabeth Pilliod, Rutgers University-Camden
Douglas B. Rosentrater, Bucks County Community College
Debra Thomas, Harrisburg Area Community College

RHODE ISLAND
Mallica Kumbera Landrus, Rhode Island School of Design

TEXAS
Mindi Bailey, Collin County Community College
Peggy Brown, Collin County Community College
Marsha Lindsay, Lone Star College-North Harris
Aditi Samarth, Richland College
Lee Ann Westman, University of Texas at El Paso

UTAH
Matthew Ancell, Brigham Young University
Terre Burton, Dixie College
Nate Kramer, Brigham Young University
Joseph D. Parry, Brigham Young University

VIRGINIA
Margaret Browning, Hampton University
Carey Freeman, Hampton University
John Long, Roanoke College
Anne Pierce, Hampton University
Jennifer Rosti, Roanoke College

No project of this scope could ever come into being without the hard work and perseverance of many more people than its author. In fact, this author has been humbled by a team at Pearson Prentice Hall that never wavered in their confidence in my ability to finish this enormous undertaking (or if they did, they had the good sense not to let me know); never hesitated to cajole, prod, and massage me to complete the project in something close to on time; and always gave me the freedom to explore new approaches to the materials at hand. At the down-and-dirty level, I am especially grateful to fact-checker, Julia Moore; to Mary Ellen Wilson for the pronunciation guides; for the more specialized pronunciations offered by David Atwill (Chinese and Japanese), Jonathan Reynolds (African), Nayla Muntasser (Greek and Latin), and Mark Watson (Native American); to Margaret Gorenstein for tracking down the readings; to Laurel Corona for her extraordinary help with Africa; to Arnold Bradford for help with critical thinking questions; and to Francelle Carapetyan for her remarkable photo research. The maps and some of the line art are the work of cartographer and artist, Peter Bull, with Precision Graphic drafting a large portion of the line art for the book. I find both in every way extraordinary.

In fact, I couldn't be more pleased with the look of the book, which is the work of Pat Smythe, senior art director. Cory Skidds, senior imaging specialist, worked on image compositing and color accuracy of the artwork. The production of the book was coordinated by Melissa Feimer, associate managing editor, Barbara Cappuccio, senior production project manager, and Marlene Gassler, production project manager, who oversaw with good humor and patience the day-to-day, hour-to-hour crises that arose. Brian Mackey, production-planning and operations specialist, ensured that this project progressed smoothly through its production route. And I want to thank Lindsay Bethoney and the staff at PreMedia Global for working so hard to make the book turn out the way I envisioned it.

The marketing and editorial teams at Prentice Hall are beyond compare. On the marketing side, Brandy Dawson, vice president of marketing, and Kate Mitchell, executive marketing manager, helped us all to understand just what students want and need. On the editorial side, my thanks to Yolanda de Rooy, president of the Social Sciences and the Arts division; to Sarah Touborg, editor-in-chief; Billy Grieco, editor; Bud Therien, special projects manager; David Nitti, assistant editor; and Theresa Graziano, editorial assistant. The combined human hours that this group has put into this project are staggering. This book was Bud's idea in the first place; Billy and Sarah have supported me every step of the way in making it as good, or even better, than I envisioned; and Yolanda's over-arching vision is responsible for helping to make Pearson such an extraordinarily good publisher to write for.

Deserving of special mention is my development team, Rochelle Diogenes, editor-in-chief of development; and Margaret Manos, development editor. Margaret has been an especially valuable partner, helping me literally to "re-vision" this revision and bringing clarity and common sense to those moments where they were lost.

Finally, I want to thank, with all my love, my beautiful wife, Sandy Brooke, who has supported this project in every way. She has continued to teach, paint, and write, while urging me on, listening to my struggles, humoring me when I didn't deserve it, and being a far better wife than I was a husband. In some ways, enduring what she did in the first edition must have been tougher in the second, since she knew what was coming from the outset. She was, is, and will continue to be, I trust, the source of my strength.

BOOK ONE

The Ancient World and the Classical Past

PREHISTORY TO 200 CE

Detail from *Nebamun Hunting Birds,* from the tomb of Nebamun, Thebes. ca. 1400 BCE (see Fig 3.2).

The history of human beings on this planet is, geologically speaking, very short. The history of their coming together in groups for their common good is even shorter, covering a span of perhaps 25,000 to 50,000 years on a planet that scientists estimate to be between 4 and 5 billion years old. We call these groups, as they become more and more sophisticated, civilizations. A **civilization** is a social, economic, and political entity distinguished by the ability to express itself through images and written language. Civilizations develop when the environment of a region can support a large and productive population. It is no accident that the first civilizations arose in fertile river valleys, where agriculture could take hold: the Tigris and the Euphrates in Mesopotamia, the Nile in Egypt, the Indus on the Indian subcontinent, and the Yellow in China. Civilizations require technologies capable of supporting the principal economy. In the ancient world, agriculture was supported by the technologies related to irrigation.

With the rise of agriculture, and with irrigation, human nature began to assert itself over and against nature as a whole. People increasingly thought of themselves as masters of their own destiny. At the same time, different and dispersed populations began to come into contact with one another as trade developed from the need for raw materials not native to a particular region. Organizing this level of trade and production also required an administrative elite to form and establish cultural priorities. The existence of such an elite is another characteristic of civilization. Finally, as the history of cultures around the world makes abundantly clear, one of the major ways in which societies have acquired the goods they want and simultaneously organized themselves is by means of war.

If a civilization is a system of organization, a **culture** is the set of common values—religious, social, and/or political—that govern that system. Out of such cultures arise scientific and artistic achievements by which we characterize different cultures. Before the invention of writing sometime around the fourth millennium BCE, these cultures created myths and legends that explained their origins and relation to the world. As we do today, ancient peoples experienced the great uncontrollable, and sometimes violent forces of nature—floods, droughts, earthquakes, and hurricanes. Prehistoric cultures understood these forces as the work of the invisible gods, who could not be approached directly but only through the mediating agency of shamans and priests, or kings and heroes. As cultures became increasingly self-assertive, in the islands between mainland Greece and Asia Minor, in Egypt, in China, on the Indian subcontinent, and on the Greek mainland, these gods seemed increasingly knowable. The gods could still intervene in human affairs, but now they did so in ways that were recognizable. It was suddenly possible to believe that if people could come to understand themselves, they might also understand the gods. The study of the natural world might well shed light on the unknown, on the truth of things.

It is to this moment—it was a long "moment," extending for centuries—that the beginnings of scientific inquiry can be traced. Humanism, the study of the human mind and its moral and ethical dimensions, was born. In China, the formalities of social interaction—moderation, personal integrity, self-control, loyalty, altruism, and justice—were codified in the writings of Confucius. In Mesopotamia and Greece, the presentation of a human character working things out (or not) in the face of adversity was the subject of epic and dramatic literature. In Greece, it was also the subject of philosophy—literally, "love of wisdom"—the practice of reasoning that followed from the Greek philosopher Socrates's famous dictum, "Know thyself." Visual artists strove to discover the perfections of human form and thought. By the time of the rise of the Roman Empire, at the end of the first millennium BCE, these traditions were carried on in more practical ways, as the Romans attempted to engineer a society embodying the values they had inherited from the Greeks.

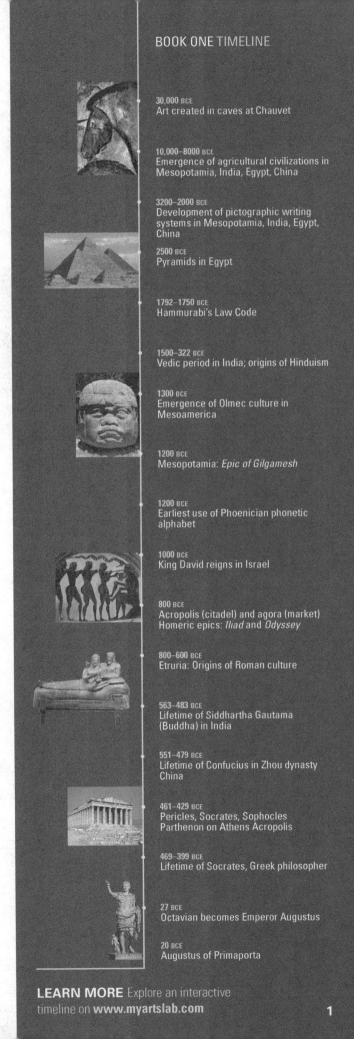

30,000 BCE
Art created in caves at Chauvet

10,000–8000 BCE
Emergence of agricultural civilizations in Mesopotamia, India, Egypt, China

3200–2000 BCE
Development of pictographic writing systems in Mesopotamia, India, Egypt, China

2500 BCE
Pyramids in Egypt

1792–1750 BCE
Hammurabi's Law Code

1500–322 BCE
Vedic period in India; origins of Hinduism

1300 BCE
Emergence of Olmec culture in Mesoamerica

1200 BCE
Mesopotamia: *Epic of Gilgamesh*

1200 BCE
Earliest use of Phoenician phonetic alphabet

1000 BCE
King David reigns in Israel

800 BCE
Acropolis (citadel) and agora (market) Homeric epics: *Iliad* and *Odyssey*

800–600 BCE
Etruria: Origins of Roman culture

563–483 BCE
Lifetime of Siddhartha Gautama (Buddha) in India

551–479 BCE
Lifetime of Confucius in Zhou dynasty China

461–429 BCE
Pericles, Socrates, Sophocles Parthenon on Athens Acropolis

469–399 BCE
Lifetime of Socrates, Greek philosopher

27 BCE
Octavian becomes Emperor Augustus

20 BCE
Augustus of Primaporta

LEARN MORE Explore an interactive timeline on **www.myartslab.com**

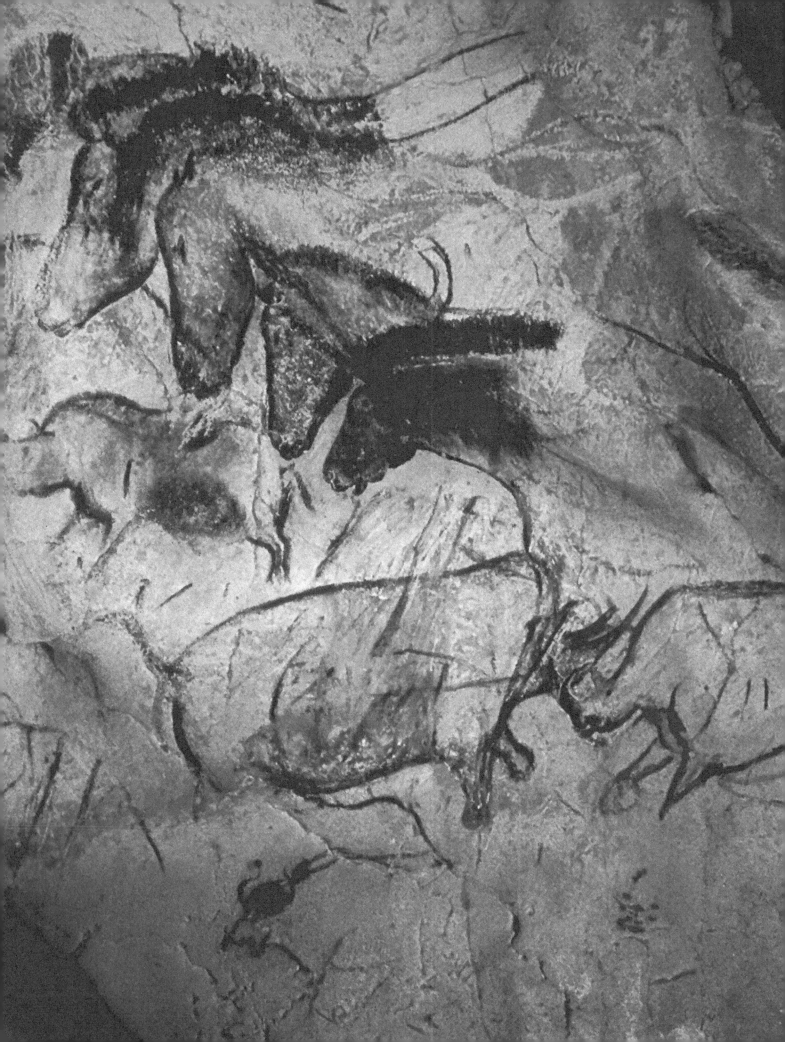

1

The Rise of Culture
From Forest to Farm

THINKING AHEAD

What features characterize the beginnings of human culture?

What characteristics distinguish the Neolithic from the Paleolithic?

What is a megalith?

How can we understand the role of myth in prehistoric culture?

On a cold December afternoon in 1994, Jean-Marie Chauvet and two friends were exploring the caves in the steep cliffs along the Ardèche River gorge in southern France. After descending into a series of narrow passages, they entered a large chamber. There, beams from their headlamps lit up a group of drawings that would astonish the three explorers—and the world (Fig. **1.1**).

Since the late nineteenth century, we have known that **prehistoric** peoples, peoples who lived before the time of writing and so of recorded history, drew on the walls of caves. Twenty-seven such caves had already been discovered in the cliffs along the 17 miles of the Ardèche gorge (Map **1.1**). But the cave found by Chauvet [shoh-veh] and his friends transformed our thinking about prehistoric peoples. Where previously discovered cave paintings had appeared to modern eyes as childlike, this cave contained drawings comparable to those a contemporary artist might have done. We can only speculate that other comparable artworks were produced in prehistoric times but have not survived, perhaps because they were made of wood or other perishable materials. It is even possible that art may have been made earlier than 30,000 years ago, perhaps as people began to inhabit the Near East, between 90,000 and 100,000 years ago.

At first, during the Paleolithic [PAY-lee-uh-LITH-ik] era, or "Old Stone Age," from the Greek *palaios*, "old," and *lithos*, "stone," the cultures of the world sustained themselves on game and wild plants. The cultures themselves were small, scattered, and nomadic, though evidence suggests some interaction among the various groups. We begin

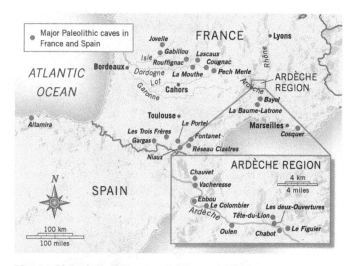

Map 1.1 Major Paleolithic caves in France and Spain.

◀ **Fig. 1.1 Wall painting with horses, Chauvet Cave, Vallon-Pont-d'Arc, Ardèche gorge, France. ca. 30,000 BCE.** Ministère de la Culture et de la Communication. Direction Regionale des Affaires Culturelles de Rhone-Alpes. Service Regional de l'Archeologie. Paint on limestone, approx. height 6'. In the center of this wall are four horses, each behind the other in a startlingly realistic space. Below them, two rhinoceroses fight.

HEAR MORE Listen to an audio file of your chapter at **www.myartslab.com**

this book, then, with the cultures of prehistoric times, evidence of which survives in wall paintings in caves and small sculptures dating back more than 25,000 years.

THE BEGINNINGS OF CULTURE IN THE PALEOLITHIC ERA

A **culture** encompasses the values and behaviors shared by a group of people, developed over time, and passed down from one generation to the next. Culture manifests itself in the laws, customs, ritual behavior, and artistic production common to the group. The cave paintings at Chauvet suggest that, as early as 30,000 years ago, the Ardèche gorge was a *center of culture*, a focal point of group living in which the values of a community find expression. There were others like it. In northern Spain, the first decorated cave was discovered in 1879 at Altamira [al-tuh-MIR-uh]. In the Dordogne [dor-DOHN] region of southern France to the west of the Ardèche, schoolchildren discovered the famous Lascaux Cave in 1940 when their dog disappeared down a hole. And in 1991, along the French Mediterranean coast, a diver discovered the entrance to the beautifully decorated Cosquer [kos-KAIR] Cave below the waterline near Marseille [mar-SAY].

Agency and Ritual: Cave Art

Ever since cave paintings were first discovered, scholars have been marveling at the skill of the people who produced them, but we have been equally fascinated by their very existence. Why were these paintings made? Most scholars believe that they possessed some sort of **agency**— that is, they were created to exert some power or authority

over the world of those who came into contact with them. Until recently, it was generally accepted that such works were associated with the hunt. Perhaps the hunter, seeking game in times of scarcity, hoped to conjure it up by depicting it on cave walls. Or perhaps such drawings were magic charms meant to ensure a successful hunt. But at Chauvet, fully 60 percent of the animals painted on its walls were never, or rarely, hunted—such animals as lions, rhinoceroses, bears, panthers, and woolly mammoths. One drawing depicts two rhinoceroses fighting horn-to-horn beneath four horses that appear to be looking on (see Fig. 1.1).

What role, then, did these drawings play in the daily lives of the people who created them? The caves may have served as some sort of **ritual** space. A ritual is a rite or ceremony habitually practiced by a group, often in religious or quasi-religious context. The caves, for instance, might be understood as gateways to the underworld and death, as symbols of the womb and birth, or as pathways to the world of dreams experienced in the dark of night, and rites connected with such passage might have been conducted in them. The general arrangement of the animals in the paintings by species or gender, often in distinct chambers of the caves, suggests to some that the paintings may have served as lunar calendars for predicting the seasonal migration of the animals. Whatever the case, surviving human footprints indicate that these caves were ritual gathering places and in some way were intended to serve the common good.

At Chauvet, the use of color suggests that the paintings served some sacred or symbolic function. For instance, almost all of the paintings near the entrance to the cave are painted with natural red pigments derived from ores rich in iron oxide. Deeper in the cave, in areas more difficult to reach, the vast majority of the animals are painted in black

Fig. 1.2 Wall painting with bird-headed man, bison, and rhinoceros, Lascaux Cave, Dordogne, France. ca. 15,000–13,000 BCE. Paint on limestone, length approx. 9′. In 1963, Lascaux was closed to the public so that conservators could fight a fungus attacking the paintings. Most likely, the fungus was caused by carbon dioxide exhaled by visitors. An exact replica called Lascaux II was built and can be visited.

pigments derived from ores rich in manganese dioxide. This shift in color appears to be intentional, but we can only guess at its meaning.

The skillfully drawn images at Chauvet raise even more important questions. The artists seem to have understood and practiced a kind of **perspectival drawing**—that is, they were able to convey a sense of three-dimensional space on a two-dimensional surface. In the painting reproduced on the opening page of this chapter, several horses appear to stand one behind the other (see Fig. 1.1). The head of the top horse overlaps a black line, as if peering over a branch or the back of another animal. In no other cave yet discovered do drawings show the use of shading, or **modeling**, so that the horses' heads seem to have volume and dimension. And yet these cave paintings, rendered over 30,000 years ago, predate other cave paintings by at least 10,000 years, and in some cases by as much as 20,000 years.

One of the few cave paintings that depicts a human figure is found at Lascaux, in the Dordogne region of southwestern France. What appears to be a male wearing a bird's-head mask lies in front of a disemboweled bison (Fig. **1.2**). Below him is a bird-headed spear thrower, a device that enabled hunters to throw a spear farther and with greater force. (Several examples of spear throwers have survived.) In the Lascaux painting, the hunter's spear has pierced the bison's hindquarters, and a rhinoceros charges off to the left. We have no way of knowing whether this was an actual event or an imagined scene. One of the painting's most interesting and inexplicable features is the discrepancy between the relatively naturalistic representation of the animals and the highly stylized, almost abstract realization of the human figure. Was the sticklike man added later by a different, less talented artist? Or does this image suggest that man and beast are different orders of being?

Before the discovery of Chauvet, historians divided the history of cave painting into a series of successive styles, each progressively more realistic. But Chauvet's paintings, by far the oldest known, are also the most advanced in their realism, suggesting the artists' conscious quest for visual **naturalism**, that is, for representations that imitate the actual appearance of the animals. Not only were both red and black animals outlined, their shapes were also modeled by spreading paint, either with the hand or a tool, in gradual gradations of color. Such modeling is extremely rare or unknown elsewhere. In addition, the artists further defined many of the animals' contours by scraping the wall behind so that the beasts seem to stand out against a deeper white ground. Three handprints in the cave were evidently made by spitting paint at a hand placed on the cave wall, resulting in a stenciled image.

Art, the Chauvet drawings suggest, does not necessarily evolve in a linear progression from awkward beginnings to more sophisticated representations. On the contrary, already in the earliest artworks, people obtained a very high degree of sophistication. Apparently, even from the earliest times, human beings could choose to represent the world naturalistically or not, and the choice not to represent the world in naturalistic terms should not necessarily be attributed to lack of skill or sophistication but to other, more culturally driven factors.

Paleolithic Culture and Its Artifacts

Footprints discovered in South Africa in 2000 and fossilized remains uncovered in the forest of Ethiopia in 2001 suggest that, about 5.7 million years ago, the earliest upright humans, or hominins (as distinct from the larger classification of **hominids**, which includes great apes and chimpanzees as well as humans), roamed the continent of Africa. Ethiopian excavations further indicate that sometime around 2.5 or 2.6 million years ago, hominid populations began to make rudimentary stone tools, though long before, between 14 million and 19 million years ago, the *Kenyapithecus* [ken-yuh-PITH-i-kus] ("Kenyan ape"), a hominin, made stone tools in east central Africa. Nevertheless, the earliest evidence of a culture coming into being are the stone artifacts of *Homo sapiens* [ho-moh SAY-pee-uhnz] (Latin for "one who knows"). *Homo sapiens* evolved about 100,000–120,000 years ago and can be distinguished from earlier hominids by the lighter build of their skeletal structure and larger brain. A 2009 study of genetic diversity among Africans found the San people of Zimbabwe to be the most diverse, suggesting that they are the most likely origin of modern humans from which others gradually spread out of Africa, across Asia, into Europe, and finally to Australia and the Americas.

Homo sapiens were **hunter-gatherers**, whose survival depended on the animals they could kill and the foods they could gather, primarily nuts, berries, roots, and other edible plants. The tools they developed were far more sophisticated than those of their ancestors. They included cleavers, chisels, grinders, hand axes, and arrow- and spearheads made of flint, a material that also provided the spark to create an equally important tool—fire. In 2004, Israeli archeologists working at a site on the banks of the Jordan River reported the earliest evidence yet found of controlled fire created by hominids—cracked and blackened flint chips, presumably used to light a fire, and bits of charcoal dating from 790,000 years ago. Also at the campsite were the bones of elephants, rhinoceroses, hippopotamuses, and small species, demonstrating that these early hominids cut their meat with flint tools and ate steaks and marrow. *Homo sapiens* cooked with fire, wore animal skins as clothing, and used tools as a matter of course. They buried their dead in ritual ceremonies, often laying them to rest accompanied by stone tools and weapons.

The Paleolithic era is the period of *Homo sapiens*' ascendancy. These Upper Paleolithic people carved stone tools and weapons that helped them survive in an inhospitable climate. They carved small sculptural objects as well, which, along with the cave paintings we have already seen, appear to be the first instances of what we have come to call "art" (see *Materials & Techniques*, page 7). Among the most remarkable of these sculptural artifacts are a large number of female figures, found at various archeological sites across Europe. The most famous of these is the limestone statuette of a woman found at Willendorf [VIL-un-dorf], in modern Austria (Fig. **1.3**), dating from about 22,000 to 21,000 BCE and often called the *Willendorf Venus*. Markings on *Woman* and other similar figures indicate that they were originally colored, but what these small sculptures meant and what they were used for remains unclear. Most are 4 to 5 inches high and fit neatly into a person's hand. This suggests that they may have had a ritual purpose. Their exaggerated breasts and bellies and their clearly delineated genitals support a connection to fertility and childbearing. We know, too, that *Woman* from Willendorf was originally painted in red ochre, suggestive of menses. And, her navel is not carved; rather, it is a natural indentation in the stone. Whoever carved her seems to have recognized, in the raw stone, a connection to the origins of life. But such figures may have served other purposes as well. Perhaps they were dolls, guardian figures, or images of beauty in a cold, hostile world where having body fat might have made the difference between survival and death.

Female figurines vastly outnumber representations of males in the Paleolithic era, which suggests that women played a central role in Paleolithic culture. Most likely, they had considerable religious and spiritual influence, and their preponderance in the imagery of the era suggests that Paleolithic culture may have been *matrilineal* (in which descent is determined through the female line) and *matrilocal* (in which residence is in the female's tribe or household). Such traditions exist in many primal societies today.

The peoples of the Upper Paleolithic period followed herds northward in summer, though temperatures during the Ice Age rarely exceeded 60 degrees Fahrenheit (16 degrees centigrade). Then, as winter approached, they retreated southward into the cave regions of northern Spain and southern France. But caves were not their only shelter. At about the same latitude as the Ardèche gorge but eastward, in present-day Ukraine, north of the Black Sea, archeologists have discovered a village with houses built from mammoth bone, dating from 16,000 to 10,000 BCE (Fig. **1.4**). Using long curving tusks as roof supports, constructing walls with pelvis bones, shoulder blades, jawbones, tusks, and skulls, and probably covering the structure with hides, the Paleolithic peoples of the region built houses that ranged from 13 to 26 feet in diameter, with the largest measuring 24 by 33 feet. The total of bones incorporated in the structure belonged to approximately ninety-five different mammoths. Here we see one of the earliest examples of architecture—the construction of living space with at least some artistic intent. The remains

Fig. 1.3 Woman (Venus of Willendorf), found at Willendorf, Austria. ca. 25,000–20,000 BCE. Limestone, height 4″. Naturhistorisches Museum, Vienna. For many years, modern scholars called this small statue the *Venus of Willendorf*. They assumed that its carvers attributed to it an ideal of female beauty comparable to the Roman ideal of beauty implied by the name Venus.

of these structures suggest that those who built them gathered together in a village of like dwellings, the fact that most underscores their common culture. They must have shared resources, cooperated in daily tasks, intermarried, and raised their children by teaching them the techniques necessary for survival in the harsh climate of the Ukraine.

Methods of Carving

Carving is the act of cutting or incising stone, bone, wood, or another material into a desired form. Surviving artifacts of the Paleolithic era were carved from stone or bone. The artist probably held a sharp instrument, such as a stone knife or a chisel, in one hand and drove it into the stone or bone with another stone held in the other hand to remove excess material and realize the figure. Finer details could be scratched into the material with a pointed stone instrument. Artists can carve into any material softer than the instrument they are using. Harder varieties of stone can cut into softer stone as well as bone. The work was probably painstakingly slow.

There are basically two types of sculpture: sculpture in the round and relief sculpture. **Sculpture in the round** is fully three-dimensional; it occupies 360 degrees of space. The Willendorf statuette (see Fig. 1.3) was carved from stone and is an example of sculpture in the round. **Relief sculpture** is carved out of a flat background surface; it has a distinct front and no back. Not all relief sculptures are alike. In *high relief* sculpture, the figure extends more than 180 degrees from the background surface. *Woman Holding an Animal Horn*, found at Laussel, in the Dordogne region of France, is carved in high relief and is one of the earliest relief sculptures known. This sculpture was originally part of a great stone block that stood in front of a Paleolithic rock shelter. In *low* or *bas relief*, the figure extends less than 180 degrees from the surface. In *sunken relief*, the image is carved, or incised, into the surface, so that the image recedes below it. When a light falls on relief sculptures at an angle, the relief casts a shadow. The higher the relief, the larger the shadows and the greater the sense of the figure's three-dimensionality.

Woman Holding an Animal Horn, Laussel (Dordogne), France. ca. 30,000–15,000 BCE. Limestone, height 17 $\frac{3}{8}$". Musée des Antiquites Nationales, St. Germain-en-Laye, France.

EXPLORE MORE To see a studio video about carving, go to **www.myartslab.com**

Fig. 1.4 Reconstruction of a mammoth-bone house, Mezhirich, Ukraine. ca. 16,000–10,000 BCE. Kiev Museum of Paleontology, Mezhirich, Ukraine. Mammoth jawbones are inserted upside down into one another to form the base of the house. About three dozen huge, curving mammoth tusks were used as arching supports for the roof.

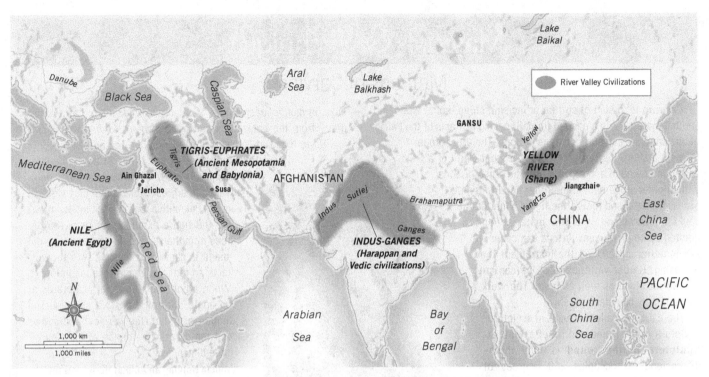

Map 1.2 The great river valley civilizations. ca. 2000 BCE. Agriculture thrived in the great river valleys throughout the Neolithic era, but by the end of the period, urban life had developed there as well, and civilization as we know it had emerged.

THE RISE OF AGRICULTURE IN THE NEOLITHIC ERA

As the ice covering the Northern Hemisphere began to recede around 10,000 BCE, the seas rose, covering, for instance, the cave entrance at Cosquer in southern France (see Map 1.1), filling what is now the North Sea and English Channel with water, and inundating the land bridge that had connected Asia and North America. Agriculture began to replace hunting and gathering, and with it, a nomadic lifestyle gave way to a more sedentary way of life. The consequences of this shift were enormous, and ushered in the Neolithic [nee-uh-LITH-ik] era, or "New Stone Age."

For 2,000 years, from 10,000 to 8000 BCE, the ice covering the Northern Hemisphere receded farther and farther northward. As temperatures warmed, life gradually changed. During this period of transition, areas once covered by vast regions of ice and snow developed into grassy plains and abundant forests. Hunters developed the bow and arrow, which were easier to use at longer range on the open plains. They fashioned dugout boats out of logs to facilitate fishing, which became a major food source. They domesticated dogs to help with the hunt as early as 11,000 BCE, and soon other animals as well—goats and cattle particularly. Perhaps most important, people began to cultivate the more edible grasses. Along the eastern shore of the Mediterranean, they harvested wheat; in Asia, they cultivated millet and rice; and in the Americas, they grew squash, beans, and corn. Gradually, farming replaced hunting as the primary means of sustaining

life. A culture of the fields developed—an agri-culture, from the Latin *ager*, "farm," "field," or "productive land."

Agricultural production seems to have originated about 10,000 BCE in the Fertile Crescent, an area arching from southwest Iran, across the foothills of the Taurus Mountains in southeastern Turkey, then southward into Lebanon. By about 8000 BCE, Neolithic agricultural societies began to concentrate in the great river valleys of the Middle East and Asia (Map **1.2**). Here, distinct centers of people involved in a common pursuit began to form. A **civilization** is a social, economic, and political entity distinguished by the ability to express itself through images and written language. Civilizations develop when the environment of a region can support a large and productive population. An increasing population requires increased production of food and other goods, not only to support itself, but to trade for other commodities. Organizing this level of trade and production also requires an administrative elite to form and to establish priorities. The existence of such an elite is another characteristic of civilization. Finally, as the history of cultures around the world makes abundantly clear, one of the major ways that societies have acquired the goods they want and simultaneously organized themselves is by means of war.

Gradually, as the climate warmed, Neolithic culture spread across Europe. By about 5000 BCE, the valleys of Spain and southern France supported agriculture, but not until about 4000 BCE is there evidence of farming in the northern reaches of the European continent and England. The Neolithic era does not end in these colder climates until about 2000 BCE,

Fig. 1.5 Early Neolithic wall and tower, Jericho, Jordan. ca. 7500 BCE. The smooth walls and sand brick at Jericho construction are architectural innovations that go far beyond the rudimentary construction techniques of the hunter-gatherers (compare Fig. 1.4, for instance).

and continues on more remote regions, such as Africa and the Americas, well into the first millennium.

Meanwhile, the great rivers of the Middle East and Asia provided a consistent and predictable source of water, and people soon developed irrigation techniques that fostered organized agriculture and animal husbandry. As production outgrew necessity, members of the community were freed to occupy themselves in other endeavors—complex food preparation (bread, cheese, and so on), construction, religion, even military affairs. Soon, permanent villages began to appear, and villages began to look more and more like cities.

Neolithic Jericho and Skara Brae

Jericho is one of the oldest known settlements of the Neolithic era. It is located in the Middle East some 15 miles east of modern Jerusalem, on the west bank of the Jordan River. Although not in one of the great river valleys, Jericho was the site of a large oasis, and by 7500 BCE, a city had developed around the water source. The homes were made of mud brick on stone foundations and had plaster floors and walls. Mud bricks were a construction material found particularly in hot, arid regions of the Neolithic Middle East, where stone and wood were in scarce supply. The city was strongly fortified (Fig. 1.5), indicating that all was not peaceful even in the earliest Neolithic times. It was surrounded by a ditch, probably not filled with water, but dug out in order to increase the height of the walls behind. The walls themselves were between 5 and 12 feet thick, and the towers rose to a height of 30 feet. What particular troubles

necessitated these fortifications is debatable, but Jericho's most precious resource was without doubt its water, and others probably coveted the site.

The most startling discovery at Jericho is the burial of ten headless corpses under the floors of the city's houses. The skulls of the dead were preserved and buried separately, the features rebuilt in plaster and painted to look like the living ancestor (Fig. 1.6). Each is unique and highly realistic, possessing the distinct characteristics of the ancestor. The purpose of the skull portraits is unknown to us. Perhaps the people of Jericho believed that the spirit of the dead lived on in the likeness. Whatever the case, the existence of the skulls indicates the growing stability of the culture, its sense of permanence and continuity.

Preserved in the cold northern climate of the Orkney Islands off the northeast coast of Scotland is Skara Brae [SKAR-uh brey]. Some 4,000 years younger than Jericho, Skara Brae is a Neolithic village dating from between 3100 and 2600 BCE. The seaside village was apparently buried long ago beneath a layer of sand during a massive storm, and then, in 1850, uncovered when another storm swept the sand away.

The houses of Skara Brae are made entirely of stone—virtually the only buildings on the treeless Orkney Islands. The walls are made by **corbeling**, a construction technique (see *Materials & Techniques*, page 18), in which layers of flat stones are piled one upon the other, with each layer projecting slightly inward as the wall rises. As the walls curve inward, they are buttressed, or supported, on the outside by earth. Nothing of the roofs has survived, suggesting that they were constructed of organic matter such as straw thatch or seaweed (seaweed remained a common roofing material in the Orkney Islands into the twentieth century). Furniture

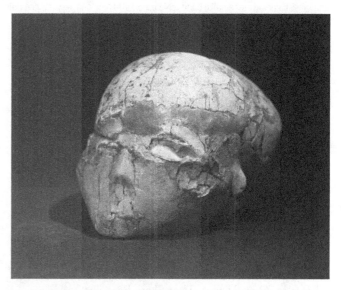

Fig. 1.6 Plastered skull from Jericho. Pre-pottery Neolithic B period. ca. 7000–6000 BCE. Life-size. Nicholson Museum, University of Sydney, Sydney, Australia. NM Inv. 57.03: presented by Dame Kathleen Kenyon, British School of Archaeology in Jerusalem. Hair was originally painted onto the head, and the eye sockets were filled with cowrie shell to give the "portrait" realism.

Fig. 1.7 House interior, Skara Brae, Orkney Islands, Scotland. ca. 3100–2600 BCE. This is a view of the interior of house 7 in Fig. 1.8. In this and other houses, archeologists have found stone cooking pots; mortars for grinding grains, including barley and wheat; carved stone balls; bone tools used for fishing and sewing; and pottery. In this view, the walls are just beginning to curve inward in corbeling.

was built into the walls—in the house shown here, rectangular stone beds at either side of a central hearth, and a stone bench along the back wall (Fig. **1.7**). The bed frames would have been filled with organic materials such as heather or straw, and covered with furs. Storage spaces have been fashioned into the walls above the beds and in the back left corner. The only light in the house would have come from the smoke hole above the hearth.

The houses in the village were connected by a series of narrow walkways that were probably covered (Fig. **1.8**). Each of the houses is more or less square, with rounded corners. They are relatively spacious, ranging in size from 12 by 14 feet to 20 by 21 feet. That Skara Brae was continually inhabited for five hundred years suggests that life in the village was relatively comfortable despite the harsh climate.

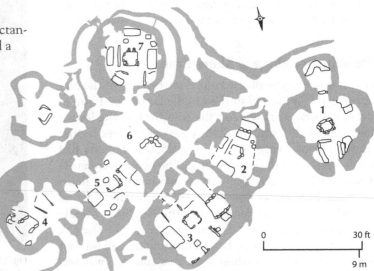

Fig. 1.8 Plan, Village of Skara Brae, Orkney Islands, Scotland. ca. 3100–2600 BCE. The numbers refer to individual houses.

Neolithic Pottery Across Cultures

The transition from cultures based on hunting and fishing to cultures based on agriculture led to the increased use of pottery vessels. Ceramic vessels are fragile, so hunter-gatherers would not have found them practical for carrying food, but people living in the more permanent Neolithic settlements could have used them to carry and store water, and to prepare and store certain types of food.

There is no evidence of pottery at the Jericho site. But, as early as 10,000 BCE, Japanese artisans were making clay pots capable of storing, transporting, and cooking food and water. Over the course of the Neolithic era, called the Jomon [joe-mon] period in Japan (12,000–300 BCE), their work became increasingly decorative. *Jomon* means "cord markings" and refers to the fact that potters decorated many of their wares by pressing cord into the damp clay. As in most Neolithic societies, women made Jomon pottery; their connection to fertility and the life cycle may have become even more important to Neolithic cultures in the transition from hunting and gathering to agricultural food production. Jomon women built their pots up from the bottom with coil upon coil of soft clay. They mixed the clay with a variety of adhesive materials, including mica, lead, fibers, and crushed shells. After forming the vessel, they employed tools to smooth both the outer and interior surfaces. Finally, they decorated the outside with cord markings and fired the pot in an outdoor bonfire at a temperature of about 1650 degrees Fahrenheit (900 degrees centigrade). By the middle Jomon period, potters had begun to decorate the normal flat-bottomed, straight-sided jars with elaborately ornate and flamelike rims (Fig. **1.9**), distinguished by their asymmetry and their unique characteristics. These rims suggest animal forms, but their significance remains a mystery.

The Neolithic cultures that flourished along the banks of the Yellow River in China beginning in about 5000 BCE also produced pottery. These cultures were based on growing rice and millet (grains from the Near East would not be introduced for another 3,000 years), and this agricultural emphasis spawned towns and villages, such as Jiangzhai, the largest Neolithic site that has been excavated in China. The Jiangzhai community, near modern Xi'an [she-an], in Shaanxi [shahn-shee] province, dates to about 4000 BCE and consisted of about 100 dwellings. At its center was a communal gathering place, a cemetery, and, most important, a *kiln*, an oven specifically designed to achieve the high temperatures necessary for firing clay. Indeed, the site yielded many pottery fragments. Farther to the east, in Gansu [gan-soo] province, Neolithic potters began to add painted decoration to their work (Fig. **1.10**). The flowing, curvilinear forms painted on the shallow basin illustrated here include "hand" motifs on the outside and round, almost eyelike forms that flow into each other on the inside.

Fig. 1.9 Deep bowl with sculptural rim, late Middle Jomon period (ca. 2500–1600 BCE), Japan. ca. 2000 BCE. Terracotta, 14 ¹/₂″ × 12 ¹/₃″. Musée des Arts Asiatiques-Guimet, Paris, France. The motifs incised on this pot may have had some meaning, but most interesting is the potter's freedom of expression. The design of the pot's flamelike rim is anything but practical.

Fig. 1.10 Basin (*pen*), Majiayao culture, Majiayao phase, Gansu Province, China. ca. 3200–2700 BCE. Earthenware with painted decoration, diameter 11″. The Metropolitan Museum of Art, New York. Anonymous Loan (L.1996.55.6). The designs on this bowl are examples of the kind of markings that would eventually develop into writing.

Some of the most remarkable Neolithic painted pottery comes from Susa [soo-suh], on the Iranian plateau. The patterns on one particular beaker (Fig. 1.11) from around 5000 to 4000 BCE are highly stylized animals. The largest of these is an ibex, a popular decorative feature of prehistoric ceramics from Iran. Associated with the hunt, the ibex may have been a symbol of plenty. The front and hind legs of the ibex are rendered by two triangles, the tail hangs behind it like a feather, the head is oddly disconnected from the body, and the horns rise in a large, exaggerated arc to encircle a decorative circular form. Hounds race around the band above the ibex, and wading birds form a decorative band across the beaker's top.

In Europe, the production of pottery apparently developed some time later, around 3000 BCE. Early pots were made either by molding clay over a round stone or by coiling long ropes of clay on top of one another and then smoothing the seams between them. Then the pots were fired at temperatures high enough to make them watertight—above 700 degrees Fahrenheit (370 degrees centigrade).

By this time, however, artisans in Egypt had begun using the potter's wheel, a revolving platter for forming vessels from clay with the fingers. It allowed artisans to produce a uniformly shaped vessel in a very short time. By 3000 BCE, the potter's wheel was in use in the Middle East as well as China. Because it is a machine created expressly to produce goods, it is in many ways the first mechanical and technological breakthrough in history. As skilled individuals specialized in making and decorating pottery, and traded their wares for other goods and services, the first elemental forms of manufacturing began to take shape.

Neolithic Ceramic Figures

It is a simple step from forming clay pots and firing them to modeling clay sculptural figures and submitting them to the same firing process. Examples of clay modeling can be found in some of the earliest Paleolithic cave sites where, at Altamira, for instance, in Spain, an artist added clay to an existing rock outcropping in order to underscore the rock's natural resemblance to an animal form. At Le Tuc d'Audoubert, south of Lascaux, an artist shaped two, two-feet-long clay bison as if they were leaning against a rock ridge.

But these Paleolithic sculptures were never fired. One of the most interesting examples of Neolithic fired clay figurines were the work of the so-called Nok peoples who lived in modern Nigeria. We do not know what they called themselves—they are identified instead by the name of the place where their artifacts were discovered. In fact, we know almost nothing about the Nok. We do not know how their culture was organized, what their lives were like, or

Fig. 1.11 Beaker with ibex, dogs, and long-necked birds, from Susa, southwest Iran. ca. 5000–4000 BCE. Baked clay with painted decoration, height 11 1/4". Musée du Louvre, Paris. The ibex was the most widely hunted game in the ancient Middle East, which probably accounts for its centrality in this design.

Fig. 1.12 Head, Nok. ca. 500 BCE–200 CE. Terracotta, height 14 $\frac{3}{16}$". © Werner Forman/Art Resource, NY. This slightly-larger-than-life-size head was probably part of a complete body, and shows the Nok people's interest in abstract geometrical representations of facial features and head shape. Holes in the eyes and nose were probably used to control temperature during firing.

what they believed. But while most Neolithic peoples in Africa worked in materials that were not permanent, the Nok fired clay figures of animals and humans that were approximately life-size.

These figures were first unearthed early in the twentieth century by miners over an area of about 100 square kilometers. Carbon-14 and other forms of dating revealed that some of these objects had been made as early as 800 BCE and others as late as 600 CE. Little more than the hollow heads have survived intact, revealing an artistry based on abstract geometrical shapes (Fig. **1.12**). In some cases, the heads are represented as ovals, and in others, as cones, cylinders, or spheres. Facial features are combinations of ovals, triangles, graceful arches, and straight lines. These heads were probably shaped with wet clay and then, after firing, finished by carving details into the hardened clay. Some scholars have argued that the technical and artistic

sophistication of works by the Nok and other roughly contemporaneous groups suggests that it is likely there are older artistic traditions in West Africa that have not as yet been discovered. Certainly, farther to the east, in the sub-Saharan regions of the Sudan, Egyptian culture had exerted considerable influence for centuries, and it may well be that Egyptian technological sophistication had worked its way westward.

The Neolithic Megaliths of Northern Europe

A distinctive kind of monumental stone architecture appears late in the Neolithic period, particularly in what is now Britain and France. Known as **megaliths** [MEG-uh-liths], or "big stones," these works were constructed without the use of mortar and represent the most basic form of architectural construction. Sometimes, they consisted merely of posts—upright

Fig. 1.13 Neolithic menhir alignments at Ménec, Carnac, Brittany, France. ca. 4250–3750 BCE. According to an ancient legend, the Carnac menhirs came into being when a retreating army was driven to the sea. Finding no ships to aid their escape, they turned to face their enemy and were transformed into stone.

stones stuck into the ground—called **menhirs** [MEN-hir], from the Celtic words *men*, "stone," and *hir*, "long." These single stones occur in isolation or in groups. The largest of the groups is at Carnac [kahr-nak], in Brittany (Fig. **1.13**), where some 3,000 menhirs arranged east to west in 13 straight rows, called *alignments*, cover a 2-mile stretch of plain. At the east end, the stones stand about 3 feet tall and gradually get larger and larger until, at the west end, they attain a height of 13 feet. This east–west alignment suggests a connection to the rising and setting of the sun and to fertility rites. Scholars disagree about their significance; some speculate that the stones may have marked out a ritual procession route; others think they symbolized the body and the process of growth and maturation. But there can be no doubt that megaliths were designed to be permanent structures, where domestic architecture was not. Quite possibly the megaliths stood in tribute to the strength of the leaders responsible for assembling and maintaining the considerable labor force required to construct them.

Another megalithic structure, the **dolmen** [DOLE-muhn], consists of two posts roofed with a capstone, or **lintel**. Because it is composed of three stones, the dolmen is a **trilithon** [try-LITH-un], from Greek *tri*, "three," and *lithos*, "rock," and it formed the basic unit of architectural structure for thousands of years. Today, we call this kind of construction **post-and-lintel** (see *Materials & Techniques*, page 18). Megaliths such

as the dolmen, in County Clare, Ireland (Fig. **1.14**), were probably once covered with earth to form a fully enclosed burial chamber, or **cairn** [karn].

A third type of megalithic structure is the **cromlech** [krahm-lek], from the Celtic *crom*, "circle," and *lech*, "place." Without doubt, the most famous megalithic structure in the world is the cromlech known as Stonehenge (Fig. **1.15**), on Salisbury Plain, about 100 miles west of modern London. A henge is a special type of cromlech, a circle surrounded by a ditch with built-up embankments, presumably for fortification.

The site at Stonehenge reflects four major building periods, extending from about 2750 to 1500 BCE. By about 2100 BCE, most of the elements visible today were in place. In the middle was a U-shaped arrangement of five post-and-lintel trilithons. The one at the bottom of the U stands taller than the rest, rising to a height of 24 feet, with a 15-foot lintel 3 feet thick. A continuous circle of sandstone posts, each weighing up to 50 tons and all standing 20 feet high, surrounded the five trilithons. Across their top was a continuous lintel 106 feet in diameter. This is the Sarsen Circle. Just inside the Sarsen Circle was once another circle, made of bluestone—a bluish dolerite—found only in the mountains of southern Wales, some 120 miles away. (See *Closer Look*, pages 16–17.)

Fig. 1.14 Neolithic dolmen. Poulnabrone Dolmen, on the Burren limestone plateau, County Clare, Ireland. ca. 2500 BCE. A mound of earth once covered this structure, an ancient burial chamber.

Why Stonehenge was constructed remains a mystery, although it seems clear that orientation toward the rising sun at the summer solstice connects it to planting and the harvest. Stonehenge embodies, in fact, the growing importance of agricultural production in the northern reaches of Europe. Perhaps great rituals celebrating the earth's plenty took place here. Together with other megalithic structures of the era, it suggests that the late Neolithic peoples who built it were extremely social beings, capable of great cooperation. They worked together not only to find the giant stones that rise at the site, but also to quarry, transport, and raise them. In other words, theirs was a culture of some magnitude and no small skill. It was a culture capable of both solving great problems and organizing itself in the name of creating a great social center. For Stonehenge is, above all, a center of culture. Its fascination for us today lies in the fact that we know so little of the culture that left it behind.

Fig. 1.15 Stonehenge, Salisbury Plain, Wiltshire, England. ca. 2750–1500 BCE. Like most Neolithic sites, Stonehenge invites speculation about its significance. Of this, however, we are certain: At the summer solstice, the longest day of the year, the sun rises directly over the Heel Stone. This suggests that the site was intimately connected to the movement of the sun.

How the Neolithic peoples of Britain constructed Stonehenge is uncertain. Scholars believe that the giant stones of the Sarsen Circle, which weigh up to 50 tons, were transported from the Marlborough Downs, roughly 20 miles to the north, by rolling them on logs. Most of the way, the going is relatively easy, but at the steepest part of the route, at Redhorn Hill, modern work studies estimate that it would have taken at least 600 men to push the stones up the hill. A relatively sophisticated understanding of basic physics—the operation of levers and pulleys—was needed to lift the stones, and their lintels, into place.

Recently, archeologists at Stonehenge have uncovered a second cromlech-like circle at Durrington Wells, about 2 miles north of the stone megalith, consisting of a circular ditch surrounding a ring of postholes out of which very large timber posts would have risen. The circle was the center of a village consisting of as many as 300 houses. The site is comparable in scale to Stonehenge itself. These discoveries—together with the ability to carbon-date human remains found at Stonehenge with increased accuracy—suggest that Stonehenge was itself a burial grounds. Archeologist Mike Parker-Pearson of the University of Sheffield speculates that villagers would have transported their dead down an avenue leading to the River Avon, then journeyed downstream, in a ritual symbolizing the passage to the afterlife, finally arriving at an avenue leading up to Stonehenge from the river. "Stonehenge wasn't set in isolation," Parker-Pearson says, "but was actually one half of this monument complex. We are looking at a pairing–one in timber to represent the transience of life, the other in stone marking the eternity of the ancestral dead."

Something to Think About . . .

The circle is a geometric form that appears in the earliest manifestations of art and architecture. Can you speculate on its appeal?

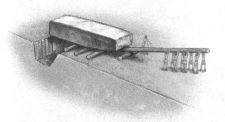

The sarsen stone is raised with a long lever. Logs are placed under the stone, and then it is rolled into place.

One by one, layers of timber are placed under the lever, both raising the stone and dropping it into the prepared pit.

As many as 200 men pull the stone upright on ropes as timbers support it from behind.

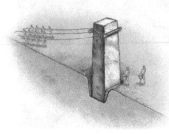

The pit around the stone is filled with stones and chalks to pack it into place.

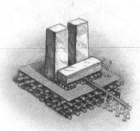

The lintel is raised on successive layers of a timber platform.

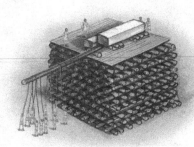

Once the platform reaches the top of the posts, the lintel is levered onto the posts.

Finally, the platform is removed, and the trilithon is complete.

The Design and Making of Stonehenge

The Heel Stone
On Midsummer's Eve, it casts a shadow directly into the circle. The stone stands 16 feet high and weighs 35 tons. It was brought from a quarry 23 miles away.

The Avenue
The shadow cast by the Heel Stone on Midsummer's Eve would extend directly down this ceremonial approach.

The Slaughter Stone
It was once believed that humans were sacrificed on this stone, which now lies flat on the ground, but it was originally part of a great portal.

The Sarsen Circle
Erected about 1500 BCE, the circle is capped by lintel stones held in place by mortise-and-tenon joints, similar to those used by woodworkers. The end of the post is narrowed and slotted into a hole in the lintel.

The Outer Bank
This ditch, 330 feet in diameter, is the oldest construction at the site, originally exposing the white limestone beneath the surface soil to form a giant circle.

Five Massive Trilithons
Inside the outer circle stood a horseshoe of trilithons, two on each side and the largest at the closed end at the southwest. Only one of the largest trilithons still stands. It rises 22 feet above ground, with 8 feet more below ground level. The stone weighs about 50 tons.

The Altar Stone
One of the most distinct stones in Stonehenge, the so-called altar stone is a 16-foot block of smoothed green sandstone located near the center of the complex.

The Bluestone Circle
This circle of 80 smallish slabs was built in about 2000 BCE from stone quarried in South Wales.

SEE MORE For a Closer Look at Stonehenge, go to **www.myartslab.com**

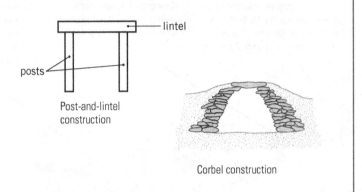
THE ROLE OF MYTH IN CULTURAL LIFE

A **myth** is a story that a culture assumes is true. It also embodies the culture's views and beliefs about its world, often serving to explain otherwise mysterious natural phenomena. Myths stand apart from scientific explanations of the nature of reality, but as a mode of understanding and explanation, myth has been one of the most important forces driving the development of culture. Although myths are speculative, they are not pure fantasy. They are grounded in observed experience. They serve to rationalize the unknown and to explain to people the nature of the universe and their place within it.

Much of our understanding of the role of myth in prehistoric cultures comes from stories that have survived in cultures around the world that developed without writing—that is, **oral cultures**—such as San cultures of Zimbabwe and the Oceanic peoples of Tahiti in the South Pacific. These cultures have passed down their myths and histories over the centuries, from generation to generation, by word of mouth. Although, chronologically speaking, many of these cultures are contemporaneous with the medieval, Renaissance, and even modern cultures of the West, they are actually closer to the Neolithic cultures in terms of social practice and organization, and, especially in terms of agency, myth, and ritual, they can help us to understand the outlook of actual Neolithic peoples.

Both nineteenth-century and more recent anthropological work among the San people suggests that their belief systems can be traced back for thousands of years. As a result, the meaning of their rock art that survives in open-air caves below the overhanging stone cliffs atop the hills of what is now Matobo National Park in Zimbabwe (Fig. **1.16**), some

of which dates back as far as 5,000 to 10,000 years ago, is not entirely lost. A giraffe stands above a group of smaller giraffes crossing a series of large, white, lozenge-shaped forms with brown rectangular centers, many of them overlapping one another. To the right, six humanlike figures are joined hand in hand, probably in a trance dance. For the San people, prolonged dancing activates *num*, a concept of personal energy or potency that the entire community can acquire. Led by a **shaman**, a person thought to have special ability to communicate with the spirit world, the dance encourages the *num* to heat up until it boils over and rises up through the spine to explode, causing the dancers to enter into a trance. Sweating and trembling, the dancers variously convulse or become rigid. They might run, jump, or fall. The San believe that in many instances, the dancer's spirit leaves the body, traveling far away, where it might enter into battle with supernatural forces. At any event, the trance imbues the dancer with almost supernatural agency. The dancers' *num* is capable of curing illnesses, managing game, or controlling the weather.

Native American Cultural Traditions

Seventeen thousand years ago, about the time that the hunter-gatherers at Lascaux painted its caves, the Atlantic and Pacific oceans were more than 300 feet below modern levels, exposing a low-lying continental shelf that extended from northeastern Asia to North America. It was a landscape of grasslands and marshes, home to the woolly mammoth, the steppe bison, wild horses, caribou, and antelope. Although recent research has found evidence of migration into North America as early as 25,000 years ago, at some point around 15,000 BCE, large numbers of hunter-gatherers in northeastern Asia followed these animals across the grasslands land bridge into the Americas. By 12,000 BCE, prehistoric hunters had settled across North America and begun to move farther south, through Mesoamerica (the region extending from central Mexico to northern Central America), and on into South America, reaching the southern end of Chile no later than 11,000 BCE.

Around 9000 BCE, for reasons that are still hotly debated—perhaps a combination of overhunting and climatic change—the peoples of the Americas developed agricultural societies. They domesticated animals—turkeys, guinea pigs, dogs, and llamas, though never a beast of burden, as in the rest of the world—and they cultivated a whole new range of plants, including maize and corn (domesticated in the Valley of Mexico by 8000 BCE), beans, squash, tomatoes, avocados, potatoes, tobacco, and cacao, the source of chocolate. The wheel remained unknown to them, though they learned to adapt to almost every conceivable climate and landscape. A **creation myth**, or story of a people's origin, told by the Maidu [MY-doo] tribe of California, characterizes this early time: "For a long time everyone spoke the same language, but suddenly people began to speak in different tongues. Kulsu (the Creator), however, could speak all languages, so he called his people together and told them the names of the animals in their own language, taught them to get food, and gave them their laws and rituals. Then he sent each tribe to a different place to live."

The Anasazi and the Role of Myth The Anasazi [ah-nuh-SAH-zee] people thrived in the American Southwest from about 900 to 1300 CE, a time roughly contemporaneous with the late Middle Ages in Europe. They left us no written record of their culture, only ruins and artifacts. As William M. Ferguson and Arthur H. Rohn, two prominent scholars of the Anasazi, have described them: "They were a Neolithic people without a beast of burden, the wheel, metal, or a written language, yet they constructed magnificent masonry

Fig. 1.16 Wall painting with giraffes, zebra, eland, and abstract shapes, San people, Inanke, Matobo National Park, Zimbabwe. Before 1000 CE. Photo: Christopher and Sally Gable © Dorling Kindersley. The animals across the bottom are elands, the largest of antelope, resembling cattle.

Fig. 1.17 Spruce Tree House, Mesa Verde, Anasazi culture. ca. 1200–1300 CE. The courtyard was formed by the restoration of the roofs over two underground kivas.

housing and ceremonial structures, irrigation works, and water impoundments." At Mesa Verde [MAY-suh VURD-ee], in what is today southwestern Colorado, their cliff dwellings (Fig. **1.17**) resemble many of the Neolithic cities of the Middle East, such as Ain Ghazal [ine gah-zahl] ("spring of the gazelles"), just outside what is now Amman, Jordan. Though Ain Ghazal flourished from about 7200 to 5000 BCE, thousands of years before the Mesa Verde community, both complexes were constructed with stone walls sealed with a layer of mud plaster. Their roofs were made of wooden beams cross-layered with smaller twigs and branches and sealed with mud. Like other Neolithic cultures, the Anasazi were accomplished in pottery-making, decorating their creations with elaborately abstract, largely geometric shapes and patterns.

The Anasazi abandoned their communities in the late thirteenth century, perhaps because of a great drought that lasted from about 1276 to 1299. Their descendants may be the Pueblo [PWEB-loh] peoples of the American Southwest today. (*Anasazi* is in fact a Navajo word meaning "enemy

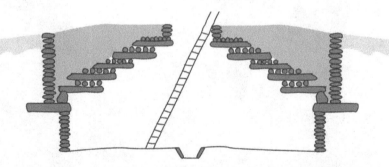

Fig. 1.18 Cribbed roof construction of a kiva. After a National Park Service pamphlet.

ancestors"—we do not know what the Anasazi called themselves.) What is remarkable about the Pueblo peoples, who despite the fact that they speak several different languages share a remarkably common culture, is that many aspects of their culture have survived and are practiced today much as they were in ancient times. For all Pueblo peoples, the village is not just the center of culture but the very center of the world. And the cultural center of village life is the **kiva**

[KEE-vuh] (Fig. **1.18**), two of which have been restored at Spruce Tree House to form the plaza visible in Fig. 1.17. They are constructed of horizontally laid logs built up to form a dome with an access hole. The roof area thus created is used as a common area. Down below, in the enclosed kiva floor, was a *sipapu* [see-paw-poo], a small, round hole symbolic of the Anasazi creation myth, which told of the emergence of the Anasazi's ancestors from the depths of the Earth. In the parched Southwestern desert country, it is equally true that water, like life itself, also seeps out of small fissures in the Earth. Thus, it is as if the Anasazi community, and everything necessary to its survival, were to emerge from Mother Earth.

Zuni Pueblo Emergence Tales The Pueblos have maintained the active practice of their ancient religious rites and ceremonies, which they have chosen not to share with outsiders. Most do not allow their ceremonial dances to be photographed. These dance performances tell stories that relate to the experiences of the Pueblo peoples, from planting, hunting, and fishing in daily life to the larger experiences of birth, puberty, maturity, and death. Still other stories explain the origin of the world, the emergence of a particular Pueblo people into the world, and their history. Most Pueblo people believe that they originated in the womb of Mother Earth and, like seeds sprouting from the soil in the springtime, were called out into the daylight by their Sun Father. This belief about origins is embodied in a type of narrative known as an **emergence tale**, a form of creation myth (**Reading 1.1**).

READING 1.1

Zuni Emergence Tale, *Talk Concerning the First Beginning*

Yes, indeed. In this world there was no one at all. Always the sun came up; always he went in. No one in the morning gave him sacred meal; no one gave him prayer sticks; it was very lonely. He said to his two children: "You will go into the fourth womb. Your fathers, your mothers, kä-eto·we, tcu-eto·we, mu-eto·we, le-eto·we, all the society priests, society pekwins, society bow priests, you will bring out yonder into the light of your sun father."

So begins this emergence tale, which embodies the fundamental principles of Zuni religious society. The Zuni, or "Sun People," are organized into groups, each responsible for a particular aspect of the community's well-being, and each group is represented by a particular -*eto·we*, or fetish, connecting it to its spiritual foundation in Earth's womb. The pekwins mentioned here are sun priests, who control the ritual calendar. Bow priests oversee warfare and social behavior. In return for corn and breath given them by the Sun Father, the Zuni offer him cornmeal and downy feathers attached to painted prayer sticks symbolizing both

clouds—the source of rain—and breath itself. Later in the tale, the two children of the Sun Father bring everyone out into the daylight for the first time:

Into the daylight of their sun father they came forth standing. Just as early dawn they came forth. After they came forth there they set down their sacred possessions in a row. The two said, "Now after a little while when your sun father comes forth standing to his sacred place you will see him face to face. Do not close your eyes." Thus he said to them. After a little while the sun came out. When he came out they looked at him. From their eyes the tears rolled down. After they had looked at him, in a little while their eyes became strong. "Alas!" Thus they said. They were covered all over with slime. With slimy tails and slimy horns, with webbed fingers, they saw one another. "Oh dear! is this what we look like?" Thus they said.

Then they could not tell which was which of their sacred possessions.

From this point on in the tale, the people and priests, led by the two children, seek to find the sacred "middle place," where things are balanced and orderly. Halona-Itiwana [ha-LOH-nah it-ee-WAH-nah] it is called, the sacred name of the Zuni Pueblo, "the Middle Ant Hill of the World." In the process, they are transformed from indeterminate, salamander-like creatures into their ultimate human form, and their world is transformed from chaos to order.

At the heart of the Zuni emergence tale is a moment when, to the dismay of their parents, many children are transformed into water-creatures—turtles, frogs, and the like—and the Hero Twins instruct the parents to throw these children back into the river. Here they become *kachinas* [kuh-CHEE-nuhs] or *katcinas*, deified spirits, who explain:

May you go happily. You will tell our parents, "Do not worry." We have not perished. In order to remain thus forever we stay here. To Itiwana but one day's travel remains. Therefore we stay nearby. . . . Whenever the waters are exhausted and the seeds are exhausted you will send us prayer sticks. Yonder at the place of our first beginning with them we shall bend over to speak to them. Thus there will not fail to be waters. Therefore we shall stay quietly nearby.

The Pueblo believe that kachina spirits, not unlike the *num* of the San people of Africa, manifest themselves in performance and dance. Masked male dancers impersonate the kachinas, taking on their likeness as well as their supernatural character. Through these dance visits the kachinas, although always "nearby," can exercise their powers for the good of the people. The nearly 250 kachina personalities embody clouds, rain, crops, animals, and even ideas such as

Fig. 1.19 **Buffalo Kachina, Zuni culture. ca. 1875.** Wood, cloth, hide, fur, shell, feathers, horse hair, tin cones. © Millicent Rogers Museum. The Buffalo Kachina is designed to increase the population of furbearing animals in the arid environment of the Southwest. Derived from a Plains Indian ritual dance, it was first danced by the Zuni near the end of the last century as the region's wildlife was becoming increasingly threatened.

Japan and the Role of Myth in the Shinto Religion

A culture's religion—that is, its understanding of the divine—is thus closely tied to and penetrated by mythical elements. Its beliefs, as embodied in its religion, stories, and myths, have always been closely tied to seasonal celebrations and agricultural production—planting and harvest in particular, as well as rain—the success of which was understood to be inextricably linked to the well-being of the community. In a fundamental sense, myths reflect the community's ideals, its history (hence, the preponderance of creation myths in both ancient societies and contemporary religions), and its aspirations. Myths also tend to mirror the culture's moral and political systems, its social organization, and its most fundamental beliefs.

A profound example is the indigenous Japanese religion of Shinto. Before 200 CE, Japan was fragmented; its various regions were separated by sea and mountain, and ruled by numerous competing and often warring states. The *Records of Three Kingdoms*, a classic Chinese text dating from about 297 CE, states that in the first half of the third century CE, many or most of these states were unified under the rule of Queen Himiko. According to the *Records*: "The country formerly had a man as ruler. For some seventy or eighty years after that there were disturbances and warfare. Thereupon the people agreed upon a woman for their ruler. Her name was Himiko." After her rule, Japan was more or less united under the Yamato emperors, who modeled their rule after the Chinese, and whose imperial court ruled from modern-day Nara Prefecture, then known as Yamato Province. Its peoples shared a mythology that was finally collected near the end of the Yamato period, in about 700 CE, called the *Kojiki* [koh-JEE-kee] or "*Chronicles of Japan*." (See **Reading 1.2**, page 29.) According to the *Kojiki*, the islands that constitute Japan were formed by two *kami* [KAH-mee], or gods—Izanagi [izah-NAH-gee] and his consort Izanami [izah-NAH-mee]. Among their offspring was the sun goddess, Amaterasu Omikami [AH-mah-teh-rah-soo OH-mee-kah-mee], from whom the Japanese Imperial line later claimed to have descended. In other words, Japanese emperors could claim not merely to have been put in position by the gods; they could claim to be direct descendants of the gods, and hence divine.

Amaterasu is the principal goddess of the early indigenous religious practices that came to be known as Shinto. She

growth and fertility. Although kachina figurines (Fig. **1.19**) are made for sale as art objects, particularly by the Hopi, the actual masks worn in ceremonies are not considered art objects by the Pueblo people. Rather, they are thought of as active agents in the transfer of power and knowledge between the gods and the men who wear them in dance, just like the African Baule mask. In fact, kachina dolls made for sale are considered empty of any ritual power or significance.

Pueblo emergence tales, and the ritual practices that accompany them, reflect the general beliefs of most Neolithic peoples. These include the following:

- belief that the forces of nature are inhabited by living spirits, which we call **animism**
- belief that nature's behavior can be compared to human behavior (we call the practice of investing plants, animals, and natural phenomena with human form or attributes **anthropomorphism**), thus explaining what otherwise would remain inexplicable
- belief that humans can communicate with the spirits of nature, and that, in return for a sacrificial offering or a prayer, the gods might intercede on their behalf

Fig. 1.20 Naiku (Inner) Shrine housing Amaterasu, Ise, Japan. Late fifth–early sixth century CE. Although the site has been sacred to Shinto since prehistoric times, beginning in the reign of the emperor Temmu (r. 673–86 CE), the Shinto shrine at Ise has been rebuilt by the Japanese ruling family, with some inevitable lapses, every 20 years. The most recent reconstruction occurred in 1993 and will occur again in 2013.

is housed in a shrine complex at Ise, a sacred site from pre-historic times. In many respects, Shinto shares much with Pueblo religions. In Shinto, trees, rocks, water, and mountains—especially Mount Fuji, the volcano just outside Tokyo which is said to look over the country as its protector—are all manifestations of the *kami*, which, like kachinas, are the spirits that are embodied in the natural world. Even the natural materials with which artists work, such as clay, wood, and stone, are imbued with the *kami* and are to be treated with the respect and reverence due to a god. The *kami* are revered in *matsuri*, festivals that usually occur on an annual basis in which, it is believed, past and present merge into one, everyday reality fades away, and people come face-to-face with their gods. The *matsuri* serve to purify the territory and community associated with the *kami*, restoring them from the degradation inevitably worked upon them by the passing of time. During the festival, people partake of the original energies of the cosmos, which they will need to re-store order to their world. Offerings such as fish, rice, and vegetables, as well as music and dancing, are presented to the *kami*, and the offerings of food are later eaten.

The main sanctuary at Ise, or *shoden* [SHOH-dehn], con-sists of undecorated wooden beams and a thatched roof (Fig. 1.20). Ise is exceptional in its use of these plain and simple materials, which not only embody the basic tenet of Shinto—reverence for the natural world—but also the

continuity and renewal of a tradition where wood, rather than stone, has always been the principal building material. The most prominent festival at Ise is the *shikinen-sengu* cere-mony, which involves the installation of the deity in a new shrine in a celebration of ritual renewal held every 20 years. The shrine buildings are rebuilt on empty ground adjacent to the older shrine, the deity is transferred to the new shrine, and the older shrine is razed, creating empty ground where the next shrine will be erected. The empty site is strewn with large white stones and is left totally bare except for a small wooden hut containing a sacred wooden pole, a practice that scholars believe dates back to very ancient times. This cycle of destruction and renewal connects the past to the present, the human community to its gods and their original energies.

The three sacred treasures of Shinto—a sword, a mirror, and a jewel necklace—were said to be given by Amaterasu to the first emperor, and they are traditionally handed down from emperor to emperor in the enthronement ceremony. The mirror is housed at Ise, the sword at the Atsuta Shrine in Nagoya, and the jewel necklace at the Imperial Palace in Tokyo. These Imperial regalia are not considered mere sym-bols of the divine but "deity-bodies" in which the powers of the gods reside, specifically wisdom in the mirror, valor in the sword, and benevolence in the jewel necklace. To this day, millions of Japanese continue to practice Shinto, and they undertake pilgrimages to Ise each year.

SACRED SITES: THE EXAMPLE OF THE AMERICAS

In some prehistoric cultures, priests or priestesses were principally responsible for mediating between the human and the divine. In others, as in Shinto, the ruler was the representative of the divine world on Earth. But in almost all prehistoric cultures, communication with the spiritual world was conducted in special precincts or places such as Ise. Many scholars believe that caves served this purpose in Paleolithic times. In Neolithic culture, sites such as Stonehenge and the Anasazi kiva served this function.

The Olmec

As early as 1300 BCE, a preliterate group known as the Olmec [OHL-mek] came to inhabit the area between Veracruz and Tabasco on the southern coast of the Gulf of Mexico (see Map 1.3), where they built huge ceremonial precincts in the middle of their communities. Many of the characteristic features of later Mesoamerican culture, such as pyramids, ball courts, mirror-making, and the calendar system, originated in the lowland agricultural zones that the Olmec inhabited.

The Olmec built their cities on great earthen platforms, probably designed to protect their ceremonial centers from rain and flood. On these platforms, they erected giant pyramidal mounds, where an elite group of ruler-priests lived, supported by the general population that farmed the rich, sometimes swampy land that surrounded them. These pyramids

may have been an architectural reference to the volcanoes that dominate Mexico, or they may have been tombs. Excavations may eventually tell us. At La Venta [luh VEN-tuh], very near the present-day city of Villahermosa [vee-yuh-er-MOH-suh], three colossal stone heads stood guard over the ceremonial center on the south end of the platform (Fig. 1.21), and a fourth guarded the north end by itself. Each head weighs between 11 and 24 tons, and each bears a unique emblem on its headgear, which is similar to old-style American leather football helmets. At other Olmec sites—San Lorenzo, for instance—as many as eight of these heads have been found, some up to 12 feet high. They are carved of basalt, although the nearest basalt quarry is 50 miles to the south in the Tuxtla [toost-luh] Mountains. They were evidently at least partially carved at the quarry, then loaded onto rafts and floated downriver to the Gulf of Mexico before going back upriver to their final resting places. The stone heads are generally believed to be portraits of Olmec rulers, and they all share the same facial features, including wide, flat noses and thick lips. They suggest that the ruler was the culture's principal mediator with the gods, literally larger than life.

The Mound Builders

Sometime between 1800 and 500 BCE, at about the same time that the Olmec were building the La Venta mound cluster in Mexico, Neolithic hunter-gatherers in eastern North America began building huge ceremonial centers of their own, consisting of large-scale embankments and burial mounds

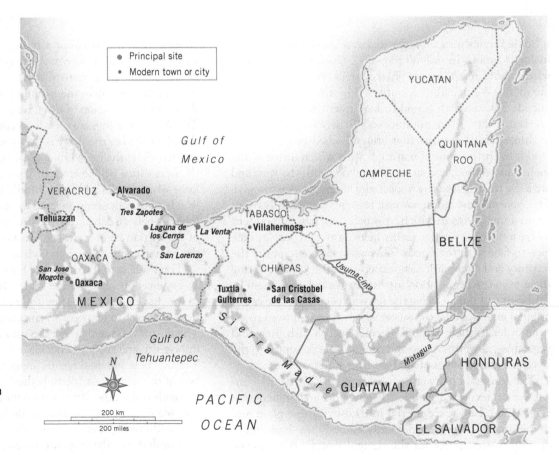

Map 1.3 Olmec civilization sites. The Olmec inhabited most of the area that we now refer to as Mesoamerica from 1300 to 400 BCE.

Fig. 1.21 Colossal head, La Venta, Mexico, Olmec culture. ca. 900–500 BCE. Basalt, height 7'50". La Venta Park, Villahermosa, Tabasco, Mexico. Giant heads such as this one faced out from the ceremonial center and evidently served to guard it.

(Map **1.4**). These people, who probably had arrived in North America sometime between 14,000 and 10,000 BCE, are known as the Woodlands peoples because the area where they lived, from the Mississippi River basin in the West to the Atlantic Ocean in the East, was originally forested.

One of these Woodlands peoples, the Hopewell culture in southern Ohio, enveloped the corpses of what we presume were their highest-ranking leaders from head to toe in freshwater pearls, weighted them down with plates of beaten copper, and then surrounded them with jewelry, sculpture, and pottery. These burials give us a fair idea of the extent of Woodlands trade. Their copper came from the Great Lakes, decorative shell from the Gulf Coast, alligator and shark teeth from Florida, and mica from the Appalachian Mountains. There are even examples of obsidian that can be traced to what is now Yellowstone National Park, and grizzly bear teeth from the Rocky Mountains.

Map 1.4 Archeological sites of the Anasazi and the mound builders' archeological sites in North America.

Fig. 1.22 Great Serpent Mound, Adams County, Ohio, Hopewell culture. ca. 600 BCE–200 CE. Length approx. 1,254'. Recently, archeologists have carbon-dated an artifact found at the Great Serpent Mound as late as 1070 CE. As a result, some now think that the mound may be related to Halley's comet, which passed by the Earth in 1066.

The most intriguing of the Hopewell mounds is the Great Serpent Mound, near Locust Grove, Ohio (Fig. **1.22**). Nearly a quarter of a mile long, it contains no burial sites. Its "head" consists of an oval enclosure that may have served some ceremonial purpose, and its tail is a spiral. The spiral would, in fact, become a favorite decorative form of the Mississippian culture, which developed out of the Woodlands-era cultures and raised ritual mound building to a new level of achievement. The great mound at Cahokia [kuh-HO-kee-uh] (Fig. **1.23**), near the juncture of the Illinois, Missouri, and Mississippi rivers at modern East St. Louis, Illinois, required the moving of over 22 million cubic feet of earth and probably three centuries to construct, beginning about 900 CE. It was the focal point of a ritual center that contained as many as 120 mounds, some of which were aligned with the position of the sun at the equinoxes, as well as nearly 400 other platforms, wooden enclosures, and houses. Evidence suggests that the Mississippians worshipped the sun: The Natchez people, one of the Mississippian peoples who survived contact with European culture, called their chief the Great Sun, and their highest social class the Suns.

The Mississippian culture sustained itself primarily by the cultivation of corn, suggesting close connections to Mexico, where cultivation of corn was originally perfected. As many as 4 million people may have lived in the Mississippi Valley. Cahokia itself thrived, with a population of 20,000 people within its six-square-mile area, until just before 1500, when the site was mysteriously abandoned.

Fig. 1.23 Reconstruction of central Cahokia, East St. Louis, Illinois, Mississippian culture. ca. 1150 CE. East–west length approx. 3 mi.; north–south length approx. 2 ¼ mi.; base of great mound, 1,037' × 790'; height approx. 100'. William Iseminger, "Reconstruction of Central Cahokia Mounds". c. 1150 CE. Courtesy of Cahokia Mounds State Historic Site. The stockade, or fence, surrounding the central area, indicates that warfare probably played an important role in Mississippian life.

Representing the Power of the Animal World

The two images shown here in some sense bracket the six volumes of *The Humanities*. The first (Fig. **1.24**), from the Chauvet Cave, is one of the earliest known drawings of a horse. The second (Fig. **1.25**), a drawing by contemporary American painter Susan Rothenberg (b. 1945), also represents a horse, though in many ways less realistically than the cave drawing. The body of Rothenberg's horse seems to have disappeared and, eyeless, as if blinded, it leans forward, its mouth open, choking or gagging or gasping for air.

In his catalog essay for a 1993 retrospective exhibition of Rothenberg's painting, Michael Auping, chief curator at the Albright-Knox Museum in Buffalo, New York, described Rothenberg's kind of drawing: "Relatively spontaneous, the drawings are Rothenberg's psychic energy made imminent . . . . [They] uncover realms of the psyche that are perhaps not yet fully explicable." The same could be said of the cave drawing executed by a nameless hunter-gatherer more than 20,000 years ago. That artist's work must have seemed just as strange as Rothenberg's, lit by flickering firelight in the dark recesses of the cave, its body disappearing, too, into the darkness that surrounded it.

It seems certain that in some measure both drawings were the expression of a psychic need on the part of the artist—whether derived from the energy of the hunt or of nature itself—to fix upon a surface an image of the power and vulnerability of the animal world. That drive, which we will see in the art of the Bronze Age of the Middle East in the next chapter—for instance, in the haunting image of a dying lion in the palace complex of an Assyrian king at Nineveh—remains constant from the beginnings of art to the present day. It is the compulsion to express the inexpressible, to visualize the mind as well as the world. ■

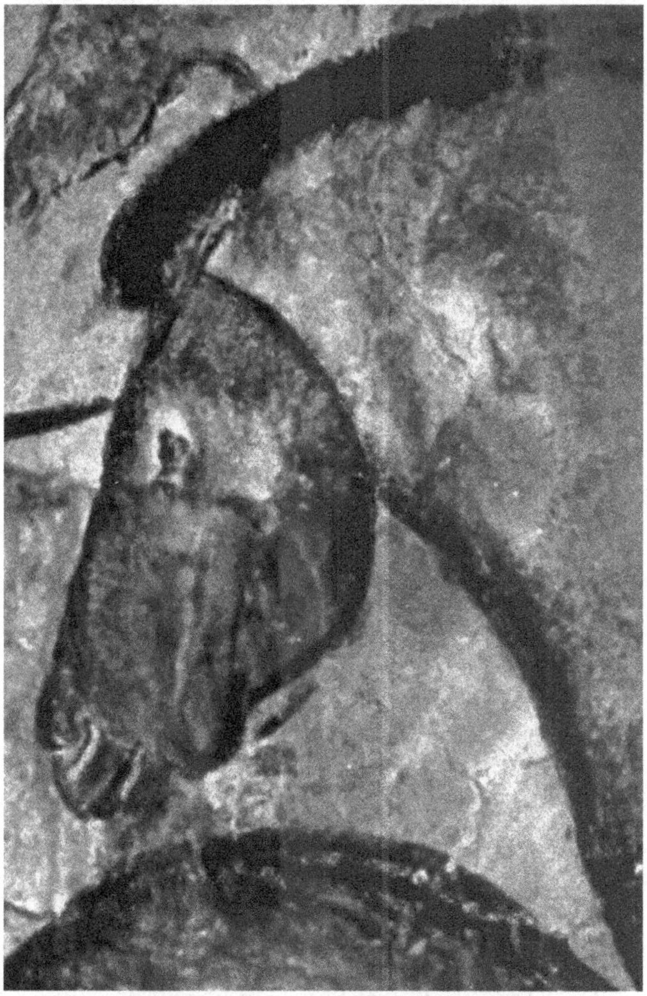

Fig. 1.24 Horse. Detail from Chauvet Cave, Vallon-Pont-d'Arc, Ardèche gorge, France (Fig. 1.1). ca. 30,000 BCE. Note the realistic shading that defines the volume of the horse's head. It is a realism that artists throughout history have sometimes sought to achieve, and sometimes ignored, in their efforts to express for the forces that drive them.

Fig. 1.25 Susan Rothenberg. Untitled. 1978. Acrylic, flashe, and pencil on paper, 20″ × 20″. Collection Walker Art Center, Minneapolis. Art Center Acquisition Fund, 1979. © 2008 Susan Rothenberg/Artist's Rights Society (ARS), NY. Part of the eeriness of this image comes from Rothenberg's use of flashe, a French vinyl-based color that is clear and so creates a misty, ghostlike surface.

What features characterize the beginnings of human culture?

The widespread use of stone tools and weapons by Homo sapiens, the hominid species that evolved around 120,000 to 100,000 years ago, gives rise to the name of the earliest era of human development, the Paleolithic era. Carvers fashioned stone figures, both in the round and in relief. In cave paintings, such as those discovered at Chauvet Cave, the artists' great skill in rendering animals helps us to understand that the ability to represent the world with naturalistic fidelity is an inherent human skill, unrelated to cultural sophistication. Culture can be defined as a way of living—religious, social, and/or political—formed by a group of people and passed on from one generation to the next. What can the earliest art tell us about the first human cultures? What questions remain a mystery?

What characteristics distinguish the Neolithic from the Paleolithic?

As the ice that covered the Northern Hemisphere slowly melted, people began cultivating edible grasses and domesticating animals. Gradually, farming supplanted hunting as the primary means of sustaining life, especially in the great river valleys where water was abundant. The rise of agriculture is the chief characteristic of the Neolithic age. Along with agriculture, permanent villages such as Skara Brae begin to appear. What does the appearance of fire-baked pottery tell us about life in Neolithic culture?

What is a megalith?

During the fifth millennium BCE, Neolithic peoples began constructing monumental stone architecture, or megaliths, in France and England. Upright, single stone posts called menhirs were placed in the ground, either individually or in groups, as at Carnac in Brittany. Elementary post-and-lintel construction was employed to create dolmens, two posts roofed with a capstone. The most famous of the third type of monumental construction, the circular cromlech, is Stonehenge, in England. What does the enormous amount of human labor required for the construction of these megaliths suggest about the societies that built them?

How can we understand the role of myth in prehistoric culture?

Neolithic culture in the Americas lasted well into the second millennium CE. Much of our understanding of the role of myth in prehistoric cultures derives from the traditions of contemporary Native American tribes that still survive in tribes such as the Hopi and Zuni, who are the direct descendents of the Anasazi. Their legends, such as the Zuni emergence tale, encapsulate the fundamental religious principles of the culture. Such stories, and the ritual practices that accompany them, reflect the general beliefs of most Neolithic peoples. Can you describe some of these beliefs? What role do sacred sites, such as those at Ise in Japan, or Cahokia in the Mississippi Valley, play?

PRACTICE MORE Get flashcards for images and terms and review chapter material with quizzes at **www.myartslab.com**

GLOSSARY

agency The idea that an object possesses qualities that help to effect change.

animism The belief that the forces of nature are inhabited by living spirits.

anthropomorphism The practice of investing plants, animals, and natural phenomena with human form or attributes.

cairn A fully enclosed burial chamber covered with earth.

carving The act of cutting or incising stone, bone, wood, or other material into a desired form.

civilization A culture that possesses the ability to organize itself thoroughly and communicates through written language.

corbeling A method for creating walls and roofs by layering stones so that they project inward over the layer beneath.

creation myth A story of a people's origin.

cromlech A circle of megaliths, usually surrounding a dolmen or mound.

culture The set of values, beliefs, and behaviors that governs or determines a common way of living formed by a group of people and passed on from one generation to the next.

dolmen A type of prehistoric megalithic structure made of two posts supporting a horizontal capstone.

emergence tale A type of narrative that explains beliefs about a people's origins.

hominids The earliest upright mammals, including humans, apes, and other related forms.

hunter-gatherer One whose primary method of subsistence depends on hunting animals and gathering edible plants and other foodstuffs from nature.

kiva A Pueblo ceremonial enclosure that is usually partly underground and serves as the center of village life.

lintel A horizontal architectural element.

megalith Literally, "big stone"; large, usually rough, stones used in a monument or structure.

menhir A large, single, upright stone.

modeling The use of shading in a two-dimensional representation to give a sense of roundness and volume.

myth A story that a culture assumes is true. A myth also embodies the culture's views and beliefs about its world, often serving to explain otherwise mysterious natural phenomena.

naturalism In art, representations that imitate the reality in appearance of natural objects.

oral culture A culture that develops without writing and passes down stories, beliefs, values, and systems by word of mouth.

perspectival drawing The use of techniques to show the relation of objects as they appear to the eye and to convey a sense of three-dimensional space on a two-dimensional surface.

post A piece fixed firmly in an upright position.

post-and-lintel A form of construction consisting of two posts (upright members) that support a lintel (horizontal member).

prehistoric Existing in or relating to the times before writing and recorded history.

relief sculpture A three-dimensional work of art carved out of a flat background surface.

ritual A rite or ceremony habitually practiced by a group, often in religious or quasi-religious context.

sculpture in the round A fully three-dimensional work of art.

shaman A person thought to have special ability to communicate with the spirit world.

trilithon A type of megalithic structure composed of three stones: two posts and a lintel; served in prehistory as the basic architectural unit.

READINGS

The Japanese Creation Myth: The *Kojiki*

The following is a beginning of a modern retelling of the Kojiki *or* Records of Ancient Matters *the oldest surviving account of ancient Japanese history. This creation myth details the origins of Japan and the sacred spirits, or* kami, *which are objects of worship for the indigenous religion of Japan, Shintoism.*

Before the heavens and the earth came into existence, all was a chaos, unimaginably limitless and without definite shape or form. Eon followed eon: then, lo! out of this boundless, shapeless mass something light and transparent rose up and formed the heaven. This was the Plain of High Heaven, in which materialized a deity called Ame-no-Minaka-Nushi-no-Mikoto (the Deity-of-the-August-Center-of-Heaven). Next the heavens gave birth to a deity named Takami-Musubi-no-Mikoto (the High-August-Producing-Wondrous-Deity), followed by a third called Kammi-Musubi-no-Mikoto (the Divine-Producing-Wondrous-Deity). These three divine beings are called the Three Creating Deities.

In the meantime what was heavy and opaque in the void gradually precipitated and became the earth, but it had taken an immeasurably long time before it condensed sufficiently to form solid ground. In its earliest stages, for millions and millions of years, the earth may be said to have resembled oil floating, medusa-like, upon the face of the waters. Suddenly like the sprouting up of a reed, a pair of immortals were born from its bosom. . . . Many gods were thus born in succession, and so they increased in number, but as long as the world remained in a chaotic state, there was nothing for them to do. Whereupon, all the Heavenly deities summoned the two divine beings, Izanagi and Izanami, and bade them descend to the nebulous place, and by helping each other, to consolidate it into terra firma. [The heavenly deities] handed them a spear called Ama-no-Nuboko, embellished with costly gems. The divine couple received respectfully and ceremoniously the sacred weapon and then withdrew from the presence of the deities, ready to perform their august commission. Proceeding forthwith to the Floating Bridge of Heaven, which lay between the heaven and the earth, they stood awhile to gaze on that which lay below. What they beheld was a world not yet condensed, but looking like a sea of filmy fog floating to and fro in the air, exhaling the while an inexpressibly fragrant odor. They were, at first, perplexed just how and where to start, but at length Izanagi suggested to his companion that they should try the effect of stirring up the brine with their spear. So saying he pushed down the jeweled shaft and found that it touched something. Then drawing it up, he examined it and observed that the great drops which fell from it almost immediately coagulated into an island, which is, to this day, the Island of Onokoro. Delighted at the result, the two deities descended forthwith from the Floating Bridge to reach the miraculously created island. In this island they thenceforth dwelt and made it the basis of their subsequent task of creating a country . . . . First, the island of Awaji was born, next, Shikoku, then, the island of Oki, followed by Kyushu; after that, the island Tsushima came into being, and lastly, Honshu, the main island of Japan. The name of Oyashi-ma-kuni (the Country of the Eight Great Islands) was given to these eight islands . . . .

READING CRITICALLY

One of the key moments in this creation myth is when the heavenly deities order Izanagi and Izanami to "descend to the nebulous place, and by helping each other, to consolidate it into terra firma." What does this tell us about Japanese culture?

2 Mesopotamia

Power and Social Order in the Early Middle East

THINKING AHEAD

What characteristics distinguish the ancient civilizations of Sumer, Akkad, Babylon, and Assyria?

How does the Epic of Gilgamesh embody the relationship between the Mesopotamian ruler and the gods?

What distinguished the Hebrews from other cultures of the Ancient Near East?

What characteristics did the Persian religion share with Judaism?

In September 1922, British Archeologist C. Leonard Woolley boarded a steamer, beginning a journey that would take him to southern Iraq. There, Woolley and his team would discover one of the richest treasure troves in the history of archeology in the ruins of the ancient city of Ur. Woolley concentrated his energies on the burial grounds surrounding the city's central **ziggurat** [ZIG-uh-rat], a pyramidal temple structure consisting of successive platforms with outside staircases and a shrine at the top. (Fig. **2.1**). Digging there in the winter of 1927, he unearthed a series of tombs with several rooms, many bodies, and masses of golden objects (Fig. **2.2**)—vessels, crowns, necklaces, statues, and weapons—as well as jewelry and lyres made of electrum and the deep-blue stone lapis lazuli. With the same sense of excitement that was felt by Jean-Marie Chauvet and his companions when they first saw the paintings on the wall of Chauvet cave, Woolley was careful to keep what he called the "royal tombs" secret. On January 4, 1928, Woolley telegrammed his colleagues in Latin. Translated to English, it read:

> *I found the intact tomb, stone built, and vaulted over with bricks of queen Shubad [later known as Puabi] adorned with a dress in which gems, flower crowns and animal figures are woven. Tomb magnificent with jewels and golden cups.*
>
> —Woolley

Fig. 2.2 Vessel in the shape of an ostrich egg, from the Royal Cemetery of Ur. ca. 2550 BCE. Gold, lapis lazuli, red limestone, shell, and bitumen, hammered from a single sheet of gold and with geometric mosaics at the top and bottom of the egg. Height 5 ¾"; Diameter 5 ⅛" University of Pennsylvania Museum of Archaeology and Anthropology. The array of materials came from trade with neighbors in Afghanistan, Iran, Anatolia, and perhaps Egypt and Nubia.

◄ **Fig. 2.1 The ziggurat at Ur (modern Muqaiyir, Iraq). ca. 2100 BCE.** The best preserved and most fully restored of the ancient Sumerian temples, this ziggurat was the center of the city of Ur, in the lower plain between the Tigris and Euphrates rivers.

HEAR MORE Listen to an audio file of your chapter at **www.myartslab.com**

When Woolley's discovery was made public, it was worldwide news for years.

Archeologists and historians were especially excited by Woolley's discoveries, because they opened a window onto the larger region we call Mesopotamia [mes-uh-po-TAY-mee-uh], the land between the Tigris [TIE-gris] and Euphrates [you-FRAY-teez] rivers. Ur was one of 30 or 40 cities that arose in Sumer, the southern portion of Mesopotamia (Map 2.1). Its people abandoned Ur more than 2,000 years ago, when the Euphrates changed its course away from the city.

The peoples of the region were, in fact, almost totally dependent on the two rivers for their livelihoods. By irrigating the lands just outside the marshes on the riverbanks, the conditions necessary for extensive and elaborate communities such as Ur began to arise: People dug canals and ditches and cooperated in regulating the flow of water in them, which eventually resulted in crops that exceeded the needs of the population. These could be transformed into foodstuffs of a more elaborate kind, including beer. Evidence indicates that over half of each grain harvest went into producing beer. Excess crops were also traded by boat with nearby communities or up the great rivers to the north, where stone, wood, and metals were available in exchange. As people congregated in central locations to exchange goods, cities began to form. Cities such as Ur became hubs of great trading networks. With trade came ideas, which were incorporated into local custom and spawned newer and greater ideas in turn. Out of the exchange of goods and ideas, then, the conditions were in place for great cultures to arise.

This chapter outlines the cultural forces that came to define Mesopotamia. After agriculture, first among these was **metallurgy**, the science of separating metals from their ores and then working or treating them to create objects. The technology probably originated in the Fertile Crescent to the north about 4000 BCE, but as it spread southward, the peoples of Mesopotamia adopted it as well.

This new technology would change the region's social organization, inaugurating what we have come to call the Bronze Age. Metallurgy required the mining of ores, specialized technological training, and skilled artisans. Although the metallurgical properties of copper were widely understood, technicians discovered that by alloying it with tin they could create bronze, a material of enormous strength and durability. Bronze weapons would transform the military and the nature of warfare. Power consolidated around the control and mastery of weaponry, and thus bronze created a new military elite of soldiers dedicated to protecting the Sumerian **city-states** from one another for control of produce and trade. The city-states, in turn, spawned governments ruled by **priest-kings**, who exercised power as intermediaries between the gods and the people. In their secular role, the priest-kings established laws that contributed to the social order necessary for maintaining successful agricultural societies. The arts developed largely as celebrations of the priest-kings' powers. In order to keep track of the production and distribution of goods, the costs of equipping the military, and records relating to enforcing laws and regulations, writing, perhaps the greatest innovation of the Bronze Age, developed. If agricultural production served to stimulate the creation of urban centers, metallurgy made possible the new military cultures of the city-states. The arts served to celebrate these new centers of power, and writing, which arose out of the necessity of tracking the workings of the state, would come to celebrate the state in a literature of its own.

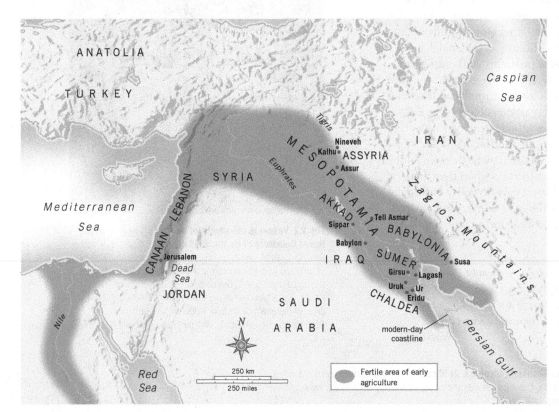

Map 2.1 **Major Mesopotamian capitals. ca. 2600–500 BCE.**

SUMERIAN UR

Ur is not the oldest city to occupy the southern plains of Mesopotamia, the region known as Sumer [SOO-mur]. That distinction belongs to Uruk [oo-RUK], just to the north. But the temple structure at Ur is of particular note because it is the most fully preserved and restored. It was most likely designed to evoke the mountains surrounding the river valley, which were the source of the water that flowed through the two rivers and, so, the source of life. Topped by a sanctuary, the ziggurat might also have symbolized a bridge between heaven and earth. Woolley, who supervised the reconstruction of the first platform and stairway of the ziggurat at Ur (Fig. 2.3), speculated that the platforms of the temple were originally not paved but covered with soil and planted with trees, an idea that modern archeologists no longer accept.

Visitors—almost certainly limited to members of the priesthood—would climb up the stairs to the temple on top. They might bring an offering of food or an animal to be sacrificed to the resident god—at Ur, it was Nanna or Sin, god of the moon. Visitors often placed in the temple a statue that represented themselves in an attitude of perpetual prayer. We know this from the inscriptions on many of the statues. One, dedicated to the goddess Tarsirsir, protector of Girsu, a city-state across the Tigris and not far upstream from Ur, reads:

> To Bau, gracious lady, daughter of An, queen of the holy city, her mistress, for the life of Nammahani . . . has dedicated as an offering this statue of the protective goddess of Tarsirsir which she has introduced to the courtyard of Bau. May the statue, to which let my mistress turn her ear, speak my prayers.

A group of such statues, found in 1934 in the shrine room of a temple at Tell Asmar, near modern Baghdad, includes seven men and two women (Fig. 2.4). The men wear belted,

Fig. 2.3 Reconstruction drawing of the ziggurat at Ur (modern Muqaiyir, Iraq). ca. 2100 BCE. British archeologist Sir Leonard Woolley undertook reconstruction of the ziggurat in the 1930s (see Fig. 2.1). In his reconstruction, a temple on top, which was the home of the patron deity of the city, crowning the three-tiered platform, the base of which measures 140 by 200 feet. The entire structure rose to a height of 85 feet. Woolley's reconstruction was halted before the second and third platforms were completed.

fringed skirts. They have huge eyes, inlaid with lapis lazuli (a blue semiprecious stone) or shell set in bitumin. The single arching eyebrow and crimped beard (only the figure in the at the right is beardless) are typical of Sumerian sculpture. The two women wear robes. All figures clasp their hands in front of them, suggestive of prayer when empty and of making an offering when holding a cup. Some scholars believe that the the tallest man represents Abu, god of vegetation, due to his especially large eyes, but all of the figures are probably worshippers.

Fig. 2.4 Dedicatory statues, from the Abu Temple, Tell Asmar, Iraq. ca. 2900–2700 BCE. Marble, alabaster, and gypsum, height of tallest figure, approx. 30″. Excavated by the Iraq Expedition of the Oriental Institute of the University of Chicago, February 13, 1934. Courtesy of the Oriental Institute of the University of Chicago. The wide-eyed appearance of these figures is probably meant to suggest they are gazing in perpetual awe at the deity.

Religion in Ancient Mesopotamia

Although power struggles among the various city-states dominate Mesopotamian history, with one civilization succeeding another, and with each city-state or empire claiming its own particular divinity as chief among the Mesopotamian gods, the nature of Mesopotamian religion remained relatively constant across the centuries. With the exception of the Hebrews, the religion of the Mesopotamian peoples was polytheistic, consisting of multiple gods and goddesses connected to the forces of nature—sun and sky, water and storm, earth and its fertility (see *Context*, this page). We know many of them by two names, one in Sumerian and the other in the Semitic language of the later, more powerful Akkadians. A famous Akkadian **cylinder seal** (Fig. 2.5), an engraved cylinder used as a signature by rolling it into a wet clay tablet in order to confirm receipt of goods or to identify ownership, represents many of the gods. The figures are recognizably gods because they wear pointed headdresses with multiple horns, though the figure on the left, beside the lion and holding a bow, has not been definitively identified. The figure with two wings standing atop the scaly mountain is Ishtar [ISH-tar], goddess of love and war. Weapons rise from her shoulders, and she holds a bunch of dates in her hand, a symbol of fertility. Beneath her, cutting his way through the mountain so that he can rise at dawn, is the sun god, Shamash [SHAH-mash]. Standing with his foot on the mountain at the right, streams of water with fish in them flowing from his shoulders, is Ea [EE-ah], god of water, wisdom, magic, and art. Behind him is his vizier [vih-ZEER], or "burden-carrier."

To the Mesopotamians, human society was merely part of the larger society of the universe governed by these gods and a reflection of it. Anu, father of the gods, represents the authority, which the ruler emulates as lawmaker and -giver. Enlil [EN-lil], god of the air—the calming breeze as well as the violent storm—is equally powerful, but he represents force, which the ruler emulates in his role as military leader. The active principles of fertility, birth, and agricultural plenty are those of the goddess Belitili [bell-eh-TEE-lee], while water, the life force itself, the creative element, is embodied in the god Ea, or Enki [EN-kee], who is also god of the arts. Both Belitili and Ea are subject to the authority of

CONTEXT

Mesopotamian Gods and Goddesses

Name	Symbol	Role
An/Anu	horned cap	Father of the gods, god of the sky
Enlil	horned cap	God of the air and storm; later replaces Anu as father of the gods
Utu/Shamash	solar disc	Sun-god, lord of truth and justice
Inanna/Ishtar	star	Goddess of love and war
Ninhursag /Belitili	'omega' symbol	Mother Earth
Enki/Ea	goat-fish	God of water, lord of wisdom, magic, art
Marduk	spade	Chief god of Babylon

Fig. 2.5 Cylinder seal impression and the Seal of Adda. Akkadian. ca. 2200–2159 BCE. Greenstone, height 1 ½". The two-line inscription at the left identifies the seal's owner as Adda, a scribe.

Anu. Ishtar is subject to Enlil, ruled by his breezes (in the case of love) and by his storm (in the case of war). A host of lesser gods represented natural phenomena, or, in some cases, abstract ideas, such as truth and justice.

The Mesopotamian ruler, often represented as a "priest-king," and often believed to possess divine attributes, acts as the intermediary between the gods and humankind. His ultimate responsibility is the behavior of the gods—whether Ea blesses the crop with rains, Ishtar his armies with victory, and so on.

Royal Tombs of Ur

Religion was central to the people of Ur, and the cemetery at Ur, discovered by Sir Leonard Woolley in 1928, tells us a great deal about the nature of their beliefs. Woolley unearthed some 1,840 graves, most dating from between 2600 and 2000 BCE. The greatest number of graves were individual burials of rich and poor alike. However, some included a built burial chamber rather than just a coffin and contained more than one body, in some cases as many as 80. These multiple burials, and the evidence of elaborate burial rituals, suggest that members of a king or queen's court accompanied the ruler to the grave. The two richest burial sites, built one behind the other, are now identified as royal tombs, one belonging to Queen Puabi [poo-AH-bee], the other to an unknown king (but it is not that of her husband, King Meskalamdug [mes-kah-LAM-doog], who is buried in a different grave).

The Golden Lyres In the grave of either the unknown king or Queen Puabi (records are confusing on this point) were two lyres, one of which today is housed in Philadelphia (Fig. 2.6), the other in London (Fig. 2.7). Both are decorated with bull's heads and are fronted by a panel of **narrative scenes**—that is, scenes representing a story or event. Although originally made of wood, which rots over time, these objects were able to be saved in their original form due to an innovation of Woolley's during the excavation. He ordered his workers to tell him whenever they came upon an area that sounded hollow. He would fill such hollows (where the original wood had long since rotted away) with wax or plaster, thus preserving, in place, the decorative effects on the object's outside. It seems likely that the mix of animal and human forms that decorate these lyres represents a funerary banquet in the realm of the dead. They are related, at least thematically, to events in the Sumerian *Epic of Gilgamesh*, which we will discuss later in the chapter. This suggests that virtually

Fig. 2.7 Lyre from Tomb 789 (alternatively identified as the unknown king's or Puabi's tomb), from the cemetery at Ur (modern Muqaiyir, Iraq). ca. 2600 BCE. Gold leaf and lapis lazuli over a wood core, height 44 ½" restored 1971–1972. © The Trustees of the British Museum.

Fig. 2.6 Soundbox panel front of the lyre from Tomb 789 (alternatively identified as the unknown king's or Puabi's tomb), from the cemetery at Ur (modern Muqaiyir, Iraq). ca. 2600 BCE. Wood with inlaid gold, lapis lazuli, and shell, height approx. 12 ¼". University of Pennsylvania Museum of Archaeology and Anthropology, Philadelphia. Museum object #B17694, (image #150848). The meaning of the scenes on the front of this lyre has always puzzled scholars. On the bottom, a goat holding two cups attends a man with a scorpion's body. Above that, a donkey plays a bull-headed lyre held by a bear, while a seated jackal plays a small percussion instrument. On the third level, animals walking on their hind legs carry food and drink for a feast. In the top panel, a man with long hair and beard, naked but for his belt, holds two human-headed bulls by the shoulders.

every element of the culture—from its music and literature to its religion and politics—was tied in some way to every other. The women whose bodies were found under the two lyres may have been singers and musicians, and the placement of the lyres over them would indicate that the lyres were put there after the celebrants died.

Such magnificent musical instruments indicate that music was important in Mesopotamian society. Surviving documents tell us that music and song were part of the funeral ritual, and music played a role in worship at the temple, as well as in banquets and festivals. Indeed, a fragment of a poem from the middle of the third millennium BCE found at Lagash [LAY-gash] indicates that Sumerian music was anything but funereal. It is music's duty, the poet says,

> To fill with joy the Temple court
> And chase the city's gloom away
> The heart to still, the passions calm,
> Of weeping eyes the tears to stay.

The _Royal Standard of Ur_ One of Woolley's most important discoveries in the Royal Cemetery was the so-called _Royal Standard of Ur_ (Fig. **2.8**). Music plays a large part here, too.

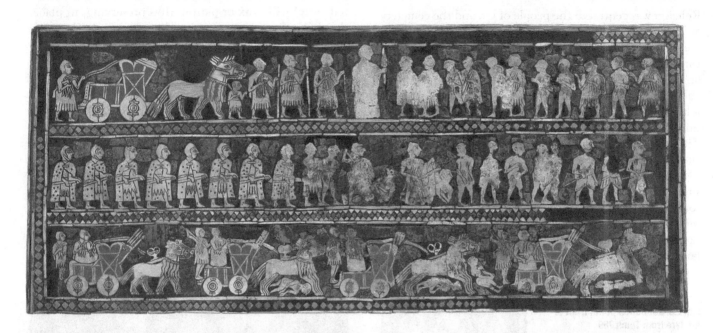

Fig. 2.8 _Royal Standard of Ur_, front ("War") and back ("Peace") sides, from tomb **779**, cemetery at Ur (modern Muqaiyir, Iraq). ca. **2600** BCE. Shell, lapis lazuli, and red limestone, originally on a wooden framework, height 8", length 19". © The Trustees of The British Museum/Art Resource, NY. For all its complexity of design, this object is not much bigger than a sheet of legal paper. Its function remains a mystery, though it may have served as a pillow or headrest. Sir Woolley's designation of it as a standard was purely conjectural.

SEE MORE To view a Closer Look feature about the _Royal Standard of Ur_, go to **www.myartslab.com**

The main panels of this rectangular box of unknown function are called "War" and "Peace," because they illustrate, on one side, a military victory and, on the other, the subsequent banquet celebrating the event, or perhaps a cult ritual. Each panel is composed of three **registers**, or self-contained horizontal bands within which the figures stand on a **ground-line**, or baseline.

At the right side of the top register of the "Peace" panel (the lower half of Fig. 2.8), a musician plays a lyre, and behind him another, apparently female, sings. The king, at the left end, is recognizable because he is taller than the others and wears a tufted skirt, his head breaking the register line on top. In this convention, known as **social perspective**, or **hierarchy of scale**, the most important figures are represented as larger than the others. In other registers on the "Peace" side of the *Standard*, servants bring cattle, goats, sheep, and fish to the celebration. These represent the bounty of the land and perhaps even delicacies from lands to the north. (Notice that the costumes and hairstyles of the figures carrying sacks in the lowest register are different from those in the other two.) This display of consumption and the distribution of food may have been intended to dramatize the power of the king by showing his ability to control trade routes.

On the "War" side of the *Standard*, the king stands in the middle of the top register. War chariots trample the enemy on the bottom register. (Note that the chariots have solid wheels; spoked wheels were not invented until approximately 1800 BCE.) In the middle register, soldiers wearing leather cloaks and bronze helmets lead naked, bound prisoners to the king in the top register, who will presumably decide their fate. Many of the bodies found in the royal tombs were wearing similar military garments. The importance of the *Royal Standard of Ur* is not simply as documentary evidence of Sumerian life but as one of the earliest examples we have of historical narrative.

AKKAD

At the height of the Sumerians' power in southern Mesopotamia, a people known as the Akkadians arrived from the north and settled in the area around modern Baghdad. Their capital city, Akkad [AK-ad], has never been discovered and in all likelihood lies under Baghdad itself. Under Sargon [SAR-gun] I (r. ca. 2332–2279 BCE), the Akkadians conquered virtually all other cities in Mesopotamia, including

those in Sumer, to become the region's most powerful city-state. Sargon named himself "King of the Four Quarters of the World" and equated himself with the gods, a status bestowed upon Akkadian rulers from Sargon's time forward. Legends about Sargon's might and power survived in the region for thousands of years. Indeed, the legend of his birth gave rise to what amounts to a **narrative genre** (a class or category of story with a universal theme) that survives to the present day: the boy from humble origins who rises to a position of might and power, the so-called "rags-to-riches" story.

As depicted on surviving clay tablets, Sargon was an illegitimate child whose mother deposited him in the Euphrates River in a basket. There, a man named Akki [AK-kee] (after whom Akkad itself is named) found him while drawing water from the river and raised him as his own son. Such stories of abandonment, orphanhood, and being a foundling raised by foster parents will become a standard feature in the narratives of mythic heroes.

Although the Akkadian language was very different from Sumerian, through most of the third millennium BCE—that is, until Sargon's dynastic ambitions altered the balance of power in the region—the two cultures coexisted peacefully. The Akkadians adopted Sumerian culture and customs (see Fig. 2.5) and their style of **cuneiform writing**, a script made of wedge-shaped characters (see *Closer Look*, pages 38–39), although not their language. In fact, many bilingual dictionaries and Sumerian texts with Akkadian translations survive. The Akkadian language was Semitic in origin, having more in common with other languages of the region, particularly Hebrew, Phoenician, and Arabic. It quickly became the common language of Mesopotamia, and peoples of the region spoke Akkadian, or dialects of it, throughout the second millennium BCE and well into the first.

Fig. 2.9 *Head of an Akkadian Man*, from Nineveh (modern Kuyunjik, Iraq). ca. 2300–2200 BCE. Copper alloy, height 14 1/8″ Iraq Museum, Baghdad.

Akkadian Sculpture

Although Akkad was arguably the most influential of the Mesopotamian cultures, few Akkadian artifacts survive, perhaps because Akkad and other nearby Akkadian cities have disappeared under Baghdad and the alluvial soils of the Euphrates plain. Two impressive sculptural works do remain, however. The first is the bronze head of an Akkadian man (Fig. 2.9), found at Nineveh [NIN-eh-vuh]. Once believed to be Sargon the Great himself, many modern scholars now think it was part of a statue of Sargon's grandson, Naramsin [nuh-RAHM-sin] (ca. 2254–2218 BCE). It may be neither, but it is certainly the bust of a king. Highly realistic, it

HEAR MORE Listen to the advice of a father to his son, written down over 4,000 years ago at **www.myartslab.com**

Writing first appeared in the middle of the fourth millennium BCE in agricultural records as **pictograms**—pictures that represent things or concepts—etched into clay tablets. For instance, the sign for "woman" is a pubic triangle, and the more complicated idea of "slave" is the sign for "woman" plus the sign for "mountains"—literally, a "woman from over the mountains":

woman   mountains   slave

Pictograms could also represent concepts. For instance, the signs for "hatred" and "friendship" are, respectively, an "X" and a set of parallel lines:

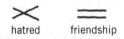

hatred   friendship

Beginning about 2900 BCE, most writing began to look more linear, for it was difficult to draw curves in wet clay. So scribes adopted a straight-line script made with a triangle-tipped **stylus** [STY-lus], or writing tool, cut from reeds. The resulting impressions looked like wedges. Cuneiform writing was named from the Latin *cuneus*, "wedge."

By 2000 BCE, another significant development in the progress of writing had appeared: Signs began to represent not things but sounds. This **phonetic writing** liberated the sign from its picture. Previously, they had been linked, as if, in English, we represented the word *belief* with pictograms for "bee" and "leaf."

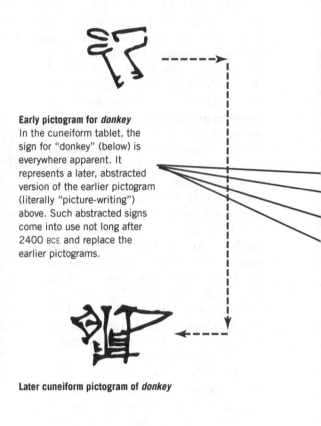

Early pictogram for *donkey*
In the cuneiform tablet, the sign for "donkey" (below) is everywhere apparent. It represents a later, abstracted version of the earlier pictogram (literally "picture-writing") above. Such abstracted signs come into use not long after 2400 BCE and replace the earlier pictograms.

Later cuneiform pictogram of *donkey*

stylus

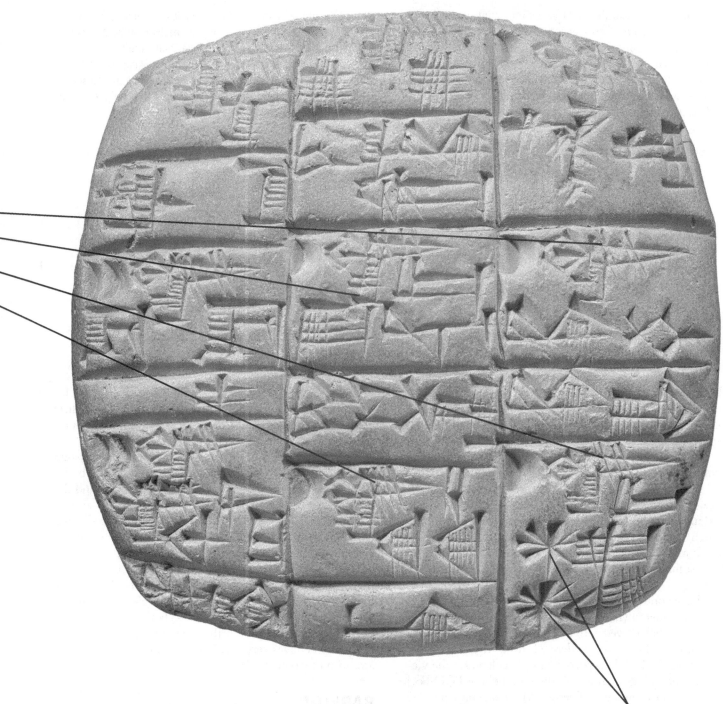

Sumerian tablet from Lagash, modern Tello, Iraq. ca. 2360 BCE. Clay. Musée du Louvre, Paris. This tablet is an economic document detailing the loan of donkeys to, among others, a farmer, a smith, and a courier.

These stars are the Sumerian sign for "god." They sometimes have many more points than the eight seen here.

Something to Think About . . .

What is it about this "document" that underscores the necessity of writing in the development of a civilization?

Lost-Wax Casting

At about the same time that cuneiform script was adopted, Mesopotamian culture also began to practice metallurgy, the process of mining and smelting ores. At first, copper was used almost exclusively; later, an alloy of copper and tin was melted and combined to make bronze. The resulting material was much stronger and more durable than anything previously known.

Because sources of copper and tin were mined in very different regions of the Middle East, the development of trade routes was a necessary prerequisite to the technology. While solid bronze pieces were made in simple molds as early as 4000 BCE, hollow bronze casts could produce larger pieces and were both more economical and lightweight. The technology for making hollow bronze casts was developed by the time of the Akkadians, in the second millennium BCE. Called **lost-wax casting**, the technique is illustrated below.

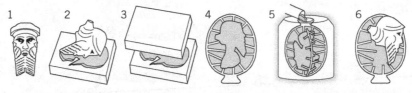

A positive model (1), often created with clay, is used to make a negative mold (2). The mold is coated with wax, the wax shell is filled with a cool fireclay, and the mold is removed (3). Metal rods, to hold the shell in place, and wax rods, to vent the mold, are then added (4). The whole is placed in sand, and the wax is burned out. Molten bronze is poured in where the wax used to be (5). When the bronze has hardened, the whole is removed from the sand and the rods and vents are removed (6).

EXPLORE MORE To see a studio video on lost-wax casting, go to **www.myartslab.com**

---

depicts a man who appears both powerful and majestic. In its damaged condition, the head is all that survives of a life-size statue that was destroyed in antiquity. Its original gemstone eyes were removed, perhaps by plundering soldiers, or possibly by a political enemy who recognized the sculpture as an emblem of absolute majesty. In the fine detail surrounding the face—in the beard and elaborate coiffure, with its braid circling the head—it testifies to the Akkadian mastery of the lost-wax casting technique, which originated in Mesopotamia as early as the third millennium BCE (see *Materials & Techniques*, above). It is the earliest monumental work made by that technique that we have.

The second Akkadian sculpture we will look at is the *Stele of Naramsin* (Fig. **2.10**). A **stele** [STEE-lee] is an upright stone slab carved with a commemorative design or inscription. (The word is derived from the Greek for "standing block.") This particular stele celebrates the victory of Sargon's grandson over the Lullubi [lool-LOO-bee] in the Zagros Mountains of eastern Mesopotamia sometime between 2252 and 2218 BCE. The king, as usual, is larger than anyone else (another example of social perspective or hierarchy of scale). The Akkadians, in fact, believed that Naramsin became divine during the course of his reign. In the stele, his divinity is represented by his horned helmet and by the physical perfection of his body. Bow and arrow in hand, he stands atop a mountain pass, dead and wounded Lullubians beneath his feet. Another Lullubian falls before

him, a spear in his neck. Yet another seems to plead for mercy as he flees to the right. Behind Naramsin, his soldiers climb the wooded slopes of the mountain—here represented by actual trees native to the region.

The sculptor abandoned the traditional register system that we saw in the *Royal Standard of Ur* and set the battle scene on a unified landscape. The lack of registers and the use of trees underscore the reality of the scene—and by implication, the reality of Naramsin's divinity. The divine and human worlds are, in fact, united here, for above Naramsin three stars (cuneiform symbols for the gods) look on, protecting both Naramsin, their representative on Earth, and his troops. Both the copper bust of the Akkadian king and *Stele of Naramsin* testify to the role of the king in Mesopotamian culture, in general, as both hero and divinity. If the king is not exactly the supreme god Marduk of the *Hymn*, he behaves very much like him, wielding the same awe-inspiring power.

BABYLON

The Akkadians dominated Mesopotamia for just 150 years, their rule collapsing not long after 2200 BCE. For the next 400 years, various city-states thrived locally. No one in Mesopotamia matched the Akkadians' power until the first decades of the eighteenth century BCE, when Hammurabi [ham-uh-RAH-bee] of Babylon [BAB-uh-lon] (r. 1792–1750 BCE) gained control of most of the region.

The Law Code of Hammurabi

Hammurabi imposed order on Babylon where laxness and disorder, if not chaos, reigned. A giant stele, the so-called *Law Code of Hammurabi*, survives (Fig. 2.11). By no means the first of its kind, though by far the most complete, the stele is a record of decisions and decrees made by Hammurabi over the course of some 40 years of his reign. Its purpose was to celebrate his sense of justice and the wisdom of his rule. Atop the stele, in sculptural relief, Hammurabi receives the blessing of Shamash, the sun god; notice the rays of light coming from his shoulders. The god is much larger than Hammurabi; in fact, he is to Hammurabi as Hammurabi, the patriarch, is to his people. If Hammurabi is divine, he is still subservient to the greater gods. At the same time, the phallic design of the stele, like such other Mesopotamian steles as the *Stele of Naramsin*, asserts the masculine prowess of the king.

Below the relief, 282 separate "articles" cover both sides of the basalt monument. One of the great debates of legal history is the question of whether these articles actually constitute a code of law. If by *code* we mean a comprehensive, systematic, and methodical compilation of all aspects of

Fig. 2.10 *Stele of Naramsin*, **from Susa (modern Shush, Iran).** **ca. 2254–2218 BCE.** Pink sandstone, height approx. 6' 6". Chuzeville/Musée du Louvre, Paris, France. This work, which was stolen by invading Elamites around 1157 BCE, as an inscription on the mountain indicates, was for centuries one of the most influential of all artworks, copied by many rulers to celebrate their own military feats.

SEE MORE To view a Closer Look feature about the *Stele of Naramsin*, go to **www.myartslab.com**

Fig. 2.11 *Stele of Hammurabi*, **from Susa (modern Shush, Iran). ca. 1760 BCE.** Diorite, height of stele, approx. 7', height of relief, 28". Musée du Louvre, Paris. Like the *Stele of Naramsin*, this stele was stolen by invading Elamites and removed to Susa, where, together with the *Stele of Naramsin*, it was excavated by the French in 1898.

Mesopotamian law, then it is not. It is instead selective, even eccentric, in the issues it addresses. Many of its articles seem to be "reforms" of already existing law, and as such they define new principles of justice.

Principles and Social Inequalities Chief among these is the principle of *talion* [TAL-ee-un]—an eye for an eye, a tooth for a tooth—which Hammurabi introduced to Mesopotamian law. (Sections of earlier codes from Ur compensate victims of crimes with money.) This principle punished the violence or injustice perpetuated by one free person upon another, but violence by an upper-class person on a lower-class person was penalized much less severely. Slaves (who might be either war captives or debtors) enjoyed no legal protection at all—only the protection of their owner.

The code tells us much about the daily lives of Mesopotamian peoples, including conflicts great and small. In rules governing family relations and class divisions in Mesopotamian society, inequalities are sharply drawn. Women are inferior to men, and wives, like slaves, are the personal property of their husbands (although protected from the abuse of neglectful or unjust husbands). Incest is strictly forbidden. Fathers cannot arbitrarily disinherit their sons—a son must have committed some "heavy crime" to justify such treatment. The code's strongest concern is the maintenance and protection of the family, though trade practices and property rights are also of major importance.

The following excerpts from the code, beginning with Hammurabi's assertion of his descent from the gods and his status as their favorite (**Reading 2.1**), give a sense of the code's scope. But the code is, finally, and perhaps above all, the gift of a king to his people, as Hammurabi's epilogue, at the end of the excerpt, makes clear:

READING 2.1

from the *Law Code of Hammurabi*
(ca. 1792–1750 BCE)

When the august god Anu, king of the Anunnaku deities, and the god Enlil, lord of heaven and earth, who determines the destinies of the land, allotted supreme power over all peoples to the god Marduk, the firstborn son of the god Ea, exalted him among the Igigu deities, named the city of Babylon with its august name and made it supreme exalted within the regions of the world, and established for him within it eternal kingship whose foundations are as fixed as heaven and earth, at that time, the gods Anu and Bel, for the enhancement of the well-being of the people, named me by my name, Hammurabi, the pious prince, who venerates the gods, to make justice prevail in the land, to abolish the wicked and the evil, to prevent the strong from oppressing the weak, to rise like the Sun-god Shamash over all humankind, to illuminate the land. . . .

1. If a man accuses another man and charges him with homicide but cannot bring proof against him, his accuser shall be killed. . . .

8. If a man steals an ox, a sheep, a donkey, a pig, or a boat—if it belongs either to the god or to the palace, he shall give thirtyfold; if it belongs to a commoner, he shall replace it tenfold; if the thief does not have anything to give, he shall be killed. . . .

32. If there is either a soldier or a fisherman who is taken captive while on a royal campaign, a merchant redeems him, and helps him get back to his city—if there are sufficient in his own estate for the redeeming, he himself shall redeem himself: if there are not sufficient means in his estate to redeem him he shall be redeemed by his city's temple; if there are not sufficient means in his city's temple to redeem him, the palace shall redeem him; but his field, orchard, or house shall not be given for his redemption. . . .

143. If [a woman] is not circumspect, but is wayward, squanders her household possessions, and disparages her husband, they shall cast that woman into the water. . . .

195. If a child should strike his father, they shall cut off his hand.

196. If an *awilu* [in general, a person subject to law] should blind the eye of another *awilu*, they shall blind his eye.

197. If he should break the bone of another *awilu*, they shall break his bone. . . .

229. If a builder constructs a house for a man but does not make his work sound, and the house he constructs collapses and causes the death of the householder, that builder shall be killed. . . .

282. If a slave should declare to his master, "You are not my master," he (the master) shall bring charge and proof against him that he is indeed his slave, and his master shall cut off his ear. . . .

These are the decisions which Hammurabi, the able king, has established, and thereby has directed the land along the course of truth and the correct way of life.

I am Hammurabi, noble king. . .

May any king who will appear in the land in the future, at any time, observe the pronouncements of justice that I have inscribed upon my stele. May he not alter the judgments that I rendered and verdicts that I gave, nor remove my engraved image. If that man has discernment, and is capable of providing just ways for his land may he heed the pronouncements I have inscribed upon my stele, may the stele reveal for him the traditions, the proper conduct, the judgements of the land that I rendered, the verdicts of the land that I gave and may he, too, provide just ways for all humankind in his care. . . .

I am Hammurabi, king of justice. . . .

Consequences of the Code Even if Hammurabi meant only to assert the idea of justice as the basis for his own divine rule, the stele established what amounts to a uniform code throughout Mesopotamia. It was repeatedly copied for over a thousand years, long after it was removed to Susa in 1157 BCE with the Naramsin stele, and it established the rule of law in

Mesopotamia for a millennium. From this point on, the authority and power of the ruler could no longer be capricious, subject to the whim, fancy, and subjective interpretation of his singular personality. The law was now, at least ostensibly, more objective and impartial. The ruler was required to follow certain prescribed procedures. But the law, so prescribed in writing, was now also much less flexible, hard to change, and much more impersonal. Exceptions to the rule were few and difficult to justify. Eventually, written law would remove justice from the discretion of the ruler and replace it by a legal establishment of learned judges charged with enacting the king's statutes.

THE ASSYRIAN EMPIRE

With the fall of Babylon in 1595 BCE to a sudden invasion of Hittites from Turkey, the entire Middle East appears to have undergone a period of disruption and instability. Only the Assyrians, who lived around the city of Assur in the north, managed to maintain a continuing cultural identity. Over the centuries, they became increasingly powerful until, beginning with the reign of Ashurnasirpal II (r. 883–859 BCE), they dominated the entire region.

Ashurnasirpal [ah-SHOOR-na-zir-pahl] II built a magnificent capital at Kalhu (modern Nimrud), on the Tigris River, surrounded by nearly 5 miles of walls, 120 feet thick and 42 feet high. A surviving inscription tells us that Ashurnasirpal invited 69,574 people to celebrate the city's dedication. The entire population of the region, of all classes, probably did not exceed 100,000, and thus many guests from throughout Mesopotamia and farther away must have been invited.

Assyrian Art Alabaster reliefs decorated many of the walls of Ashurnasirpal's palace complex, including a depiction of *Ashurnasirpal II Killing Lions* (Fig. **2.12**). The scene uses many of the conventions of Assyrian pictorial representation. For instance, to create a sense of deep space, the sculptor used the device of overlapping, which we first encountered in prehistoric cave paintings (see Fig. 1.2). This is done convincingly where the king stands in his chariot in front of its driver, but less so in the case of the horses drawing the chariot. For instance, there are three horse heads but only six visible legs—three in front and three in back. Furthermore, Assyrian artists never hid the face of an archer (in this case, the king himself) by realistically having him aim down the shaft of the arrow, which would have the effect of covering his eye with his hand. Instead, they drop the arrow to shoulder level and completely omit the bowstring so that it appears to pass (impossibly) behind the archer's head and back.

The scene is also a **synoptic** view, that is, it depicts several consecutive actions at once: As soldiers drive the lion toward the king from the left, he shoots it; to the right, the same lion lies dying beneath the horses' hooves. If Assyrian artists seem unconcerned about accurately portraying the animals, that is because the focus of the work is on the king himself, whose prowess in combating the lion, traditional symbol of power, underscores his own invincibility. And it is in the artists' careful balance of forms—the relationship between the positive shapes of the relief figures and the negative space between them—that we sense the importance placed on an orderly arrangement of parts. This orderliness reflects, in all probability, their sense of the orderly character of their society.

Fig. 2.12 *Ashurnasirpal II Killing Lions*, **from the palace complex of Ashurnasirpal II, Kalhu (modern Nimrud, Iraq). ca. 850 BCE.** Alabaster, height approx. 39″. The British Museum, London. The repetition of forms throughout this relief helps create a stunning design. Notice especially how the two shields carried by the soldiers are echoed by the chariot wheel and the king's arched bow.

Cultural Propaganda Rulers in every culture and age have used the visual arts to broadcast their power. These reliefs were designed to celebrate and underscore for all visitors to Ashurnasirpal's palace the military prowess of the Assyrian army and their king. They are thus a form of cultural propaganda, celebrating the kingdom's achievements even as they intimidate its potential adversaries. In fact, the Assyrians were probably the most militant civilization of ancient Mesopotamia, benefactors of the invention of iron weaponry. By 721 BCE, the Assyrians had used their iron weapons to conquer Israel, and by the middle of the seventh century BCE, they controlled most of Asia Minor from the Nile Valley to the Persian Gulf.

The Assyrians also used their power to preserve Mesopotamian culture. Two hundred years after the reign of Ashurnasirpal, Ashurbanipal (r. 668–627 BCE) created the great library where, centuries later, the clay tablets containing the Sumerian *Epic of Gilgamesh*, discussed in the following pages, were stored. Its still partially intact collection today consists of 20,000 to 30,000 cuneiform tablets containing approximately 1,200 distinct texts, including a nearly complete list of ancient Mesopotamian rulers. Each of its many rooms was dedicated to individual subjects—history and government, religion and magic, geography, science, poetry, and important government materials.

As late as Ashurbanipal's reign, reliefs of the lion hunt were still a favored form of palace decoration, but those depicted from his palace at Nineveh, in what is now northern Iraq, reveal that the lions were caged and released for the king's hunt, which was now more ritual than real, taking place in an enclosed arena. The lions were sacrificed as an offering to the gods. In one section of the relief, Ashurbanipal, surrounded by musicians, pours a libation, a liquid offering to the gods, over the dead animals as servants bring more bodies to the offering table. This ritual was implicit in all kingly hunts, even Ashurnasirpal's 200 years earlier, for in his pursuit and defeat of the wild beast, the ruler masters the most elemental force of nature—the cycle of life and death itself.

The Assyrian kings represented their might and power not only through the immense size of their palaces and the decorative programs within, but also through massive gateways that greeted the visitor. Especially impressive are the gateways with giant stone monuments, such as those in Iraq at the Khorsabad [KOR-suh-bahd] palace of Sargon II (r. 721–705 BCE), who named himself after Sargon of Akkad. These monuments (Fig. 2.13) are **composites**, part man, part bull, and part eagle, the bull signifying the king's strength and the eagle his vigilance. The king himself wears the traditional horned crown of Akkad and the beard of Sumer, thus containing within himself all Mesopotamian history. Such composites, especially in monumental size, were probably intended to amaze and terrify the visitor and to underscore the ruler's embodiment of all the forces of nature, which is to say, his embodiment of the very gods.

MESOPOTAMIAN LITERATURE

Sumerian literature survives on nearly 100,000 clay tablets and fragments. Many deal with religious themes in the form of poems, blessings, and incantations to the gods.

The Blessing of Inanna

One particularly interesting Sumerian religious work is *The Blessing of Inanna* (**Reading 2.2**). It recounts the myth of the goddess Inanna, here depicted as a young girl from Uruk who decides to visit Enki, the god of wisdom. Inanna travels south to Eridu, the chief seaport of Sumer, where Enki lives. Apparently taken with Inanna, Enki offers a series of toasts, each time bestowing upon her one of his special powers, including the highest powers of all:

Fig. 2.13 *Human-Headed Winged Bull*, **one of a pair from the entrance to the palace of Sargon II, Khorsabad, Iraq. ca. 720 BCE.** Limestone, height approx. 13′ 10″. Musée du Louvre, France. Seen from a three-quarter view, as here, this hybrid beast that guarded the palace entrance has five legs. He stands firmly before you when seen from the front, and seems to stride by you when seen from the side.

The Blessing of Inanna (ca. 2300 BCE)

Enki and Inanna drank beer together.
They drank more beer together.
They drank more and more beer together.
With their bronze vessels filled to overflowing,
With the vessels of Urash, Mother of the Earth
They toasted each other; they challenged each other.
Enki, swaying with drink,
   toasted Inanna: "In the name of my power!
In the name of my holy shrine!
To my daughter Inanna I shall give
The high priesthood! Godship!
The noble, enduring crown! The throne of kingship!"
Inanna replied: "I take them!"

Having gathered all 80 of Enki's mighty powers, Inanna piles them all into her boat and sails back up river. The drunken Enki realizes what he has done and tries to recover his blessings, but Inanna fends him off. She returns to Uruk, blessed as a god, and enters the city triumphantly, bestowing now her own gifts on her people, who subsequently worship her. Enki and the people of Eridu are forced to acknowledge the glory of Inanna and her city of Uruk, assuring peace and harmony between the two competing city-states.

The Sumerians worshipped Inanna as the goddess of fertility and heaven. In this tale, she and Enki probably represent the spirits of their respective cities and the victory of Uruk over Eridu. That Inanna appears in the work first as a mere mortal is a classic example of *anthropomorphism*, endowing the gods and the forces of nature that they represent with humanlike traits. The story has some basis in fact, since Uruk and Eridu are the two oldest Mesopotamian cities, and surviving literary fragments suggest that the two cities were at war sometime after 3400 BCE.

The *Epic of Gilgamesh*

One of the great surviving manuscripts of Mesopotamian culture and the oldest story ever recorded is the *Epic of Gilgamesh*. It consists of some 2,900 lines written in Akkadian cuneiform script on eleven clay tablets, none of them completely whole (Fig. **2.14**). It was composed sometime before Ashurbanipal's reign, possibly as early as 1200 BCE, by Sinleqqiunninni [sin-lek-KEE-un-nin-nee] a scholar-priest of Uruk. This would make Sinleqqiunninni the oldest known author. We know that Gilgamesh was the fourth king of Uruk, ruling sometime between 2700 and 2500 BCE. (The dates of his rule were recorded on a clay tablet, the *Sumerian King List*.) Recovered fragments of his story date back nearly to his actual reign, and the story we have, known as the Standard Version, is a compilation of these earlier versions.

The work is the first example we have of an **epic,** a long, narrative poem in elevated language that follows characters of a high position through a series of adventures, often including a visit to the world of the dead. For many literary scholars, the epic is the most exalted poetic form. The central figure is a legendary or historical figure of heroic proportion, in this case the Sumerian king Gilgamesh. Homer's *Iliad* and *Odyssey* (see Chapter 4) had been considered the earliest epic, until late in the nineteenth century, when *Gilgamesh* was discovered in the library of King Ashurbanipal at

Fig. 2.14 Fragment of Tablet 11 of the *Epic of Gilgamesh*, containing the Flood Story. From the Library of Ashurbanipal, Nineveh (modern Kuyunjik, Iraq). Second millennium BCE. © The Trustees of the British Museum/Art Resource, NY. This example, which is relatively complete, shows how difficult it is to reconstruct the *Gilgamesh* epic in its entirety.

Nineveh, believed to be the first library of texts in history systematically collected and organized.

The scope of an epic is large. The supernatural world of gods and goddesses usually plays a role in the story, as do battles in which the hero demonstrates his strength and courage. The poem's language is suitably dignified, often consisting of many long, formal speeches. Lists of various heroes or catalogs of their achievements are frequent.

Epics are often compilations of preexisting myths and tales handed down generation to generation, often orally, and finally unified into a whole by the epic poet. Indeed, the main outline of the story is usually known to its audience. The poet's contribution is the artistry brought to the subject, demonstrated through the use of epithets, metaphors, and similes. **Epithets** are words or phrases that characterize a person (for example, "Enkidu, the protector of herdsmen," or "Enkidu, the son of the mountain"). **Metaphors** are words or phrases used in place of another to suggest a similarity between the two, as when Gilgamesh is described as a "raging flood-wave who destroys even walls of stone." **Similes** compare two unlike things by the use of the word "like" or "as" (for example, "the land shattered like a pot").

Perhaps most important, the epic illuminates the development of a nation or race. It is a national poem, describing a people's common heritage and celebrating its cultural identity. It is hardly surprising, then, that Ashurbanipal preserved the *Epic of Gilgamesh*. Just as Sargon II depicted himself at the gates of Khorsabad in the traditional horned crown of Akkad and the beard of Sumer, containing within himself all Mesopotamian history, the *Epic of Gilgamesh* preserves the historical lineage of all Mesopotamian kings—Sumerian, Akkadian, Assyrian, and Babylonian. The tale embodies their own heroic grandeur, and thus the grandeur of their peoples.

The poem opens with a narrator guiding a visitor (the reader) around Uruk. The narrator explains that the epic was written by Gilgamesh himself and was deposited in the city's walls, where visitors can read it for themselves. Then the narrator introduces Gilgamesh as an epic hero, two parts god and one part human. The style of the following list of his deeds is the same as in hymns to the gods (**Reading 2.3a**):

READING 2.3a

from the *Epic of Gilgamesh*, Tablet I
(ca. 1200 BCE)

Supreme over other kings, lordly in appearance,
he is the hero, born of Uruk, the goring wild bull.
He walks out in front, the leader,
and walks at the rear, trusted by his companions.
Mighty net, protector of his people,
raging flood-wave who destroys even walls of stone! . . .
It was he who opened the mountain passes,
who dug wells on the flank of the mountain.

It was he who crossed ocean, the vast seas, to the rising sun,
who explored the world regions, seeking life.
It was he who reached by his own sheer strength the Utanapishtim, the Faraway,
who restored the cities that the Flood had destroyed! . . .
Who can compare to him in kingliness?
Who can say like Gilgamesh: "I am King!"?

After a short break in the text, Gilgamesh is described as having originally oppressed his people. Hearing the pleas of the people for relief, the gods create a rival, Enkidu [EN-kee-doo], to challenge Gilgamesh (**Reading 2.3b**):

READING 2.3b

from the *Epic of Gilgamesh*, Tablet I
(ca. 1200 BCE)

Enkidu
born of Silence, endowed with the strength of Ninurta.
His whole body was shaggy with hair,
he had a full head of hair like a woman. . . .
He knew neither people nor settled living. . . .
He ate grasses with the gazelles,
and jostled at the watering hole with the animals.

Enkidu is, in short, Gilgamesh's opposite, and their confrontation is an example of the classic struggle between nature, represented by Enkidu, and civilization, by Gilgamesh. Seduced by a harlot (see **Reading 2.3c**, page 47), Enkidu loses his ability to commune with the animals (i.e., he literally loses his innocence), and when he finally wrestles Gilgamesh, the contest ends in a draw. The two become best friends.

Gilgamesh proposes that he and Enkidu undertake a great adventure, a journey to the Cedar Forest (either in present-day southern Iran or Lebanon), where they will kill its guardian, Humbaba [hum-BAH-buh] the Terrible, and cut down all the forest's trees. Each night on the six-day journey to the forest, Gilgamesh has a terrible dream, which Enkidu manages to interpret in a positive light. As the friends approach the forest, the god Shamash informs Gilgamesh that Humbaba is wearing only one of his seven coats of armor and is thus extremely vulnerable. When Gilgamesh and Enkidu enter the forest and begin cutting down trees, Humbaba comes roaring up to warn them off. An epic battle ensues, and Shamash intervenes to help the two heroes defeat the great guardian. Just before Gilgamesh cuts off Humbaba's head, Humbaba curses Enkidu, promising that he will find no peace in the world and will die before his friend Gilgamesh. In a gesture that clearly evokes the triumph of civilization over nature, Gilgamesh and Enkidu cut down the tallest of the cedar trees to make a great cedar gate for the city of Uruk.

At the center of the poem, in Tablet VI, Ishtar, goddess of both love and war, offers to marry Gilgamesh. Gilgamesh refuses, which unleashes Ishtar's wrath. She sends the Bull of Heaven to destroy them, but Gilgamesh and Enkidu slay it instead (see Reading 2.3c)

READING 2.3c

from the *Epic of Gilgamesh*, Tablet VI
(ca. 1200 BCE)

A Woman Scorned

. . .When Gilgamesh placed his crown on his head
Princess, Ishtar raised her eyes to the beauty of Gilgamesh.
  "Come along, Gilgamesh, be you my husband,
  to me grant your lusciousness.[1]
  Be you my husband, and I will be your wife.
  I will have harnessed for you a chariot of lapis
      lazuli and gold,
  with wheels of gold . . .
  Bowed down beneath you will be kings, lords,
      and princes.
  The Lullubu people[2] will bring you the produce of the
      mountains and countryside as tribute.
  Your she-goats will bear triplets, your ewes twins,
  your donkey under burden will overtake the mule,
  your steed at the chariot will be bristling to gallop,
  your ox at the yoke will have no match."
Gilgamesh addressed Princess Ishtar saying:
  Do you need oil or garments for your body?
  Do you lack anything for food or drink?
  I would gladly feed you food fit for a god,
  I would gladly give you wine fit for a king . . .
  a half-door that keeps out neither breeze nor blast,
  a palace that crushes down valiant warriors,
  an elephant who devours its own covering,
  pitch that blackens the hands of its bearer,
  a waterskin that soaks its bearer through,
  limestone that buckles out the stone wall,
  a battering ram that attracts the enemy land,
  a shoe that bites its owner's feet!
  Where are your bridegrooms that you keep
      forever? . . .
  You loved the supremely mighty lion,
  yet you dug for him seven and again seven pits.
  You loved the stallion, famed in battle,
  yet you ordained for him the whip, the goad,
      and the lash,
  ordained for him to gallop for seven and seven
      hours,
  ordained for him drinking from muddied waters,[3]

[1]Literally "fruit."
[2]The Lullubu were a wild mountain people living in the area of modern-day western Iran. The meaning is that even the wildest, least controllable of peoples will recognize Gilgamesh's rule and bring tribute.
[3]Horses put their front feet in the water when drinking, churning up mud.

  you ordained for his mother Silili to wail
      continually.
  You loved the Shepherd, the Master Herder,
  who continually presented you with bread
      baked in embers,
  and who daily slaughtered for you a kid.
  Yet you struck him, and turned him into a wolf,
  so his own shepherds now chase him
  and his own dogs snap at his shins.
  You loved Ishullanu, your father's date gardener,
  who continually brought you baskets of dates,
  and brightened your table daily.
  You raised your eyes to him, and you went to him:
      'Oh my Ishullanu, let us taste of your strength,
      stretch out your hand to me, and touch our
          "vulva."'[4]
  Ishullanu said to you:
      'Me? What is it you want from me?. . .'
  As you listened to these his words
  you struck him, turning him into a dwarf(?),[5] . . .
  And now me! It is me you love, and you will ordain
for me as for them!"

Her Fury

When Ishtar heard this
in a fury she went up to the heavens,
going to Anu, her father, and crying,
going to Antum, her mother, and weeping:
  "Father, Gilgamesh has insulted me over and over,
  Gilgamesh has recounted despicable deeds
      about me,
  despicable deeds and curses!"
Anu addressed Princess Ishtar, saying:
  "What is the matter? Was it not you who
      provoked King Gilgamesh?
  So Gilgamesh recounted despicable deeds about
      you,
  despicable deeds and curses!"
Ishtar spoke to her father, Anu, saying:
  "Father, give me the Bull of Heaven,
  so he can kill Gilgamesh in his dwelling.
  If you do not give me the Bull of Heaven,
  I will knock down the Gates of the Netherworld,
  I will smash the door posts, and leave the doors
      flat down,
  and will let the dead go up to eat the living!
  And the dead will outnumber the living!"
Anu addressed Princess Ishtar, saying:
  "If you demand the Bull of Heaven from me,
  there will be seven years of empty husks for the
      land of Uruk.
  Have you collected grain for the people?
  Have you made grasses grow for the animals?"
Ishtar addressed Anu, her father, saying:
  "I have heaped grain in the granaries for the people,

[4]This line probably contains a word play on *hurdatu* as "vulva" and "date palm," the latter being said (in another unrelated text) to be "like the vulva."
[5]Or "frog"?

I made grasses grow for the animals,
    in order that they might eat in the seven years of
        empty husks.
I have collected grain for the people,
I have made grasses grow for the animals. . . ."
When Anu heard her words,
he placed the nose-rope of the Bull of Heaven in her
    hand.
Ishtar led the Bull of Heaven down to the earth.
When it reached Uruk. . .
It climbed down to the Euphrates . . .
At the snort of the Bull of Heaven a huge pit opened
    up,
and 100 Young Men of Uruk fell in.
At his second snort a huge pit opened up,
and 200 Young Men of Uruk fell in.
At his third snort a huge pit opened up,
and Enkidu fell in up to his waist.
Then Enkidu jumped out and seized the Bull of
    Heaven by its horns.
The Bull spewed his spittle in front of him,
with his thick tail he flung *his dung behind him* (?).
Enkidu addressed Gilgamesh, saying:
    "My friend, we can be bold(?) . . .
    Between the nape, the horns, and . . . thrust your
        sword."
Enkidu stalked and *hunted down* the Bull of Heaven.
He grasped it by the thick of its tail
and held onto it with both his hands (?),
while Gilgamesh, like an *expert butcher*,
boldly and *surely approached the Bull of Heaven*.
Between the nape, the horns, and . . . he thrust his
    sword. . . .
Ishtar went up onto the top of the Wall of Uruk-
    Haven,
cast herself into the pose of mourning, and hurled
    her woeful curse:
    "Woe unto Gilgamesh who slandered me and
        killed the Bull of Heaven!"
When Enkidu heard this pronouncement of Ishtar,
he wrenched off the Bull's hindquarter and flung it in her
    face:
    "If I could only get at you I would do the same to
        you!
    I would drape his innards over your arms!". . .
Gilgamesh said to the palace retainers:
    "Who is the bravest of the men?
    Who is the boldest of the males?
    —Gilgamesh is the bravest of the men,
    the boldest of the males!
    She at whom we flung the hindquarter of the Bull
        of Heaven in anger,
    Ishtar has no one that pleases her . . ."

But Gilgamesh and Enkidu cannot avoid the wrath of
the gods altogether. One of them, the gods decide, must die,
and so Enkidu suffers a long, painful death, attended by his
friend, Gilgamesh, who is terrified (**Reading 2.3d**):

Dismayed at the prospect of his own mortality, Gilgamesh
embarks on a journey to find the secret of eternal life from
the only mortal known to have attained it, Utnapishtim [ut-
na-PISH-tim], who tells him the story of the Great Flood.
Several elements of Utnapishtim's story deserve explanation.
First of all, this is the earliest known version of the flood
story that occurs also in the Hebrew Bible, with Utnapishtim
in the role of the biblical Noah. The motif of a single man
and wife surviving a worldwide flood brought about by the
gods occurs in several Middle Eastern cultures, suggesting a
single origin or shared tradition. In the Sumerian version, Ea
(Enki) warns Utnapishtim of the flood by speaking to the
wall, thereby technically keeping the agreement among the
gods not to warn mortals of their upcoming disaster. The passage in which Ea tells Utnapishtim how to explain his actions to his people without revealing the secret of the gods is
one of extraordinary complexity and wit (**Reading 2.3e**).
The word for "bread" is *kukku*, a pun on the word for "darkness," *kukkû*. Similarly, the word for "wheat," *kibtu*, also
means "misfortune." Thus, when Ea says, "He will let loaves
of bread shower down, / and in the evening a rain of wheat,"
he is also telling the truth: "He will let loaves of darkness
shower down, and in the evening a rain of misfortune."

Ea, the Clever Prince, was under oath with them
so he repeated their talk to the reed house:
'Reed house, reed house! Wall, wall!
Hear, O reed house! Understand, O wall!
O man of Shuruppak, son of Ubartutu:
Tear down the house and build a boat!
Abandon wealth and seek living beings!
Spurn possessions and keep alive human beings!
Make all living beings go up into the boat.
The boat which you are to build,
its dimensions must measure equal to each other:
its length must correspond to its width,
Roof it over like the Apsu.'
I understood and spoke to my lord, Ea:
'My lord, thus is your command.
I will heed and will do it.
But what shall I answer the city, the populace, and
    the Elders?'

Ea spoke, commanding me, his servant:
'. . . this is what you must say to them:
"It appears that Enlil is rejecting me
so I cannot reside in your city,
nor set foot on Enlil's earth.
I will go . . . to live with my lord, Ea,
and upon you he will rain down abundance,
a profusion of fowls, myriad fishes.
He will bring you a harvest of wealth,
in the morning he will let loaves of bread shower down,
and in the evening a rain of wheat."' . . .

I butchered oxen for the meat(?),
and day upon day I slaughtered sheep.
I gave the workmen(?) ale, beer, oil, and wine, as if it
    were river water,
so they could make a party like the New Year's
    Festival. . . .
The boat was finished. . . .
Whatever I had I loaded on it:
whatever silver I had I loaded on it,
whatever gold I had I loaded on it.
Al the living beings that I had I loaded on it,
I had all my kith and kin go up into the boat,
all the beasts and animals of the field and the
    craftsmen I had go up. . . .

I watched the appearance of the weather—
the weather was frightful to behold!
I went into the boat and sealed the entry. . . .
Just as dawn began to glow
there arose on the horizon a black cloud.
Adad rumbled inside it. . . .
Stunned shock over Adad's deeds overtook the heavens,
and turned to blackness all that had been light.
The . . . land shattered like a . . . pot.
All day long the South Wind blew . . . ,
blowing fast, submerging the mountain in water,
overwhelming the people like an attack.
No one could see his fellow,
they could not recognize each other in the torrent.
The gods were frightened by the Flood,
and retreated, ascending to the heaven of Anu.

The gods were cowering like dogs, crouching by the
    outer wall.
Ishtar shrieked like a woman in childbirth. . . .
Six days and seven nights
came the wind and flood, the storm flattening the land.
When the seventh day arrived, the storm was pounding,
the flood was a war—struggling with itself like a
    woman writhing (in labor).
The sea calmed, fell still, the whirlwind (and) flood
    stooped up.
I looked around all day long—quiet had set in
and all the human beings had turned to clay!
The terrain was flat as a roof.
I opened a vent and fresh air (daylight?) fell upon the
    side of my nose.
I fell to my knees and sat weeping,
tears streaming down the side of my nose.
I looked around for coastlines in the expanse of the sea,
and at twelve leagues there emerged a region (of land).
On Mt. Nimush the boat lodged firm,
Mt. Nimush held the boat, allowing no sway.

When the gods discover Utnapishtim alive, smelling his incense offering, they are outraged. They did not want a single living being to escape. But since he has, they grant him immortality and allow him to live forever in the Faraway. As a reward for Gilgamesh's own efforts, Utnapishtim tells Gilgamesh of a secret plant that will give him perpetual youth. "I will eat it," he tells the boatman who is returning him home, "and I will return to what I was in my youth." But when they stop for the night, Gilgamesh decides to bathe in a cool pool, where the scent of the plant attracts a snake who steals it away, an echo of the biblical story of Adam and Eve, whose own immortality is stolen away by the wiles of a serpent—and their own carelessness. Broken-hearted, Gilgamesh returns home empty-handed.

The *Epic of Gilgamesh* is the first known literary work to confront the idea of death, which is, in many ways, the very embodiment of the unknown. Although the hero goes to the very ends of the earth in his quest, he ultimately leaves with nothing to show for his efforts except an understanding of his own, very human, limitations. He is the first hero in Western literature to yearn for what he can never attain, to seek to understand what must always remain a mystery. And, of course, until the death of his friend Enkidu, Gilgamesh had seemed, in his self-confident confrontation with Ishtar and in the defeat of the Bull of Heaven, as near to a god as a mortal might be. In short, he embodied the Mesopotamian hero-king. Even as the poem asserts the hero-king's divinity—Gilgamesh is, remember, two parts god—it emphasizes his humanity and the mortality that accompanies it. By making literal the first words of the *Sumerian King List*—"After the kingship had descended from heaven"—the *Epic of Gilgamesh* acknowledges what many Mesopotamian kings were unwilling to admit, at least publicly: their own, very human, limitations, their own powerlessness in the face of the ultimate unknown—death.

THE HEBREWS

The Hebrews (from *Habiru*, "outcast" or "nomad") were a people forced out of their homeland in the Mesopotamian basin in about 2000 BCE. According to their tradition, it was in the delta of the Tigris and Euphrates rivers that God created Adam and Eve in the Garden of Eden. It was there that Noah survived the same great flood that Utnapishtim survived in the *Epic of Gilgamesh*. And it was out of there that Abraham of Ur led his people into Canaan [KAY-nun], in order to escape the warlike Akkadians and the increasingly powerful Babylonians. There is no actual historical evidence to support these stories. We know them only from the Hebrew Bible—a word that derives from the Greek, *biblia*, "books"—a compilation of hymns, prophecies, and laws transcribed by its authors between 800 and 400 BCE, some 1,000 years after the events the Hebrew Bible describes. Although the archeological record in the Near East confirms some of what these scribes and priests wrote, especially about more contemporaneous events, the stories themselves were edited and collated into the stories we know today. They recount the Assyrian conquest of Israel, the Jews' later exile to Babylon after the destruction of Jerusalem by the Babylonian king Nebuchadnezzar [neb-uh-kud-NEZ-ur] in 587 BCE, and their eventual return to Jerusalem after the Persians conquered the Babylonians in 538 BCE. The stories represent the Hebrews' attempt to maintain their sense of their own history and destiny. But it would be a mistake to succumb to the temptation to read the Hebrew Bible as an accurate account of the historical record. Like all ancient histories, passed down orally through generation upon generation, it contains its fair share of mythologizing.

The Hebrews differed from other Near Eastern cultures in that their religion was *monotheistic*—they worshipped a single god, whereas others in the region tended to have gods for their clans and cities, among other things. According to Hebrew tradition, God made an agreement with the Hebrews, first with Noah after the flood, later renewed with Abraham and each of the subsequent **patriarchs** (scriptural fathers of the Hebrew people): "I am God Almighty; be fruitful and multiply; a nation and a company of nations shall come from you. The land which I gave to Abraham and Isaac I will give to you, and I will give the land to your descendants after you" (Genesis 35: 11–12). In return for this promise, the Hebrews, the "chosen people," agreed to obey God's will. "Chosen people" means that the Jews were chosen to set an example of a higher moral standard (a light unto the nations), not chosen in the sense of favored, which is a common misunderstanding of the term.

Genesis, the first book of the Hebrew Bible, tells the story of the creation of the world out of a "formless void." It describes God's creation of the world and all its creatures, and his continuing interest in the workings of the world, an interest that would lead, in the story of Noah, to God's near-destruction of all things. It also posits humankind as easily tempted by evil. It documents the moment of the introduction of sin (and shame) into the cosmos, associating these with the single characteristic separating humans from animals—knowledge. And it shows, in the example of Noah, the reward for having "walked with God," the basis of the covenant. (See **Reading 2.4**, pages 61–63, for two selections from Genesis, the story of Adam and Eve and the story of Noah.)

Moses and the Ten Commandments

The biblical story of Moses and the Ten Commandments embodies the centrality of the written word to Jewish culture. The Hebrew Bible claims that in about 1600 BCE, drought forced the Hebrew people to leave Canaan for Egypt, where they prospered until the Egyptians enslaved them in about 1300 BCE. Defying the rule of the pharaohs, the Jewish patriarch Moses led his people out of Egypt. According to tradition, Moses led the Jews across the Red Sea (which miraculously parted to facilitate the escape) and into the desert of the Sinai [SYE-nye] peninsula. (The story became the basis for the book of Exodus.) Most likely, they crossed a large tidal flat, called the Sea of Reeds; subsequently, that body of water was misidentified as the Red Sea. Unable to return to Canaan, which was now occupied by local tribes of considerable military strength, the Jews settled in an arid region of the Sinai desert near the Dead Sea for a period of 40 years, which archeologists date to sometime between 1300 and 1150 BCE.

In the Sinai desert, the Hebrews forged the principal tenets of a new religion that would eventually be based on the worship of a single god. There, too, the Hebrew god supposedly revealed a new name for himself—YHWH, a name so sacred that it could neither be spoken nor written. The name is not known and YHWH is a cipher for it. There are, however, many other names for God in the Hebrew Bible, among them Elohim [eh-loe-HEEM], which is plural in Hebrew, meaning "gods, deities"; Adonai [ah-dun-EYE] ("Lord"); and El Shaddai [shah-die], literally "God of the fields" but usually translated "God Almighty." Some scholars believe that this demonstrates the multiple authorship of the Bible. Others argue that the Hebrews originally worshipped many gods, like other Near Eastern peoples. Still other scholars suggest that God has been given different names to reflect different aspects of his divinity, or the different roles that he might assume—the guardian of the flocks in the fields, or the powerful master of all. Translated into Latin as "Jehovah" [ji-HOH-vuh] in the Middle Ages, the name is now rendered in English as "Yahweh." This God

Fig. 2.15 The Ark of the Covenant and sanctuary implements, mosaic floor decorations from Hammath near Tiberias, Israel. Fourth century CE. Z. Radovan/www.BibleLandPictures.com. Israel Antiquities Authority, Jerusalem. Two menorahs (seven-branched candelabras) flank each side of the Ark. The menorah is considered a symbol of the nation of Israel and its mission to be "a light unto the nations" (Isaiah 42:6). Instructions for making it are outlined in Exodus 25:31–40. Relatively little ancient Jewish art remains. Most of it was destroyed as the Jewish people were conquered, persecuted, and exiled.

also gave Moses the Ten Commandments, carved onto stone tablets, as recorded in Deuteronomy 5:6–21. Subsequently, the Hebrews carried the commandments in a sacred chest, called the Ark of the Covenant (Fig. **2.15**), which was lit by seven-branched candelabras known as *menorahs* [men-OR-uhz]. The centrality to Hebrew culture of these written words is even more apparent in the words of God that follow the commandments (**Reading 2.4a**):

READING 2.4a

from the Hebrew Bible (Deuteronomy 6:6–9)

6 Keep these words that I am commanding you today in your heart.

7 Recite them to your children and talk about them when you are at home and when you are away, when you lie down and when you rise.

8 Bind them as a sign on your hand, fix them as an emblem on your forehead,

9 and write them on the doorposts of your house and on your gates.

Whenever the Hebrews talked, wherever they looked, wherever they went, they focused on the commandments of their God. Their monotheistic religion was thus also an ethical and moral system derived from an omnipotent God. The Ten Commandments were the centerpiece of the Torah [tor-AH], or Law (literally "instructions"), consisting of the books of Genesis, Exodus, Leviticus, Numbers, and Deuteronomy. (Christians would later incorporate these books into their Bible as the first five books of the Old Testament.) The Hebrews considered these five books divinely inspired and attributed their original authorship to Moses himself, although, as we have noted, the texts as we know them were written much later.

The body of laws outlined in the Torah is quite different from the code of Hammurabi. The code was essentially a list of punishments for offenses; it is not an *ethical* code (see Fig. 2.11 and Reading 2.1). Hebraic and Mesopotamian laws are distinctly different. Perhaps because the Hebrews were once themselves aliens and slaves, their law treats the lowest members of society as human beings. As Yahweh declares in Exodus 23:6: "You will not cheat the poor among you of their rights at law." At least under the law, class distinctions, with the exceptions of slaves, did not exist in Hebrew society, and punishment was levied equally. Above all else, rich and poor alike were united for the common good in a common enterprise, to follow the instructions for living as God provided.

After 40 years in the Sinai had passed, it is believed that the patriarch Joshua led the Jews back to Canaan, the Promised Land, as Yahweh had pledged in the covenant. Over the next 200 years, they gradually gained control of the region through a protracted series of wars described in the books of Joshua, Judges, and Samuel in the Bible. They named themselves the Israelites [IZ-ree-uh-lites], after Israel, the name that was given by God to Jacob. The nation consisted of 12 tribes, each descending from one of Jacob's 12 sons. By about 1000 BCE, Saul had established himself as king of Israel, followed by David, who as a boy rescued the Israelites from the Philistines [FIL-uh-steenz] by killing the giant Goliath with a stone thrown from a sling, as described in First Samuel, and later united Israel and Judah into a single state.

Map 2.2 The United Monarchy of Israel under David and Solomon. ca. 1000 BCE.

Kings David and Solomon, and Hebrew Society

King David reigned until 961 BCE. It was he who captured Jerusalem from the Canaanites and made it the capital of Israel (Map **2.2**). As represented in the books of Samuel, David is one of the most complex and interesting individuals in ancient literature. A poet and musician, he is author of some of the Psalms. Although he was capable of the most deceitful treachery—sending one of his soldiers, Uriah [you-RYE-uh], to certain death in battle so that he could marry his widow, Bathsheba [bath-SHE-buh]—he also suffered the greatest sorrow, being forced to endure the betrayal and death of his son Absalom. David was succeeded by his other son, Solomon, famous for his fairness in meting out justice, who ruled until 933 BCE.

Solomon undertook to complete the building campaign begun by his father, and by the end of his reign, Jerusalem was, by all reports, one of the most beautiful cities in the Near East. A magnificent palace and, most especially, a splendid temple dominated the city. First Kings claims that Yahweh himself saw the temple and approved of it.

The rule of the Hebrew kings was based on the model of the scriptural covenant between God and the Hebrews. This covenant was the model for the relationship between the king and his people. Each provided protection in return for obedience and fidelity. The same relationship existed between the family patriarch and his household. His wife

and children were his possessions, whom he protected in return for their unerring faith in him.

Although women were their husbands' possessions, the Hebrew Scriptures provide evidence that women may have had greater influence in Hebrew society than this patriarchal structure would suggest. In one of the many texts later incorporated into the Hebrew Bible and written during Solomon's reign, the "The Song of Songs, which is Solomon's" (as Chapter 1, Verse 1 of this short book reads), the woman's voice is particularly strong. It is now agreed that the book is not the work of Solomon himself, but rather a work of secular poetry, probably written during his reign. It is a love poem, a dialogue between a man (whose words are reproduced here in regular type) and a younger female lover, a Shulamite [SHOO-luh-mite], or "daughter of Jerusalem" (whose voice is in italics) (**Reading 2.4b**). This poem of sexual awakening takes place in a garden atmosphere reminiscent of Eden, but there is no Original Sin here, only fulfillment:

READING 2.4b

from the Hebrew Bible
(Song of Solomon 4:1–6, 7:13–14)

The Song of Songs (translated by Ariel and Chana Bloch)

How beautiful you are, my love,
My friend! The doves of your eyes
looking out
from the thicket of your hair.

Your hair
like a flock of goats
bounding down Mount Gilead. . . .

Your breasts are two fauns
twins of a gazelle,
grazing in a field of lilies.

An enclosed garden is my sister, my bride,
A hidden well, a sealed spring. . . .

Awake, north wind! O south wind, come,
breathe upon my garden,
let its spices stream out.
Let my lover come into his garden
and taste its delicious fruit. . . .

Let us go early to the vineyards
to see if the vine has budded,
if the blossoms have opened
and the pomegranate is in flower.

There I will give you my love . . .
rare fruit of every kind, my love,
I have stored away for you.

So vivid are the poem's sexual metaphors that many people have wondered how the poem found its way into the Scriptures. But the Bible is frank enough about the attractions of sex. Consider Psalms 30:18–19: "Three things I marvel at, four I cannot fathom: the way of an eagle in the sky, the way of a snake on a rock, the way of a ship in the heart of the sea, the way of a man with a woman." The Song of Songs is full of **double entendres** [on-TAHN-druh], expressions that can be understood in two ways, one of them often sexual or risqué. Although the implications of such language are almost unavoidable, embarrassed Christian interpreters of the Bible for centuries worked hard to avoid the obvious and assert a higher purpose for the poem, reading it, especially, as a description of the relation between Christ and his "Bride," the Church.

Generations of translators also sought to obscure the powerful voice of the female protagonist in the poem by presenting the young woman as chaste and submissive, but of the two voices, hers is the more active and authoritative. In a world in which history is traced through the patriarchs, and genealogies are generally written in the form of the father "begetting" his sons, the young woman asserts herself here in a way that suggests that if in Hebrew society the records of lineage was in the hands of its men, the traditions of love-making—and by extension, the ability to propagate the lineage itself—were controlled by its women. It is even possible that a woman composed all or large parts of the poem, since women traditionally sang songs of victory and mourning in the Bible, and the daughters of Jerusalem actually function as a chorus in the poem, asking questions of the Shulamite.

The Prophets and the Diaspora

After Solomon's death, the United Monarchy of Israel split into two separate states. To the north was Israel, with its capital in Samaria [suh-MAR-ee-uh], and to the south, Judah, with its capital in Jerusalem. In this era of the two kingdoms, Hebrew culture was dominated by **prophets**, men who were prophetic not in the sense of foretelling the future, but rather in the sense of serving as mouthpieces and interpreters of Yahweh's purposes, which they claimed to understand through visions. The prophets instructed the people in the ways of living according to the laws of the Torah, and they more or less freely confronted anyone guilty of wrongful actions, even the Hebrew kings. They attacked, particularly, the wealthy Hebrews whose commercial ventures had brought them unprecedented material comfort and who were inclined to stray from monotheism and worship Canaanite [KAY-nuh-nite] fertility gods and goddesses. The moral laxity of these wealthy Hebrews troubled the prophets, who urged the Hebrew nation to reform spiritually.

In 722 BCE, Assyrians attacked the northern kingdom of Israel and scattered its people, who were thereafter known as the Lost Tribes of Israel. The southern kingdom of Judah survived another 140 years, until Nebuchadnezzar and the Babylonians overwhelmed it in 587 BCE, destroying the Temple of Solomon in Jerusalem and deporting the Hebrews to Babylon (Fig. **2.16**). Not only had the Hebrews lost their homeland and their temple,

Fig. 2.16 *Exile of the Israelites, from the palace of Sennacherib, Nineveh, Assyria.* **Late eighth century BCE.** Limestone. This relief shows a family of Israelites, their cattle yoked to a cart carrying their household into exile after being defeated by the Assyrians in 722 BCE. The relief seems to depict three generations of a family: the father in front with the cattle, the son behind carrying baggage, the wife of the father seated on the front of the cart, the son's wife and children seated behind her.

but the Ark of the Covenant itself disappeared. For nearly 60 years, the Hebrews endured what is known as the Babylonian Captivity. As recorded in Psalm 137: "By the rivers of Babylon, there we sat down, yea we wept, when we remembered Zion."

Finally, invading Persians, whom they believed had been sent by Yahweh, freed them from the Babylonians in 520 BCE. They returned to Judah, known now, for the first time, as the Jews (after the name of their homeland). They rebuilt a Second Temple of Jerusalem, with an empty chamber at its center, meant for the Ark of the Covenant should it ever return. And they welcomed back other Jews from around the Mediterranean, including many whose families had left the northern kingdom almost 200 years earlier. Many others, however, were by now permanently settled elsewhere, and they became known as the Jews of the Diaspora [die-AS-puh-ruh], or the "dispersion."

Hebrew culture would have a profound impact on Western civilization. The Jews provided the essential ethical and moral foundation for religion in the West, including Christianity and Islam, both of which incorporate Jewish teachings into their own thought and practice. In the Torah, we find the basis of the law as we understand and practice it today. So moving and universal are the stories recorded in the Torah that over the centuries they have inspired—and continue to inspire—countless works of art, music, and literature. Most important, the Hebrews introduced to the world the concept of ethical monotheism, the idea that there is only one God, and that God demands that humans behave in a certain way, and rewards and punishes accordingly. Few, if any, concepts have had a more far-reaching effect on history and culture.

NEO-BABYLONIA

From the eighth through the seventh century BCE, Babylon fell in and out of Assyrian rule, until Nabopolassar (r. 626–604 BCE), the first king of Babylonia, defeated the Assyrians, sacking Nineveh in 612 BCE. The Assyrian Empire collapsed completely in 609 BCE. Nabopolassar was followed by his son and heir, Nebuchadnezzar (r. 604–562 BCE), who continued on with his father's plan to restore Babylon's palace as the center of Mesopotamian civilization. It was here that the Hebrews lived in exile for nearly 50 years (586–538 BCE) after Nebuchadnezzar captured the people of Jerusalem.

Nebuchadnezzar wished to remake Babylon as the most remarkable and beautiful city in the world. It was laid out on both sides of the Euphrates River, joined together by a single bridge. Through the middle of the older, eastern sector, ran the Processional Way, an avenue also called "May the Enemy Not Have Victory" (Fig. 2.17). It ran from the Euphrates bridge eastward through the temple district, past the Marduk ziggurat. (Many believe this ziggurat was the legendary Tower of Babel [BAB-ul], described in Genesis 11 as the place where God, confronted with the prospect of "one people. . . one language," chose instead to "confuse the language of all the earth," and scatter people "abroad

Fig. 2.17 Reconstruction drawing of Babylon with the Processional Way and the Ishtar Gate as it might have appeared in the sixth century BCE. Courtesy of the Oriental Institute of the University of Chicago. In the distance is the Marduk Ziggurat, and between the ziggurat and the Ishtar Gate are the famous Hanging Gardens in the palace of Nebuchadnezzar II.

over the face of the earth.") Then it turned north, ending at the Ishtar Gate, the northern entrance to the city. Processions honoring Marduk, the god celebrated above all others in Babylonian lore and considered the founder of Babylon itself, regularly filled the street, which was as much as 65 feet wide at some points and paved with large stone slabs. Marduk's might is celebrated in the *Hymn to Marduk* (**Reading 2.5**), found in Ashurbanipal's library:

READING 2.5
_____

from the *Hymn to Marduk* (1000–700 BCE)

Lord Marduk, Supreme god, with
   unsurpassed wisdom. . . .
When you leave for battle the Heavens shake,
   when you raise your voice, the Sea is wild!
When you brandish your sword, the gods turn
   back.
There is none who can resist your furious blow!
Terrifying lord, in the Assembly of the gods no
   one equals you! . . .
Your weapons flare in the tempest!
Your flame annihilates the steepest mountain.

No trace of the city's famous Hanging Gardens survives, once considered among the Seven Wonders of the World, and only the base and parts of the lower stairs of the Marduk ziggurat still remain. But in the fifth century BCE, the Greek historian Herodotus [he-ROD-uh-tus] (ca. 484–430/420 BCE) described the ziggurat as follows:

> There was a tower of solid masonry, a furlong in length and breadth, on which was raised a second tower, and on that a third, and so on up to eight. The ascent to the top

is on the outside, by a path which winds round all the towers. . . . On the topmost tower, there is a spacious temple, and inside the temple stands a couch of unusual size, richly adorned with a golden table by its side. . . . They also declare that the god comes down in person into this chamber, and sleeps on the couch, but I do not believe it.

Although the ziggurat has disappeared, we can glean some sense of the city's magnificence from the Ishtar Gate (Fig. **2.18**), named after the Babylonian goddess of fertility.

Fig. 2.18 Ishtar Gate (restored), from Babylon. ca. 575 BCE. Glazed brick. Staatliche Museen, Berlin. The dark blue bricks are glazed—that is, covered with a film of glass—and they would have shown brilliantly in the sun.

SEE MORE To view a Closer Look feature about the Ishtar Gate, go to **www.myartslab.com**

Today, the gate is restored and reconstructed inside one of the Berlin State Museums. It was made of glazed and unglazed bricks, and decorated with animal forms. The entire length of the Processional Way was similarly decorated on both sides, so the ensemble must have been a wondrous sight. The gate's striding lions are particularly interesting. They are traditional symbols of Ishtar herself. Alternating with rows of bulls with blue horns and tails, associated with deities such as Adad [AD-dad], god of the weather, are fantastic dragons with long necks, the forelegs of a lion, and the rear legs of a bird of prey, an animal form sacred to the god Marduk. Like so much other Mesopotamian art, it is at once a monument to the power of Nebuchadnezzar, an affirmation of his close relation to the gods, and a testament to his kingdom's wealth and well-being.

THE PERSIAN EMPIRE

In 520 BCE, the Persians, formerly a minor nomadic tribe that occupied the plateau of Iran, defeated the Babylonians and freed the Jews. Their imperial adventuring had begun in 559 BCE with the ascension of Cyrus II (called the Great, r. 559–530 BCE), the first ruler of the Achaemenid dynasty, named after Achaemenes [eck-KEE-min-ees], a warrior-king whom Persian legend says ruled on the Iranian plateau around 700 BCE. By the time of Cyrus's death, the Persians had taken control of the Greek cities in Ionia on the west coast of Anatolia. Under King Darius [duh-RY-us] (r. 522–486 BCE), they soon ruled a vast empire that stretched from Egypt in the south, around Asia Minor, to the Ukraine [you-KRAIN] in the north. The capital of the empire was Parsa, which the Greeks called Persepolis [per-SEP-uh-lis], or city of the Persians, located in the Zagros [ZAG-rus] highlands of present-day Iran (Fig. 2.19). Built by artisans and workers from all over the Persian Empire, including Greeks from Ionia, it reflected Darius's multicultural ambitions. If he was, as he said, "King of King, King of countries, King of the earth," his palace should reflect the diversity of his peoples.

The columns reflect Egyptian influence, and, especially in their **fluting**, the vertical channels that exaggerate their height and lend them a feeling of lightness, they reflect, as we will later see, in Chapter 4, the influence of the Greeks. Rulers are depicted in relief sculptures with Assyrian beards and headdresses (Fig. 2.20). In typical Mesopotamian fashion, they are larger than other people in the works. These decorations further reflect the Persians' sense that all the peoples of the region owed allegiance. This relief, from stairway to the audience hall where Darius and his son Xerxes received visitors, is covered with images of their subjects bringing gifts to the palace—23 subject nations in all—Ionian, Babylonian, Syrian, Susian, and so on—each culture recognizable by its beards and costumes. Darius can be seen receiving tribute as Xerxes stands behind him as if waiting to take his place as the Persian ruler. Huge winged bulls with the heads of bearded kings, reminiscent of the human-headed winged bulls that guard the Khorsabad palace of Assyrian king Sargon II (see Fig. 2.13), dominated the approach to the south gateway. Thus, Mesopotamian, Assyrian, Egyptian, and Greek styles all intermingle in the palace's architecture and decoration.

The Persians also perfected the art of metalwork. The rhyton, or ritual cup, illustrated here (Fig. 2.21), is related to the many mythological creatures that can be

Fig. 2.19 Palace of Darius and Xerxes, Persepolis, Iran. 518–ca. 460 BCE. The palace stands on a rock terrace 545 yards deep and 330 yards wide. Approached by a broad staircase decorated with men carrying gifts, its centerpiece was the Hall of One Hundred Columns, a forest of stone comprised of ten rows of ten columns, each rising to a height of 40 feet.

Fig. 2.20 *Darius and Xerxes Receiving Tribute*, **detail of a relief from a stairway leading to the Apadana, ceremonial complex, Persepolis, Iran. 491–486 BCE.** Limestone, height 8′ 4″. Iranbastan Museum, Teheran. This panel was originally painted in blue, scarlet, green, purple, and turquoise. Objects such as Darius's necklace and crown were covered in gold.

Fig. 2.21 Rhyton. Achaemenid, fifth–third centuries BCE. Gold. Archaeological Museum, Teheran, Iran. This elaborate gold vessel would have probably served as both a drinking cup and a wine decanter.

found throughout Mesopotamian art—the hybrid human and bull creature that guarded the palace gate at Parsa, for instance, or the dragon with lion's feet decorating the Ishtar Gate in Babylon. This gold rhyton has been fashioned into a *simurgh*, a mythical creature with the body of a lion, the head of a dog, the wings of a griffin, and a peacock's tail.

The rhyton would have been used in rituals connected to the Zoroastrian religion practiced by the Persians. Zoroaster (the Greek name for the Iranian Zarathustra) was a Persian prophet who according to tradition lived in the sixth century BCE. However, linguistic analysis of the writings that are attributed to him places him ca. 1000 BCE. Whatever the case, his writings and other ritual hymns, prayers, and laws associated with the religion were collected in the sixth century into the *Zend-Avesta* [zen-dah-VES-tah], or Book of Knowledge, the holy book of the Zoroastrian faith. Ahura Mazda, "the Wise Lord," is its supreme deity, creator of heaven and earth, and in almost all inscriptions, the one and only god. But Zoroastrianism is only semi-monotheistic: there are lesser gods—many of them remnants of earlier religious practices—but all of them created by Ahura Mazda himself. The Zend-Avesta sets up a dualistic universe in which *asha* (literally, "truth") is opposed to *druj* ("lie" or "deceit"). The physical order of the universe is the chief manifestation of *asha* and is wholly the work of Ahura Mazda. *Druj* manifests itself as anything that is opposed to this physical order—chaos, natural decay, evil deeds. Perhaps Zoroaster's greatest contribution to religious thought is his emphasis on free will. As the *Zend-Avesta* says, Ahura Mazda "has left it to men's wills" to choose for themselves whether to lead a life of "good thoughts, good words, good deeds." Those who do—thus helping Ahura Mazda to maintain the order of the universe—will be admitted to heaven. Those who choose to follow the path of evil will be condemned to hell.

In Zoroastrian tradition, the *simurgh* whose image is invoked on the rhyton lives on Mount Alburz, the highest mountain in the world, around which circled the sun, moon, and stars. From the summit of the mountain, the legendary Chinwad bridge, the "bridge of judgment," extended to heaven. There, the souls of the good men and women are greeted by a beautiful maiden and led across an ever-widening pathway to *pairidaeza*, from which the English word "paradise" derives, and the souls of the bad are greeted by an ugly old hag and led across an ever-narrowing bridge until they fall into hell. The bridge is described at some length in the *Zend-Avesta* (Reading 2.6):

READING 2.6

from the *Zend-Avesta* (ca. 600 BCE)

27. O Maker of the material world, thou Holy One! Where are the rewards given? Where does the rewarding take place? Where is the rewarding fulfilled? Whereto do men come to take the reward that, during their life in the material world, they have won for their souls?

28. Ahura Mazda answered: "When the man is dead, when his time is over, then the wicked, evil-doing Daevas[1] cut off his eyesight. On the third night, when the dawn appears and brightens up, when Mithra, the god with beautiful weapons, reaches the all-happy mountains, and the sun is rising

29. 'Then the fiend, named Vizaresha[2], O Spitama[3] Zoroaster, carries off in bonds the souls of the wicked Daeva-worshippers who live in sin. The soul enters the way made by Time, and open both to the wicked and to the righteous. At the head of the Chinwad bridge, the holy bridge made by Mazda, they ask for their spirits and souls the reward for the worldly goods which they gave away here below.

30. "Then comes the beautiful, well-shapen, strong and well-formed maid, with the dogs at her sides, one who can distinguish, who has many children, happy, and of high understanding. She makes the soul of the righteous one go up above . . . the Chinwad bridge; she places it in the presence of the heavenly gods themselves."

[1]**Daevas**: supernatural entities with variously disagreeable characteristics; in the oldest Zoroastrian works they are "wrong" or "false" gods that are to be rejected in favor of the worship of the one God, Ahura-Mazda.
[2]**Vizaresh**: a demon who, during that struggle of three days and three nights with the souls of the departed, wages terror on them and beats them. He sits at the gate of hell.
[3]**Spitama**: the original name of Zoroaster, who as a prince gave up his royal duties to meditate, spending fifteen years searching for enlightenment before a vision of Ahura-Mazda gave him the answers to his many questions.

In this context, it is worth recalling that the Zend-Avesta was compiled at about the same time as the Hebrew Bible. Its teachings would, in fact, influence all three of the great religions of the Western world—Judaism, Christianity, and Islam.

The Stability of Egyptian Culture

Civilization in Mesopotamia developed across the last three millennia BCE almost simultaneously with civilization in Egypt, a region on the northeastern corner of the African continent in close proximity to Mesopotamian and Mediterranean cultures. The civilizations of Egypt and Mesopotamia have much in common. Both formed around river systems—the Tigris and Euphrates in Mesopotamia; the Nile in Egypt. Both were agrarian societies that depended on irrigation, and their economies were hostage to the sometimes fickle, sometimes violent flow of their respective river systems. As in Mesopotamia, Egyptians learned to control the river's flow by constructing dams and irrigation canals, and it was probably the need to cooperate with one another in such endeavors that helped Mesopotamia and Egypt to create the civilization that would eventually arise in the Nile Valley.

The Mesopotamians and the Egyptians built massive architectural structures dedicated to their gods—the ziggurat in Mesopotamia and the pyramid in Egypt (see Figs. 2.1 and 3.6). Both unite the Earth and the heavens in a single architectural form, although the Mesopotamian ziggurat is topped by a temple and is considered the house of the city-state's god, and the Egyptian pyramid is funerary in nature with a royal burial in the bottom. Both cultures developed forms of writing, although the cuneiform style of Mesopotamian culture and the hieroglyph style of Egyptian society were very different. There is ample evidence that the two civilizations traded with one another, and to a certain degree influenced one another.

Fig. 2.22 Obelisk of Luxor in the Place de la Concorde, Paris. Dynasty 19, ca. 1279–1213 BCE. Height 75′. The obelisk was a gift of the Egyptian government to the French, presented to them in 1829 by the Egyptian viceroy, Mehemet Ali. Gilded images on the pedestal portray the monumental task of transporting the monolith to Paris and erecting it in the city's most central square, the Place de la Concorde.

What most distinguishes Mesopotamian from Egyptian culture, however, is the relative stability of the latter. Mesopotamia was rarely, if ever, united as a single entity. Whenever it was united, it was through force, the power of an army, not the free will of a people striving for the common good. In contrast, political transition in Egypt was *dynastic*—that is, rule was inherited by members of the same family, sometimes for generations. As in Mesopotamia, however, the ruler's authority was cemented by his association with divine authority. He was, indeed, the manifestation of the gods on Earth. As a result, the dynastic rulers of Egypt sought to immortalize themselves through art and architecture. In fact, there is clear reason to believe that the sculptural image of a ruler was believed to be, in some sense, the ruler himself.

Embodying the ruler's sense of his own permanence is an obelisk—a four-sided stone shaft topped by a pyramid-shaped block—which once marked the entrance to the Amon temple at Luxor during the reigns of the pharaohs Ramses II and Ramses III (Fig. **2.22**). Some 3,300 years old, it stands today at the center of the Place de la Concorde in Paris, a gift to the French from the Egyptian government in the nineteenth century. The inscription, carved in hieroglyphics, says it all: "Son of Ra [the sun god]: Ramses-Meryamum ["Beloved of Amun"]. As long as the skies exist, your monuments shall exist, your name shall exist, firm as the skies." ∎

What characteristics distinguish the ancient civilizations of Sumer, Akkad, Babylon, and Assyria?

The royal tombs at the Sumerian city of Ur reveal a highly developed Bronze Age culture, based on the social order of the city-state, which was ruled by a priest-king acting as the intermediary between the gods and the people. The rulers also established laws and encouraged record-keeping, which in turn required the development of a system of writing—cuneiform script. In Sumer and subsequent Mesopotamian cultures, monumental architecture such as ziggurats were dedicated to the gods, and in each city-state, one of the gods rose to prominence as the city's protector. Under the rule of Hammurabi of Babylon, Mesopotamian law was codified, specifically in the stele that records the *Law Code of Hammurabi*. How would you characterize the general relationship between Mesopotamian rulers and the gods?

How does the Epic of Gilgamesh embody the relationship between the Mesopotamian ruler and the gods?

Preserved in the library of the Assyrian king Ashurbanipal, the *Epic of Gilgamesh* remains one of the greatest expressions of world literature. The sense of cultural continuity in Mesopotamia is underscored by the fact that the *Epic of Gilgamesh* preserves the historical lineage of all Mesopotamian kings—Sumerian, Akkadian, Babylonian, and Assyrian. While asserting the king's divinity, the story also admits the king's human mortality. What are the characteristics of its epic form? What are its principal themes?

What distinguished the Hebrews from other cultures of the Ancient Near East?

The Hebrews practiced a monotheistic religion. They considered themselves the "chosen people" of God, whom they called Yahweh. The written word is central to their culture, and it is embodied in a body of law, the Torah, and more specifically in the Ten Commandments. What does the Torah have in common with the Law Code of Hammurabi? How does it differ? How do the stories in Genesis, the first book of the Hebrew Bible, compare to the *Epic of Gilgamesh*?

What characteristics did the Persian religion share with Judaism?

The last of the great Mesopotamian empires arose on the Iranian plateau. The Persian kings practiced the Zoroastrian religion. Like the Jews, the Persians' beliefs were collected in a single holy book, compiled at about the same time as the Hebrew Bible. However, the Persian religion was only semi-monotheistic. Their supreme deity, Ahura Mazda, was the creator of many lesser gods. In what way was Zoroastrian religion dualistic?

PRACTICE MORE Get flashcards for images and terms and review chapter material with quizzes at **www.myartslab.com**

GLOSSARY

city-states Governments based in urban centers of the Mesopotamian basin that controlled neighboring regions; also an independent self-governing city.

composite Made up of distinct parts.

cuneiform writing A writing system composed of wedge-shaped characters.

cylinder seal An engraved piece of stone or other material used as a signature, confirmation of receipt, or identification of ownership.

double entendre A word or expression that can be understood two ways, with one often having a sexual or risqué connotation.

epic A long narrative poem in elevated language that follows characters of a high position through a series of adventures, often including a visit to the world of the dead.

epithet A word or phrase that characterizes a person.

fluting The vertical channels in a column shaft.

ground-line A baseline.

hierarchy of scale A pictorial convention in which the most important figures are represented in a larger size than the others; see also *social perspective*.

lost-wax casting A sculptural process in which a figure is modeled in wax and covered in plaster or clay; firing melts away the wax and hardens the plaster or clay, which then becomes a mold for molten metal.

metallurgy The science of separating metals from their ores.

metaphor A word or phrase used in place of another to suggest a likeness.

narrative genre A class or category of story with a universal theme.

narrative scene A scene that represents a story or event.

patriarch A scriptural father of the Hebrew people.

phonetic writing A writing system in which signs represent sounds.

pictogram A picture that represents a thing or concept.

priest-king In ancient Mesopotamia, a government leader who acted as an intermediary between gods and people and established laws.

prophet One who serves as a mouthpiece for and interpreter of Yahweh's purposes, which is understood through visions.

register A self-contained horizontal band.

simile A comparison of two unlike things using the word *like* or *as*.

social perspective A pictorial convention in which the most important figures are represented in a larger size than the others; see also *hierarchy of scale*.

stele An upright stone slab carved with a commemorative design or inscription.

stylus A writing tool.

synoptic A view that depicts several consecutive actions at once.

ziggurat A pyramidal temple structure consisting of successive platforms with outside staircases and a shrine at the top.

READINGS

from the *Epic of Gilgamesh*, Tablet I (ca. 1200 BCE) *(translated by Maureen Gallery Kovacs)*

The Epic of Gilgamesh describes the exploits of the Sumerian ruler Gilgamesh and his friend Enkidu. The following passage, from the first of the epic's 12 tablets, recounts how Enkidu, the primal man raised beyond the reach of civilization and fully at home with wild animals, loses his animal powers, and with them his innocence, when a trapper, tired of Enkidu freeing animals from his traps, arranges for a harlot from Uruk to seduce him. The story resonates in interesting ways with the biblical tale of Adam and Eve and their loss of innocence in the Garden of Eden.

TABLET I

THE HARLOT

The trapper went, bringing the harlot, Shamhat, with him,
they set off on the journey, making direct way.
On the third day they arrived at the appointed place,
and the trapper and the harlot sat down at their posts(?).
A first day and a second they sat opposite the watering hole.
The animals arrived and drank at the watering hole,
the wild beasts arrived and slaked their thirst with water.
Then he, Enkidu, offspring of the mountains,
who eats grasses with the gazelles,
came to drink at the watering hole with the animals,   10
with the wild beasts he slaked his thirst with water.
Then Shamhat saw him—a primitive,
a savage fellow from the depths of the wilderness!
    "That is he, Shamhat! Release your clenched arms,
    expose your sex so he can take in your voluptuousness.
    Do not be restrained—take his energy!
    When he sees you he will draw near to you.
    Spread out your robe so he can lie upon you,
    and perform for this primitive the task of womanhood!
    His animals, who grew up in his wilderness, will become   20
      alien to him,
      and his lust will groan over you."

Shamhat unclutched her bosom, exposed her sex, and he
      took in her voluptuousness.
She was not restrained, but took his energy.
She spread out her robe and he lay upon her,
she performed for the primitive the task of womankind.
His lust groaned over her;
for six days and seven nights Enkidu stayed aroused,
and had intercourse with the harlot   30
until he was sated with her charms.
But when he turned his attention to his animals,
the gazelles saw Enkidu and darted off,
the wild animals distanced themselves from his body.
Enkidu . . . his utterly depleted (?) body,
his knees that wanted to go off with his animals went rigid;
Enkidu was diminished, his running was not as before.
But then he drew himself up, for his understanding had
      broadened.

READING CRITICALLY

In giving in to the temptation of the harlot Shamhat, Enkidu loses much here, but he also gains something. What is it that he comes to understand? How does it differ from the physical prowess that he has evidently lost?

from the Hebrew Bible, Genesis (Chapters 2–3, 6–7)

The following excerpts from the first book of both the Hebrew Torah and the Christian Old Testament describe the story of Adam and Eve and the story of Noah. Together they demonstrate some of the characteristics of Hebrew monotheism—belief in the direct agency of their God in the workings of the world and his creation of a universe that is systematically planned and imbued with a moral order that derives from him. The passages also demonstrate the power and authority the Hebrews invested in their God.

CHAPTER 2

1 Thus the heavens and the earth were finished, and all their multitude.

2 And on the seventh day God finished the work that he had done, and he rested on the seventh day from all the work that he had done.

3 So God blessed the seventh day and hallowed it, because on it God rested from all the work that he had done in creation . . .

7 then the LORD God formed man from the dust of the ground, and breathed into his nostrils the breath of life; and   10
the man became a living being.

8 And the LORD God planted a garden in Eden, in the east; and there he put the man whom he had formed.

9 Out of the ground the LORD God made to grow every tree that is pleasant to the sight and good for food, the tree of life also in the midst of the garden, and the tree of the knowledge of good and evil.

10 A river flows out of Eden to water the garden, and from there it divides and becomes four branches.

11 The name of the first is Pishon; it is the one that flows   20
around the whole land of Havilah, where there is gold;

12 and the gold of that land is good; odellium and onyx stone are there.

13 The name of the second river is Gihon; it is the one that flows around the whole land of Cush.

14 The name of the third river is Tigris, which flows east of Assyria. And the fourth river is the Euphrates.

15 The LORD God took the man and put him in the garden of Eden to till it and keep it.

16 And the LORD God commanded the man, "You may freely eat of every tree of the garden; 30

17 but of the tree of the knowledge of good and evil you shall not eat, for in the day that you eat of it you shall die."

18 Then the LORD God said, "It is not good that the man should be alone; I will make him a helper as his partner."

19 So out of the ground the LORD God formed every animal of the field and every bird of the air, and brought them to the man to see what he would call them; and whatever the man called every living creature, that was its name.

20 The man gave names to all cattle, and to the birds of the 40 air, and to every animal of the field; but for the man there was not found a helper as his partner.

21 So the LORD God caused a deep sleep to fall upon the man, and he slept; then he took one of his ribs and closed up its place with flesh.

22 And the rib that the LORD God had taken from the man he made into a woman and brought her to the man.

23 Then the man said, "This at last is bone of my bones and flesh of my flesh; this one shall be called Woman, for out of Man this one was taken." 50

24 Therefore a man leaves his father and his mother and clings to his wife, and they become one flesh.

25 And the man and his wife were both naked, and were not ashamed.

THE TEMPTATION AND EXPULSION

CHAPTER 3

1 Now the serpent was more crafty than any other wild animal that the LORD God had made. He said to the woman, "Did God say, 'You shall not eat from any tree in the garden'?"

2 The woman said to the serpent, "We may eat of the fruit of the trees in the garden;

3 but God said, 'You shall not eat of the fruit of the tree that 60 is in the middle of the garden, nor shall you touch it, or you shall die.'"

4 But the serpent said to the woman, "You will not die;

5 for God knows that when you eat of it your eyes will be opened, and you will be like God, knowing good and evil."

6 So when the woman saw that the tree was good for food, and that it was a delight to the eyes, and that the tree was to be desired to make one wise, she took of its fruit and ate; and she also gave some to her husband, who was with her, and he ate. 70

7 Then the eyes of both were opened, and they knew that they were naked; and they sewed fig leaves together and made loincloths for themselves.

8 They heard the sound of the LORD God walking in the garden at the time of the evening breeze, and the man and his wife hid themselves from the presence of the LORD God among the trees of the garden.

9 But the LORD God called to the man, and said to him, "Where are you?"

10 He said, "I heard the sound of you in the garden, and I 80 was afraid, because I was naked; and I hid myself."

11 He said, "Who told you that you were naked? Have you eaten from the tree of which I commanded you not to eat?"

12 The man said, "The woman whom you gave to be with me, she gave me fruit from the tree, and I ate."

13 Then the LORD God said to the woman, "What is this that you have done?" The woman said, "The serpent tricked me, and I ate."

14 The LORD God said to the serpent, "Because you have done this, cursed are you among all animals and among all 90 wild creatures; upon your belly you shall go, and dust you shall eat all the days of your life.

15 I will put enmity between you and the woman, and between your offspring and hers; he will strike your head, and you will strike his heel."

16 To the woman he said, "I will greatly increase your pangs in childbearing; in pain you shall bring forth children, yet your desire shall be for your husband, and he shall rule over you."

17 And to the man he said, "Because you have listened to 100 the voice of your wife, and have eaten of the tree about which I commanded you, 'You shall not eat of it,' cursed is the ground because of you; in toil you shall eat of it all the days of your life;

18 thorns and thistles it shall bring forth for you; and you shall eat the plants of the field.

19 By the sweat of your face you shall eat bread until you return to the ground, for out of it you were taken; you are dust, and to dust you shall return."

20 The man named his wife Eve, because she was the 110 mother of all living.

21 And the LORD God made garments of skins for the man and for his wife, and clothed them.

22 Then the LORD God said, "See, the man has become like one of us, knowing good and evil; and now, he might reach out his hand and take also from the tree of life, and eat, and live forever"—

23 therefore the LORD God sent him forth from the garden of Eden, to till the ground from which he was taken.

24 He drove out the man; and at the east of the garden of 120 Eden he placed the cherubim, and a sword flaming and turning to guard the way to the tree of life.

THE STORY OF NOAH

CHAPTER 6

5 The LORD saw that the wickedness of humankind was great in the earth, and that every inclination of the thoughts of their hearts was only evil continually.

6 And the LORD was sorry that he had made humankind on the earth, and it grieved him to his heart.

7 So the LORD said, "I will blot out from the earth the human beings I have created—people together with animals and creeping things and birds of the air, for I am sorry that I have 130 made them."

8 But Noah found favor in the sight of the LORD. . . .

13 And God said to Noah, "I have determined to make an end of all flesh, for the earth is filled with violence because of them; now I am going to destroy them along with the earth.

14 Make yourself an ark of cypress wood; make rooms in the ark, and cover it inside and out with pitch. . . .

17 For my part, I am going to bring a flood of waters on the earth, to destroy from under heaven all flesh in which is the breath of life; everything that is on the earth shall die. 140

18 But I will establish my covenant with you; and you shall come into the ark, you, your sons, your wife, and your sons' wives with you.

19 And of every living thing, of all flesh, you shall bring two of every kind into the ark, to keep them alive with you; they shall be male and female.

20 Of the birds according to their kinds, and of the animals according to their kinds, of every creeping thing of the ground according to its kind, two of every kind shall come in to you, to keep them alive. 150

21 Also take with you every kind of food that is eaten, and store it up; and it shall serve as food for you and for them."

22 Noah did this; he did all that God commanded him.

CHAPTER 7

6 Noah was six hundred years old when the flood of waters came on the earth.

7 And Noah with his sons and his wife and his sons' wives went into the ark to escape the waters of the flood.

8 Of clean animals, and of animals that are not clean, and of birds, and of everything that creeps on the ground, 160

9 two and two, male and female, went into the ark with Noah, as God had commanded Noah.

10 And after seven days the waters of the flood came on the earth. . . .

11 . . . on that day all the fountains of the great deep burst forth, and the windows of the heavens were opened.

12 The rain fell on the earth forty days and forty nights. . . .

18 The waters swelled and increased greatly on the earth; and the ark floated on the face of the waters.

19 The waters swelled so mightily on the earth that all the 170 high mountains under the whole heaven were covered; . . .

21 And all flesh died that moved on the earth, birds, domestic animals, wild animals, all swarming creatures that swarm on the earth, and all human beings;

22 everything on dry land in whose nostrils was the breath of life died.

23 He blotted out every living thing that was on the face of the ground, human beings and animals and creeping things and birds of the air; they were blotted out from the earth. Only Noah was left, and those that were with him in the 180 ark. . . .

READING CRITICALLY

The story of Noah is, in some sense, a parable of the value of choosing to "walk with God." How does it reflect, then, the idea of the covenant, God's agreement with the Hebrews?

3

The Stability of Ancient Egypt

Flood and Sun

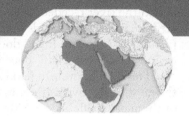

THINKING AHEAD

How did the idea of cycles shape Egyptian civilization?

Originally, what purposes did Egyptian sculpture and architecture serve?

What important change distinguishes the Middle Kingdom?

Who was Amenhotep IV? Why did he change his name to Akhenaten?

How did Egypt decline and fall?

"Can you see anything?" "Yes, wonderful things!" English archeologist Howard Carter was peering into a chamber of a tomb that had been sealed for over three thousand years. On November 26, 1922, he had pried loose a stone from the wall and inserted a candle through the hole. "At first I could see nothing," he later wrote, ". . . but presently, as my eyes grew accustomed to the light, details of the room within emerged slowly from the mist, strange animals, statues, and gold—everywhere the glint of gold. For the moment I was struck dumb with amazement, and when Lord Carnarvon [Carter's financial supporter] . . . inquired . . . 'Can you see anything?' It was all I could do to get out the words 'Yes, wonderful things.'"

The tomb was that of Tutankhamun, and among the most spectacular of the "wonderful things" Carter and Carnarvon would find inside was a coffin consisting of three separate coffins placed one inside the other. These were in turn encased in a quartzite **sarcophagus**, a rectangular stone coffin that was encased in four gilded, boxlike wooden shrines, also nestled one inside the other. Inside the innermost coffin, itself made of solid gold, a gold funerary mask had been placed over the upper body of the young king's mummified body (Fig. **3.1**). As news of

Carter's discovery leaked out, the world press could hardly contain its enthusiasm. "This has been, perhaps, the most extraordinary day in the whole history of Egyptian excavation," *The Times* of London wired *The New York Times* on February 18, 1922, the day that the sealed door to the burial chamber was finally opened. "Whatever one may have guessed or imagined of the secret of Tut-ankh-Amen's tomb, they [*sic*] surely cannot have dreamed the truth that is now revealed. The entrance today was made into the sealed chamber of the tomb of Tut-ankh-Amen, and yet another door opened beyond that. No eyes have seen the King, but to practical certainty we know that he lies there close at hand in all his original state, undisturbed." It would be another year until the quartzite lid to Tutankhamen's coffin, weighing nearly 1.25 tons, was hoisted off, and yet another nine months before the inner coffins were removed to reveal the king's body. Carter's discovery revealed the wealth that defined the Egyptian kingship, as well as the elaborate rituals surrounding the burial of the king himself.

The Egyptian kingship was deeply connected to the lifeblood and heart of Egyptian culture, the Nile River. Like the Tigris and Euphrates in Mesopotamia, the Nile could be said to have made Egypt possible. The river begins in

◀ **Fig. 3.1 Funerary mask of Tutankhamun. Dynasty 18, ca. 1327 BCE.** Gold inlaid with glass and semiprecious stones, height 21 ¹/₄". Egyptian Museum, Cairo. So many items of extraordinary value were found in Tutankhamen's tomb—furniture, perfumes, chariots, weapons, jewelry, clothing, utensils, cups, and on and on—that it took Carter ten years to empty it and inventory its contents.

HEAR MORE Listen to an audio file of your chapter at **www.myartslab.com**

central eastern Africa, one tributary in the mountains of Ethiopia and another at Lake Victoria in Uganda, from which it flows north for nearly 4,000 miles. Egyptian civilization developed along the last 750 miles of the river's banks, extending from the granite cliffs at Aswan, north to the Mediterranean Sea (see Map **3.1**).

Nearly every year, torrential rains caused the river to rise dramatically. Most years, from July to November, the Egyptians could count on the Nile flooding their land. When the river receded, deep deposits of fertile silt covered the valley floor. Fields would then be tilled, and crops planted and tended. If the flooding was either too great or too minor, especially over a period of years, famine could result. The cycle of flood and sun made Egypt one of the most productive cultures in the ancient world and one of the most stable. For 3,000 years, from 3100 BCE until the defeat of Mark Antony and Cleopatra by the Roman general Octavian in 31 BCE, Egypt's institutions and culture remained remarkably unchanged. Its stability contrasted sharply with the conflicts and shifts in power that occurred in Mesopotamia. The constancy and achievements of Egypt's culture are the subject of this chapter.

THE NILE AND ITS CULTURE

As a result of the Nile's annual floods, Egypt called itself Kemet, meaning "Black Land." In Upper Egypt, from Aswan to the Delta, the black, fertile deposits of the river covered an extremely narrow strip of land. Surrounding the river's alluvial plain was the "Red Land," the desert environment that could not support life, but where rich deposits of minerals and stone could be mined and quarried. Lower Egypt consists of the Delta itself, which today begins some 13 miles north of Giza [GHEE-zuh], the site of the largest pyramids, across the river from what is now

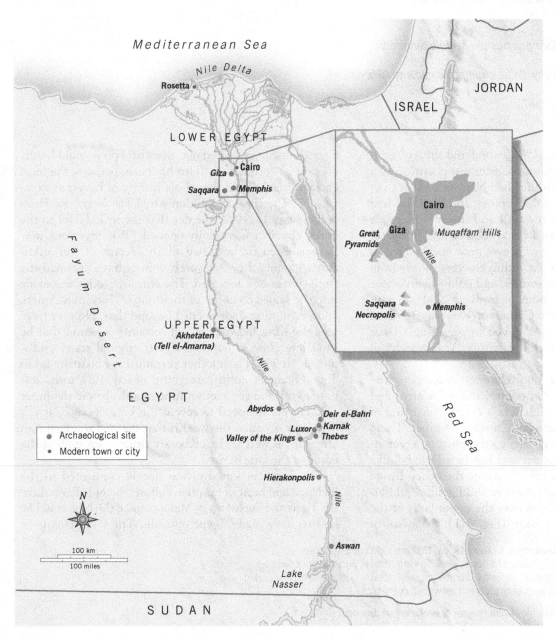

Map 3.1 Nile River Basin with archeological sites in relation to modern Cairo.
The broad expanse of the Lower Nile Delta was crisscrossed by canals, allowing for easy transport of produce and supplies.

Fig. 3.2 *Nebamun Hunting Birds*, from the tomb of Nebamun, Thebes. Dynasty 18, ca. 1400 BCE. Fresco on dry plaster, approx. 2′ 8″ high. The British Museum, London. The fish and the birds, and the cat, are completely realistic, but this is not a realistic scene. It is a conventional representation of the deceased, in this case Nebamun, spearing fish or hunting fowl, almost obligatory for the decoration of a tomb. The pigments were applied directly to a dry wall, a technique that has come to be known as *fresco secco* [FRES-coh SEK-koh], dry fresco. Such paintings are extremely fragile and susceptible to moisture damage, but Egypt's arid climate has preserved them.

modern Cairo. But in ancient times, it began 18 miles south of Giza, near the city of Memphis.

In this land of plenty, great farms flourished, and wildlife abounded in the marshes. In fact, the Egyptians linked the marsh to the creation of the world and represented it that way in the famous hunting scene that decorates the tomb of Nebamun [NEB-ah-mun] at Thebes [theebz] (Fig. 3.2). Nebamun is about to hurl a snake-shaped throwing stick into a flock of birds as his wife and daughter look on. The painting is a sort of visual pun, referring directly to sexual procreation. The verb "to launch a throwing stick" also means "to ejaculate," and the word for "throwing stick" itself, to "create." The hieroglyphs written between Nebamun and his wife translate as "enjoying oneself, viewing the beautiful, . . . at the place of constant renewal of life."

Scholars divide Egyptian history into three main periods of achievement. Almost all of the conventions of Egyptian art were established during the first period, the *Old Kingdom*. During the *Middle Kingdom*, the "classical" literary language that would survive through the remainder of Egyptian history was first produced. The *New Kingdom* was a period of prosperity that saw a renewed interest in art and architecture. During each of these periods, successive dynasties—or royal houses—brought peace and stability to the country. Between them were "Intermediate Periods" of relative instability (see *Context*, page 68).

Egypt's continuous cultural tradition—lasting over 3,000 years—is history's clearest example of how peace and prosperity go hand in hand with cultural stability. As opposed to the warring cultures of Mesopotamia, where city-state vied with city-state and empire with successive empire, Egyptian culture was predicated on unity. It was a **theocracy**, a state ruled by a god or by the god's representative—in this case a king (and very occasionally a queen), who ruled as the living representative of the sun god, Re [reh]. Egypt's government was indistinguishable from its religion, and its religion manifested itself in nature, in the flow of the Nile, the heat of the sun, and in the journey of the sun through the day and night and through the seasons. In the last judgment of the soul after death, Egyptians believed that the heart was weighed to determine whether it was "found true by trial of the Great Balance." Balance in all things—in nature, in social life, in art, and in rule—this was the constant aim of the individual, the state, and, Egyptians believed, the gods.

Whereas in Mesopotamia the flood was largely a destructive force (recall the flood in the *Epic of Gilgamesh*), in Egypt it had a more complex meaning. It could, indeed, be destructive, sometimes rising so high that great devastation resulted. But without it, the Egyptians knew, their culture could not endure. So, in Egyptian art and culture, a more complex way of thinking about nature, and about life itself, developed. Every aspect of Egyptian life is countered by an

Major Periods of Ancient Egyptian History

The dates of the periods of Egyptian history, as well as the kingships within them, should be regarded as approximate. Each king numbered his own regal years, and insufficient information about the reign of each king results in dates that sometimes vary, especially in the earlier periods, by as much as 100 years. Although there is general consensus on the duration of most individual reigns and dynasties, there is none concerning starting and ending points.

5500–2972 BCE	**Predynastic Period** *No formal dynasties*	Reign of Narmer and unification of Upper and Lower Egypt
2972–2647 BCE	**Early Dynastic Period** *Dynasties 1–2*	A unified Egypt ruled from Memphis
2647–2124 BCE	**Old Kingdom** *Dynasties 3–8*	The stepped pyramids at Saqqara in Dynasty 3; Pyramids at Giza in Dynasty 4
2123–2040 BCE	**First Intermediate Period** *Dynasties 9–10*	Egypt divided between a Northern power center at Hierakonpolis and a Southern one at Thebes
2040–1648 BCE	**Middle Kingdom** *Dynasties 11–16*	Reunification of Upper and Lower Egypt
1648–1540 BCE	**Second Intermediate Period** *Dynasty 17*	Syro-Palestinian invaders, the Hyksos, hold Lower Egypt and much of Upper Egypt until the Thebans defeat them
1540–1069 BCE	**New Kingdom** *Dynasties 18–20*	Reunification of Egypt; an extended period of prosperity and artistic excellence
1069–715 BCE	**Third Intermediate Period** *Dynasties 21–24*	More political volatility
715–332 BCE	**Late Period** *Dynasties 25–31*	Foreign invasions, beginning with the Kushites from the south and ending with Alexander the Great from the north

opposite and equal force, which contradicts and negates it, and every act of negation gives rise to its opposite again. As a result, events are cyclical, as abundance is born of devastation and devastation closely follows abundance. Likewise, just as the floods brought the Nile Valley back to life each year, the Egyptians believed that rebirth necessarily followed death. So their religion, which played a large part in their lives, reflected the cycle of the river itself.

Egyptian Religion: Cyclical Harmony

The religion of ancient Egypt, like that of Mesopotamia, was *polytheistic*, consisting of many gods and goddesses who were associated with natural forces and realms (see *Context*, page 69). When represented, gods and goddesses have human bodies and human or animal heads, and wear crowns or other headgear that identifies them by their attributes. The religion reflected an ordered universe in which the stars and planets, the various gods, and basic human activities were thought to be part of a grand and harmonious design. A person who did not disrupt this harmony did not fear death because his or her spirit would live on forever.

At the heart of this religion were creation stories that explained how the gods and the world came into being. Chief among the Egyptian gods was Re, god of the sun. According to these stories, at the beginning of time, the Nile created a great mound of silt, out of which Re was born. It was understood that Re had a close personal relationship with the king, who was considered the son of Re. But the king could also identify closely with other gods. The king was simultaneously believed to be the personification of the sky god, Horus [HOR-us], and was identified with deities associated with places like Thebes or Memphis when his power resided in those cities. Though not a full-fledged god, the king was *netjer nefer* [net-jer nef-er], literally, a "junior god." That made him the representative of the people to the gods, whom he contacted through statues of divine beings placed in all temples. Through these statues, Egyptians believed, the gods manifested themselves on earth. Not only did the orderly functioning of social and political events depend upon the king's successful communication with the gods, but so did events of nature—the ebb and flow of the river chief among them.

Like the king, all the other Egyptian gods descend from Re, as if part of a family. As we have said, many can be traced back to local deities of predynastic times who later assumed greater significance at a given place—at Thebes, for instance, the trinity of Osiris, Horus, and Isis gained a special significance. Osiris [oh-SY-ris], ruler of the underworld and god of the dead, was at first a local deity in the eastern Delta. According to myth, he was murdered by his wicked brother Seth, god of storms and violence, who chopped his brother into pieces and threw them into the Nile. But Osiris's wife and sister, Isis [EYE-zis], the goddess of fertility, collected all these parts, put the god back together, and restored him to life. Osiris was therefore identified with the Nile itself, with its annual flood and renewal. The child of Osiris and Isis was Horus, who defeated Seth and became the mythical first king of Egypt. The actual, living king was considered the earthly manifestation of Horus (as well as the son of Re). When the living king died, he became Osiris, and his son took the throne as Horus. Thus, even the kingship was cyclical.

At Memphis, the triad of Ptah, Sakhmet, and Nefertum held sway. A stone inscription at Memphis describes Ptah as the supreme artisan and creator of all things **(Reading 3.1)**:

READING 3.1

from Memphis, "This It Is Said of Ptah"
(ca. 2300 BCE)

This it is said of Ptah: "He who made all and created the gods." And he is Ta-tenen, who gave birth to the gods, and from whom every thing came forth, foods, provisions, divine offerings, all good things. This it is recognized and understood that he is the mightiest of the gods. Thus Ptah was satisfied after he had made all things and all divine words.

He gave birth to the gods, He made the towns,
He established the nomes [provinces],
He placed the gods in their shrines,
He settled their offerings,
He established their shrines,
He made their bodies according to their wishes,
Thus the gods entered into their bodies,
Of every wood, every stone, every clay,
Every thing that grows upon him
In which they came to be.

Sekhmet is Ptah's female companion. Depicted as a lioness, she served as protector of the king in peace and war. She is also the mother of Nefertum, a beautiful young man whose name means "perfection," small statues of whom were often carried by Egyptians for good luck.

The cyclical movement through opposing forces, embodied in stories such as that of Osiris and Isis, is one of the earliest instances of a system of religious and philosophic thought that survives even in contemporary thought. Life and death, flood and sun, even desert and oasis were part of a larger harmony of nature, one that was predictable in both the diurnal cycle of day and night but also in its seasonal patterns of repetition. A good deity like Osiris was necessarily balanced by a bad deity like Seth. The fertile Nile Valley was balanced by the harsh desert surrounding it. The narrow reaches of the upper Nile were balanced by the broad marshes of the Delta. All things were predicated upon the return of their opposite, which negates them, but

CONTEXT

Some of the Principal Egyptian Gods

A Horus, son of Osiris, a sky god closely linked with the king; pictured as a hawk, or hawk-headed man.

B Seth, enemy of Horus and Osiris, god of storms; pictured as an unidentifiable creature (some believe a wild donkey), or a man with this animal's head.

C Thoth, a moon deity and god of writing, counting, and wisdom; pictured as an ibis, or ibis-headed man, often with a crescent moon on his head.

D Khnum, originally the god of the source of the Nile, pictured as a bull who shaped men out of clay on his potter's wheel; later, god of pottery.

E Hathor, goddess of love, birth, and death; pictured as a woman with cow horns and a sun disk on her head.

F Sobek, the crocodile god, associated both with the fertility of the Nile, and, because of the ferocity of the crocodile, with the army's power and strength.

G Re, the sun god in his many forms; pictured as a hawk-headed man with a sun disk on his head.

which in the process completes the whole and regenerates the cycle of being and becoming once again.

Pictorial Formulas in Egyptian Art

This sense of duality, of opposites, informs even the earliest Egyptian artifacts, such as the *Palette of Narmer*, found at Hierakonpolis [hy-ruh-KAHN-puh-liss], in Upper Egypt (see *Closer Look*, pages 70–71). A palette is technically an everyday object used for grinding pigments and making body- or eye paint. The scenes on the *Palette of Narmer* are in low relief. Like the *Royal Standard of Ur* (see Fig. 2.8), they are arranged in registers that provide a ground-line upon which the figures stand (the two lion-tamers are an exception). The figures typically face to the right, though often, as is the case here, the design is **symmetrical**, balanced left and right. The artist represents the various parts of the human figure in what the Egyptians thought was their most characteristic view. So, the face, arms, legs, and feet are in profile, with the left foot advanced in front of the right. The eye and shoulders are in front view. The mouth, navel and hips, and knees are

The Egyptians created a style of writing very different from that of their northern neighbors in Mesopotamia. It consists of **hieroglyphs**, "writing of the gods," from the Greek *hieros*, meaning "holy," and *gluphein*, "to engrave." Although the number of signs increased over the centuries from about 700 to nearly 5,000, the system of symbolic communication underwent almost no major changes from its advent in the fourth millennium BCE until 395 CE, when Egypt was conquered by the Byzantine Empire. It consists of three kinds of signs: **pictograms**, or stylized drawings that represent objects or beings, which can be combined to express ideas; **phonograms**, which are pictograms used to represent sounds; and **determinatives**, signs used to indicate which category of objects or beings is in question. The *Palette of*

Narmer is an early example of the then-developing hieroglyphic style. It consists largely of pictograms, though in the top center of each side, Narmer's name is represented as a phonogram.

The round circle formed by the two elongated lions' heads intertwined on the *recto*, or front, of the palette is a bowl for mixing pigments. The palette celebrates the defeat by Narmer (r. ca. 3000 BCE) of his enemies and his unification of both Upper and Lower Egypt, which before this time had been at odds. So on the recto side, Narmer wears the red cobra crown of Lower Egypt, and on the *verso*, or back, he wears the white crown of Upper Egypt—representing his ability (and duty) to harmonize antagonistic elements.

Flanking the top of each side of the palette is a goddess wearing cow's horns; such headdresses represent the divine attributes of the figure. Later, **Hathor**, the sky mother, a goddess embodying all female qualities, would possess these attributes, but this early image probably represents the cow-goddess, **Bat**.

The **mace** was the chief weapon used by the king to strike down enemies, and the scene here is emblematic of his power.

As on the other side of the palette, the king is here accompanied by his sandal-bearer, who stands on his own ground-line. He carries the king's sandals to indicate that the king, who is barefoot, stands on **sacred ground**, and that his acts are themselves sacred.

Narmer, wearing the white crown of Upper Egypt, strikes down his enemy, probably the embodiment of **Lower Egypt** itself, especially since he is, in size, comparable to Narmer himself, suggesting he is likewise a leader.

Two more figures represent the defeated enemy. Behind the one on the left is a small aerial view of a **fortified city;** behind the one on the right, a **gazelle trap**. Perhaps together they represent Narmer's victory over both city and countryside.

The hawk is a symbolic representation of the god **Horus**. The king was regarded as the earthly embodiment of Horus. Here, Horus has a human hand with which he holds a rope tied to a symbolic representation of a conquered land and people.

A human head grows from the same ground as six **papyrus** blossoms, possibly the symbol of Lower Egypt.

This hieroglyph identifies the man that Narmer is about to kill, a name otherwise unknown.

Palette of Narmer, verso side, from Hierakonpolis. Dynasty 1, ca. 3000 BCE. Schist, height 25¼" Egyptian Museum, Cairo.

SEE MORE For a Closer Look at the *Palette of Narmer*, go to **www.myartslab.com**

Reading the *Palette of Narmer*

Narmer's Palette was not meant for actual use. Rather, it is a **votive**, or ritual object, a gift to a god or goddess that was placed in a temple to ensure that the king, or perhaps some temple official, would have access to a palette throughout eternity. It may or may not register actual historical events, although, in fact, Egypt marks its beginnings with the unification of its Upper and Lower territories. Subsequent kings, at any rate, presented themselves in almost identical terms, as triumphing over their enemies, mace in hand, even though they had no role in a similar military campaign. It is even possible that by the time of Narmer such conventions were already in place, although our system of numbering Egyptian dynasties begins with him. Whether the scene depicted is symbolic, the **pictorial formulas**, or conventions of representation, that Egyptian culture used for the rest of its history are fully developed in this piece.

Something to Think About . . .

Do you see any connection between the Egyptian hieroglyphs, as seen on the *Palette of Narmer*, and Sumerian cuneiform writing?

These are two instances of the hieroglyphic sign for **Narmer**, consisting of a catfish above a chisel. Each individual hieroglyph is a pictogram but is utilized here for its phonetic sound. The word for "catfish" is *nar,* and the word for "chisel" is *mer* (or, perhaps, "sickly")—hence "Narmer." In the lower instance, the hieroglyph identifies the king. In the instance at the top, the king's name is inside a depiction of his palace seen simultaneously from above, as a ground plan, and from the front, as a facade. This device, called a *serekh*, is traditionally used to hold the king's name.

We are able to identify **Narmer** not only from his hieroglyphic name, next to him, but by his relative size. As befits the king, he is larger than anyone else.

Similarly positioned on the other side of the palette and identified by the accompanying hieroglyph, this is the king's **sandal-bearer**.

The **bull** here strikes down his victim and is another representation of the king's might and power. Note that in the depictions of Narmer striking down his victim and in procession, a bull's tail hangs from his waistband.

The defeated **dead** lie in two rows, their decapitated heads between their feet. Narmer in sacred procession reviews them, while above them, a tiny Horus (the hawk) looks on.

This is the **mixing bowl** of the palette. The lions may represent competing forces brought under control by the king. Each is held in check by one of the king's **lion-tamers**, figures that in some sense represent state authority.

This is a representation of a **fortified city** as seen both from above, as a floor plan, and from the front, as a facade. It is meant to represent the actual site of Narmer's victory.

Palette of Narmer, recto side, from Hierakonpolis. **Dynasty 1, ca. 3000 BCE.** Schist, height 25 1/4". Egyptian Museum, Cairo.

in three-quarter view. As a result, the viewer sees each person in a **composite view**, the integration of multiple perspectives into a single unified image.

In Egyptian art, not only the figures but the scenes themselves unite two contradictory points of view into a single image. In the *Palette of Narmer*, the king approaches his dead enemies from the side, but they lie beheaded on the ground before him as seen from above. Egyptian art often represents architecture in the same terms. At the top middle of the *Palette of Narmer*, the external facade of the palace is depicted simultaneously from above, in a kind of ground plan, with its niched facade at the bottom. The design contains Narmer's Horus-name, consisting of a catfish and a chisel. The hieroglyphic signs for Narmer could not be interpreted until the Rosetta Stone was discovered (see *Context*, page 75), but we are still not sure whether it is to be read "Narmer," which are the later phonetic values of the signs. In fact, later meanings of these signs suggest that it might be read "sick catfish," which seems rather unlikely.

THE OLD KINGDOM

Although the *Palette of Narmer* probably commemorates an event in life, as a votive object it is devoted, like most surviving Egyptian art and architecture, to burial and the afterlife. The Egyptians buried their dead on the west side of the Nile, where the sun sets, a symbolic reference to death and rebirth, since the sun always rises again. The pyramid was the first monumental royal tomb. A massive physical manifestation of the reality of the king's death, it was also the symbolic embodiment of his eternal life. It would endure for generations as, Egyptians believed, would the king's *ka* [kah]. This idea is comparable to an enduring "soul" or "life force," a concept found in many other religions. The *ka*, which all persons possessed, was created at the same time as the physical body, itself essential for the person's existence since it provided

Fig. 3.3 Possibly the work of Imhotep. Stepped pyramid and funerary complex of Djoser, Saqqara. Dynasty 3, 2610 BCE. Limestone, height of pyramid 197′. The base of this enormous structure measures 460 feet east to west, and 388 feet north to south. It is the earliest known use of cut stone for architecture. The architect, Imhotep, was Djoser's prime minister. He is the first architect in history known to us by name.

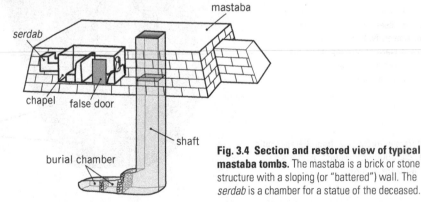

Fig. 3.4 Section and restored view of typical mastaba tombs. The mastaba is a brick or stone structure with a sloping (or "battered") wall. The *serdab* is a chamber for a statue of the deceased.

the *ka* with an individual identity in which its personality, or *ba* [bah], might also manifest itself. This meant that it was necessary to preserve the body after death so that the *ba* and *ka* might still recognize it for eternity. All the necessities of the afterlife, from food to furniture to entertainment, were placed in the pyramid's burial chamber with the king's body.

Funerary temples and grounds surrounded the temple so that priests could continuously replenish these offerings in order to guarantee the king's continued existence after death. Pyramids are the massive architectural product of what is known as the Old Kingdom, which dates from 2647 to 2124 BCE, a period of unprecedented achievement that solidified the accomplishments of the Early Dynastic Period initiated by Narmer.

The Stepped Pyramid at Saqqara

The first great pyramid was the Stepped Pyramid of Djoser [DJOH-zer] (r. ca. 2628–2609 BCE), who ruled at Saqqara [suh-KAHR-uh], just south of modern Cairo (Figs. **3.3**, **3.4**). It pre-dates the Ziggurat at Ur by nearly 500 years and is therefore the first great monumental architecture in human history to have survived. It consists of a series of stepped platforms rising to a height of 197 feet, but since it sits on an elevated piece of ground, it appears even taller to the approaching visitor.

Above ground level, the pyramid of Djoser contains no rooms or cavities. The king's body rested below the first level of the pyramid, in a chamber some 90 feet beneath the original **mastaba** [MAS-tuh-buh]—a trapezoidal tomb structure that derives its name from the Arabic word for "bench." Such mastabas predate Djoser's pyramid but continued to be used for the burial of figures of lesser importance

for centuries. The pyramid is situated in a much larger, ritual area than this earlier form of tomb. The total enclosure of this enormous complex originally measured 1,800 by 900 feet—or six football fields by three.

The idea of stacking six increasingly smaller mastabas on top of one another to create a monumental symbol of the everlasting spirit of the king was apparently the brainchild of Imhotep [im-HO-tep], Djoser's chief architect. He is the first artist or architect whose name survives, and his reputation continued to grow for centuries after his death. Graffiti written on the side of the pyramid a thousand years after Djoser's death praises Imhotep for a building that seems "as if heaven were within it" and as though "heaven rained myrrh and dripped incense upon it."

Three Pyramids at Giza

From Djoser's time forward, the tomb of the king was dramatically distinguished from those of other members of the royal family. But within 50 years, the stepped form of Djoser's pyramid was abandoned and replaced with a smooth-sided, starkly geometric monument consisting of four triangular sides slanting upward from a square base to an apex directly over the center of the square. The most magnificent examples of this form are found at Giza, just north of Djoser's tomb at Saqqara.

Khufu's Pyramid Of the three pyramids at Giza, Khufu's (r. 2549–2526 BCE) is both the earliest and the grandest one (Fig. **3.5**), measuring 479 feet high on a base measuring 755 feet square, built from an estimated 2.3 million stone blocks, weighing between 2 and 5 tons each. Historians

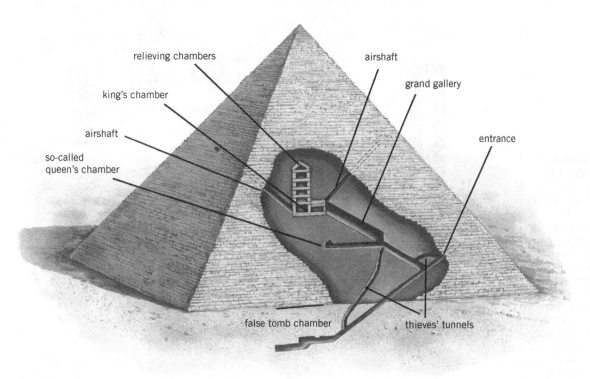

relieving chambers

king's chamber

airshaft

so-called
queen's chamber

airshaft

grand gallery

entrance

false tomb chamber

thieves' tunnels

Fig. 3.5 Cutaway elevation of the pyramid of Khufu.

Fig. 3.6 The pyramids at Menkaure (ca. 2470 BCE), Khafre (ca. 2500 BCE), and Khufu (ca. 2530 BCE). Giza was an elaborate complex of ritual temples, shrines, and ceremonial causeways, all leading to one or another of the three giant pyramids.

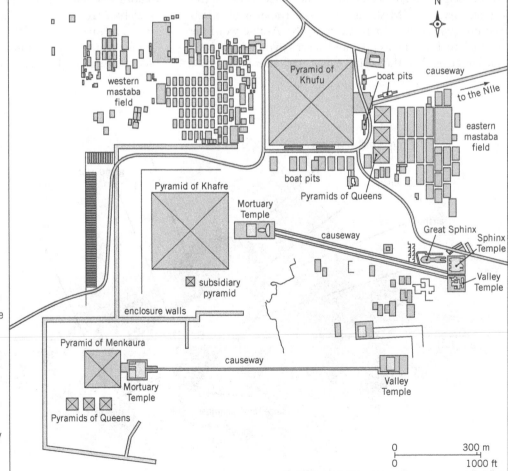

Fig. 3.7 Plan of the pyramids at Giza. Surrounding the northernmost pyramid of Khufu were mastaba fields, a royal cemetery in which were buried various officials, priests, and nobility of the king's court. When a king died in the royal palaces on the east bank of the Nile, his body was transported across the river to a valley temple on the west bank. After a ritual ceremony, it was carried up the causeway to the temple in front of the pyramid where another ritual was performed—the "opening of the mouth," in which priests "fed" the deceased's *ka* a special meal. The body was then sealed in a relatively small tomb deep in the heart of the pyramid (see Fig. 3.5).

The Rosetta Stone

Until the nineteenth century, Egyptian hieroglyphs remained untranslated. The key to finally deciphering them was the Rosetta Stone, a discovery made by Napoleon's army in 1799 and named for the town in the Egyptian Delta near where it was found. On the stone was a decree issued in 196 BCE by the priests of Memphis honoring the ruler Ptolemy V, recorded in three separate languages—Greek, demotic Egyptian (an informal and stylized form of writing used by the people—the "demos"), which first came into use in the eighth century BCE, and finally hieroglyphs, the high formal communication used exclusively by priests and scribes.

The stone was almost immediately understood to be a key to deciphering hieroglyphs, but its significance was not fully realized until years later. French linguist Jean-François Champollion began an intensive study of the stone in 1808 and concluded that the pictures and symbols in hieroglyphic writing stood for specific phonetic sounds, or, as he described it, constituted a "phonetic alphabet." A key to unlocking the code was a **cartouche**, an ornamental and symbolic frame reserved for the names of rulers. Champollion noticed that the cartouche surrounded a name, and deciphered the phonetic symbols for P, O, L, and T—four of the letters in the name Ptolemy. In another cartouche, he found the symbols for Cleopatra's name. By 1822, he had worked out enough of the writing system and the language to translate two texts, but Egyptologists have continued to improve and refine our understanding of the language to this day.

The Rosetta Stone. 196 BCE. Basalt, 46 $\frac{1}{2}$" × 30 $\frac{1}{8}$". © The Trustees of the British Museum/Art Museum, NY. The top, parts of which have been lost, contains the formal hieroglyphs; the middle, demotic Egyptian; and the bottom, the Greek text of the decree.

---

speculate that the stones were dragged up inclined ramps made of compacted rubble bonded and made slippery with a kind of lime-clay, called *tafl*, although they may well have been raised from tier to tier up the side of the pyramid by means of levers not unlike those used by the workers at Stonehenge (see *Closer Look*, pages 16–17 Chapter 1). Whatever feats of engineering accomplished the transport of so much stone into such an enormous configuration, what still dazzles us is this pyramid's astronomical and mathematical precision. It is perfectly oriented to the four cardinal points of the compass (as are the other two pyramids, which were positioned later, probably using Khufu's alignment as a reference point).

The two airshafts that run from the two top chambers seem oriented to specific stars, including Sirius, the brightest star in the night sky. The relationship between the various sides of the structure suggests that the Egyptians understood and made use of the mathematical value π (pi). All of this has led to considerable theorizing about "the secret of the pyramids," the other two of which are Khafre's (r. 2518–2493 BCE), and Menkaure's (r. 2488–2460 BCE) (Figs. **3.6** and **3.7**). Most convincing is the theory that the pyramid's sides represented the descending rays of the sun god Re, whose cult was particularly powerful at the time the pyramids were built. Because they were covered in a polished limestone sheath (the only remnant survives atop Khafre's pyramid), the sun must have glistened off them. And one convincing text survives: "I have trodden these rays as ramps under my feet where I mount up to my mother Uraeus on the brow of Re." Whatever their symbolic significance, they are above all extraordinary feats of human construction.

Monumental Royal Sculpture: Perfection and Eternity

The Sphinx's monumentality indicates the growing importance of sculpture to the Egyptian funerary tradition. The word for sculpture in Egyptian is, in fact, the same as for giving birth, and funerary sculpture served the same purpose as the pyramids themselves—to preserve and guarantee the king's existence after death, thereby providing a kind of rebirth. Although there are thousands of limestone and not a few sandstone funerary monuments, the materials of choice were diorite, schist, and granite, stones as durable

Fig. 3.8 The Great Sphinx (with the pyramid of Khafre in the background), Giza. Dynasty 4, ca. 2500 BCE. Limestone, height approx. 65′. Over the years, legend has had it that the artillery forces of Napoleon's invading army shot off the Sphinx's nose and ears. In truth, a fanatical Muslim cleric from Cairo severely damaged the statue in an attack in 1378.

The Great Sphinx In front of the pyramid dedicated to Khufu's son Khafre, and near the head of the causeway leading from the valley temple to the mortuary temple (see Fig. 3.6), is the largest statue ever made in the ancient world, the Great Sphinx [sfinks], carved out of an existing limestone knoll (Fig. **3.8**). As in Egyptian depictions of the gods, the Sphinx is half man and half animal. But where the gods are normally depicted with an animal's head and a human body, the Sphinx is just the opposite: a lion's body supports the head of a king wearing the royal headcloth. The sculpture probably represents Khafre himself protecting the approach to his own funerary complex, and thus it requires Khafre's physical likeness, but its combination of animal and human forms also suggests the king's connection to the gods.

Fig. 3.9 Seated statue of Khafre, from valley temple of Khafre, Giza. Dynasty 4, ca. 2500 BCE. Diorite, height 66″. Egyptian Museum, Cairo. On the side of Khafre's throne, intertwining lotus and papyrus blossoms signify his rule of both Upper and Lower Egypt.

and enduring as the *ka* itself. These stones can also take on a high polish and, because they are not prone to fracture, can be finely detailed when carved. These stones were carved into three main types of male statue: (1) a seated figure, looking directly ahead, his feet side by side, one hand resting flat on the knee, the other clenched in a fist; (2) a standing figure, his gaze fixed into the distance, left foot forward, both hands alongside the body with fists clenched; and (3) a figure seated on the ground with legs crossed. The first two types were used for kings as well as important officials. The third was used for royal scribes. Also popular were statue pairs of husband and wife, either seated or standing.

The statue of Khafre from his valley temple at Giza (see Fig. 3.5) is an example of the first type (Fig. **3.9**). The king sits rigidly upright and frontal, wearing a simple kilt and the same royal headdress as the Great Sphinx outside the valley temple. His throne is formed of the bodies of two stylized lions. Behind him, as if caressing his head, is a hawk, a manifestation of the god Horus, extending its wings in a protective gesture. In Egyptian society, the strong care for and protect the weak; so too Horus watches over Khafre as Khafre watches over his people. Because Khafre is a king and a divinity, he is shown with a perfectly smooth, proportioned face and a flawless, well-muscled body. This idealized anatomy was used in Egyptian sculpture regardless of the actual age and body of the king portrayed, its perfection mirroring the perfection of the gods themselves. Most Egyptian statues were *monolithic*, or carved out of a single piece of stone, even those depicting more than a single figure.

The same effect is apparent in the statue of Menkaure with a woman—perhaps his queen, his mother, or even a goddess—that was also found at his valley temple at Giza (Fig. **3.10**). Here, the deep space created by carving away the side of the stone to expose fully the king's right side seems to free him from the stone. He stands with one foot ahead of the other in the second traditional pose, the conventional depiction of a standing figure. He is not walking. Both feet are planted firmly on the ground (and so his left leg is, of necessity, slightly longer than his right). His back is firmly implanted in the stone panel behind him, but he seems to have emerged farther from it than the female figure who accompanies him, as if to underscore his power and might. Although the woman is almost the same size as the man, her stride is markedly shorter than his. She embraces him, her arm reaching round his back, in a gesture that reminds us of Horus's protective embrace of Khafre, but suggests also the simple marital affection of husband and wife. The ultimate effect of both of these sculptures—their solidity and unity, their sense of resolute purpose—testifies finally to their purpose, which is to endure for eternity.

Fig. 3.10 ***Menkaure with a Queen*, probably Khamerernebty, from valley temple of Menkaure, Giza. Dynasty 4, ca. 2460 BCE.** Schist, height 54 ¼". Museum of Fine Arts, Boston. Harvard University-Boston Museum of Fine Arts, 11.1738. Photograph © 2008 Museum of Fine Arts, Boston. Note that the woman's close-fitting attire is nearly transparent, indicating a very fine weave of linen.

Fig. 3.11 *Seated Scribe,* **from his mastaba, Saqqara. Dynasty 5, ca. 2400 BCE.** Painted limestone, height 21″. Musée du Louvre, Paris, France. Scribes were the most educated of Egyptians—not only able to read and write but accomplished in arithmetic, algebra, religion, and law. Their ka statues necessarily accompanied those of their kings into the afterlife.

Fig. 3.12 *Lector Priest Ka-aper* **(also known as the "Sheikh el-Beled"), from mastaba of Ka-aper, Saqqara. Dynasty 5, ca. 2450 BCE.** Plaster and painted wood, height 3′7″. Egyptian Museum, Cairo. This paunchy priest lacks the idealized physique reserved for more eminent nobility.

The Sculpture of the Everyday

Idealized athletic physiques, austere dignity, and grand scale were for royalty and officials only. Lesser figures were depicted more naturally, with flabby physiques or rounded shoulders, and on a more human scale. The third traditional type of male figure in Egyptian sculpture was the royal scribe, and in Figure **3.11**, we can see that a soft, flabby body replaces the hardened chest of a king. But the scribe's pose, seated cross-legged on the floor, marks him as literate and a valuable official of the king. The stone was carved out around his arms and head so that, instead of the monumental space of the king's sculpture, which derives from its compactness and its attachment to the slab of stone behind it, the scribe seems to occupy real space. The scribe's task was important: His statue would serve the king through eternity as he had served the king in life.

Statues of lesser persons were often made of less permanent materials, such as wood. Carved from separate pieces, with the arms attached to the body at the shoulders, such statues as that of the priest Ka-aper, found in his own tomb at Saqqara, could assume a more natural pose (Fig. **3.12**). The eyes, made of rock crystal, seem vital and lively. Originally, the statue was covered with plaster and painted (men were usually red-brown, like the seated scribe, and women yellow). Small statues of servants, especially those who made food, have also been found in the tombs of officials.

THE MIDDLE KINGDOM AT THEBES

The Old Kingdom collapsed for a variety of reasons—drought, a weakened kingship, greater autonomy of local administrators—all of which led to an Egypt divided between competing power centers in the North and South. After over 150 years of tension, Nebhepetre Mentuhotep II (2040–1999 BCE) assumed the rule of the Southern capital at Thebes, defeated the Northern kings, and reunited the country. The Middle Kingdom begins with his reign.

Thebes, on the west bank of the Nile, was the primary capital of the Middle Kingdom and included within its outer limits Karnak, Luxor, and other sites on the east bank (see Map 3.1). Although certain traditions remained in place from the Old Kingdom, change was beginning to occur.

Middle Kingdom Literature

One of the greatest changes took place in literature. Earlier, most writing and literature served a sacred purpose. But, during the Middle Kingdom, writers produced stories, instructive literature, satires, poems, biography, history, and scientific writings. Much of the surviving writing is highly imaginative, including tales of encounters with the supernatural. Among the most interesting texts is *The Teachings of Khety* [KEH-tee], a satiric example of instructive literature in which a scribe tries to convince his son to follow him into the profession. He begins by extolling the virtues of the scribe's life: "I shall make you love books more than your mother, and I shall place their excellence before you. It is greater than any office. There is nothing like it on earth." But he goes on to defend his own work by detailing all that is wrong with every other profession available to him:

> I have seen a coppersmith at his work at the door of his furnace. His fingers were like the claws of the crocodile, and he stank more than fish excrement. . . .
>
> I shall also describe to you the bricklayer. His kidneys are painful. When he must be outside in the wind, he lays bricks without a garment. His belt is a cord for his back, a string for his buttocks. His strength has vanished through fatigue and stiffness. . . .
>
> The sandal maker is utterly wretched carrying his tubs of oil. His stores are provided with carcasses, and what he bites is hides.

The work provides us with a broad survey of daily life in the Middle Kingdom. It ends in a series of admonitions about how a young scribe must behave—advice that parents have been giving children for millennia (see **Reading 3.2**, page 93 for more of the text).

Middle Kingdom Sculpture

Although a new brand of literature began to appear in the Middle Kingdom, sculpture remained firmly rooted in tradition. The only innovation in the traditional seated king funerary statue of Nebhepetre Mentuhotep II is that the pose has been slightly modified (Fig. **3.13**). Most noticeably, the king crosses his arms tightly across his chest. The pose is reminiscent of a **mummy**, an embalmed body wrapped for burial (see *Materials & Techniques*, page 84). The king's mummy-like pose probably refers to the growing cult of the god Osiris, discussed earlier. As early as the late Fifth Dynasty, the dead king was called "Osiris [King's Name]." By the time of the Middle Kingdom, ordinary, nonroyal people were beginning to be identified with Osiris as well. Osiris, god of the underworld, overseer of the judgment of souls, is usually depicted wrapped in white linen, but unlike Nebhepetre Mentuhotep II, whose legs and hands are exposed, Osiris is usually completely wrapped.

Fig. 3.13 *Nebhepetre Mentuhotep II*, from his funerary temple at Deir el-Bahri, Western Thebes. Dynasty 11, ca. 2000 BCE. Painted sandstone, height 72". Egyptian Museum, Cairo. The king's dark color here may refer to the "black land" of the Nile Valley, another symbol of the cycle of death and resurrection that is embodied in the Osiris myth.

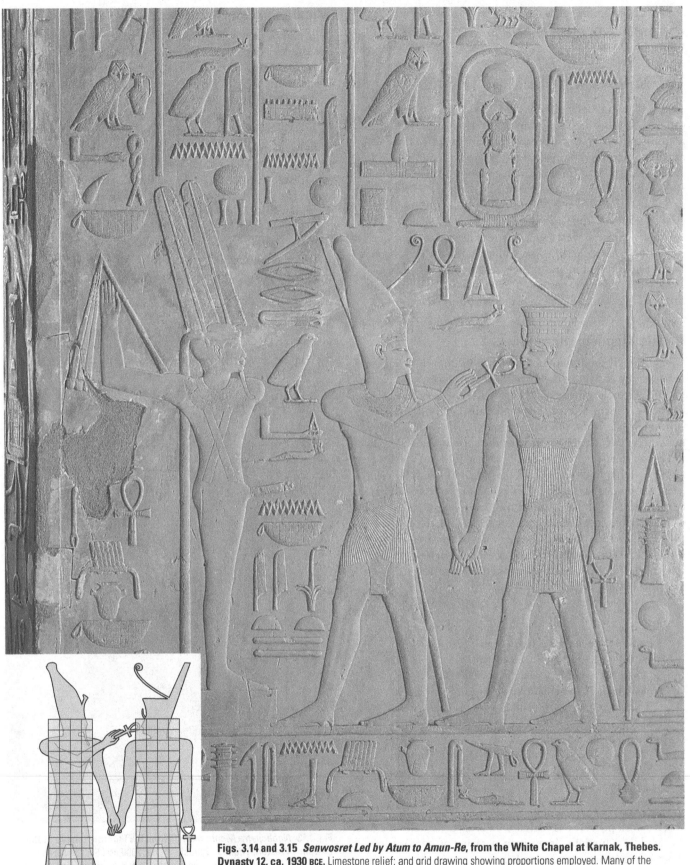

Figs. 3.14 and 3.15 *Senwosret Led by Atum to Amun-Re*, **from the White Chapel at Karnak, Thebes. Dynasty 12, ca. 1930 BCE.** Limestone relief; and grid drawing showing proportions employed. Many of the elements visible in the *Palette of Narmer*, which dates from over 1,000 years earlier, are still visible here. Not only are the bodies depicted in the conventional poses, but note the two figures on the right: King Senwosret wears the crown of Upper Egypt, and the god Atum wears the double crown of both Upper and Lower Egypt. Note also that just like Narmer, Senwosret and Atum each wears a bull's tail draped from his waist.

In relief carvings found in the temples of the Middle Kingdom, the traditional pose of the figure, which dates back to Narmer's time, still survives. The figures in a Twelfth Dynasty relief from the White Chapel at Karnak are depicted with right foot forward, feet and face in profile, and the shoulders and hips frontal (Fig. 3.14). But we have learned that figures were now conceived according to a *grid*. Much like a piece of graph paper, a grid is a system of regularly spaced horizontally and vertically crossed lines. Used in the initial design process, it enables the artist to transfer a design or enlarge it easily (Fig. 3.15). In the Egyptian system, the height of the figure from the top of the forehead (where it disappears beneath the headdress) to the soles of the feet is 18 squares. The top of the knee is 6 squares high, the waist, 11. The elbows are at the twelfth square, the armpits at the fourteenth, and the shoulders at the sixteenth. Each square also relates to the human body as a measure, representing the equivalent of one clenched fist.

This particular relief depicts the rise of yet another god in the Middle Kingdom—Amun, or, to associate him more closely with the sun, Amun-Re. Originally the chief god of Thebes, as the city became more prominent, Amun became the chief deity of all of Egypt. His name would appear (sometimes as "Amen") in many subsequent royal names—such as Amenhotep [ah-men-HO-tep] ("Amun is Satisfied") or, most famously, Tutankhamun [too-tahnk-AH-mun] ("The Living Image of Amun"). In the relief from the White Chapel, Atum, the god of the city of Heliopolis, just north of Memphis, that Nebhepetre Mentuhotep II had defeated four generations earlier, leads King Senwosret [sen-WAHZ-ret] I (1960–1916 BCE) to Amun, who stands at the left on a pedestal with an erect penis, signifying fertility. Atum turns to Senwosret and holds the hieroglyph **ankh** [ahnk], signifying life, to his nose. The king is depicted as having received the gift, since he holds it in his left hand.

The continuity and stability implied by this relief ended abruptly in 1648 BCE, when a Hyksos [HIK-sohs] king declared himself king of Egypt. The Hyksos were foreigners who had apparently lived in Egypt for some time. They made local alliances, introduced the horse-drawn chariot (which may well have helped them achieve their military dominance), and led Egypt into another "intermediate" period of disunity and disarray. Dissatisfaction with Hyksos rule originated, once again, in Thebes, and finally, in 1540 BCE, the Theban king Ahmose [AH-moh-seh] defeated the last Hyksos ruler and inaugurated the New Kingdom.

THE NEW KINGDOM

The worship of Amun that developed in the Twelfth Dynasty continued though the Middle Kingdom and into the Eighteenth Dynasty of the New Kingdom, 500 years later. In fact, there is clear evidence that the rulers of the Eighteenth Dynasty sought to align themselves closely with the aims and aspirations of the Middle Kingdom. The funerary temple of Hatshepsut [hat-SHEP-sut] in western Thebes is an interesting case in point.

Temple and Tomb Architecture and Their Rituals

Hatshepsut (r. ca. 1479–1457 BCE) was the daughter of Thutmose [TOOT-mo-zeh] I (r. ca. 1504–1492 BCE) and married her half-brother Thutmose II. When her husband died, she became regent for their young son, Thutmose III, and ruled for 20 years as king (priests of Amun, in fact, declared her king). As her reign continued, sculptures of Hatshepsut increasingly lost many of their female characteristics until she is barely distinguishable, given family resemblances, from later sculptures of her son, Thutmose III (Fig. 3.16). Her breasts are barely visible, and she wears the false beard of the

Fig. 3.16 Kneeling statue of Hatshepsut. New Kingdom, Dynasty 18, Joint reign of Hatshepsut and Thutmose III. ca. 1473–1458 BCE. Granite, paint, Height 34 ¼"; width 12 ¹³/₁₆"; diameter 20 ¼". © The Metropolitan Museum of Art/Art Resource, NY. This is one of at least eight, perhaps twelve, small kneeling statues of Hatshepsut believed to have lined the processional way of her temple at Deir el-Bahri.

Fig. 3.17 Senenmut. Funerary temple of Hatshepsut, Deir el-Bahri, Western Thebes. Dynasty 18, ca. 1460 BCE. At the far left is the ramp and funerary temple of Nebhepetre Mentuhotep II. Dynasty 11 (Middle Kingdom). ca. 2000 BCE. Senenmut's name is associated with the tomb because he has titles that suggest he oversaw the project, and he had little images of himself carved behind doors, where they would not be seen. But he may or may not have been the actual architect.

SEE MORE For a Closer Look at the Temple of Queen Hatshepsut, go to www.myartslab.com

Egyptian kings, the traditional symbol of the king's power and majesty.

Hatshepsut's temple, built on three levels, is modeled precisely on the two-level funerary temple of Nebhepetre Mentuhotep II, next to which it stands. Hatshepsut's temple is partly freestanding and partly cut into the rock cliffs of the hill (Fig. **3.17**). The first level consisted of a large open plaza backed by a long **colonnade**, a sequence or row of columns supporting a lintel and roof. A long ramp led up to a second court that housed shrines to Anubis (god of embalming and agent of Osiris) and Hathor (the sky mother, probably a reference to Hatshepsut's gender). Another ramp led to another colonnade fronted with colossal royal statues, two more colonnades, a series of chapels, and behind them, cut into the cliff, a central shrine to Amun-Re.

The Great Temple of Amun at Karnak Directly across the valley from Hatshepsut's temple, and parallel to it, is the Great Temple of Amun at Karnak. It is a product of the age in which the Egyptian king came to be known as **pharaoh** [FAY-roh], from Egyptian *per-aa*, "great house," meaning the palace of the king. In the same way that we refer to the presidency as "the White House," or the government of England as "10 Downing Street," so the Egyptians, beginning in the Eighteenth Dynasty, came to speak of their rulers by invoking their place of residence. (The modern practice of referring to all Egyptian kings as "pharaoh," incidentally, can probably be attributed to its use in the Hebrew Bible to refer to both earlier and later Egyptian kings.)

The pharaohs engaged in massive building programs during the New Kingdom, lavishing as much attention on their temples as their tombs. Not only was Amun a focus of worship, but so was his wife, Mut, and their son Khonsu. Although each temple is unique, all of the New Kingdom temples share a number of common architectural premises. They were fronted by a **pylon**, or massive gateway with sloping walls, which served to separate the disorderly world of everyday existence from the orderly world of the temple. Behind the pylon was one or more open courtyards leading to a roofed **hypostyle hall**, a vast space filled with

the many massive columns required to hold up the stone slabs forming the roof. The columns in the hypostyle hall of the Great Temple of Amun at Karnak have flower and bud capitals (Figs. **3.18**, **3.19**). Behind the hypostyle hall was the **sanctuary**, in which the statue of the deity was placed. To proceed into the temple was to proceed out of the light of the outside world and into a darker and more spiritual space. The temple was therefore a metaphor for birth and creation.

Fig. 3.18 Hypostyle hall, Great Temple of Amun, Karnak, Thebes. Dynasty 19. ca. 1294–1212 BCE. It is difficult to sense the massive scale of these columns from a photo. Dozens of people could easily stand on the top of one of them, and it takes at least eight people, holding hands, to span the circumference of a given column near its base. An average person is no taller than the base and first drum, or circular disk of stone, forming the column.

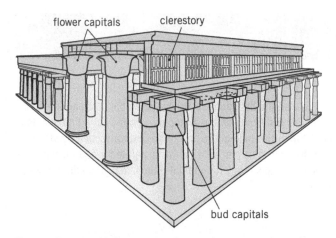

flower capitals   clerestory

bud capitals

Fig. 3.19 Reconstruction drawing of the hypostyle hall, Great Temple of Amun, Karnak. Dynasty 19, ca. 1294–1212 BCE. The foreground columns have bud capitals, and the hall's central columns are taller with flower capitals. The center columns are taller than the outer columns in order to admit light into the hall through windows along the upper walls. (Note that in this drawing the first five rows of columns in the front have been omitted for clarity. There are seven rows of columns on each side of the center rows.)

Each day, priests washed the deity statue, clothed it with a clean garment, and offered it two meals of delicious food. It was the "spirit" of the food that the gods enjoyed, and after the offering, the priests themselves ate the meals. Only kings and priests were admitted to the sanctuary, but at festival times, the cult statue of the deity was removed to lead processions—perhaps across the Nile to the funerary temples of the kings or to visit other deities in their temples (Mut regularly "visited" Amun, for instance).

The Great Temple of Amun at Karnak was the largest temple in Egypt. Although the temple was begun in the Middle Kingdom period, throughout the New Kingdom period pharaohs strove to contribute to its majesty and glory by adding to it or rebuilding its parts. The pharaohs built other temples to Amun as well. Each year, in an elaborate festival, the image of Amun from Karnak would travel south to visit his temple at Luxor. The most monumental aspects of both temples were the work of the Nineteenth Dynasty pharaoh Ramses [RAM-zeez] II (1279–1213 BCE), whose 66-year rule was longer than that of all but one

other Egyptian king. It was he who, with his father, was responsible for decorating the enormous hypostyle hall at Karnak, and it was he who built the massive pylon gate at Luxor (Fig. 3.20).

Ramses's Pylon Gate at Luxor In front of the pylon stand two enormous statues of the king and, originally, a pair of **obelisks**—square, tapered stone columns topped by a pyramid shape—although only the eastern one remains in place; the other is in the Place de la Concorde in Paris (see Fig. 2.22). The outside of the pylon was decorated with reliefs and texts describing the king's victory over the Hittites, at a battle fought on the river separating modern Syria and Lebanon. The battle was not the unqualified military success depicted by the reliefs, so these may be an

Fig. 3.20 Pylon gate of Ramses II with obelisk in the foreground, at Luxor, Thebes. Dynasty 19, ca. 1279–1212 BCE. The inscriptions on the pylon celebrate Ramses II's victory at the Battle of Qadesh over the Hittites as the two empires fought for control of Syria.

Mummification

In the belief that the physical body was essential to the *ka's* survival in the afterlife, the Egyptians developed a sophisticated process to preserve the body, **mummification**. This was a multi-staged, highly ritualized process.

The oldest evidence of mummification was recently found near Saqqara and dates from 3100 to 2890 BCE. Mummification methods changed over time, and the techniques used between 1085 and 945 BCE were the most elaborate. Upon death, the body was carried across to the west bank of the Nile, symbolically "going into the west" like the setting sun. There it was taken to "the place of purification," where it was washed with natron. (Natron is a hydrated form of sodium carbonate used to absorb the body's fluids; it also turned the body black.) After this first step in its symbolic rebirth, the body was transferred to the House of Beauty, where it was properly embalmed, its inner organs removed, dried, coated in resin, and either preserved in their own special containers, called canopic jars, or wrapped in linen and put back inside the body. The body itself was stuffed with linen and other materials in order to maintain its shape and was surrounded by bags of natron for 40 days. The entire process was overseen by an Overseer of Mysteries, God's Seal-Bearer, who served as chief surgeon, and a lector priest who recited the required texts and incantations.

After 40 days, the body was cleaned with spices and perfumes, rubbed with oils to restore some of its suppleness, and then coated with resin to waterproof it. Its nails were sewn back on and artificial eyes put into its eye sockets. Cosmetics were applied to the face and a wig put on its head. Dressed and decked out in jewels, the body was, finally, wrapped in a shroud of bandages from head to foot, along with small figurines and amulets as protection on the journey through the underworld. Finally, a mask was placed on the head and shoulders. The wrapping process involved several stages: First the head and neck were wrapped, then fingers and toes individually, and the same for the arms and legs, which were then tied together. The embalmers also placed a papyrus scroll with spells from the Book of the Dead between the wrapped hands (**a**). After several more layers of wrapping impregnated with liquid resin to glue the bandages together, the embalmers painted a picture of the god Osiris on the wrapping surface, did a final bandaging of the entire mummy with a large cloth attached by strips of linen (**b**), and then placed a board of painted wood on top. The mummy was now ready for its final ritual burial. The entire process took 70 days!

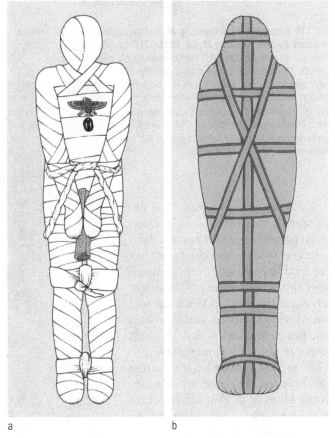

a   b

Two stages in the wrapping of a mummy. © The Trustees of the British Museum

early example of art used as propaganda, a theme that continues up to the present. It may be better to think of these reliefs as symbolic rather than historical, as images of the king restoring order to the land. Inside the pylon, around the walls of the courtyard, were complex reliefs depicting the king, in the company of deities, together with his chief wife, 17 of his sons, and some of the nearly 100 other royal children whom he fathered with 8 other official wives.

Such complexity typifies New Kingdom decoration. We see it clearly in the many surviving wall paintings in the rock-cut tombs across the river from Thebes. Earlier, we discussed the variety of fish and bird life in the painting of *Nebamun Hunting Birds* (see Fig. 3.2). In a feast scene from the same tomb, the guests receive food from a servant in the top register, while below them, musicians and dancers entertain the group (Fig. **3.21**). Very little is known about how Egyptian music actually sounded. Evidently, hymns were chanted at religious festivals, and song was a popular part of daily life. As in Mesopotamia, musical instruments—flutes, harps, lyres, trumpets, and metal rattles called *sistrums*—were often found in Egyptian tombs. In this wall painting, the two nude dancers are posed in a complex intertwining of limbs. Furthermore, of the four seated figures on the left—one of whom plays a double flute while the others appear to be clapping and, perhaps, chanting—two are depicted

Fig. 3.21 *Female Musicians and Dancers Entertaining Guests at a Meal*, detail of a fresco from the tomb of Nebamun, Western Thebes. Dynasty 18, ca. 1360 BCE. Paint on plaster, height of fragment 24″. The British Museum, London. © The Trustees of The British Museum/Art Resource, NY. The inclusion of such a scene in a tomb suggests that, in the New Kingdom, the dead demanded not only that they be accompanied by the usual necessities into the afterlife, but that they be entertained there as well.

frontally, a rarity in Egyptian art. The women wear cones of a scented fatty substance on their heads (as the cones melted, the women were bathed in its perfume), and the soles of their feet are turned toward us. In this luxurious atmosphere, a new informality seems to have introduced itself into Egyptian art.

Akhenaten and the Politics of Religion

Toward the end of the Eighteenth Dynasty, Egypt experienced one of the few real crises of its entire history when, in 1353 BCE, Amenhotep IV (r. 1353–1337 BCE) assumed the throne of his father Amenhotep III (r. 1391–1353 BCE). It was the father who had originally begun construction of the greater (southern) part of the Temple of Amun-Mut-Khonsu at Luxor and who built the third and tenth pylons at the Temple of Amun at Karnak. The great additions to these temples undertaken by Ramses II some 70 years later may have been a conscious return to the style—and traditions—of Amenhotep III. Certainly, they represent a massive, even overstated rejection of the ways of the son,

for Amenhotep IV had forsaken not only the traditional conventions of Egyptian representation but the very gods themselves.

Although previous Egyptian kings may have associated themselves with a single god whom they represented in human form, Egyptian religion supported a large number of gods. Even the Nile was worshipped as a god. Amenhotep IV abolished the pantheon of Egyptian gods and established a religion in which the sun disk Aten was worshipped exclusively. Other gods were still acknowledged, but they were considered to be too inferior to Aten to be worth worshipping. Whether Amenhotep's religion was *henotheism*—as we have seen before, in the Zoroastrian worship of Athura Mazda in Persia (see Chapter 2)—or truly monotheistic is a matter of some debate.

Amenhotep IV believed the sun was the creator of all life, and he may have composed *The Hymn to the Sun*, inscribed on the west wall of the tomb of Ay (r. 1327–1323 BCE) at el-Amarna [uh-MAHR-nuh] and in many other tombs as well (**Reading 3.3**):

from *Akhenaten's Hymn to the Sun*
(14th century BCE)

Let your holy Light shine from the height of heaven,
    O living Aton, source of all life!
From eastern horizon risen and streaming,
    you have flooded the world with your beauty.
You are majestic, awesome, bedazzling, exalted,
      overlord over all earth,
     yet your rays, they touch lightly, compass the lands
       to the limits of all your creation.
There in the Sun, you reach to the farthest of those
    you would gather in for your Son,
      whom you love;
Though you are far, your light is wide upon earth;
    and you shine in the faces of all
      who turn to follow your journeying.
When you sink to rest below western horizon
    earth lies in darkness like death,
Sleepers are still in bedchambers, heads veiled,
    eye cannot spy a companion;
All their goods could be stolen away,
    heads heavy there, and they never knowing!
Lions come out from the deeps of their caves,
    snakes bite and sting;
Darkness muffles, and earth is silent:
    he who created all things lies low in his tomb.
Earth-dawning mounts the horizon,
    glows in the sun-disk as day:
You drive away darkness, offer your arrows of shining,
    and the Two Lands are lively with morningsong.
Sun's children awaken and stand,
    for you, golden light, have upraised the sleepers;
Bathed are their bodies, who dress in clean linen,
    their arms held high to praise your Return.
Across the face of the earth
    they go to their crafts and professions.
The herds are at peace in their pastures,
    trees and the vegetation grow green;
Birds start from their nests,
    wings wide spread to worship your Person;
Small beasts frisk and gambol, and all
    who mount into flight or settle to rest
      live, once you have shone upon them;
Ships float downstream or sail for the south,
    each path lies open because of your rising;
Fish in the River leap in your sight,
    and your rays strike deep in the Great Green Sea.
It is you create the new creature in Woman,
    shape the life-giving drops into Man,
Foster the son in the womb of his mother,
    soothe him, ending his tears . . . .

Re is clearly the life force and source of all good, the very origin of creation itself.

Amenhotep IV was so dedicated to Aten that he changed his own name to Akhenaten [ah-ken-AH-ten] ("The Shining Spirit of Aten") and moved the capital of Egypt from Thebes to a site many miles north that he also named Akhetaten (modern Tell el-Amarna). This move transformed Egypt's political and cultural as well as religious life. At this new capital he presided over the worship of Aten as a divine priest and his queen as a divine priestess. Temples to Aten were open courtyards, where the altar received the sun's direct rays.

Why would Amenhotep IV/Akhenaten have substituted monotheism for Egypt's traditional polytheistic religion? Many Egyptologists argue that the switch had to do with enhancing the power of the pharaoh. With the pharaoh representing the one god who mattered, all religious justification for the power held by a priesthood dedicated to the traditional gods was gone. As we have seen, the pharaoh was traditionally associated with the sun god Re. Now in the form of the sun disk Aten, Re was the supreme deity, embodying the characteristics of all the other gods, therefore rendering them superfluous. By analogy, Amenhotep IV/Akhenaten was now supreme priest, rendering all other priests superfluous as well. Simultaneously, the temples dedicated to the other gods lost prestige and influence. These changes also converted the priests into dissidents.

A New Art: The Amarna Style Such significant changes had a powerful effect on the visual arts as well. Previously, Egyptian art had been remarkably stable because its principles were considered a gift of the gods—thus perfect and eternal. But now, the perfection of the gods was in question, and the principles of art were open to reexamination as well. A new art replaced the traditional canon of proportion—the familiar poses of king and queen—with realism, and a sense of immediacy, even intimacy. So Akhenaten allowed himself and his family to be portrayed with startling realism, in what has become known, from the modern name for the new capital, as the Amarna style.

An example is a small relief from Akhenaten's new capital: The king is depicted with a skinny, weak upper body, his belly protruding over his skirt; his skull is elongated behind an extremely long, narrow facial structure; and he sits in a slumped, almost casual position (Fig. **3.22**). (One theory holds that Akhenaten had Marfan syndrome, a genetic disorder that leads to skeletal abnormalities.) This depiction contrasts sharply with the idealized depictions of the pharaohs in earlier periods. Akhenaten holds one of his children in his arms and seems to have just kissed her. His two other children sit with the queen across from him, one turning to speak with her mother, the other touching the queen's cheek. The queen herself, Nefertiti [nef-er-TEE-tee], sits only slightly below her husband and appears to share his position and authority. In fact, one of the most striking features of the Amarna style is Nefertiti's prominence in the decoration of the king's temples. In one, for example, she is shown slaughtering prisoners, an image traditionally reserved for the king himself. It is likely that her prominence was part of Akhenaten's attempt to substitute the veneration of his own family (who, after all, represent Aten on earth) for the traditional Amun-Mut-Khonsu family group.

In a house in the southern part of Akhenaten's new city at Amarna, the famous bust of Queen Nefertiti was discovered along with drawings and sculptures of the royal family (Fig. **3.23**). This was the workshop of Thutmose, one of the king's royal artists. It seems likely that many other sculptures and reliefs were modeled on the bust of Nefertiti. At any rate, the queen's beauty cannot be denied, and this image of her has become famous worldwide. Even in her own time, she was known by such epitaphs as "Fair of Face" and "Great in Love."

The Return to Thebes and to Tradition

Akhenaten's revolution was short-lived. Upon his death, Tutankhaten (r. 1336–1327 BCE), probably Akhenaten's son, assumed the throne and changed his name to Tutankhamun (indicating a return to the more traditional gods, in this case Amun). The new king abandoned el-Amarna, moved the royal family to Memphis in the north, and reaffirmed Thebes as the nation's religious center. He died shortly after and was buried in the west bank of the Nile at Thebes, near the tomb of Hatshepsut.

The Tomb of Tutankhamun Tutankhamun's is the only royal tomb in Egypt to have escaped the discovery of looters. In addition to the royal sarcophagus discovered by Carter (see Fig. 3.1), there were also vast quantities of beautiful furniture in the tomb, including a golden throne that dates from early in the king's rule and still bears the indelible stamp of

Fig. 3.24 Back of Tutankamun's "Golden Throne," from his tomb, Valley of the Kings, Western Thebes. Dynasty 18, ca. 1335 BCE. Wood, gold, faience, and semiprecious stones, height of entire throne 41″, height of detail approx. 12 ¼″. Egyptian Museum, Cairo. This throne shows that early in his life, at least, Tutankamun was still portrayed in the Armana style.

the Armana style, with Aten shining down on both the king and queen (Fig. **3.24**). Jewelry of exquisite quality abounded, as did textiles—rarest of all archeological finds because they deteriorate over time. Carter and his team also found a golden *canopic* [kuh-NOPE-ik] chest—which held the king's embalmed internal organs—a shrine-shaped box of alabaster, carved with four compartments, each of which had a carved and gilded stopper depicting the king. It had an alabaster lid that covered the stoppers, and it was set in a larger shrine of gilded wood, protected by three gilded statues of goddesses, and covered by a shroud covered with gold rosettes.

The Final Judgment The elaborate burial process was not meant solely to guarantee survival of the king's *ka* and *ba*. It also prepared him for a "last judgment," a belief system that

would find expression in the Hebrew faith as well. In this two-part ritual, deities first questioned the deceased about their behavior in life. Then their hearts, the seat of the *ka*, were weighed against an ostrich feather, symbol of Maat [mah-aht], the goddess of truth, justice, and order. Egyptians believed the heart contained all the emotions, intellect, and character of the individual, and so represented both the good and bad aspects of a person's life. If the heart did not balance with the feather, then the dead person was condemned to nonexistence, to be eaten by a creature called Ammit [AH-mit], the vile "Eater of the Dead," part crocodile, part lion, and part hippopotamus. Osiris, wrapped in his mummy robes, oversaw this moment of judgment. Tut himself, depicted on his sarcophagus with his crossed arms holding crook and flail, was clearly identified with Osiris.

Books of Going Forth by Day At the time of Tut's death, the last judgment was routinely illustrated in Books of Going Forth by Day (also known as Books of the Dead), collections of magical texts or spells buried with the deceased to help them survive the ritual of judgment. One such magical text was the "Negative Confession" (**Reading 3.4**), which the deceased would utter upon entering the judgment hall:

READING 3.4

from *The Book of Going Forth by Day*

I have come unto you; I have committed no faults; I have not sinned; I have done no evil; I have accused no man falsely; therefore let nothing be done against me. I live in right and truth, and I feed my heart upon right and truth. That which men have bidden I have done, and the gods are satisfied thereat. I have pacified the god, for I have done his will. I have given bread unto the hungry and water unto those who thirst, clothing unto the naked, and a boat unto the shipwrecked mariner. I have made holy offerings unto the gods; and I have given meals of the tomb to the sainted dead. O, then, deliver ye me, and protect me; accuse me not before the great god. I am pure of mouth, and I am pure of hands . . .

I offer up prayers in the presence of the gods, knowing that which concerneth them. I have come forward to make a declaration of right and truth, and to place the balance upon its supports within the groves of amaranth. Hail, thou who art exalted upon thy resting place, thou lord of the *atef* crown,[1] who declarest thy name as the lord of the winds, deliver thou me from thine angels of destruction, who make dire deeds to happen and calamities to arise, and who have no covering upon their faces, because I have done right and truth, O thou Lord of right and truth. I am pure, in my fore-parts have I been made clean, and in my hinder parts have I been purified; my reins have been bathed in the Pool of right and truth, and no member of my body was wanting. I have been purified in the pool of the south . . .

[1] A conical headdress decorated with two ostrich feathers, joined with ram's horns and a sun disk, and associated particularly with Osiris.

LEARN MORE Gain insight about Books of the Dead from a primary source document at **www.myartslab.com**

Fig. 3.25 *Last Judgment of Hunefer by Osiris*, from a Book of Going Forth by Day in his tomb at Thebes. Dynasty 19, ca. 1285 BCE. Painted papyrus scroll, height 15 ⅝″. The British Museum, London. At the top, Hunefer, having passed into eternity, is shown adoring a row of deities.

The following moment of judgment is depicted in one such Book of Going Forth by Day, a papyrus scroll created for an otherwise anonymous man known as Hunefer [HOO-nef-er] (Fig. 3.25). The scene reads from left to right in a continuous pictorial narrative. To the left, Anubis [uh-NOO-bis], overseer of funerals and cemeteries, brings Hunefer into the judgment area. Hunefer's heart, represented as a pot, is being weighed against the ostrich feather. In this image, Hunefer passes the test—not surprising, given that the work is dedicated to ensuring that Hunefer's *ka* survive in the afterlife. Horus brings Hunefer to Osiris, seated under a canopy, with his sisters at the right.

THE LATE PERIOD, THE KUSHITES, AND THE FALL OF EGYPT

From Tutankhamun's time through the Late Period (715–332 BCE) and until the fall of Egypt to the Romans in 30 BCE, the conventions of traditional representation remained in place. For example, the pose we saw in Menkaure's funeral sculpture of 2460 BCE (see Fig. 3.10) is repeated in the seventh-century BCE statue of *Mentuemhet*, the Governor (Fig. 3.26). Mentuemhet [men-too-EM-het] strides forward into eternal life, nearly 2,000 years after that Old Kingdom pharaoh, a strong visual signal of the stability of Egyptian culture.

Mentuemhet was probably the most influential official of the Twenty-fifth Dynasty (ca. 715–656 BCE). He was appointed governor of Thebes by the Kushites [KOOSH-ites] (from Kush, the Egyptian name for the southern region of Nubia, in today's Sudan). Nubia had long been an important neighbor, appearing in Egyptian records as far back as

Fig. 3.26 *Mentuemhet*, from Karnak, Thebes. Dynasty 25, ca. 660 BCE. Granite, height 54″. Egyptian Museum, Cairo. The only concession to naturalistic representation in this sculpture is in the governor's facial features.

Fig. 3.27 *Nubians Bringing Tribute*, from the tomb of Amenhotep Huy, the Nubian viceroy under Tutankhamen, Qurnet Murai, Western Thebes. **Dynasty 18, ca. 1330 BCE.** Painting on plaster. Editions Gallimard, Paris. This painting represents the kind of trade relations that Egypt enjoyed with Nubia and Kush.

the Old Kingdom. Nubia served as a corridor for trade between Egypt and sub-Saharan Africa and was the main means by which Egypt procured gold and incense, as well as ivory, ebony, and other valuable items (Fig. **3.27**). Because of its links with tropical Africa, over time, the population of Nubia became a diverse mixture of ethnicities.

Nubia had been the location of several wealthy urban centers, including Kerma, whose walls, mud-brick buildings, and lavish tombs were financed and built by indigenous Nubian rulers around 1650 BCE. Napata was built during an Egyptian annexation of the area in approximately 1500 BCE, during the reign of Thutmose I. Napata became the provincial capital of southern Nubia, an area the Egyptians knew as Kush.

The Kushites

The Kushites had an immense appetite for assimilating Egyptian culture. They adopted Egyptian religion and practices, worshipping Egyptian gods, particularly Amun, the Egyptian state god. The main religious center of Kush was at Jebel Barkal [JEB-uh bar-kahl], a mountain near the fourth cataract of the Nile where the Kushites believed Amun dwelled. Their adoption of Egyptian ways nevertheless retained their distinctly Nubian identity. The Kushites developed hieroglyphs to express their own language, continued to worship many of their own gods, and though they also began to erect pyramids over their royal tombs, theirs started from smaller bases and were distinctly steeper and more needle-like than their Egyptian counterparts. There are nearly 300 of these pyramids in modern Sudan, more than in Egypt itself. Although annexed to Egypt, Kush was essentially an independent state toward the end of the New Kingdom. Egypt relied upon Kush to supply gold and other resources (including Nubian soldiers, among the most feared warriors in the region), but as Egypt struggled with its own enemies to the east, the rulers of Kush eventually found themselves in a position to take control of Egypt

themselves. In the eighth century BCE, the Egyptians turned to Kush for the leadership they needed to help hold off the mounting threat of an Assyrian invasion, and the Egyptianized African rulers of Kush became the Twenty-fifth Dynasty of pharaohs. As pharaohs, the Kushite kings ruled an empire that stretched from the borders of Palestine possibly as far upstream as the Blue and White Niles, uniting the Nile Valley from Khartoum [KAR-toom] to the Mediterranean. They were expelled from Egypt by the Assyrians after a rule of close to 100 years.

Egypt Loses Its Independence

The Assyrians left rule of Egypt to a family of local princes at Saïs [SAY-is], in the western portion of the Nile Delta, inaugurating the Twenty-sixth, or Saite [SAY-eet] Dynasty (664–525 BCE). With Memphis as their administrative center, they emphasized Mediterranean trade, which in turn produced over 100 years of economic prosperity. But Egypt was anything but secure in power struggles that dominated the larger political climate of the region. In 525 BCE, the Persians invaded from the north and made the country a mere province in its empire. For the next 200 years, Egypt enjoyed brief periods of independence, until the Persians invaded again in 343 BCE. They had ruled for not much more than a decade when the Macedonian [mass-uh-DOH-nee-un] conqueror Alexander the Great drove them out and asserted his own authority. According to legend, the god Amun spoke to Alexander through an oracle, acknowledging him as his son and therefore legitimate ruler of Egypt. Its independence as a state had come to an end. When Alexander died, the country fell to the rule of one of his generals, Ptolemy [TAHL-uh-mee], and beginning in 304 BCE, the final Ptolemaic [tahl-MAY-ik] Dynasty was under way. A kingdom in the Greek constellation, Egypt would finally fall to an invading Roman army in 30 BCE. But remarkably, until this moment, its artistic and religious traditions, as well as its daily customs, remained largely in place, practiced as they had been for 3,000 years.

Mutual Influence through Trade

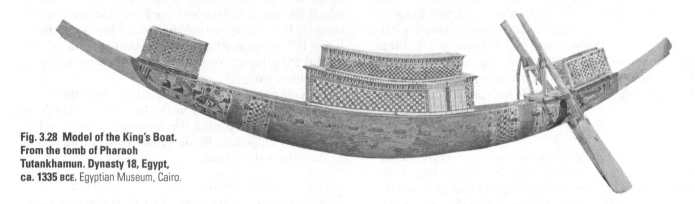

Fig. 3.28 Model of the King's Boat. From the tomb of Pharaoh Tutankhamun. Dynasty 18, Egypt, ca. 1335 BCE. Egyptian Museum, Cairo.

Although Egyptian art and culture remained extraordinarily stable for over 3,000 years, it would be a mistake to assume that this was because the region was isolated. In fact, Egypt was a center of trade for the entire Mediterranean basin. Spiral and geometric designs on Egyptian pottery from as early as the Twelfth Dynasty (1980–1801 BCE) suggest the influence of Aegean civilizations, and during the reign of Hatshepsut's young son, Thutmose III, connections with Aegean cultures appear to have been extremely close. Evidence from surviving images of both cultures' ship designs—ships that would have facilitated Aegean trade—suggests a mutual influence. A small-scale model of the king's boat from the tomb of King Tut shows a stern cabin, decorated with images of the king, where the steersmen would have guided the boat (Fig. **3.28**). Ships such as this were equipped with a mast that could be raised and fitted with a sail to catch the Nile winds from astern.

Egypt's influence in the Mediterranean was far-flung, although it is unlikely that its ships set out to sea. Rather, their boats would have generally hugged the coast. But Egypt was a port of call, and traders from around the Mediterranean visited there. Archeologists excavating at Mycenae [my-SEE-nee], a center of culture that was firmly established on the Greek Peloponnesus [pel-uh-puh-NEE-sus] by 1500 BCE, have discovered Egyptian scarabs at the site, including one bearing the name of Queen Tiy [tee], mother of Akhenaten. Scarabs are amulets in the shape of a beetle, and since the Egyptian word for beetle, *kheprer*, is derived from the word *kheper*, "to come into being," scarabs were associated with rebirth in the afterlife. Those displaying names were generally used as official seals. A shipwreck discovered off the coast of southern Turkey in 1982 gives us some sense of the extent of Mediterranean trade. Carbon dating of firewood found on board suggests the ship sank in about 1316 BCE. Its cargo included gold from Egypt, weapons from Greece, a scarab bearing Nefertiti's name (Fig. **3.29**), amber from northern Europe, hippopotamus and elephant ivory, and tin from Afghanistan. Such trade resulted not only in the transfer of goods between various regions, but in a broader cultural diffusion as well, for ideas, styles, religions, and technologies spread from one culture to another throughout the region. Much work remains to be done on the interconnections and lines of continuity and change among the peoples of the Aegean, the broader Mediterranean, Mesopotamia, and Egypt, but it is clear that they knew of one another, traded with one another, and were stimulated by one another's presence.

Fig. 3.29 Scarab of Queen Nefertiti, wreck of the *Uluburun*. ca. 1330 BCE. The Bodrum Museum of Underwater Archaeology, Bodrum, Turkey.

How did the idea of cycles shape Egyptian civilization?

The annual cycle of flood and sun, the inundation of the Nile River Valley that annually deposited deep layers of silt followed by months of sun in which crops could grow in the fertile soil, helped to define Egyptian culture. This predictable cycle helped to create a cultural belief in the stability and balance of all things that lasted for over 3,000 years. Can you describe this belief in terms of cyclical harmony? How does the Egyptian religion reflect this belief system?

Originally, what purposes did Egyptian sculpture and architecture serve?

Most surviving Egyptian art and architecture was devoted to burial and the afterlife, the cycle of life, death, and rebirth. The pyramids at Saqqara and Giza and the statuary of kings and queens were especially dedicated to this cycle. How do sculptures of lesser figures serve the same ends?

What important change distinguishes the Middle Kingdom?

Whereas in the Old Kingdom, writing had been used almost exclusively in a religious context, in the Middle Kingdom a vast secular literature developed. What does this secular literature tell us about Egyptian society?

Who was Amenhotep IV? Why did he change his name to Akhenaten?

The New Kingdom kings, now called "pharaoh," undertook massive, elaborately decorated building projects at Karnak and Thebes. Toward the end of the Eighteenth Dynasty, Amenhotep IV forsook traditional conventions of Egyptian representation, abolished the pantheon of Egyptian gods, established a monotheistic religion in which the sun disk Aten was worshiped exclusively, and changed his own name to Akhenaten. How does Amenhotep IV's religion differ from Egyptian religion in general? What other changes to Egyptian tradition occurred during his reign?

Funeral practices soon included the incantation of texts and spells collected in Books of Going Forth by Day, which accompanied the deceased as they underwent a last judgment. What significance do you attach to the title of these books?

How did Egypt decline and fall?

After the end of the New Kingdom, traditional representational practices remained in place, even when Kushite kings from the south in modern Sudan ruled the country. How did the Nubians and Kushites contribute to Egyptian culture? Egypt became susceptible to invasion, and after it fell to Alexander the Great in 332 BCE, its independence as a state came to an end, even though the new Greek Ptolemaic Dynasty continued traditional Egyptian ways until Rome conquered the country in 30 BCE.

PRACTICE MORE Get flashcards for images and terms and review chapter material with quizzes at **www.myartslab.com**

GLOSSARY

ankh A hieroglyph of a cross topped with a loop; a symbol of life in ancient Egypt.

ba In ancient Egypt, an idea comparable to a person's personality.

cartouche In ancient Egyptian art, an ornamental and symbolic frame reserved for the names of rulers and their wives.

colonnade A sequence or row of columns supporting a lintel and a roof.

composite view A view that integrates multiple perspectives into a single unified representation.

determinative A sign used in Egyptian hieroglyphs to indicate the category of an object or being.

fresco secco "Dry fresco"; the technique of painting on dry plaster.

hieroglyph A sign used in hieroglyphic writing, a writing system consisting mainly of pictorial characters.

hypostyle hall A vast space filled with columns supporting a roof.

ka In ancient Egypt, an idea comparable to a "soul" or "life force."

mastaba A trapezoidal tomb structure.

mummification The process of embalming, drying, and preserving a body.

mummy An embalmed body wrapped for burial.

obelisk A square, tapered stone column topped by a pyramid shape.

pharaoh A ruler of ancient Egypt.

phonogram A pictogram used to represent a sound.

pictogram A drawing that represents an object or being; often combined in hieroglyphic writing to express ideas.

pictorial formula A convention of representation in art.

pylon A massive gateway with sloping walls.

sanctuary The most sacred place of a religious building.

sarcophagus A rectangular stone coffin.

serekh A hieroglyphic device representing a pharaoh's palace seen simultaneously from above and the front, usually with a falcon on top of it (though not on *Narmer's Palette*; used to hold the pharaoh's name.

symmetrical Balanced on the left and right sides.

theocracy A state ruled by a god or by the god's representative.

votive A ritual object.

READINGS

The Teachings of Khety (ca. 2040–1648 BCE)

In the following example of instructive literature, dating from the Middle Kingdom, a royal scribe tries to convince his son to follow him into the profession by debunking virtually every other career path the young man might choose to follow. The work is as instructive as it is amusing, since it presents a wonderfully complete picture of daily life in the Middle Kingdom.

The beginning of the teaching which the man of Tjel named Khety made for his son named Pepy, while he sailed southwards to the Residence to place him in the school of writings among the children of the magistrates, the most eminent men of the Residence.

So he spoke to him: Since I have seen those who have been beaten, it is to writings that you must set your mind. Observe the man who has been carried off to a work force. Behold, there is nothing that surpasses writings! They are a boat upon the water. Read then at the end of the Book of Kemyet this state- 10
ment in it saying:

As for a scribe in any office in the Residence, he will not suffer want in it. When he fulfills the bidding of another, he does not come forth satisfied. I do not see an office to be compared with it, to which this maxim could relate. I shall make you love books more than your mother, and I shall place their excellence before you. It is greater than any office. There is nothing like it on earth. When he began to become sturdy but was still a child, he was greeted (respectfully). When he was sent to carry out a task, before he returned he was dressed in adult garments. 20

I do not see a stoneworker on an important errand or a goldsmith in a place to which he has been sent, but I have seen a coppersmith at his work at the door of his furnace. His fingers were like the claws of the crocodile, and he stank more than fish excrement.

Every carpenter who bears the adze is wearier than a fieldhand. His field is his wood, his hoe is the axe. There is no end to his work, and he must labor excessively in his activity. At nighttime he still must light his lamp . . . .

The barber shaves until the end of the evening. But he must 30
be up early, crying out, his bowl upon his arm. He takes himself from street to street to seek out someone to shave. He wears out his arms to fill his belly, like bees who eat (only) according to their work.

The reed-cutter goes downstream to the Delta to fetch himself arrows. He must work excessively in his activity. When the gnats sting him and the sand fleas bite him as well, then he is judged.

The potter is covered with earth, although his lifetime is still among the living. He burrows in the field more than swine to bake his cooking vessels. His clothes being stiff with mud, his 40
head cloth consists only of rags, so that the air which comes forth from his burning furnace enters his nose. He operates a pestle with his feet with which he himself is pounded, penetrating the courtyard of every house and driving earth into every open place.

I shall also describe to you the bricklayer. His kidneys are painful. When he must be outside in the wind, he lays bricks without a garment. His belt is a cord for his back, a string for his buttocks. His strength has vanished through fatigue and stiffness, kneading all his excrement. He eats bread with his fin- 50
gers, although he washes himself but once a day . . . .

The weaver inside the weaving house is more wretched than a woman. His knees are drawn up against his belly. He cannot breathe the air. If he wastes a single day without weaving, he is beaten with 50 whip lashes. He has to give food to the doorkeeper to allow him to come out to the daylight . . . .

See, there is no office free from supervisors, except the scribe's. He is the supervisor!

But if you understand writings, then it will be better for you than the professions which I have set before you . . . . What I 60
have done in journeying southward to the Residence is what I have done through love of you. A day at school is advantageous to you . . . .

Be serious, and great as to your worth. Do not speak secret matters. For he who hides his innermost thoughts is one who makes a shield for himself. Do not utter thoughtless words when you sit down with an angry man.

When you come forth from school after midday recess has been announced to you, go into the courtyard and discuss the last part of your lesson book. 70

When an official sends you as a messenger, then say what he said. Neither take away nor add to it . . . .

See, I have placed you on the path of God . . . . See, there is no scribe lacking sustenance, (or) the provisions of the royal house . . . . Honour your father and mother who have placed you on the path of the living.

READING CRITICALLY

Although the scribe Dua-Khety spends much time describing the shortcomings of other lines of work, he also reminds his son how he should behave at school. What do the father's words of advice tell us about the values of Egyptian society?

7 Other Empires
Urban Life and Imperial Majesty in China and India

THINKING AHEAD

What were early China's lasting contributions to Chinese civilization?

How was China unified as an empire?

How did religious outlooks shape ancient India?

The North China plain lies in the large, fertile valley of the Yellow River (Map **7.1**). Around 7000 BCE, when the valley's climate was much milder and the land more forested than it is today, the peoples inhabiting this fertile region began to cultivate the soil, growing primarily millet. Archeologists recognize at least three separate cultural groups in this region during this period, distinguished by their different pottery styles and works in jade. As Neolithic tribal people, they used stone tools, and although they domesticated animals very early on, they maintained the shamanistic practices of their hunter-gatherer heritage. Later inhabitants of this region would call this area the "Central Plain" because they believed it was the center of their country. During the ensuing millennia, Chinese culture in the Central Plain coalesced in ways that parallel developments in the Middle East and Greece during the same period, as China transformed itself from an agricultural society into a more urban-centered state.

By the third century BCE, at about the same time that Rome began establishing its imperial authority over the Mediterranean world, the government of China was sufficiently unified that it could build a Great Wall (Fig. **7.1**) across the hills north of the Central Plain to protect the realm from the intruding Central Asians who lived beyond its

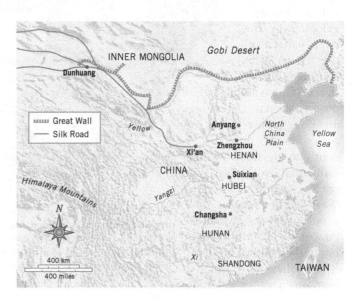

Map 7.1 Map of China. 1000–200 BCE.

northern borders. Some sections of the wall were already in place, built in previous centuries to protect local areas. These were rebuilt and connected to define a frontier stretching some 1,500 miles from northeast to northwest China. New roads and canal systems were built linking the entire nation, a

◀ **Fig. 7.1 The Great Wall, near Beijing, China. Begun late third century BCE.** Length approx. 4,100 miles, average height 25′. In the third century BCE, the Chinese Emperor Shihuangdi ordered his army to reconstruct, link, and augment walls on the northern frontier of China in order to form a continuous barrier protecting his young country from northern Mongol "barbarians."

HEAR MORE Listen to an audio file of your chapter at **www.myartslab.com**

large salaried bureaucracy was established, and a new imperial government headed by an emperor collected taxes, codified the law, and exerted control over a domain of formerly rival territories. Unification—first achieved here by the Qin dynasty—has remained a preeminent problem throughout China's long history.

This ritual jade disc, or *bi* [bee], made sometime in the fourth or third century BCE (Fig. 7.2), is emblematic of the continuity of Chinese historical traditions and ethnic identity. The earliest *bi* disks are found in burials dating from around 4000 BCE, and are thought to be part of the archaic paraphernalia of the shaman. While their original significance is unknown, by the time this one was made they were said to symbolize heaven. This example is decorated with a dragon and two tigers, auspicious symbols likewise emerging from China's prehistoric past. The first part of this chapter surveys the rise of the Chinese culture into a unified state capable of such an enormous undertaking as the Great Wall as well as the artistic refinement of the jade *bi* disk seen here.

At the same time, another culture was developing in the river valleys of the Asian subcontinent of India. In both China and India, national literatures arose, as did religious and philosophical practices that continue to this day and are influential worldwide. But in the ancient world, East and West had not yet met. The peoples of the Mediterranean world and those living in the Yellow and Indus River valleys were isolated from one another. As trade routes stretched across the Asian continent, these cultures would eventually cross paths. Gradually, Indian thought, especially Buddhism, would find its way into China, and Chinese goods would find their way to the West. Even more gradually, intellectual developments in ancient China and India, from Daoism to the teachings of Confucius [kun-FYOO-shus] and Buddha [BOO-duh], would come to influence cultural practice in the Western world. But throughout the period studied in this chapter, up until roughly 200 CE, the cultures of China and India developed independently of those in the West.

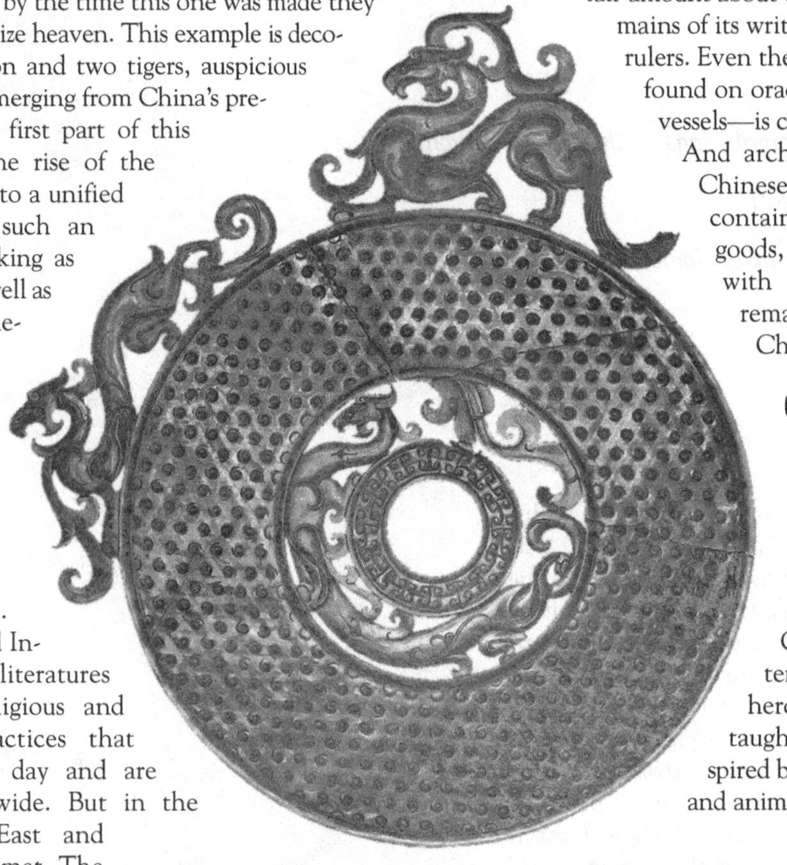

Fig. 7.2 Ritual disc *(bi)* with dragon and phoenix motif. Eastern Zhou dynasty, Warring States period, fourth–third century BCE. Jade, diameter 6 1/4". The Nelson-Atkins Museum of Art, Kansas City, Missouri. Purchase: Nelson Trust 33-81. This disc was discovered in a tomb, probably placed there because the Chinese believed that jade preserved the body from decay.

EARLY CHINESE CULTURE

Very few of the built edifices of ancient Chinese civilization have been found. We know that by the middle of the second millennium BCE, Chinese leaders ruled from large capitals, rivaling those in the West in their size and splendor. Beneath present-day Zhengzhou [juhng-joe], for instance, lies an early metropolitan center with massive earthen walls. Stone was scarce in this area, but abundant forests made wood plentiful, so it was used to build cities. As impressive as they were, cities built of wood were vulnerable to fire and military attack, and no sign of them remains. Nevertheless, we know a fair amount about early Chinese culture from the remains of its written language and the tombs of its rulers. Even the most ancient Chinese writing—found on oracle bones and ceremonial bronze vessels—is closely related to modern Chinese. And archeologists discovered that royal Chinese tombs, like Egyptian burial sites, contain furnishings, implements, luxury goods, and clothing that—together with the written record—give us a remarkably vivid picture of ancient China.

Chinese Calligraphy

Sometime during the Bronze Age, the Chinese developed a writing system that used individual pictographic characters to stand for distinct ideas and specific spoken words. According to Chinese legend, this writing system was invented by the culture-hero Fu Xi [foo shee] (who also taught the clans to hunt and fish), inspired by both the constellations and bird and animal footprints. Abundant surviving examples of writing from around 1400 to 1200 BCE—engraved with a sharp point on oracle bones made of turtle plastrons and ox scapula—record answers received from the spirit world during rituals asking about the future. We know as much as we do about the day-to-day concerns of the early Chinese rulers from these oracular fragments, on which a special order of priests, or diviners, posed questions of importance and concern (Fig. 7.3). They might ask about the harvest, the outcome of a war, the threat of flood, the course of an illness, or the wisdom of an administrative decision. To find answers, bones were heated with hot pokers, causing fissures to form with a loud crack. The patterns of these fissures were interpreted, and the bones were then inscribed. The first Chinese signs were pictograms, which, as in

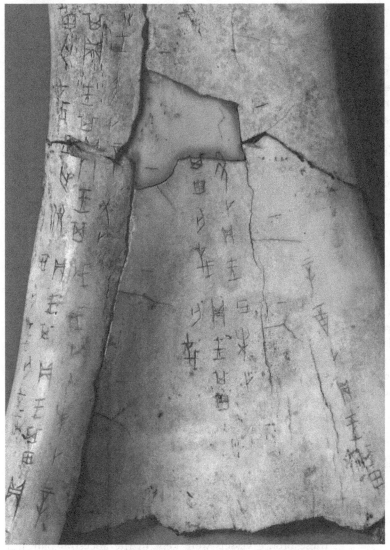

Fig. 7.3 Inscribed oracle bone. Shang period, ca. 1765–1122 BCE. The priests inscribed the characters representing the question from top to bottom in columns.

Fig. 7.4 Chinese characters. Shown are ancient characters (left) and modern ones (right). From top to bottom, they mean "sun," "mountain," "tree," "middle," "field," "frontier," and "door."

Mesopotamia, soon became stylized, particularly after the brush became the principal writing instrument (see Chapter 2, *Closer Look*, pages 38–39 for comparison.) The essence of Chinese written language is that a single written character has a fairly fixed significance, no matter how its pronunciation might vary over time or from place to place. This stability of meaning has allowed the Chinese language to remain remarkably constant through the ages. In the figure above right, 3,000 years separate the characters on the right from those on the left (Fig. 7.4).

The Shang Dynasty (ca. 1700–105 BCE)

Chinese records say that King Tang established the Shang dynasty. The Shang state was a linked collection of villages, stretching across the plains of the lower Yellow River valley. But it was not a contiguous state with distinct borders; other villages separated some of the Shang villages from

one another, and were frequently at war with the Shang. The royal family surrounded itself with shamans, who soon developed into a kind of nobility and, in turn, walled urban centers formed around the nobles' palaces or temples. The proliferation of bronze vessels, finely carved jades, and luxury goods produced for the Shang elite suggests that well-organized centers of craft production were located nearby. The Shang nobility organized itself into armies—surviving inscriptions describe forces as large as 13,000 men—that controlled the countryside and protected the king.

***The Book of Changes*: The First Classic Chinese Text** The Shang priests were avid interpreters of oracle bones. From a modern Western perspective, cracks in burnt bones are a matter of pure chance, but to the Shang, no event was merely random. The belief that the cosmos is pervaded by a greater logic and order lies at the heart of Chinese culture. In other words, there is no such thing as chance, and no transformation is without significance, not even a crack in a bone. The challenge lies in conducting one's affairs in accordance with the transformations of the cosmos.

The first classic of Chinese literature, *The Book of Changes*, or *Yi Jing*, compiled later from ideas that developed in the Shang era, is a guide to interpreting the workings of the universe. A person seeking to understand some aspect of his or her life or situation poses a question and tosses a set of straws or coins. The arrangement they make when they fall leads to one of 64 readings (or hexagrams) in the *Yi Jing*. (Fu Xi, the culture-hero who invented writing, is also said to have invented the eight trigrams that combine in pairs to form the 64 hexagrams.) Each hexagram describes the circumstances of the specific moment, which is, as the title suggests, always a moment of transition, a movement from one set of circumstances to the next. The *Yi Jing* prescribes certain behaviors appropriate to the moment. Thus, it is a book of wisdom.

This wisdom is based on a simple principle—that order derives from balance, a concept that the Chinese share with the ancient Egyptians. The Chinese believe that over time, through a series of changes, all things work toward a condition of balance. Thus, when things are out of balance, diviners might reliably predict the future by understanding that the universe tends to right itself. For example the eleventh hexagram, entitled *T'ai* [tie], or "Peace," indicated the unification of heaven and earth. The image reads:

> Heaven and earth unite: the image of PEACE.
> Thus the ruler
> Divides and completes the course of heaven and
>   earth,
> And so aids the people.

In fact, according to the Shang rulers, "the foundation of the universe" is based on the marriage of *Qian* [chee-an] (at once heaven and the creative male principle) and *Kun* (the earth, or receptive female principle), symbolized by the Chinese symbol of *yin-yang* (Fig. **7.5**). *Yin* is soft, dark, moist, and cool; *yang* is hard, bright, dry, and warm. The two combine to create the endless cycles of change, from night to day, across the four seasons of the year. They balance the five elements (wood, fire, earth, metal, and water) and the five powers of creation (cold, heat, dryness, moisture, and wind). The yin-yang sign, then, is a symbol of harmonious integration, the perpetual interplay and mutual relation among all things. And note that each side contains a circle of the same values as its opposite—neither side can exist without the other.

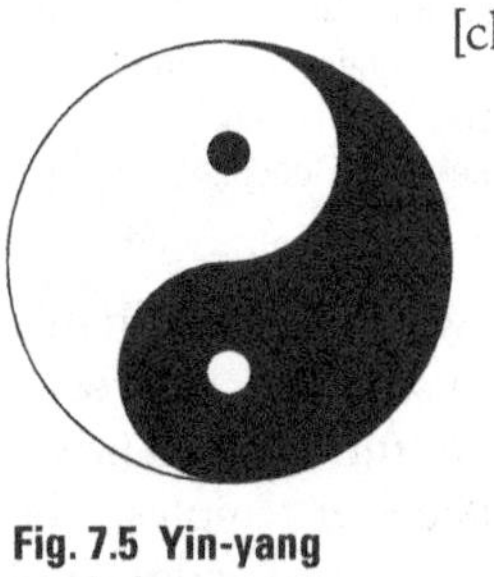

Fig. 7.5 Yin-yang symbol.

Shang Bronze The interlocking of opposites illustrated by the yin-yang motif is also present in the greatest artistic achievement of the Shang, their bronze casting. In order to cast bronze, a negative shape must be perfected first, into which the molten metal is then poured to make a positive

Fig. 7.6 Five-eared *ding* with dragon pattern. ca. 1200 BCE. Bronze, height 48″, diameter at mouth, 32 ¼″. Chinhua County Cultural Museum. One of the key features of Shang bronze decoration is the bilateral symmetry of the animal motifs, suggesting the importance of balance and order in ancient Chinese culture.

shape. Through the manufacture of ritual vessels, the Shang developed an extremely sophisticated bronze-casting technology, as advanced as any ever used. Made for offerings of food, water, and wine during ceremonies of ancestor worship, these bronze vessels were kept in the ancestral hall and brought out for banquets. Like formal dinnerware, each type of vessel had a specific shape and purpose; the *ding* (Fig. **7.6**), for example, was used for cooked food.

The conduct of the ancestral rites was the most solemn duty of a family head, with explicit religious and political significance. While the vessel shapes derived from the shapes of Neolithic pottery, in bronze they gradually became decorated with fantastic, supernatural creatures, especially dragons. For the Shang, the bronzes came to symbolize political power and authority. Leaders made gifts of bronze as tokens of political patronage, and strict rules governed the number of bronzes a family might possess according to rank. Like the oracle bones, many of these bronzes are inscribed with written characters.

At the last Shang capital and royal burial center, Yinxu [yin-shoo] (modern Anyang [ahn-yahng]), archeologists have unearthed the undisturbed royal tomb of Lady Fu Hao [foo how] (died ca. 1250 BCE), consort to the king Wu Ding. Consisting of a deep pit over which walled buildings were constructed as ritual sites to honor the dead, Lady Fu Hao's grave contained the skeletons of horses and dogs; about 440 cast and decorated bronzes, which probably originally held food and drink; 600 jade objects; chariots; lacquered items; weapons; gold and silver ornaments; and about 7,000 cowrie shells, which the Shang used as money. One of the most remarkable objects found in her grave is an ivory goblet inlaid with turquoise (Fig. **7.7**). Ivory was a local product, harvested from elephants that ranged, in the warmer Chinese climate of 3,000 years ago, much farther north than today. But the turquoise had to have come from far away. The goblet has a handle in the shape of a bird with a hooked beak, and a similar bird has been found far to the south in Sichuan province at a site roughly contemporary with Fu Hao's tomb, suggesting the jade's source. In addition, the turquoise inlay forms horned monsters with two bodies reminiscent of those seen on Shang bronze. As in Sumerian royal burials, Lady Fu Hao was not buried alone. The bodies of 16 people, apparently slaves, were found in the grave. Whether they submitted voluntarily to their deaths is a matter of pure conjecture.

Fig. 7.7 Ivory goblet inlaid with turquoise. ca. 1200 BCE. Height 8″. From Tomb 5, Xiaotun Locus North, at Yinxu, Anyang, Henan Province. Excavated in 1976. The Institute of Archaeology, Chinese Academy of Social Sciences, Beijing. Both the ivory and the turquoise inlay have been heavily restored.

Though geographically separate, the Bronze Age tombs of the Sumerians, Egyptians, Mycenaeans, and Shang demonstrate the widespread belief in life after death. They also testify to the enormous wealth that Bronze Age rulers were capable of accumulating.

The Zhou Dynasty (1027–256 BCE)

The Shang believed that their leaders were the sole conduit to the heavenly ancestors. However, in 1027 BCE, a rebel tribe known as the Zhou [joe] overthrew the Shang dynasty, claiming that the Shang had lost the Mandate of Heaven by not ruling virtuously. The Zhou asserted that the legitimacy of a ruler derived from divine approval, and that the Shang had lost this favor because of their decadent extravagances. Even so, the Zhou took measures to intermarry with the elite whom they had overthrown and took pains to conserve and restore what they admired of Shang culture. In fact, both the *Book of Changes* and the yin-yang symbol were originated by the Shang but codified and written down by the Zhou.

The Zhou ushered in an era of cultural refinement and philosophical accomplishment. One example is the oldest collection of Chinese poetry, the *Book of Songs* (*Shi jing* [she jee-ung]), still taught in Chinese schools today. According to tradition, government officials were sent into the countryside to record the lyrics of songs that expressed the feelings of the people. The collection that survives, first compiled by the Zhou, consists of 305 poems from between the eleventh and seventh centuries BCE. The poems address almost every aspect of life. There are love poems, songs celebrating the king's rule, sacrificial hymns, and folk songs. Descriptions of nature abound—over 100 kinds of plants are mentioned, as well as 90 kinds of animals and insects. Marriage practices, family life, clothing, and food are all subjects of poems. One of the oldest celebrates the harvest as an expression of the family's harmony with nature, the symbol that the family's ancestors are part of the same natural cycle of life and death, planting and harvest, as the universe as a whole (**Reading 7.1a**; for more selections from the *Book of Songs*, see **Reading 7.1**, page 237):

READING 7.1a

from the *Book of Songs*

Abundant is the year, with much millet, much rice;
But we have tall granaries,
To hold myriads, many myriads and millions of grain.
We make wine, make sweet liquor,
We offer it to ancestor, to ancestress,
We use it to fulfill all the rites,
To bring down blessings upon each and all.

Zhou Music The *Book of Songs* lists 29 different types of percussion, wind, and stringed instruments. The Chinese classified their instruments according to from which of eight different materials they were made: bronze (bells), bamboo (flutes), bone (flutes), clay (simple wind instruments), animal skin (drums), calabash (mouth-organs), and wood (zithers and lutes with silk strings). Like the Shang, the Zhou were masterful bronze artisans, and they carried this mastery into crafting their bells. A magnificent set of bronze bells (Fig. 7.8), found in the tomb of Marquis Yi [MAR-kee yee] of Zeng [dzung], brother of the Zhou ruler, gives us some feeling for the accomplishment of the Zhou in both bronze and music. The carillon consists of 65 bells, each capable of producing two distinct tones when hit either at the center or the rim. Thus, musicians playing the carillon had 130 different pitches or notes (compared to 88 on a modern piano) available in octaves of up to 10 notes. Seven zithers, two pipes, three flutes, and three drums were also found in the tomb (together with the bodies of eight young women and a dog). It is reasonable to suppose that these bells and instruments were designed for ceremonial and ritual use, as well as the simple pleasure of Marquis Yi.

Spiritual Beliefs: Daoism and Confucianism The songs in the *Shi jing* are contemporary with the poems that make up the *Dao de jing* [dow duh jee-ung] (*The Way and Its Power*), the primary philosophical treatise, written in verse, of Daoism, the Chinese mystical school of thought. The *Dao* ("the way") is deeply embedded in nature, and to attain it, the individual must accord by it, by "not-doing." (It is said that those who speak about the Dao do not know of it, and those who know about the Dao, do not speak of it.) The book, probably composed in the third century BCE, is traditionally ascribed to Lao Zi [lou zuh] ("the Old One") who lived during the sixth

century BCE. In essence, it argues for a unifying principle in all nature, the interchangeability of energy and matter, a principle the Chinese call *qi* [chee]. The *qi* can be understood only by those who live in total simplicity, and to this end the Daoist engages in strict dietary practices, breathing exercises, and meditation. In considering such images as the one expressed in the following poem, the first in the volume, the Daoist finds his or her way to enlightenment (**Reading 7.2**):

READING 7.2

from the *Dao de jing*

There are ways but the Way is uncharted;
There are names but not nature in words:
Nameless indeed is the source of creation
But things have a mother and she has a name.

The secret waits for the insight
Of eyes unclouded by longing;
Those who are bound by desire
See only the outward container.

These two come paired but distinct
By their names.
Of all things profound,
Say that their pairing is deepest,
The gate to the root of the world.

The final stanza seems to be a direct reference to the principle of yin-yang, itself a symbol of the *qi*. But the chief argument here, and the outlook of Daoism as a whole, is that enlightenment lies neither in the visible world nor in

Fig. 7.8 Set of 65 bronze bells, from the tomb of Marquis Yi of Zeng, Suixian, Hubei. 433 BCE. Bronze, frame, frame height 9', length 25'. Hubei Provincial Museum, Wuhan. Each of these bells is inscribed with the names of its two notes and with a *taotie*, a masklike image combining animal and human features that is found on many ritual bronze objects. Similar half-animal half-human figures are painted on Marquis Yi's coffin, suggesting that the ancient Chinese connected the afterlife with these supernatural figures.

Fig. 7.9 *Admonitions of the Imperial Instructress to Court Ladies* (detail), attributed to Gu Kaizhi. Six Dynasties period, ca. 344–464 CE. Handscroll, ink, and colors on silk, 9 ³/₄″ × 11′ 6″. © The Trustees of the British Museum/Art Resource, NY. This handscroll, painted nearly 900 years after the death of Confucius, shows his impact on Chinese culture.

language, although to find the "way" one must, paradoxically, pass through or use both. Daoism thus represents a spiritual desire to transcend the material world.

If Daoism sought to leave the world behind, another great canon of teachings developed during the Zhou dynasty sought to define the proper way to behave *in* the world. For 550 years, from about 771 BCE to the final collapse of the Zhou in 221 BCE, China was subjected to ever greater political turmoil as warring political factions struggled for power. Reacting to this state of affairs was the man many consider China's greatest philosopher and teacher, Kong Fuzi [kung-fu-zuh], or, as he is known in the West, Confucius.

Confucius was born to aristocratic parents in the province of Shandong in 551 BCE, the year before Peisistratus [pie-SIS-trah-tus] came to power in Athens. By his early twenties, Confucius had begun to teach a way of life, now referred to as Confucianism, based on self-discipline and proper relations among people. If each individual led a virtuous life, then the family would live in harmony. If the family lived in harmony, then the village would follow its moral leadership. If the village exercised proper behavior toward its neighbor villages, then the country would live in peace and thrive.

Traditional Chinese values—values that Confucius believed had once guided the Zhou, such as self-control, propriety, reverence for one's elders, and virtuous behavior—lie at the core of this system. Tradition has it that Confucius compiled and edited *The Book of Changes*, *The Book of Songs* (which he edited down to 305 verses), and four other "classic" Chinese texts: *The Book of History*, containing speeches and pronouncements of historical rulers; *The Book of Rites*, which is essentially a code of conduct; *The Spring and Autumn Annals*, a history of China up to the fifth century BCE; and a lost treatise on music.

Confucius particularly valued *The Book of Songs*. "My little ones," he told his followers, "why don't you study the

Songs? Poetry will exalt you, make you observant, enable you to mix with others, provide an outlet for your vexations; you learn from it immediately to serve your parents and ultimately to serve your prince. It also provides wide acquaintance with the names of birds, beasts, and plants."

After his death, in 479 BCE, Confucius's followers transcribed their conversations with him in a book known in English as the *Analects*. (For a selection, see **Reading 7.3** on page 238.) Where the *Dao de jing* is a spiritual work, the *Analects* is a practical one. At the heart of Confucius's teaching is the principle of *li* [lee]—propriety in the conduct of the rites of ancestor worship. The courtesy and dignity required when performing the rites lead to the second principle, *ren*, or benevolent compassion and fellow feeling, the ideal relationship that should exist among all people. Based on respect for oneself, *ren* extends this respect to all others, manifesting itself as charity, courtesy, and above all, justice. *De* [duh], or virtue, is the power of moral example that an individual, especially a ruler, can exert through a life dedicated to the exercise of *li* and *ren*. Finally, *wen*, or culture, will result. Poetry, music, painting, and the other arts will all reveal an inherent order and harmony reflecting the inherent order and harmony of the state. Like an excellent leader, brilliance in the arts illuminates virtue. The Chinese moral order depended not upon divine decree or authority, but instead upon the people's own right actions. A scene from a painted handscroll of a later period, known as *Admonitions of the Imperial Instructress to Court Ladies* (Fig. **7.9**), illustrates a Confucian story of wifely virtue and proper behavior. As the viewer unrolled the scroll (handscrolls were not meant to be viewed all at once, as displayed in modern museums, but unrolled right to left a foot or two at a time, as a tabletop might allow), he or she would observe a bear, who having escaped from his cage threatens the Emperor, seated at the right. Until two guards arrive to try to keep the bear at bay, Lady Feng [fung] has stepped forward, courageously placing herself between the bear and her lord. She illustrates the fifth rule of Confucian philosophy—*yi* [yee], or duty, the obligation of the wife to her husband and of the subject to her ruler.

Its emphasis on respect for age, authority, and morality made Confucianism extremely popular among Chinese leaders and the artists they patronized. It embraced the emperor, the state, and the family in a single ethical system with a hierarchy that was believed to mirror the structure of the cosmos. As a result, the Han [hahn] dynasty (206 BCE–220 CE) adopted Confucianism as the Chinese state religion, and a thorough knowledge of the Confucian classics was subsequently required of any politically ambitious person. Despite the later ascendancy among intellectuals of Daoism and Buddhism (which would begin to flourish in China after the collapse of the Han dynasty, Confucianism continued to be the core of civil service training in China until 1911, when the Chinese Republic ended the dynastic system. Even though Mao Zedong [mao zuh-dong], chairman of the Chinese Communist Party from 1945 until his death in 1976, conducted a virulent campaign against Confucian thought, many in China now believe that Confucianism offers the most viable alternative to the nation's political status quo. In fact, the noncommunist "Little Dragons" of East Asia—Hong Kong, Singapore, Taiwan, and South Korea—would all attribute their economic success in the 1980s to their Confucian heritage.

IMPERIAL CHINA

At the same time that Rome rose to dominance in the West (see Chapter 6), a similar empire arose in China. But whereas Rome's empire derived from outward expansion, China's empire arose from consolidation at the center. From about the time of Confucius onward, seven states vied for control. They mobilized armies to battle one another; iron weapons replaced bronze; they organized bureaucracies and established legal systems; merchants gained political power; and a "hundred schools of thought" flowered.

The Qin Dynasty (221–206 BCE): Organization and Control

This period of warring states culminated when the western state Qin [chin] (the origin of our name for China) conquered the other states and unified them under the Qin empire in 221 BCE. Under the leadership of Qin Shihuangdi [chin shuh-hwang-dee] (r. 221–210 BCE), who declared himself "First Emperor," the Qin worked very quickly to achieve a stable society. To discourage nomadic invaders from the north, they built a wall from the Yellow Sea east of modern Beijing far into Inner Mongolia, known today as the Great Wall of China (see Fig. 7.1).

The wall was constructed by soldiers, augmented by accused criminals, civil servants who found themselves in disfavor, and conscripts from across the countryside. Each family was required to provide one able-bodied adult male to work on the wall each year. It was made of rammed earth, reinforced by continuous, horizontal courses of brushwood, and faced with stone. Watchtowers were built at high points, and military barracks were built in the valleys below. At the same time, the Chinese constructed nearly 4,350 miles of roads, linking even the furthest reaches of the country to the Central Plain. By the end of the second century CE, China had some 22,000 miles of roads serving a country of nearly 1.5 million square miles.

Such massive undertakings could only have been accomplished by an administrative bureaucracy of extraordinary organizational skill. Indeed, in the 15 years that the Qin ruled China, the written language was standardized, a uniform coinage was introduced, all wagon axles were required to be the same width so that they would uniformly fit in the existing ruts on the Chinese roads (thus accommodating trade and travel), a system of weights and measures was introduced, and the country was divided into the administrative and bureaucratic provinces much as they exist to the present day.

Perhaps nothing tells us more about Qin organization and control than the tomb of its first emperor, Qin Shihuangdi (see *Closer Look*, pages 222–223). When he died, battalions of life-size earthenware guards in military formation were buried in pits beside his tomb. (More than 8,000 have been excavated so far.) Like the Great Wall, this monumental undertaking required an enormous workforce, and we know that the Qin enlisted huge numbers of workers in this and its other projects.

The Philosophy of Han Feizi To maintain control, in fact, the Qin suppressed free speech, persecuted scholars, burned classical texts, and otherwise exerted absolute power. They based their thinking on the writings of Han Feizi [hahn-fay-dzuh], who had died in 233 BCE, just before the Qin took power. Orthodox Confucianism had been codified by Meng-zi [mung-dzuh], known as Mencius [men-shus] (ca. 370–300 BCE), an itinerant philosopher and sage who argued for the innate goodness of the individual. He believed that bad character was a result of society's inability to provide a positive, cultivating atmosphere in which individuals might realize their capacity for goodness. Han Feizi, on the other hand, argued that human beings were inherently evil and innately selfish (exactly the opposite of Mencius's point of view). **Legalism**, as Han Feizi's philosophy came to be called, required that the state exercise its power over the individual, because no agency other than the state could instill enough fear in the individual to elicit proper conduct. The Qin Legalist bureaucracy, coupled with an oppressive tax structure imposed to pay for their massive civil projects, soon led to rebellion, and after only 15 years in power, the Qin collapsed.

The Han Dynasty (206 BCE–220 CE): The Flowering of Culture

In place of the Qin, the Han dynasty came to power, inaugurating over 400 years of intellectual and cultural growth. The Han emperors installed Confucianism as the official state philosophy and established an academy to train civil servants. Where the Qin had disenfranchised scholars, the Han honored them, even going so far as to give them an essential role in governing the country.

Han prosperity was constantly threatened by incursions of nomadic peoples to the north, chiefly the Huns, whom the Chinese called Xiongnu [she-ong-noo], and whose impact would later be felt as far away as Rome. In 138 BCE, Emperor Wu (r. 141–87 BCE) attempted to forge military alliances with Huns, sending General Zhang Qian [jahng chee-an] with 100 of his best fighting men into the northern territories. The Huns held General Zhang captive for ten years. When he returned, he spoke of horses that were far stronger and faster than those in China. Any army using them, he believed, would be unbeatable. In fact, horses could not be bred successfully in China owing to a lack of calcium in the region's water and vegetation, and until General Zhang's report, the Chinese had known horses only as small, shaggy creatures of Mongolian origin. To meet the Huns on their own terms, with cavalry instead of infantry, China needed horses from the steppes of western Asia.

"The Heavenly Horses" A small bronze horse found in the tomb of General Zhang at Wuwei [woo-way] in Gansu [gahn-soo] represents the kind of horse to which the Chinese aspired (Fig. 7.10). Its power is captured in the energetic lines of its composition, its flaring nostrils and barreled chest. But it is, simultaneously, perfectly, almost impossibly, balanced on one leg, as if defying gravity, having stolen the ability to fly from the bird beneath its hoof. In 101 BCE, the Emperor Wu, awaiting delivery of 30 such horses in the Chinese capital of Chang'an [chahng-ahn], composed a hymn in their honor (**Reading 7.4**):

READING 7.4

from Emperor Wu's *"Heavenly Horses"*

The Heavenly Horses are coming,
Coming from the Far West . . .
The Heavenly Horses are coming
Across the pastureless wilds
A thousand leagues at a stretch,
Following the eastern road . . .
Should they choose to soar aloft,
Who could keep pace with them?
The Heavenly Horses are coming . . .

Fig. 7.10 *Flying Horse Poised on One Leg on a Swallow,* **from the tomb of Governor-General Zhang at Wuwei, Gansu. Late Han dynasty, second century CE.** Bronze, 13 1/2" × 17 3/4". Gansu Provincial Museum. According to Chinese tradition, these horses sweated blood, perhaps the result of a parasitic infection. The Chinese, incidentally, also imported grass seed to feed these horses.

One day in 1974, peasants digging a well on the flat plain 1,300 yards east of the huge Qin dynasty burial mound of the Emperor Qin Shihuangdi in the northern Chinese province of Shaanxi [shahn-shee] unearthed parts of a life-size clay soldier—a head, hands, and body. Archeologists soon discovered an enormous subterranean pit beneath the fields containing an estimated 6,000 infantrymen, most standing four abreast in eleven parallel trenches paved with bricks. In 1976 and 1977, two smaller but equally spectacular sites were discovered north of the first one, containing another 1,400 individual warriors and horses, complete with metal weaponry.

Qin Shihuangdi's actual tomb has never been excavated. It rises 140 feet above the plain. Historical records indicated that below the mound is a subterranean palace estimated to be about 400 feet by 525 feet. According to the *Shi Ji* [shr jee] (*Historical Records*) of Sima Qian [shee-mah chee-an], a scholar from the Han dynasty, the emperor was buried there

The Tomb of Qin Shihuangdi

in a bronze casket surrounded by a river of mercury. Scientific tests conducted by Chinese archeologists confirm the presence of large quantities of mercury in the soil of the burial mound. Magnetic scans of the tomb have also revealed large numbers of coins, suggesting the emperor was buried with his treasury.

Something to Think About . . .

Why do you suppose this ceramic army was deployed outside the tomb of Qin Shihuangdi and not in it?

Two terra-cotta soldiers from the burial mound of Qin Shihuangdi, Shaanxi province, China. Both ca. 210 BCE. On the left, an infantryman poised for hand-to-hand combat, height 70″; below, a kneeling archer, height 48″. The bodies of most of the soldiers in the tomb appear to have been mass-produced in molds. After each stylized body was baked, head and hands were added. No two heads are alike. Many seem to possess unique, individual facial features, and they exhibit a variety of hairstyles. They were subsequently painted in vivid colors, and most carried actual weapons. Knives, spears, swords, and arrowheads have been found at the site.

Soldiers and horses, from the pits near the tomb of Emperor Qin Shihuangdi, Lintong, Shaanxi, China. Qin dynasty, ca. 210 BCE. Terra-cotta, life-size. The practice of fashioning clay replicas of humans for burial at mausoleum sites replaced an earlier practice of actual human sacrifice. Over 700,000 people were employed in preparing the tomb.

SEE MORE For a Closer Look at the Tomb of Shihuangdi, go to **www.myartslab.com**

Han Poetry Under Emperor Wu, Chinese literary arts flourished. In 120 BCE, he established the *Yue fu* [yoo-eh foo], the so-called Music Bureau, which would come to employ some 829 people charged with collecting the songs of the common people. The folk style of the *yuefu* songs was widely imitated, both by court poets during the Han and throughout the history of Chinese poetry. The lines are of uneven length, although often of five characters, and emphasize the joys and vicissitudes of daily life. A case in point is a poem by Liu Xijun [lee-ooh shee-june], a Chinese princess who, around 110 BCE, was married for political reasons to the chief of the Wusun, a band of nomads who lived in the steppes of northwest China. Her husband, as it turned out when she arrived, was old and decrepit, spoke almost no Chinese, and by and large had nothing to do with her, seeing her every six months or so. This is her "Lament" (**Reading 7.5**):

READING 7.5

Liu Xijun, "Lament"

My family married me off
to the King of the Wusun.
and I live in an alien land
a million miles from nowhere.
My house is a tent,
My walls are of felt.
Raw flesh is all I eat,
with horse milk to drink.
I always think of home
and my heart strings,
O to be a yellow snow-goose
floating home again!

The poem's last two lines—what might be called the flight of Liu Xijun's imagination—are typical of Chinese poetry, where time and again the tragic circumstances of life are overcome through an image of almost transcendent natural beauty.

As Liu Xijun's poem suggests, women poets and scholars were common—and respected—during the Han dynasty. But as the circumstances surrounding Liu Xijun's poem also suggest, women did not enjoy great power in society. The traditional Chinese family was organized around basic Confucian principles: Elder family members were wiser, and therefore superior to the younger, and males were superior to females. Thus, while a grandmother might hold sway over her grandson, a wife owed unquestioning obedience to her husband. The unenviable plight of women is the subject of a poem by Fu Xuan [foo schwan], a male poet of the late Han dynasty who apparently was one of the most prolific poets of his day, although only 63 of his poems survive (**Reading 7.6**):

READING 7.6

Fu Xuan, "To Be a Woman"

It is bitter to be a woman,
the cheapest thing on earth.

A boy stands commanding in the doorway
like a god descended from the sky.
His heart hazards the four seas,
thousands of miles of wind and dust,
but no one laughs when a girl is born.
The family doesn't cherish her.
When she's a woman she hides in back rooms,
scared to look a man in the face.
They cry when she leaves to marry—
a brief rain, then mere clouds.
Head bowed she tries to compose her face,
her white teeth stabbing red lips.
She bows and kneels endlessly,
even before concubines and servants.
If their love is strong as two stars
she is like a sunflower in the sun,
but when their hearts are water and fire
a hundred evils descend on her.
The years change her jade face
and her lord will find new lovers.
Who were close like body and shadow
will be remote as Chinese and Mongols.
Sometimes even Chinese and Mongols meet
but they'll be far as polar stars.

The poem is notable for the acuity and intensity of its imagery—her "white teeth stabbing red lips," the description of a close relationships as "like body and shadow," and, in the last lines, the estrangement of their relationship to a point as far apart as "polar stars," farther apart even than the Chinese and Mongols. (And who, one must ask, is more like the barbarian hordes, the male or the female?)

Han Architecture What we know about the domestic setting of Han dynasty society we can gather mostly from surviving poetic images describing everyday life in the home, but our understanding of domestic architecture derives from ceramic models. A model of a house found in a tomb, presumably provided for the use of the departed in the afterlife, is four stories high and topped by a watchtower (Fig. **7.11**). The family lived in the middle two stories, while livestock, probably pigs and oxen, were kept in the gated lower level with its courtyard extending in front of the house.

Architecturally, the basic form of the house is commonly found across the world—rectangular halls with columns supporting the roof or the floor above. The walls serve no weight-bearing function. Rather, they serve as screens separating the inside from the outside, or one interior room from another. Distinctive to Chinese architecture are the broad eaves of the roof, which would become a standard feature of East Asian construction. Adding playful charm is the elaborate decoration of the facade, including painted trees flanking the courtyard.

Han Silk Aside from their military value, horses advanced the growth of trade along the Silk Road. Nearly 5,000 miles long, this trade route led from the Yellow River valley to the Mediterranean, and along it, the

Fig. 7.11 Model of a House, Eastern Han Dynasty (25-200 C.E.), 1st century C.E. Painted earthenware with unfired coloring, 52 × 33 ½ × 27″ (132.1 × 85.1 × 68.6 cm) The Nelson-Atkins Museum of Art, Kansas City, Missouri. This is one of the largest and most complete models of a Han house known.

Fig. 7.12 Painted banner from the tomb of the wife of the Marquis of Dai, Mawangdui, Changsha, Hunan. Han dynasty, ca. 160 BCE. Colors on silk, height 6'8½". Hunan Provincial Museum. The banner was found in the innermost of the nested coffins opened in 1972.

Chinese traded their most exclusive commodity, silk. (See *Continuity & Change*, page 235.) The quality of Han silk is evident in a silk banner from the tomb of the wife of the Marquis of Dai, discovered on the outskirts of present-day Changsha [chahng-shah] in Hunan [hoo-nahn] (Fig. **7.12**). Painted with scenes representing the underworld, the earthly realm, and the heavens, it represents the Han conception of the cosmos. Long, sinuous lines representing dragons' tails, coiling serpents, long-tailed birds, and flowing draperies unify the three realms. In the right corner of the heavenly realm, above the crossbar of the T, is an image of the sun containing a crow, and in the other corner is a crescent moon supporting a toad. Between them is a deity entwined within his own long, red serpent tail. The deceased noblewoman herself stands on the white platform in the middle region of the banner. Three attendants stand behind her and two figures kneel before her, bearing gifts. On a white platform in the lower realm, bronze vessels contain food and wine for the deceased.

Papermaking and Other Han Technologies One of the important characteristics of Han poetry is that, as opposed to the poems in the *Book of Songs*, many poems did not emerge out of oral traditions but originated as written works. In the West, the limitations of papyrus as a writing medium had led to the invention of parchment at Pergamon (see Chapter 5), but the Chinese invention of cellulose-based paper in 105 CE by Cai Lun [tsai lwun], a eunuch and attendant to the Imperial Court who held a post responsible for manufacturing instruments and weapons, enabled China to develop widespread literacy much more rapidly than the West. Paper made of hemp had already been produced by the Han for over 200 years, but Cai Lun improved both the techniques used and its quality while using a variety of materials, such as tree bark, hemp, and rags. Although modern technologies have simplified the process, his method remains basically unchanged—the suspension in water of softened plant fibers that are formed in moulds into thin sheets, couched (pressed), drained, and then dried.

The Han were especially inventive. Motivated by trade, the Han began to make maps, becoming the world's first cartographers. They invented important agricultural technologies such as the wheelbarrow and horse collar. They learned to measure the magnitude of earthquakes with a crude but functional seismograph. But persistent warring with the Huns required money to support military and bureaucratic initiatives. Unable to keep up with increased taxes, many peasants were forced off the land and popular rebellion ensued. By the third century CE, the Han dynasty had collapsed. China reentered a period of political chaos lasting from 220 until 589 CE, when imperial rule finally regained its strength.

ANCIENT INDIA

Indian civilization was born along the Indus [IN-duhs] River in the northwest corner of the Indian subcontinent in present-day Pakistan somewhere around 2700 BCE in an area

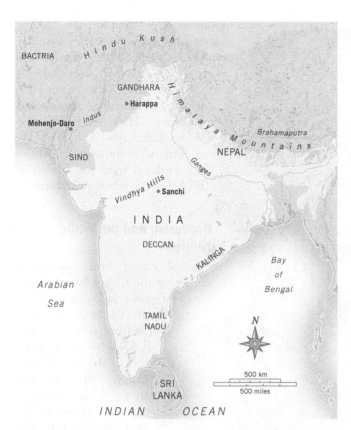

Map 7.2 India around 1500 BCE. Cut off from the rest of Asia by high mountains to the north, India was nevertheless a center of trade by virtue of its prominent maritime presence.

known as Sind—from which the words *India* and *Hindu* originate (see Map **7.2**). The earliest Indian peoples lived in at least two great cities in the Indus valley, Mohenjo-Daro [moh-HEN-joh-DAR-oh], on the banks of the Indus, and Harappa [huh-RAH-puh], on the river Ravi [RAH-vee], downstream from modern Lahore [luh-HORE]. These great cities thrived until around 1900 BCE and were roughly contemporaneous with Sumerian Ur, the Old Kingdom of Egypt, and Minoan civilization in the Aegean.

The cities were discovered by chance in the early 1920s, and excavations have continued since. The best preserved of the sites is Mohenjo-Daro. Built atop a citadel is a complex of buildings, presumably a governmental or religious center, surrounded by a wall 50 feet high. Set among the buildings on the citadel is a giant pool (Fig. **7.13**). Perhaps a public bath or a ritual space, its finely fitted bricks, laid on edge and bound together with gypsum plaster, made it watertight. The bricks on the side walls of the tank were covered with a thick layer of bitumen (natural tar) to keep water from seeping through the walls and up into the superstructure. The pool was open to the air and surrounded by a brick colonnade.

Outside the wall and below the citadel, a city of approximately 6 to 7 square miles, with broad avenues and narrow side streets, was laid out in a rough grid. It appears to have been home to a population of between 20,000 and 50,000. Most of the houses were two stories tall and built around a central courtyard. A network of covered drainage systems

Fig. 7.13 Large water tank, possibly a public or ritual bathing area, from Mohenjo-Daro, Indus valley civilization. ca. 2600–1900 BCE. It measures approximately 39 1/2 feet north-south and 23 feet wide, with a maximum depth of almost 8 feet.

ran through the streets, channeling waste and rainwater into the river. The houses were built with standard sizes of baked brick, each measuring 2¾ × 5½ × 11 inches, a ratio of 1:2:4. A brick of identical ratio but larger— 4 × 8 × 16 inches—was used in the building of platforms and city walls. Unlike the sun-dried bricks used in other cultures at the time, Mohenjo-Daro's bricks were fired, which made them much more durable. All of this suggests a civilization of considerable technological know-how and sophistication.

The arts of the Indus civilizations include human figurines and animal figurines made of stone, terra-cotta, bronze, and other materials— including the so-called "priest-king" found at Mohenjo-Daro (Fig. 7.14)—terra-cotta pottery, and various styles of decorative ornaments for human wear including beads and stoneware bangles. Over 2,000 small seals have been unearthed. Carved from steatite stone, coated with alkali, and then fired to produce a luminous white surface, many depict animals with an extraordinary naturalism, especially considering that they are rendered in such miniature detail (Fig. 7.15). Depictions of warfare or conquered enemies are strikingly absent in representational art. As the top of this seal shows, the peoples of the valley had a written language, although it remains undeciphered.

Sometime around 1500 BCE the Aryans [AIR-ee-uhnz], nomads from the north, invaded the Indus River Valley and conquered its inhabitants, making them slaves. Thus began the longest-lasting set of rigid, class-based societal divisions in world history, the Indian caste system. By the beginning of the first millennium BCE, these castes consisted of five principal groups, based on occupation: At the bottom of the ladder

Fig. 7.14 Torso of a "priest-king" from Mohenjo-Daro, Indus valley civilization. ca. 2000–1900 BCE. Steatite, height 6⁷⁄₈". National Museum of Pakistan, Karachi, Pakistan. The look created by the figure's half-closed eyes suggests that this might be a death mask of some sort. The *trefoil*, or three-lobed decorations on the garment that crosses his chest, were originally filled with red paint.

was a group considered "untouchable," people so scorned by society that they were not even considered a caste. Next in line were the Shudras [SHOO-druhz], unskilled workers. Then came the Vaishyas [VYSH-yuhz], artisans and merchants. They were followed by the Kshatriyas [kuh-SHAHT-ree-uhz], rulers and warriors. At the highest level were the Brahmins [BRAH-minz], priests and scholars.

Hinduism and the Vedic Tradition

The social castes were sanctioned by the religion the Aryans brought with them, a religion based on a set of sacred hymns to the Aryan gods. These hymns, called *Vedas* [VAY-duhz], were written in the Aryan language, Sanskrit, and they gave their name to an entire period of Indian civilization, the Vedic [VAY-dik] period (ca. 1500–322 BCE). From the *Vedas* in turn came the *Upanishads* [oo-PAHN-ih-shadz], a book of mystical and philosophical texts that date from sometime after 800 BCE. Taken together, the *Vedas* and the *Upanishads* form the basis of the Hindu religion, with Brahman, the universal soul, at its center. The religion has no single body of doctrine, nor any standard set of practices. It is defined above all by the diversity of its beliefs and deities. Indeed, several images of mother goddesses, stones in the phallic form, as well as a seal with an image that resembles the Hindu god Shiva, have been excavated at various Indus sites, leading scholars to believe that certain aspects and concepts of Hinduism survived from the Indus civilizations and were incorporated into the Vedic religion.

The *Upanishads* argue that all existence is a fabric of false appearances. What appears to the senses is entirely illusory. Only Brahman is real. Thus, in a famous story illustrating the point, a tiger, orphaned as a cub, is raised by

Fig. 7.15 Seal depicting a horned animal, Indus valley civilization. ca. 2500–1900 BCE. Steatite, approx. 1¼ × 1¼". National Museum of Pakistan, Karachi, Pakistan. The function of these seals remains unknown.

goats. It learns, as a matter of course, to eat grass and make goat sounds. But one day it meets another tiger, who takes it to a pool to look at itself. There, in its reflection in the water, it discovers its true nature. The individual soul needs to discover the same truth, a truth that will free it from the endless cycle of birth, death, and rebirth and unite it with the Brahman in **nirvana** [nir-VAH-nuh], a place or state free from worry, pain, and the external world.

Brahman, Vishnu, and Shiva As Hinduism [HIN-doo-iz-um] developed, the functions of Brahman, the divine source of all being, were split among three gods: Brahma, the creator; Vishnu [VISH-noo], the preserver; and Shiva [SHEE-vuh], the destroyer. Vishnu was one of the most popular of the Hindu deities. In his role as preserver, he is the god of benevolence, forgiveness, and love, and like the other two main Hindu gods, he was believed capable of assuming human form, which he did more often than the other gods due to his great love for humankind. Among Vishnu's most famous incarnations is his appearance as Rama [rah-mah] in the oldest of the Hindu epics, the *Ramayana* [rah-mah-yuh-nuh] (*Way of Rama*), written by Valmiki [vahl-MIH-kee] in about 550 BCE. Like Homer in ancient Greece, Valmiki gathered together many existing legends and myths into a single story, in this case narrating the lives of Prince Rama and his queen, Sita [SEE-tuh]. The two serve as models of Hindu life. Rama is the ideal son, brother, husband, warrior, and king, and Sita loves, honors, and serves her husband with absolute and unquestioning fidelity. These characters face moral dilemmas to which they must react according to **dharma** [DAHR-muh], good and righteous conduct reflecting the cosmic moral order that underlies all existence. For Hindus, correct actions can lead to cosmic harmony; bad actions, violating dharma, can trigger cosmic tragedies such as floods and earthquakes.

An equally important incarnation of Vishnu is as the charioteer Krishna [KRISH-nuh] in the later Indian epic the *Mahahbarata* [muh-ha-BAHR-uh-tuh], composed between 400 BCE and 400 CE. In the sixth book of the *Mahahbarata*, titled the *Bhagavad Gita* [BUH-guh-vud GHEE-tuh]

(see **Reading 7.7**, pages 238–240), Krishna comes to the aid of Arjuna [ahr-JOO-nuh], a warrior who is tormented by the conflict between his duty to fight and kill his kinsmen in battle and the Hindu prohibition against killing. Krishna explains to Arjuna that as a member of the Kshatriya caste—that is, as a warrior—he is freed from the Hindu sanction against killing. In fact, by fighting well and doing his duty, he can free himself from the endless cycle of birth, death, and reincarnation, and move toward spiritual union with the Brahman.

But Vishnu's popularity is probably most attributable to his celebration of erotic love, which to Hindus symbolizes the mingling of the self and the absolute spirit of Brahman. In the *Vishnu Puranas* [poor-AH-nuhz] (the "old stories" of Vishnu), collected about 500 CE, Vishnu, in his incarnation as Krishna, is depicted as seducing one after another of his devotees. In one story of the *Vishnu Puranas*, he seduces an entire band of milkmaids: "They considered every instant without him a myriad of years; and prohibited (in vain) by husbands, fathers, brothers, they went forth at night to sport with Krishna, the object of their affection." Allowing themselves to be seduced does not suggest that the milkmaids were immoral, but shows an almost inevitable manifestation of their souls' quest for union with divinity.

If Brahma is the creator of the world, Shiva takes what Brahma has made and embodies the world's cyclic rhythms. Since in Hinduism the destruction of the old world is followed by the creation of a new world, Shiva's role as destroyer is required and a positive one. In this sense, he possesses reproductive powers, and in this part of his being, he is represented as a *linga* [LING-uh] (phallus), often carved in stone on temple grounds or at shrines.

The Goddess Devi Goddess worship is fundamental to Hindu religion. Villages usually recognize goddesses as their protectors, and the goddess Devi is worshipped in many forms throughout India. She is the female aspect without whom the male aspect, which represents consciousness or discrimination, remains impotent and void. For instance, in the *Devi Mahatmayam*, another of the Puranas, composed like the *Vishnu Puranas* around 500 CE, Vishnu was asleep on the great cosmic ocean, and due to his slumber, Brahma was unable to create. Devi intervenes, kills the demons responsible for Vishnu's slumber, and helps wake up Vishnu. Thus continues the cycle of life.

Devi is synonymous with Shakti, the primordial cosmic energy, and represents the dynamic forces that move through the entire universe. Shaktism, a particular brand of Hindu faith that regards Devi as the Supreme Brahman itself, believes that all other forms of divinity, female or male, are themselves simply forms of Devi's diverse manifestations. But she has a number of particular manifestations. In an extraordinary miniature carving from the

LEARN MORE Gain insight from a primary source document from the sermon of the Buddha at **www.myartslab.com**

Fig. 7.16 *The Goddess Durga Killing the Buffalo Demon, Mahisha (Mahishasuramardini).* **Bangladesh or India, Pala period, twelfth century.** Argillite, height. 5⁵⁄₁₆″. Image copyright © The Metropolitan Museum of Art/Art Resource, NY. Durga represents the warrior aspect of Devi.

twelfth century, Devi is seen in her manifestation as Durga (Fig. **7.16**), portrayed as the sixteen-armed slayer of a buffalo inhabited by the fierce demon Mahisha. Considered invincible, Mahisha threatens to destroy the world, but Durga comes to the rescue. In this image, she has just severed the buffalo's head and Mahisha, in the form of a tiny, chubby man, his hair composed of snake heads, emerges from the buffalo's decapitated body and looks up admiringly at Durga even as his toes are being bitten by her lion. Durga smiles serenely as she hoists Mahisha by his hair and treads gracefully on the buffalo's body.

Buddhism: "The Path of Truth"

Because free thought and practice mark the Hindu religion, it is hardly surprising that other religious movements drew on it and developed from it. Buddhism is one of those. Its founder, Shakyamuni [SHAHK-yuh-moo-nee] Buddha, lived from about 563 to 483 BCE. He was born Prince Siddhartha Gautama [sid-DAR-thuh gau-tah-muh], child of a ruler of the Shakya [SHAK-yuh] clan—Shakyamuni means "sage of the Shakyas"—and was raised to be a ruler himself. Troubled by what he perceived to be the suffering of all human beings, he abandoned the luxurious lifestyle of his father's palace to live in the wilderness. For six years he meditated, finally attaining complete enlightenment while sitting under a banyan tree at Bodh Gaya [bod GUY-ah]. Shortly thereafter he gave his first teaching, at the Deer Park at Sarnath, expounding the Four Noble Truths:

1. Life is suffering.
2. This suffering has a cause, which is ignorance.
3. Ignorance can be overcome and eliminated.
4. The way to overcome this ignorance is by following the Eightfold Path of right view, right resolve, right speech, right action, right livelihood, right effort, right mindfulness, and right concentration.

Living with these truths in mind, one might overcome what Buddha believed to be the source of all human suffering—the desire for material things, which is the primary form of ignorance. In doing so, one would find release from the illusions of the world, from the cycle of birth, death, and rebirth, and ultimately reach nirvana. These principles are summed up in the *Dhammapada* [dah-muh-PAH-duh], the most popular canonical text of Buddhism, which consists of 423 aphorisms, or sayings, attributed to Buddha and arranged by subject into 26 chapters (see **Reading 7.8**, pages 240–241). Its name is a compound consisting of *dhamma*, the vernacular form of the formal Sanskrit word *dharma*, mortal truth, and *pada*, meaning "foot" or "step"— hence it is "the path of truth." The aphorisms are widely admired for their wisdom and their sometimes stunning beauty of expression.

The Buddha (which means "Enlightened One") taught for 40 years until his death at age 80. His followers preached that anyone could achieve buddhahood, the ability to see the ultimate nature of the world. Persons of very near total enlightenment, but who have vowed to help others achieve buddhahood before crossing over to nirvana, came to be known as **bodhisattvas** [boh-dih-SUT-vuhz], meaning "those whose essence is wisdom." In art, bodhisattvas wear the princely garb of India, while Buddhas wear a monk's robe.

The Maurya Empire Buddhism would become the official state religion of the Maurya Empire, which ruled India from 321 to 185 BCE. The Empire was founded by Chandragupta Maurya [chan-druh-GOOP-tuh MA-ur-ya] (r. ca. 321–297 BCE) in eastern India. Its capital was Pataliputra (modern Patna) on the Ganges River, but Chandragupta rapidly expanded the empire westward, taking advantage of the vacuum of power in the Indus Valley that followed in the wake of Alexander the Great's invasion of 326 BCE (see Chapter 5). In 305 BCE, the Hellenistic Greek ruler Suleucus I, ruler of the one of the three states that succeeded Alexander's empire, the kingdom of the Suleucids, tried to reconquer India once again. He and Chandragupta eventually signed a peace treaty, and diplomatic relations between Suleicid Greece and the Maurya Empire were established. Several Greeks ambassadors were soon residing in the Mauryan court, the beginning of substantial relations between East and West. Chandragupta was succeeded by his son Bindusara [BIN-doo-sah-rah] (r. ca. 297–273 BCE), who also had a Greek ambassador at his court, and who extended the empire southward, conquering almost all the Indian peninsula and establishing the Maurya Empire as the largest empire of its time. He was in turn succeeded by his son Ashoka [uh-SHOH-kuh] (r. ca. 273–232 BCE).

It was Ashoka who established Buddhism as the official state religion. On a battlefield in 261 BCE, Ashoka was appalled by the carnage he had inflicted in his role as a warrior king. As he watched a monk walking slowly among the dead, Ashoka was moved to decry violence and force of arms and to spread the teachings of Buddha. From that point, Ashoka, who had been described as "the cruel Ashoka," began to be known as "the pious Ashoka." At a time when Rome was engaged in the Punic Wars, Ashoka pursued an official policy of nonviolence. The unnecessary slaughter or mutilation of animals was forbidden. Sport hunting was banned, and although the limited hunting of game for the purpose of consumption was tolerated, Ashoka promoted vegetarianism. He built hospitals for people and animals alike, preached the humane treatment of all living things, and regarded all his subjects as equals, regardless of politics, religion, or caste. He also embarked on a massive Buddhist architectural campaign, erecting as many as 8,400 shrines and monuments to Buddha throughout the empire. Soon, Buddhism would spread beyond India, and Buddhist monks from China traveled to India to observe Buddhist practices.

Buddhist Monuments: The Great Stupa Among the most famous of the Buddhist monuments that Ashoka erected is

Fig. 7.17 The Great Stupa, Sanchi, Madhya Pradesh, India, view of the West Gateway. Founded third century BCE, enlarged ca. 150–50 BCE. Shrine height 50', diameter 105'. In India, the stupa is the principal monument to Buddha. The stupa symbolizes, at once, the World Mountain, the Dome of Heaven, and the Womb of the Universe.

SEE MORE For a Closer Look at the Great Stupa at Sanchi, go to **www.myartslab.com**

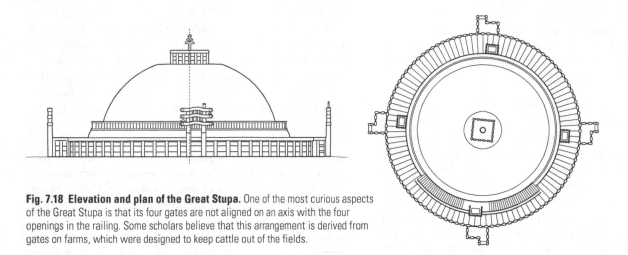

Fig. 7.18 Elevation and plan of the Great Stupa. One of the most curious aspects of the Great Stupa is that its four gates are not aligned on an axis with the four openings in the railing. Some scholars believe that this arrangement is derived from gates on farms, which were designed to keep cattle out of the fields.

the Great Stupa [STOO-puh] at Sanchi [SAHN-chee] (Fig. **7.17**), which was enlarged in the second century BCE. A **stupa** is a kind of burial mound. The earliest eight of them were built around 483 BCE as reliquaries for Buddha's remains, which were themselves divided into eight parts. In the third century, Ashoka opened the original eight stupas and further divided Buddha's relics, scattering them among a great many other stupas, probably including Sanchi.

The stupa as a form is deeply symbolic, consisting first and foremost of a hemispheric dome, built of rubble and dirt and faced with stone, evoking the Dome of Heaven (see the plan, Fig. **7.18**). Perched on top of the dome is a small square platform, in the center of which is a mast supporting three circular discs or "umbrellas," called *chatras* [CHAH-truz]. These signify both the banyan tree beneath which Buddha achieved enlightenment and the three levels of Buddhist consciousness—desire, form,

Fig. 7.19 Column capital on the East Gate of the Great Stupa, Sanchi. Stone, height of gate, 32′. The carved elephants that serve as the capital to the gateway column are traditional symbols of Buddha, signs of his authority and spiritual strength. A *yakshi* figure serves as a bracket at the right front of the elephant.

formlessness—through which the soul ascends to enlightenment. The dome is set on a raised base, around the top of which is a circumambulatory walkway. As pilgrims to the stupa circle the walkway, they symbolically follow Buddha's path, awakening to enlightenment. The whole is a **mandala** [MUN-duh-luh] (literally "circle"), the Buddhist diagram of the cosmos.

Leading out from the circular center of the stupa are four gates, positioned at the cardinal points, that create directional "rays," or beams of teaching, emanating from the "light" of the central mandala. They are 32 feet high and decorated with stories from the life of Buddha, as well as other sculptural elements including vines, lotuses, peacocks, and elephants (Fig. **7.19**). Extending as a sort

of bracket from the sides of the gateways were *yakshis* [YAK-shees]—some 24 in all—female spirit figures that probably derives from Vedic tradition. The *yakshi* symbolizes the productive forces of nature. As in Hinduism, sexuality and spirituality are visually represented here as forms of an identical cosmic energy, and the sensuous curves of the *yakshi* emphasize her deep connection to the creative force. In fact, here she seems to cause the fruit in the tree above her head to ripen, as if she is the source of its nourishment.

The *yakshi* and the gate she decorates embody the distinctive sense of beauty that is characteristic of Indian art. Both are images of abundance that reflect a belief in the generosity of spirit that both Buddha and the

Fig. 7.20 Lion capital, Ashokan pillar at Sarnath, Uttar Pradesh, India. Maurya period, ca. 250 BCE. Polished sandstone, height, 7′. Archeological Museum, Sarnath. Some scholars speculate that the pillars upon which such capitals rested represent the *axis mundi*, or "axis of the world," joining the earth with the heavens.

were inscribed with inscriptions relating to dharma, the rules of good conduct that Vedic kings such as Rama were required to uphold in the *Ramayana*. But Buddhists quickly interpreted the writings as referring to Buddhist teachings. At the top of each pillar was a capital carved in the shape of an animal.

The pillar at Sarnath, the site of Buddha's first sermon, was crowned with a sculpture of four lions facing in the cardinal directions and standing back-to-back on a slab decorated with four low-relief sculptures of wheels and, between each wheel, four different animals—lion, horse, bull, and elephant (Fig. **7.20**). Beneath these features are the turned-down petals of a lotus flower, which, since the lotus emerges from dirty water without blemish, traditionally symbolized the presence of divine purity (which is to say, Buddha and his teachings) in an imperfect world. All of the other elements on the capital have similar symbolic significance.

The lions probably refer to Buddha himself, who was known "the lion of the Shakya," the clan into which he was born as prince, and whose teachings spread in all directions like the roar of the lions. The wheels, too, are a universal symbol of Buddha's teachings at Sarnath, where, it is said, "he set the wheel of the law [*dharma*] in motion." In fact, the lions originally supported a large copper wheel, now lost.

Ashoka's missionary ambition matched his father's and grandfather's military zeal, and he sent Buddhist emissaries as far as west as Syria, Egypt, and Greece. No Western historical record of these missions survives, and their impact on Western thought remains a matter of speculation.

Hindu gods share. Sensuous form, vibrant color, and a profusion of ornament dominate Indian art as a whole, and the rich textures of this art are meant to capture the very essence of the divine. Originally, all four gates at Sanchi were flanked with a total of 24 such female figures.

Buddhist Monuments: The Pillar Ashoka also erected a series of pillars across the empire, primarily at sites related to Buddha's life. These pillars, made of sandstone, usually rested on a stone foundation sunk more than 10 feet into the ground. They rose to a height of about 50 feet. They

The Silk Road

Under the Han, (206 BCE–220 CE), Chinese trade flourished. Western linen, wool, glass, and gold, Persian pistachios, and mustard originating in the Mediterranean, were imported in exchange for the silk, ceramics, fur, lacquered goods, and spices that made their way west along the "Silk Road" that stretched from the Yellow River across Asia to the Mediterranean (see Map 7.3). The road followed the westernmost spur of the Great Wall to the oasis town of Dunhuang [doon-hwahng], where it split into northern and southern routes, passing through smaller oasis towns until converging again at Kashgar [KAHSH-gahr] on the western edge of the western Chinese deserts. From there, traders could proceed into present-day Afghanistan, south into India, or westward through present-day Uzbekistan, Iran, and Iraq into Syria and the port city of Antioch [AN-tee-awk]. Goods passed through many hands, trader to trader, before reaching the Mediterranean, and according to an official history of the Han dynasty compiled in the fifth century CE, it was not until 97 CE that one Gan Ying went "all the way to the Western sea and back." According to Gan Ying, there he encountered an empire with "over four hundred walled cities" to which "tens of small states are subject"—some of them probably outposts of the Roman Empire, but others, like the city of Bam, with its towering citadel first constructed in about 55 BCE (Fig. 7.21), Persian strongholds.

Goods and ideas spread along the Silk Road, as trade spurred the cultural interchange between East and West, India and China. As early as the first century BCE, silk from China reached Rome, where it captured the Western imagination, but the secret of its manufacture remained a mystery in the West until the sixth century CE. Between the first and third centuries CE, Buddhist missionaries from India carried their religion over the Silk Road into Southeast Asia and north into China and Korea, where it quickly became the dominant religion. By the last half of the first millennium, the Chinese capital of Chang'an, at the eastern terminus of the Silk Road, hosted Korean, Japanese, Jewish, and Christian communities, and Chinese emperors maintained diplomatic relations with Persia. Finally, the Venetian merchant Marco Polo (ca. 1254–1324), bearing a letter of introduction from Pope Gregory X, crossed the Asian continent on the Silk Road in 1275. He arrived at the new Chinese capital of Beijing, and served in the imperial court for nearly two decades. His *Travels*, written after his return to Italy in 1292, constitute the first eyewitness account of China available in Europe. ∎

Fig. 7.21 The Arg-é Bam ("Bam Citadel"), Iran.
© Isabelle Vayron/Sygma/ Corbis. All Rights Reserved. The citadel was largest adobe structure in the world until approximately 80% of it was destroyed in a massive earthquake in 2003. The Iranian government has undertaken its reconstruction.

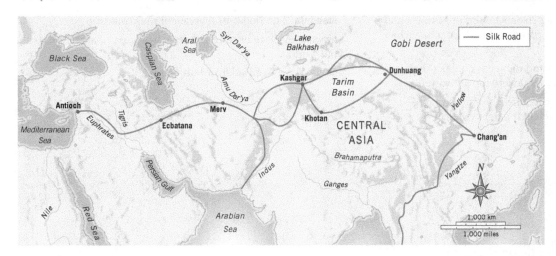

Map 7.3 The Silk Road, the trading route between the east and west and between southeast Asia and China.

What were early China's lasting contributions to Chinese civilization?

As inscribed on oracle bones and bronze vessels, the earliest Chinese written language is so closely related to modern Chinese written language that it remains legible. During the Shang (ca. 1700–1045 BCE) and Chou (1045–221 BCE) dynasties, with the production of the *Book of Changes*, or *I Jing*, and the collection of a national poetry in the *Book of Songs*, or *Shi Jing*, a lasting national literature began to arise. The two great strains of Chinese philosophy—Daoism, a mystical quietism based on harmony with Nature, and Confucianism, a pragmatic political philosophy based on personal cultivation—came into full flower at this time as well. The philosophical symbol of the yin-yang was devised during this early period too. Can you detect the workings of the yin-yang philosophy in the poetry of the *Book of Songs*? in the *Dao de jing*? in Confucianism? How did Confucianism contribute to the workings of the Chinese state? Why is Daoism less suited as a political philosophy?

How was China unified as an empire?

Under the leadership of the Emperor Qin Shihuangdi, the Qin dynasty (221–206 BCE) unified China and undertook massive building projects, including the 4,000-mile-long Great Wall, enormous networks of roads, and the emperor's own tomb, guarded by nearly 8,000 life-size ceramic soldiers, projects that required the almost complete reorganization of Chinese society. This reorganization was made possible by placing totalitarian authority in the hands of a ruthless dictator.

What philosophy supported the emperor's approach? How does Imperial China compare to the Roman Empire in the West?

During the Han dynasty (206 BCE–220 CE), the scholars and writers disenfranchised by the Qin were restored to respectability, but women remained disenfranchised. How does *yuefu* poetry reflect women's lot? How does it compare to the poetry of the *Book of Songs*? Paper was invented during the Han dynasty. What effect did this invention have on Chinese culture?

How did religious outlooks shape ancient India?

Before 2000 BCE, in the Indus Valley, sophisticated cultures arose at cities such as Mohenjo-Daro and Harappa. What archeological evidence gives credence to the idea that these were indeed sophisticated cultures?

After the invasion of the Aryans in about 1500 BCE, the Hindu religion took hold in India. The *Vedas* and *Upanishads* were its two basic texts. Its three major gods were Brahma, the creator; Vishnu, the preserver, and god of benevolence, forgiveness, and love; and Shiva, the destroyer, who is also a great dancer, embodying the sacred rhythms of creation and destruction, birth, death, and rebirth. Vishnu was an especially popular god, who appeared in human form as Rama in the epic *Ramayana* and as Krishna in the epic *Mahahbarata*. What place do female divinities hold in Hindu religion? What does this religion share with the official Indian state religion adopted by the Maurya emperor Ashoka, Buddhism? In what ways did Ashoka seek to spread Buddhism as the dominant Indian faith?

PRACTICE MORE Get flashcards for images and terms and review chapter material quizzes at **www.myartslab.com**

GLOSSARY

bodhisattva In Buddhism, a person who refrains from achieving total enlightenment in order to help others achieve buddhahood.

dharma In Hinduism, good and righteous conduct that reflects the cosmic moral order underlying all existence.

legalism A philosophy that requires the state to exercise power over the individual to elicit proper conduct.

mandala The Buddhist diagram of the cosmos.

nirvana A place or state free from worry, pain, and the external world.

stupa A type of Buddhist burial mound.

READINGS

From the *Book of Songs*

The Book of Songs *is the earliest collection of Chinese poetry. Like all subsequent Chines poetry, for which these poems, not coincidentally, provide the tradition, the poems provide a telling glimpse into everyday Chinese life. But they also demonstrate the centrality of the natural world and its rhythms and cycles to Chinese thought and feeling.*

IN THE WILDS IS A DEAD RIVER-DEER

In the wilds is a dead river-deer
wrapped in white rushes.
A lady yearned for spring
and a fine man seduced her.

In the woods are clusters of bushes
and in the wilds a dead river-deer
wrapped in white rushes.
There was a lady fine as jade.

Oh! Slow down, don't be so rough,
let go of my girdle sash.
Shhh! You'll make the dog bark.

READING CRITICALLY

The poem contrasts the dead deer to the lady's desire. What is the point? How does time, the sense of human urgency versus the natural rhythm of nature, play into this theme?

WHEN THE GOURD HAS DRIED LEAVES

When the gourd has dried leaves
you can wade the deep river.
Keep your clothes on if the water's deep;
hitch up your dress when it's shallow.

The river is rising,
pheasants are chirping.
The water is just half a wheel deep,
and the hen is chirping for the cock.

Wild geese are trilling,
the rising sun starts dawn.
If you want to marry me,
come before the river is frozen.

The ferryman is gesturing,
other people are going, but not me,
other people are going, but not me,
I'm waiting for you.

READING CRITICALLY

Who is the speaker? How does the cycle of the seasons play into the poem's argument? Are there any double entendres at work in this argument?

ALL THE GRASSLANDS ARE YELLOW

All the grasslands are yellow
and all the days we march
and all the men are conscripts
sent off in four directions.

All the grasslands are black
and all the men like widowers.
So much grief! Are soldiers
not men like other men?

We aren't bison! We aren't tigers
crossing the wilderness,
but our sorrows
roam from dawn till dusk.

Hairy tailed foxes slink
through the dark grass
as we ride tall chariots
along the wide rutted roads.

READING CRITICALLY

Clearly, the speaker of this poem is very different from the speakers of the first two. But in what ways are the themes of the first two poems reiterated here?

Confucius, from the *Analects*

The Analects *of Confucius are a collection of his dialogues and utterances, probably recorded by his disciples after his death. They reflect Confucius's dream of an ideal society of hardworking, loyal people governed by wise, benevolent, and morally upright officials—a government based on moral principles that would be reflected in the behavior of its populace.*

2-1 The Master said, "He who exercises government by means of his virtue may be compared to the north polar star, which keeps its place and all the stars turn towards it."

2-2 The Master said, "In the Book of Poetry are three hundred pieces, but the design of them all may be embraced in one sentence 'Having no depraved thoughts.'"

2-3 The Master said, "If the people be led by laws, and uniformity sought to be given them by punishments, they will try to avoid the punishment, but have no sense of shame."

"If they be led by virtue, and uniformity sought to be given 10 them by the rules of propriety, they will have the sense of shame, and moreover will become good." . . .

4-3 The Master said, "It is only the truly virtuous man, who can love, or who can hate, others."

4-4 The Master said, "If the will be set on virtue, there will be no practice of wickedness."

4-5 The Master said, "Riches and honors are what men desire. If they cannot be obtained in the proper way, they should not be held. Poverty and meanness are what men dislike. If they cannot be avoided in the proper way, they should not be 20 avoided." . . .

4-6 The Master said, "I have not seen a person who loved virtue, or one who hated what was not virtuous. He who loved virtue, would esteem nothing above it. He who hated what is not virtuous, would practice virtue in such a way that he would not allow anything that is not virtuous to approach his person." . . .

4-9 The Master said, "A scholar, whose mind is set on truth, and who is ashamed of bad clothes and bad food, is not fit to be discoursed with." 30

4-10 The Master said, "The superior man, in the world, does not set his mind either for anything, or against anything; what is right he will follow."

4-11 The Master said, "The superior man thinks of virtue; the small man thinks of comfort. The superior man thinks of the sanctions of law; the small man thinks of favors which he may receive."

4-12 The Master said, "He who acts with a constant view to his own advantage will be much murmured against." . . .

4-17 The Master said, "When we see men of worth, we 40 should think of equaling them; when we see men of a contrary character, we should turn inwards and examine ourselves."

4-18 The Master said, "In serving his parents, a son may remonstrate with them, but gently; when he sees that they do not incline to follow his advice, he shows an increased degree of reverence, but does not abandon his purpose; and should they punish him, he does not allow himself to murmur." . . .

4-22 The Master said, "The reason why the ancients did not readily give utterance to their words, was that they feared lest their actions should not come up to them." 50

4-23 The Master said, "The cautious seldom err."

4-24 The Master said, "The superior man wishes to be slow in his speech and earnest in his conduct." . . .

READING CRITICALLY

Give two or three examples, from the previous passages, of the principle of *li* at work, and explain how *li* leads to *jen* (these terms are defined in the chapter).

READING 7.7

from "The Second Teaching" in the *Bhagavad Gita: Krishna's Counsel in Time of War*

The Bhagavad Gita *constitutes the sixth book of the first-century* CE *epic Sanskrit poem, the* Mahahbarata. *It represents, in many ways, a summation of Hindu thought and philosophy. The bulk of the poem consists of the reply of Krishna, an avatar, or incarnation, of Vishnu, to Arjuna, leader of the Pandavas, who on the battlefield has decided to lay down his arms. In the following passage, Arjuna declares his unwillingness to fight. The charioteer Sanjaya, the narrator of the entire* Mahahbarata, *then introduces Krishna, who replies to Arjuna's decision and goes on to describe, at Arjuna's request, the characteristics of a man of "firm concentration and pure insight."*

FROM THE SECOND TEACHING

SANJAYA:

Arjuna sat dejected,
filled with pity,
his sad eyes blurred by tears.
Krishna gave him counsel.

LORD KRISHNA:

Why this cowardice
in time of crisis, Arjuna?
The coward is ignoble, shameful,
foreign to the ways of heaven.
Don't yield to impotence!

It is unnatural in you! 10
Banish this petty weakness from your heart.
Rise to the fight, Arjuna!

ARJUNA:

Krishna, how can I fight
against Bhishma and Drona
with arrows
when they deserve my worship?
It is better in this world
to beg for scraps of food
than to eat meals
smeared with the blood 20
of elders I killed

at the height of their power
while their goals
were still desires.
We don't know which weight
is worse to bear—
our conquering them
or their conquering us.
We will not want to live
if we kill   30
the sons of Dhritarashtra
assembled before us.
The flaw of pity
blights my very being
conflicting sacred duties
confound my reason.
I ask you to tell me
decisively—Which is better?
I am your pupil.
Teach me what I seek!   40
I see nothing
that could drive away
the grief
that withers my senses;
even if I won kingdoms
of unrivaled wealth
on earth
and sovereignty over gods.

SANJAYA:

Arjuna told this
To Krishna—then saying,   50
"I shall not fight,"
he fell silent.
Mocking him gently,
Krishna gave this counsel
as Arjuna sat dejected,
between the two armies.

LORD KRISHNA:

You grieve for those beyond grief,
and you speak words of insight;
but learned men do not grieve
for the dead or the living.   60
Never have I not existed,
nor you, nor these kings;
and never in the future
shall we cease to exist.
Just as the embodied self
enters childhood, youth, and old age,
so does it enter another body:
this does not confound a steadfast man.
Contacts with matter make us feel
heat and cold, pleasure and pain.   70
Arjuna, you must learn to endure
fleeting things—they come and go!
When these cannot torment a man,
when suffering and joy are equal
for him and he has courage,
he is fit for immortality.
Nothing of nonbeing comes to be,
nor does being cease to exist;

the boundary between these two
is seen by men who see reality.   80
Indestructible is the presence
that pervades all this;
no one can destroy
this unchanging reality.
Our bodies are known to end,
but the embodied self is enduring,
indestructible, and immeasurable;
therefore, Arjuna, fight the battle!
He who thinks this self a killer
and he who thinks it killed,   90
both fail to understand;
it does not kill, nor is it killed. . . .

ARJUNA:

Krishna, what defines a man
deep in contemplation whose insight
and thought are sure? How would he speak?
How would he sit? How would he move?

LORD KRISHNA:

When he gives up desires in his mind,
is content with the self within himself,
then he is said to be a man
whose insight is sure, Arjuna.   100

When suffering does not disturb his mind,
when his craving for pleasures has vanished,
when attraction, fear, and anger are gone,
he is called a sage whose thought is sure.

When he shows no preference
in fortune or misfortune
and neither exults nor hates,
his insight is sure.
When, like a tortoise retracting its limbs
he withdraws his senses   110
completely from sensuous objects,
his insight is sure.

So, Great Warrior, when withdrawal
of the senses
from sense objects is complete,
discernment is firm.

When it is night for all creatures,
a master of restraint is awake;
when they are awake, it is night
for the sage who sees reality.   120

As the mountainous depths
of the ocean
are unmoved when waters
rush into it,
so the man unmoved
when desires enter him
attains a peace that eludes
the man of many desires.

When he renounces all desires
and acts without craving,   130
possessiveness,
or individuality, he finds peace.

This is the place of the infinite spirit;
achieving it, one is freed from delusion;
abiding in it even at the time of death,
one finds the pure calm of infinity.

READING CRITICALLY

What does Krishna mean when he says, "Nothing of nonbeing comes to be / nor does being cease to exist; / the boundary between these two / is seen by men who see reality"?

READING 7.8

from the *Dhammapada*

The Dhammapada, *or "path of truth," consists of 423 sayings, or aphorisms, of Buddha divided by subject into 26 books. They are commonly thought to be the answers to questions put to Buddha on various occasions, and as such they constitute a summation of Buddhist thought. The following passages, consisting of different aphorisms from five different books, emphasize the Buddhist doctrine of self-denial and the wisdom inherent in pursuing the "path."*

from 5. *The Fool*

. . . Should a traveler fail to find a companion
Equal or better,
Rather than suffer the company of a fool,
He should resolutely walk alone.
"I have children; I have wealth."
These are the empty claims of an unwise man.
If he cannot call himself his own,
How can he then claim children and wealth as his own?
To the extent that a fool knows his foolishness,
He may be deemed wise.   10
A fool who considers himself wise
Is indeed a fool. . . .

from 6. *The Wise*

Irrigators contain the flowing waters.
Arrowsmiths fashion arrows.
Carpenters shape wood to their design.
Wise men mold their characters. . . .

from 11. *Old Age*

Can there be joy and laughter
When always the world is ablaze?
Enshrouded in darkness
Should you not seek a light?   20
Look at the body adorned,
A mass of wounds, draped upon a heap of bones,
A sickly thing, this subject of sensual thoughts!
Neither permanent, nor enduring!
The body wears out,
A nest of disease,
Fragile, disintegrating,
Ending in death.
What delight is there in seeing the bleached bones,
Like gourds thrown away,   30
Dried and scattered in the autumn sun?
A citadel is this structure of bones,
Blood and flesh, within which dwell
Decay, death, conceit, and malice.
The royal chariots surely come to decay
Just as the body, too, comes to decay.
But the shining truth and loving kindness live on.
So speak the virtuous to the virtuous.

from 18. *Blemishes*

. . . The wise man, carefully, moment by moment,
One by one,   40
Eliminates the stains of his mind,
As a silversmith separates the dross from the silver.
Just as rust produced by iron
Corrodes the iron,
So is the violator of moral law
Destroyed by his own wrong action.
Disconnection from scripture is learning's taint,
Neglect is the taint of houses,
Uncared-for beauty withers,
Negligence is the taint of one who keeps watch.   50
A woman behaving badly loses her femininity.
A giver sharing grudgingly loses his generosity.
Deeds done from bad motives remain everlastingly tainted.
But there is nothing more tainted than ignorance.
Eliminate ignorance, O disciples,
And purity follows. . . .
Be aware, everyone, that those flawed in their nature
Have no control of themselves.
Do not let greed and anger cause you suffering
By holding you in their grasp.   60
Men give for different reasons,
Such as devotion or appreciation.
Whoever finds fault with the food or drink given by others
Will have no peace, day or night.
However, whoever gives up this habit of finding fault
With others' offerings
Will know peace, day and night.
There is no fire like lust,
No vise like hatred,
No trap like delusion,   70
And no galloping river like craving.

from 24. *Craving*

. . . Unchecked craving strangles the careless man,
Like a creeper growing in the jungle.
He leaps from lifetime to lifetime,
Like a monkey seeking fruit.
This craving, this clinging,
Overpowers the man caught in it,
And his sorrows multiply,
Like prairie grass fed by rain.

Although it is hard to gain this freedom, 80
Sorrow leaves the man who overcomes this toxic craving,
This clinging to the world,
Just as drops of water fall from a lotus leaf.
Therefore, I admonish you all who are here assembled.
You have my blessings.
Eradicate craving at the root, as you would weeds.
Find the sweet root.
Do not succumb to temptation over and over again.
The tree may be cut down but the roots remain,
Uninjured and strong, 90
And it springs up again.
Likewise, suffering returns, again and again,
If the dormant craving is not completely eradicated. . . .
Craving grows in the man aroused by worldly thoughts.
Tied to his senses, he makes his fetters strong.
Taking delight in calming sensual thoughts,
Ever mindful, meditating on the impurities of the body and so on,
One will certainly get rid of craving.
Such a one will cut off Mara's bond.
The diligent monk 100
Has reached the summit,
Fearless, free of passion.
This is the final birth of such a man.

Free of craving and grasping,
Skilled in the knowledge of the meanings within meanings,
The significance of terms, the order of things.
This great man, greatly wise,
Need return no more.
I have conquered all, I know all,
I am detached from all, I have renounced all, 110
I am freed through destruction of craving.
Having myself realized all,
Whom shall I call my teacher?
The gift of truth is the highest gift.
The taste of truth is the sweetest taste.
The joy of truth is the greatest joy.
The extinction of craving is the end of suffering.

READING CRITICALLY

The *Dhammapada* is rich in metaphors, figures of speech that draw direct comparison between two seemingly unrelated things (from "Cravings," for instance, the comparison of a craving to the entangling creeper called *birana* [bir-AH-nuh]). How does Buddha's use of metaphor reflect his status as the "Enlightened One"?

The Medieval World and the Shaping of Culture

200 CE TO 1400

Simone Martini, *Maestà*, Council Chamber, Palazzo Pubblico, Siena. ca. 1311–17, repaired 1321 (see Fig 13.6).

Following the last 300 years of the Roman Empire, from 200 to about 500 CE, the Middle Ages span a period of about a thousand years of European history, from the collapse of the Empire to the beginning of the fifteenth century. Its opening centuries, until about 800 CE, were once commonly referred to as the "Dark Ages." During this time, the great cultural achievements of the Greeks and Romans were forgotten, so-called barbarian tribes from the North overran the continent, and ignorance reigned. But this era was followed by an age of remarkable innovation and achievement, marked by the ascendancy of three great religions—Christianity, Buddhism, and newborn Islam. Because of the way these three religions dominated their respective cultures, the centuries covered in Book Two might be best thought of as the Age of Faith.

This was the age of the monastery, the religious pilgrimage, the cathedral, the mosque, and the spread of Buddhism across Asia. By the sixth century, a new Christian mode of representation, reflecting a new ideal of beauty, had asserted itself in Byzantium, the Eastern Roman Empire. Unlike the Romans and Greeks, Byzantine artists showed little interest in depicting the visual appearance of the material world. They abandoned perspectival depth and rendered figures as highly stylized, almost geometric configurations. In other words, they depicted a spiritual rather than physical ideal.

In the first half of the seventh century, after the death of the prophet Muhammad, Islam began its rapid spread from Arabia across the Middle East to North Africa and into Spain. At the same time, in the rest of Europe, Christian and feudal traditions gradually merged. By the time Charlemagne was crowned emperor by Pope Leo III in the year 800, fidelity to one's chief could be understood as analogous to fidelity to one's God. By the late twelfth century, this brand of loyalty had found its way into the social habits of court life, where it took the form known as courtly love. In the love songs of the troubadour poets, the loyalty that a knight or nobleman had once conferred upon his lord was now transferred to a lady.

Charlemagne's passionate interest in education and the arts was broadcast across Europe through the development first of monastic schools and later of universities, which were themselves made possible by a resurgence of economic activity and trade. The Christian Crusades to recapture the Holy Land, principally Jerusalem, from Muslim control contributed to this economic revitalization, as did the practice of pilgrimage journeys to the Holy Land and to churches that housed sacred relics. The art of creating monumental stone sculpture was revived to decorate these churches, which grew ever larger to accommodate the throngs that visited them. The culmination of this trend was the Gothic cathedral, adorned with stained glass and rising to formerly unachieved heights. The sacred music of the liturgy became more complex and ornate as well, reflecting the architecture of the buildings in which it was played. To appeal to the masses of worshippers, the sculpture and painting that decorated these churches became increasingly naturalistic. Similarly, poetry and prose were more frequently written in the vernacular—the everyday language of the people—and less often in Latin. In both literature and art, the depiction of universal types, or generalized characters, gave way to the depiction of real characters and actual personalities.

We can begin to account for this shift by recognizing that, by the late Middle Ages, the center of intellectual life had shifted from the monastery to the town. From the great metropolis of Hangzhou, China that Marco Polo visited in 1271, to the cities of Teotihuacán and Palenque in Mesoamerica, daily life was an increasingly urban experience. In Asia and the Americas, these centers reflected the aspirations and power of the ruling nobility. But in Europe, towns like Florence and Siena flourished as a result of ever-enlarging trade networks. Now, suddenly, merchants and bankers began to assert themselves with as much or more power than either pope or king, ruling local governments and commissioning civic and religious works of architecture and art.

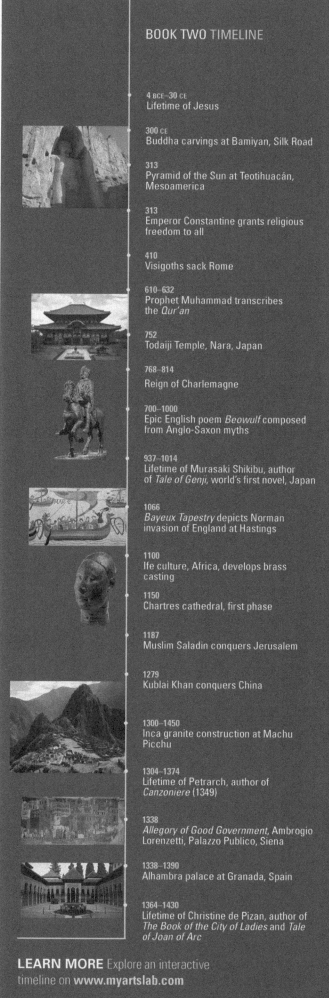

BOOK TWO TIMELINE

4 BCE–30 CE
Lifetime of Jesus

300 CE
Buddha carvings at Bamiyan, Silk Road

313
Pyramid of the Sun at Teotihuacán, Mesoamerica

313
Emperor Constantine grants religious freedom to all

410
Visigoths sack Rome

610–632
Prophet Muhammad transcribes the *Qur'an*

752
Todaiji Temple, Nara, Japan

768–814
Reign of Charlemagne

700–1000
Epic English poem *Beowulf* composed from Anglo-Saxon myths

937–1014
Lifetime of Murasaki Shikibu, author of *Tale of Genji*, world's first novel, Japan

1066
Bayeux Tapestry depicts Norman invasion of England at Hastings

1100
Ife culture, Africa, develops brass casting

1150
Chartres cathedral, first phase

1187
Muslim Saladin conquers Jerusalem

1279
Kublai Khan conquers China

1300–1450
Inca granite construction at Machu Picchu

1304–1374
Lifetime of Petrarch, author of *Canzoniere* (1349)

1338
Allegory of Good Government, Ambrogio Lorenzetti, Palazzo Publico, Siena

1338–1390
Alhambra palace at Granada, Spain

1364–1430
Lifetime of Christine de Pizan, author of *The Book of the City of Ladies* and *Tale of Joan of Arc*

LEARN MORE Explore an interactive timeline on **www.myartslab.com**

9

The Rise and Spread of Islam

A New Religion

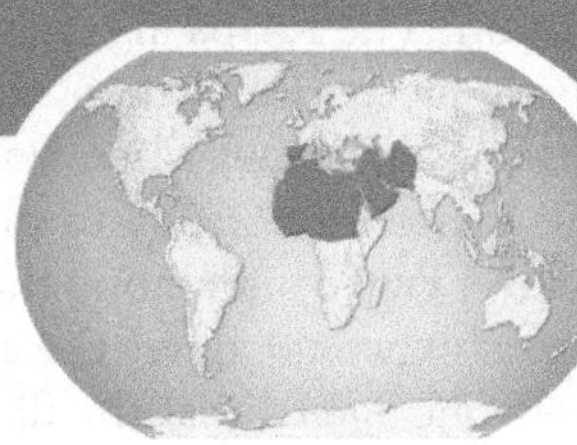

THINKING AHEAD

What was the message of the Prophet Muhammad?

Why did Islam spread so rapidly?

How did Islam come to Africa and Spain?

What place do the arts hold in the Islamic world?

The Dome of the Rock (Fig. **9.1**) stands atop the Temple Mount in Jerusalem, on the site where, in Jewish tradition, Abraham prepared to sacrifice his son Isaac. The Jewish Temple of Solomon originally stood here, and the site is further associated—by Jews, Christians, and Muslims alike—with God's creation of Adam. The Second Temple of Jerusalem also stood on this spot until it was destroyed by Roman soldiers when they sacked the city in 70 CE to put down a Jewish revolt (see Fig. 6.21). Only the Wailing Wall remains, part of the original retaining wall for the platform supporting the Temple Mount and for Jews the most sacred site in Jerusalem. To this day, the plaza in front of the wall functions as an open-air synagogue where daily prayers are recited and other Jewish rituals are performed. On Tisha B'Av, the ninth day of the month of Av, which occurs either in July or August, a fast is held commemorating the destruction of the successive temples on this site, and people sit on the ground before the wall reciting the Book of Lamentations.

One of the earliest examples of Muslim architecture, built in the 680s, the Dome's ambulatory—its circular, colonnaded walkway—encloses a projecting rock that lies directly beneath its golden dome. By the sixteenth century, Islamic faithful claimed that the Prophet Muhammad ascended to heaven from this spot, on a winged horse named Buraq, but there is no evidence that this story was in circulation when the Dome was originally built. Others thought that it represents the ascendancy of Islam over Christianity in the Holy Land. Still others believed the rock is the center of the world, or that it could refer to the Temple of Solomon, the importance of which is fully acknowledged by Muslims, who consider Solomon a founding father of their own faith. All of this suggests that the Dome was meant to proselytize, or convert, both Jews and Christians to the Muslim faith.

The sanctity of this spot, then, at the heart of Jerusalem, is recognized equally by the three great faiths of the Western world—Judaism, Christianity, and Islam—but it is the rise of Islam that is the subject of this chapter, and if the Dome of the Rock is one of Islam's most venerated sites, its holiest city is Mecca, located 760 miles to the south, about 50 miles inland from the Red Sea in modern Saudi Arabia (Map **9.1**). Its natural spring originally made it an important stopping point for nomadic Arabs, known as Bedouins, who traded along caravan routes across the arid peninsula.

◀ **Fig. 9.1 The Dome of the Rock, Jerusalem. Late 680s–691.** The golden dome of the building, one of the earliest Muslim constructions, rises above a projecting rock that is surrounded by an ambulatory. The building's function remains unclear. It is not a mosque, although it is certainly some kind of religious memorial. Inscriptions from the Qur'an decorate its interior. These are the oldest excerpts from the text to have survived.

HEAR MORE Listen to an audio file of your chapter at **www.myartslab.com**

Until the seventh century CE, they worshiped more than one god. They stored images of those gods in a square structure in the center of the city that came to be known as the *Kaaba* [KAAH-buh], literally "cube" (Fig. **9.2**). Scholars believe that the original Kaaba was linked to the astronomical year, containing an array of 360 idols, each associated with seasonal rituals and the passing of the days and months. Built with a bluish-gray stone from the hills surrounding Mecca, it is now usually covered with a black curtain. The Kaaba also held a sacred Black Stone, probably a meteorite, which reportedly "fell from heaven." Legend has it that when workers who had been rebuilding the Kaaba were ready to place the sacred stone inside, a quarrel broke out among the principal Arab tribes regarding who would have the privilege of laying the stone. Everyone agreed that the first passerby would do the honor. That passerby turned out to be the Muslim prophet Muhammad (ca. 570–632), who placed the stone on his cloak and then gave a corner of the cloak to the head of each tribe to carry into the building (Fig. **9.3**). The story establishes Muhammad as a political as well as spiritual leader, and, perhaps more important, as a prophet capable of uniting the diverse elements of Arab culture.

Today, practitioners of the Muslim faith from all over the world face toward the Kaaba when they pray. They believe it is their place of origin, the site of the first "house of God," built at God's command by the biblical Abraham and his son Ismael, the ancestors of all Muslims, on the spot where, in Muslim tradition, Abraham prepared to sacrifice Ismael (not Isaac, as in the Jewish tradition, at the Dome of the Rock). Thus, walking around the Kaaba is a key ritual in the Muslim pilgrimage to Mecca, for the cube represents the physical center of the planet and the universe. It is the physical center of Muslim life, around which all things turn and to which all things in the universe are connected, symbolic of the cosmos itself. The Islamic transformation of Middle Eastern and Western culture, which began in Mecca in the seventh century and spread outward from that city, is the subject of this chapter.

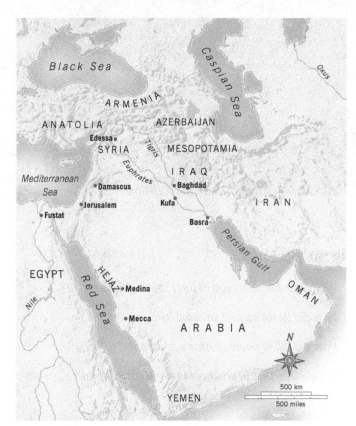

Map 9.1 The Muslim world. ca. 700 CE.

Fig. 9.2 The Kaaba, center of the Haram Mosque, Mecca, Saudi Arabia. Traditionally, all Muslims must make a pilgrimage to Mecca, in Syria, at least once in their lives. Once there, they must walk around the Kaaba seven times. The Kaaba has been rebuilt many times over the years, the last time in 1631.

اونادقاصرجل وضعواالاساس على الاساس ابرهيم واسمعيل عليهما السلم وصلوا لناوصلواالى الاساس رهيم عليه السلم وكان الاساس من حجر احمض
بجلان ينقض من ذلك الاساس جما هام نزل عالم الاسنية فلا قطعة تنازل جميعه يتنازل ذلك الحجر و عالجة الاساس غير جارقم

Fig. 9.3 *Muhammad Placing the Black Stone on His Cloak*, from Rashid al-Din's *Jami al-Tawarikh (Universal History)*, copied and illustrated at Tabriz, Iran. 1315. $5\frac{1}{8}'' \times 10\frac{1}{4}''$. University Library, Edinburgh. Notice that the figures in back of the central section are lifting a veil that covers the Kaaba. Today, the veil, the meaning of which is obscure, is black, with quotations from the Qur'an woven across it in gold thread.

Just as Muslims physically turn toward Mecca when they pray, they turn their thoughts toward the teachings of their prophet Muhammad. Wherever Muslims found themselves—and Islam rapidly spread across the Middle East, North Africa, and even into Spain—they built places of worship modeled on Muhammad's home in Medina, the city on the Arabian peninsula where Muhammad moved when he was driven from Mecca (see Map 9.1). And, as individuals, they submitted themselves to the authority of their faith, so much so that the Muslim religion quickly became synonymous with the Islamic state itself. Because Arabic, as the language of divine revelation, was believed to have a sacred nature, writing too was revered, and **calligraphy** developed into the preeminent form of visual art in Islam, creating an almost wholly abstract standard of beauty devoid of figurative elements. As a faith that considered sensory satisfaction, love, luxury, sensuality, and enjoyment to be manifestations of divine grace, the Muslim religion enveloped Islamic culture, its art, music, and literature, in the pursuit of beauty.

THE PROPHET MUHAMMAD

Born in Mecca in about 570 to a prominent family that traced its ancestry back to Ismael, son of Abraham, Muhammad was orphaned at age six and received little formal education. He worked in the desert caravan trade, first as a camel driver for his uncle, and then, after marrying a wealthy widow 15 years his senior, as head of his wife's flourishing caravan firm. At the age of 40, in 610, he heard a voice in Arabic—the Archangel Gabriel's, as the story goes—urging him, "Recite!" He responded, "What shall I recite?" And for the next 22 years, he claimed to receive messages, or "recitations," from God through the agency of Gabriel. These he memorized and dictated to scribes, who collected them to form the scriptures of Islam, the **Qur'an** [kuh-RAN] (or Koran), which means "recitations." Muhammad also claimed that Gabriel commanded him to declare himself the "Seal of the Prophets," that is, the messenger of the one and only Allah (the Arab word for God) and the final prophet in a series of prophets extending from Abraham and Moses to Jesus.

At the core of Muhammad's revelations is the concept of submission to God—the word *Islam*, in fact, means "submission" or "surrender." God, or Allah, is all—all-powerful, all-seeing, all-merciful. Because the universe is his creation, it is necessarily good and beautiful, and the natural world reflects Allah's own goodness and beauty. To immerse oneself in nature is thus to be at one with God. But the most beautiful creation of Allah is humankind, which God made in his own image. Like Christians, Muslims believe that human beings possess immortal souls and that they can live eternally in heaven if they surrender to Allah and accept him as the one and only God.

Muslims, or practitioners of Islam, dedicate themselves to the "five pillars" of the religion:

1. **Witness (Shahadah):** The repetition of the *shahadah* [sha-HAH-dah], or "witness," which consists of a single sentence, "There is no God but Allah; Muhammad is the messenger of Allah."
2. **Prayer (Salat):** The practice of daily prayer, recited facing Mecca, five times each day, at dawn, midday, mid-afternoon, sunset, and nightfall, and the additional requirement for all men to gather for a noon prayer and sermon on Fridays.
3. **Alms (Zakat):** The habit of giving alms to the poor and needy, consisting of at least one-fortieth of a Muslim's assets and income.
4. **Fasting (Sawm):** During the lunar month of Ramadan (which, over a 33-year period, will occur in every season of the year), the ritual obligation to fast by abstaining from food, drink, medicine, tobacco, and sexual intercourse from sunrise to sundown each day.
5. **Pilgrimage (Hajj):** At least once in every Muslim's life, in the twelfth month of the Muslim calendar, the undertaking of a pilgrimage to Mecca.

The five pillars are supported by the teachings of the Qur'an, which, slightly shorter than the New Testament, consists of 114 *surahs* [SOO-rahs], or chapters, each numbered but more commonly referred to by their titles. Each begins, as do most Muslim texts, with the **bismillah** [bees-mee-LAH], a sacred invocation that can be translated "In the name of Allah, the Beneficent, Ever-Merciful" (see *Closer Look*, pages 290–291). When, after Muhammad's death in 632, the Qur'an's text was established in its definitive form, the 114 *surahs* were arranged from the longest to the shortest. Thus, the first *surah* contains 287 *ayas* [ay-YAS], or verses, while the last consists of only 3. The mandatory ritual prayer (*salat*) [sah-LAAT] that is performed five times a day consists of verses from *Surahs* 2, 4, and 17.

The Qur'an

The Qur'an is a work of poetry, and in pre-Islamic Arabia, poetry was the highest form of art. Poets recited their own works, or professional reciters performed the works of others. The beauty of the poetry inspired the creation of many beautiful editions of the work (Fig. **9.4**) and, as we shall see, the art of calligraphy. But unfortunately, the beautiful, melodic qualities of the Arabic language are completely lost in translation, a fact that has helped to inspire generations of non-Arabic-speaking Muslims to learn the language. Almost all Muslims regularly read the Qur'an in Arabic, and many have memorized it completely. Translations of the Qur'an are problematic on another, more important level. Since the Qur'an is believed to be the direct word of God, it cannot be modified, let alone translated—a translation of the Qur'an is no longer the Qur'an. Nevertheless, something of the power of the poem's imagery can be understood

Fig. 9.4 Left page of double frontispiece to volume VII of the Qur'an of Baybars Jashnagir, from Egypt. 1304–06. Illuminated manuscript, 18½" × 12½". British Library, London. The most elaborate Qur'ans, such as this one, were financed by endowments created by wealthy individuals in support of a mosque and attendant buildings.

in translation. Consider a passage describing paradise from the *Surah* 76, known as "Time" (**Reading 9.1a**):

READING 9.1a

from the Qur'an, Surah 76

76.11 Therefore Allah will guard them from the evil of that day and cause them to meet with ease and happiness;
76.12 And reward them, because they were patient, with garden and silk,
76.13 Reclining therein on raised couches, they shall find therein neither (the severe heat of) the sun nor intense cold.
76.14 And close down upon them (shall be) its shadows, and its fruits shall be made near (to them), being easy to reach.
76.15 And there shall be made to go round about them vessels of silver and goblets which are of glass,

76.16 (Transparent as) glass, made of silver; they have measured them according to a measure.

76.17 And they shall be made to drink therein a cup the admixture of which shall be ginger,

76.18 (Of) a fountain therein which is named Salsabil [sal-sa-BEEL].

76.19 And round about them shall go youths never altering in age; when you see them you will think them to be scattered pearls.

76.20 And when you see there, you shall see blessings and a great kingdom.

76.21 Upon them shall be garments of fine green silk and thick silk interwoven with gold, and they shall be adorned with bracelets of silver, and their Lord shall make them drink a pure drink.

76.22 Surely this is a reward for you, and your striving shall be recompensed.

This vision of paradise addresses all the senses—touch, taste, and smell (the fruit so "easy to reach," the drink of ginger), sight ("when you see there, you shall see blessings"), and sound (in the very melody of the verse itself). All is transformed into riches. Even the young people in attendance will appear to be "scattered pearls."

The promise of heaven, so richly described here, is balanced by a moral dimension reminiscent of both the Old and New Testaments of the Christian Bible. Note particularly the call for believers to "let not hatred of a people incite you not to act equitably." Other parts of the Qur'an explicitly appeal to Jews and Christians to accept the teachings of Islam (**Reading 9.1b**):

READING 9.1b

from the Qur'an, *Surah* 5

5.8 O you who believe! Be upright for Allah, bearers of witness with justice, and let not hatred of a people incite you not to act equitably; act equitably, that is nearer to piety, and be careful of (your duty to) Allah; surely Allah is Aware of what you do.

5.9 Allah has promised to those who believe and do good deeds (that) they shall have forgiveness and a mighty reward. . . .

5.68 Say: O followers of the Book! . . .

5.69 Surely those who believe and those who are Jews and the Sabians and the Christians whoever believes in Allah and the last day and does good—they shall have no fear nor shall they grieve. . . .

5.75 The Messiah,[1] son of Marium, is but an apostle; apostles before him have indeed passed away; and his mother was a truthful woman; they both used to eat food. See how we make the communications clear to them, then behold, how they are turned away.

[1]**Messiah:** Jesus.

In the context of the present-day political climate in the Middle East, it is worth remembering that such moral positioning—and apparent tolerance—is fundamental to the Islamic tradition. However, like both Christianity and Judaism, the Qur'an also contains less tolerant messages. In the *surah* "Muhammad," the Prophet calls for his followers to "smite the necks" of those "who disbelieve" (for excerpts from the *surah*, see **Reading 9.1,** page 311). In other words, as is the case with the Bible, what one takes from the Qur'an depends on what one chooses to emphasize.

The Hadith

In addition to the Qur'an, another important source of Islamic tradition is the **hadith** [ha-DEET], meaning "narrative" or "report," which consists of sayings of Muhammad and anecdotes about his life. The story of Muhammad and the Black Rock of the Kaaba comes from the hadith (**Reading 9.2**).

The hadith literature was handed down orally, as was common in Arab society until about 100 years after Muhammad's death, when followers began to write the sayings down.

READING 9.2

from the Hadith

"Actions are but by intention and every man shall have but that which he intended."

"None of you [truly] believes until he wishes for his brother what he wishes for himself."

"Get to know Allah in prosperity and He will know you in adversity. Know that what has passed you by was not going to befall you; and that what has befallen you was not going to pass you by. And know that victory comes with patience, relief with affliction, and ease with hardship."

"If you feel no shame, then do as you wish."

"Everyone starts his day and is a vendor of his soul, either freeing it or bringing about its ruin."

"O My servants, it is but your deeds that I reckon up for you and then recompense you for, so let him who finds good [i.e., in the hereafter] praise Allah, and let him who finds other than that blame no one but himself."

"Renounce the world and Allah will love you, and renounce what people possess and people will love you."

The *Hijra* and Muslim Practice

In 622, Muhammad was forced to flee Mecca when its polytheistic leadership became irritated at his insistence on the worship of only one God. In a journey known as the **hijra** [HIJ-rah] (or *hegira*, "emigration"), he and his followers fled to the oasis of Yathrib [YA-trub], 200 miles north, which they renamed al-Medina, meaning "the city of the Prophet." Here Muhammad created a community based not on kinship, the traditional basis of Arab society, but on common

---

LEARN MORE Gain insight from a primary source from the Qur'an at **www.myartslab.com**

The *bismillah* consists of the phrase "In the name of Allah, the Beneficent, Ever-Merciful." Every pious Muslim begins any statement or activity with it, and it inaugurates each chapter of the Qur'an. For Arab calligraphers, to write the *bismillah* in as beautiful a form as possible brings the scribe forgiveness for sins, and the phrase appears in the Islamic world in many different forms—even in the shape of a parrot. From the time that Abd al-Malik took control of the Umayyad family in 692, it became an important part of architectural practice as well. It first appears in written form on a band of mosaic script around the interior walls and above the entrance of Dome of the Rock in Jerusalem (see Fig. 9.1). On the next page, the fourteenth-century ceramic tile decoration on a mihrab niche, a design feature in all Islamic mosques commemorating the spot at Medina where Mohammad planted his lance to indicate the direction in which people should pray, gives some indication of how the calligraphic script could blend with floral motifs and geometric designs to create an elaborate ornamental surface.

Ahmed Karahisari. **Calligraphic Qur'an frontispiece, from Istanbul. ca. 1550.** Ink, gold, and color on paper, 19²/₃" × 13³/₄". Museum of Turkish and Islamic Art, Istanbul. Karahisari (1469–1560) was the most famous calligrapher of his day. He placed the *bismillah* in black script between two square scripts. On top, the words "Praise God" are repeated four times. The bottom block contains the entire text of *Surah* 112 of the Qur'an: "Say: 'He is Allah, the only one [that is, indivisible]. Allah, the eternally Besought of all! He begetteth not nor was begotten. And there is none comparable to Him.'"

The importance of writing in spreading the new faith suggests one reason that Muslim calligraphers were held in such high esteem. Most Westerners think of handwriting as a form of self-expression. But the Muslim calligrapher's style has a much more important role to play: to attract the attention of the reader, eliciting admiration for the beauty of the script, and in turn reflecting the beauty of the Muslim faith. The Muslim calligrapher is considered the medium through which Allah expresses himself. The more beautiful the calligraphic script, the more fully Allah's beauty is realized. Hence, over time, many styles of elaborate cursive script developed, as illustrated on the next page. At the same time, everyday affairs required the development of simpler, less artistic forms, and the *riq'a* script is an example.

Mastering the art of calligraphy was, in this sense, a form of prayer, and it was practiced with total dedication. A famous story about an incident that happened in the city of Tabriz, in northern Iran, during the great earthquake of 1776–77, illustrates this. The quake struck in the middle of the night and buried many in the rubble. Survivors stumbled through the

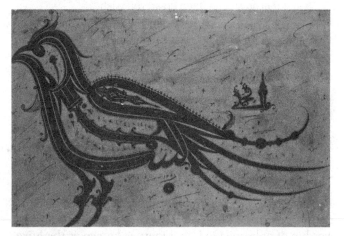

Bismillah in the form of a parrot, from Iran. **1834–35.** Ink on paper under wax coating. Cincinnati Art Museum, Franny Bryce Lehmer Fund. 1977.65. The parrot reads right to left, beginning over the large dot beneath its tail. The word *Allah* appears at the back of its head. The parrot is to humankind as humankind is to Allah. That is, it mimics human language without understanding it, just as humans recite the words of Allah without fully understanding them.

SEE MORE For a Closer Look at the *bismillah* in the Dome of the Rock, go to **www.myartslab.com**

Naskh

Thuluth

Muhaqqaq

Nastaliq

© M. Sakkal 2010

Riq'a

Five examples of the *bismillah* in different Islamic cursive scripts. *Naskh,* literally "copying," was developed in the tenth century, and refined into a fine art form in Turkey in the sixteenth century. *Thuluth* evolved over the centuries into a more impressive, stately calligraphic style, often used for titles or epigrams rather than lengthy texts, and often found in many variations on architectural monuments, as well as on glass, metalwork, textiles, and wood. It is the script employed on the mihrab niche below. *Muhaqqaq* emerged in the eleventh century in the art of making manuscripts of the Qur'an. *Nastaliq* developed in Iran in the fourteenth and fifteenth centuries. It is the most fluid and expressive of the scripts presented here, and is used extensively in copying romantic and mystical epics in Persian. *Riq'a,* the simpler style of everyday writing, is very economical and easy to write.

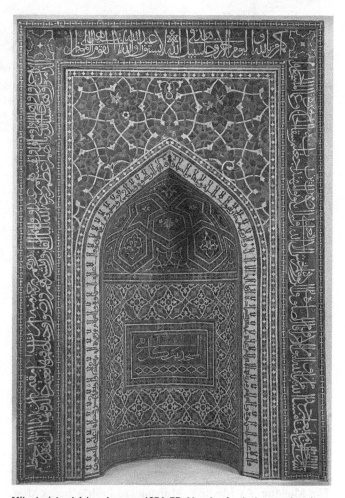

Mihrab niche, Isfahan, Iran. ca. 1354–55. Mosaic of polychrome-glazed cut tiles on fritware body; set into plaster, 135$\frac{1}{16}$" × 113$\frac{11}{16}$". ©1982 The Metropolitan Museum of Art/Art Resource, NY. Harris Brisbane Dick Fund, 1939. 39.20. The *bismillah* is contained in the rectangle in the center of the niche. The verses surrounding the niche are from the Qur'an, *Surah* 9: 18–22, beginning with this exhortation: "The mosques of Allah shall be visited and maintained by such as believe in Allah."

debris looking for signs of life. In the basement of a ruined house, rescuers discovered a man sitting on the floor absolutely absorbed in his work. He did not respond to their yells for him to hurry out before an aftershock buried him. Finally, he looked up and complained that they were disturbing him. They told him that thousands had been killed in an earthquake, and if he did not hurry up, he would be next. "What is all that to me?" he replied. "After many thousands of attempts I have finally made a perfect 'waw' [meaning 'and']." He showed them the letter, indeed a very difficult letter to make. "Such a perfect letter," he exclaimed, "is worth more than the whole city!"

Something to Think About . . .

How might modern technologies—from type to the Internet—pose a challenge to the calligraphic tradition in Islam?

Fig. 9.5 The Mosque of al-Mutawakkil, Samarra, Iraq. 848–52. The huge dimensions of the mosque can be accounted for by the fact that all worshipers must face the same direction—that is, toward Mecca—arranging themselves in parallel lines to kneel prostrate. Thus, each worshiper requires a good deal of individual space. As early as 670, many mosques were large enough to accommodate as many as 3,000 worshipers.

submission to the will of God. Such submission did not need to be entirely voluntary. Muslims were obligated to pursue the spread of their religion, and they did so by means of the **jihad** [jee-HAAD], the impassioned religious struggle that could take either of two forms: a lesser form, holy war; or a greater form, self-control over the baser human appetites. In order to enforce submission, Muhammad raised an army of some 10,000 men and returned to Mecca, conquering the city and destroying the idols in the Kaaba, with the exception of the Black Stone. Confronted by a Muslim army defined by both piety and zealotry, soon the entire western region of Arabia came under Muslim sway, and by the time of Muhammad's death even Mecca had submitted.

The community of all Muslims would come to be known as the *Umma* [OOM-mah]. It represented such a departure from tradition that its creation required a new calendar. Based on lunar cycles, the Muslim year is about 11 days shorter than the Christian year, resulting in a difference of about three years per century. The calendar began in 622 CE. Thus, in the year 2007, the Muslims celebrated the start of their year 1428.

The Mosque At Medina, Muhammad built a house that surrounded a large, open courtyard, which served as a community gathering place. There the men of the community would gather on Fridays to pray and listen to a sermon delivered by Muhammad. It thus inspired the *masjid* [mahs-JEED], the Arabic word for **mosque**, or "place of prostration." On the north and south ends of the courtyard,

covered porches supported by palm tree trunks and roofed by thatched palm fronds protected the community from the hot Arabian sun. This many-columned covered area, known as a **hypostyle** space (from the Greek *hupostulos* [hye-pos-TOO-lus], "resting upon pillars"), would later become a feature of many Muslim mosques. An important feature was the **qibla** [KIB-lah], a wall that indicated the direction of Mecca. On this wall were both the **minbar** [MIN-bur], or stepped pulpit for the preacher, and the **mihrab** [MEER-uhb], a niche commemorating the spot at Medina where Muhammad planted his lance to indicate the direction in which people should pray.

The Prophet's Mosque in Medina has been rebuilt so many times that its original character has long since been lost. But at Samarra, some 60 miles north of Baghdad on the Tigris River in modern Iraq, the remnants of the Mosque of al-Mutawakkil [al moo-ta-WAK-kul], built in the mid-ninth century, as well as a similar floorplan from a relatively contemporary mosque in Muslim Spain, show how large the mosque would soon develop (Figs. **9.5** and **9.6**). Built between 848 and 852, the mosque measures 800 by 500 feet, an area of over 10 acres. For centuries, it was the largest mosque in the world. It demonstrates the extraordinary popularity of the Muslim religion, since its central courtyard and hypostyle spaces would have been filled with many thousands of worshipers each Friday. About half the site was covered with a wooden roof on 464 supports, under which worshipers could pray. Although in a state of

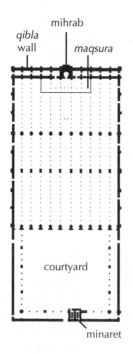

Hypostyle mosque
Great Mosque, Córdoba, Spain,
after extension by
al-Hakam II

Fig. 9.6 Plan of the Great Mosque, Córdoba, Spain. After its extension ca. 961–976. See Fig. **9.8**.

ruin today, the walls of the mosque were originally richly decorated with glass mosaic and marble panels.

The most remarkable feature of the surviving mosque at Samarra is the spiral tower opposite the mihrab. Some speculate that this tower, originally 165 feet tall, is a minaret, the tower from which the *muezzin* [moo-EZ-un] (crier) calls the faithful to prayer. But none of the earliest mosques had minarets, and although the call to prayer has become standard Muslim practice, even the earliest minarets may have been modeled on lighthouses (the root of *minaret* is *nur* [NOOR], meaning "light"), serving as sentinels to guide the faithful across the desert to the mosque. Others theorize that the tower was inspired by the ziggurats of ancient Mesopotamia (see Fig. 2.1).

Women in Islam Although Muslim practice today varies widely, in Muhammad's time, women were welcome in the mosque. In the Qur'an, Muhammad teaches that women and men are equal partners: "The faithful men and the faithful women are protecting friends for each other" (*Surah* 9:7). The husband's honor becomes an integral part of his wife's honor, and vice versa. They share equally in each other's prosperity and adversity. But Muhammad further allowed for Muslim men to have up to four wives, provided that they treated all justly and gave each equal attention. (Polygamy was widely practiced in the Arab world at the time, and marrying the widow of a deceased comrade, for instance, was understood to be an act of protective charity.) Muhammad himself—and subsequently other leaders as well—was exempt from the four-wife limitation. Although he had only one wife for 28 years, after she died when he was 53, he married at least 10 other women. The Qur'an describes the wives of Muhammad—and by extension, the wives of all Muslim men—as "Mothers of the Faithful" whose duty was the education of the *Umma*'s children. They helped them along their spiritual path, transmitting and explaining the teaching of Muhammad in all spheres of life.

One of the most discussed and most controversial aspects of Muslim faith (even among Muslims) is the *hajib* [hih-JAHB], literally "curtain," the requirement that women be covered or veiled. Its origins can be traced to

Islam's Jewish heritage and the principle of *tzenuit* [dzen-WEET], which in Hebrew means "modesty" in both dress and behavior and which requires, among other strictures, that all married women cover their hair whenever non-family members are present. Islamic covering ranges from a simple scarf covering the hair to the **chador** [CHA-dohr], which covers the wearer from head to toe, leaving only her hands and her face (or part of her face) exposed. This full covering is currently popular, especially in Iran. Interestingly, the Qur'an is not explicit about the covering. Women are advised to dress in a way that enables them to avoid harassment by not drawing attention to their beauty, or *zinat* [ZEE-nat], a word that means both physical beauty and material adornment in Arabic. The basic message and instruction expressed in the Qur'an is for Muslims to act modestly and dress modestly, a rule that applies to men and women.

Both men and women are entitled to equal treatment before the law, and justice is considered to be genderless. Both have the right to have disputes settled by an arbiter of *shari'a* [sha-REE-ah], the divine law. In the manuscript page showing a husband complaining about his wife before a state-appointed judge, or *qadi* (Fig. **9.7**) [QAH-dee], the wife,

Fig. 9.7 *A Qadi Sits in Judgment*, Baghdad. 1327. 14½" × 11". Illuminated manuscript. Bibliothèque Nationale, Paris. The women wear the *hajib*, in this instance, a full-length scarf.

accompanied by two other women who serve as witnesses, points an accusing finger at her husband. In such disputes, the first duty of the *qadi* is to reconcile the couple and avoid divorce, which, though legal in Islam, is discouraged. But all in all, the *shari'a* regulated gender relations in ways that favored males. It defined marriage as a reciprocal relationship in which a man owed his wife material support, and a wife owed her husband unwavering obedience. It asserted the male right of polygamy and outlined the terms in which males were to treat their multiple wives equally. A man could unilaterally repudiate a wife, but a woman could only bargain with her husband to end a marriage. And the *shari'a* affirmed the patrilineal structure of Muslim society by granting mothers only temporary custody of their children after the termination of a marriage, giving ultimate custody to the father or father's family.

Many modern scholars see the *shari'a* as a social revolution providing new rights and security for women in the cultures of the Middle East. But others regard the rules and regulations of the *shari'a* as a stifling suppression of the marriage practices of pre-Islamic Arab society, which was far less patriarchal. Traditional Arab society provided, among other things, for unilateral divorce by women and a woman's right to remain in her own clan and keep her children after divorce. It seems clear as well, that as Islam spread across the Middle East in the eighth and ninth centuries, the *shari'a* was adapted to and modified by local customs and practices. A clear example is the *shari'a's* stated punishment for adultery. The Qur'an ordains that

adulterers be given 100 lashes. But the standard punishment outlined in the *shari'a* by the early ninth century is death by stoning, justified by a hadith attributed to the prophet but probably originating in pre-Islamic tribal practices.

THE SPREAD OF ISLAM

Following the death of the Prophet in 632, the **caliphs** [KAY-lifs], or successors to Muhammad, assumed political and religious authority, and Islam spread with a rapidity that is almost unimaginable (Map **9.2**). Damascus fell to the caliphs in 634, Persia in 636, Jerusalem in 638, and Egypt in 640. By 710, all of North Africa and Spain were under Muslim rule.

The speed of the conquest can be partially accounted for by the fact that the Byzantine and Persian empires were exhausted by a long war. Soon after the Byzantine emperor Heraclius [heh-RAK-lius] (r. 610–40) captured Egypt, Palestine, Syria, and Asia Minor from the Persians, Muslim armies struck, driving the Byzantine armies out of their newly acquired territories and overrunning most of the Persian Empire as well. Most of the peoples in these territories, although Christian, were of the same linguistic and ethnic background as their new Muslim conquerors. Furthermore, the brand of Greek Orthodox Christianity that the Byzantine rulers had imposed on them was far too conservative for many. From Persia to Egypt, many peoples accepted their Muslim conquerors as preferable to the Byzantine rulers who had preceded them.

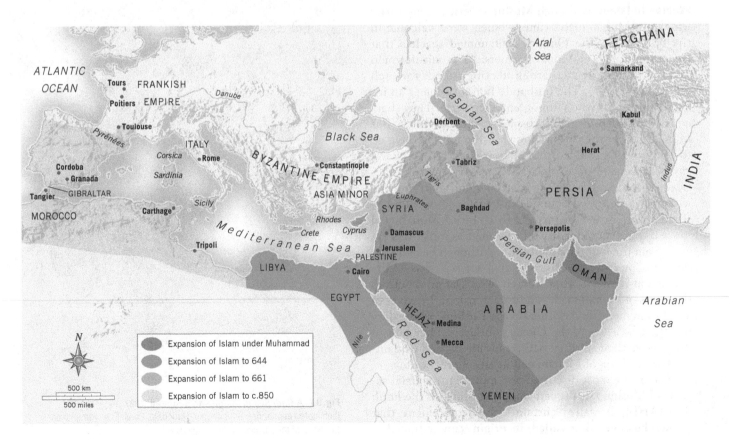

Map 9.2 The expansion of Islam to 850.

The successes of Islam must also be attributed to its appeal both as a religion and as a form of social organization. It denied neither Judaism nor Christianity, but merely superseded them. As opposed to the Jewish faith, which was founded on a common ethnic identity, Islam opened its arms to any and all comers—a feature it shared with Christianity. But unlike Christianity, it did not draw any special distinction between the clergy and the laity. It brought people together in the mosque, which served as a community meetinghouse, courthouse, council chamber, military complex, and administrative center. Traders naturally migrated to it, as did poets, artists, and scholars. In fact, the mosque was closer in function to the classical agora than to the Christian tabernacle. The sense of community that the mosque inspired played a central role in the spread of Islam.

By the eleventh century, *madrasas* [mud-RAD-sas], or teaching colleges, were attached to the mosques, and mosques became centers of learning as well. Here students studied the Qur'an, the hadith, and Islamic law, as well as mathematics, poetry, and astronomy. The madrasas eventually contributed to the rise of an intellectual elite, the *ulama* [OO-la-mah] (people possessing "correct knowledge"), a group that functioned more or less in the manner of Christian priests or Jewish rabbis. Yet any man of great religious learning could serve as an *alim* [AA-lum] (the singular form of *ulama*), and *ulama* had the singular role of overseeing the rulers of Islam, guaranteeing that they followed the letter of the law as stated in the Qur'an.

Works of the Umayyad Caliphs: The Great Mosque of Damascus

If, in the Muslim world, Mecca was the center of culture, mosques sprang up everywhere as Islam extended its reach. One of the earliest was in Damascus (Fig. **9.8**). Originally, the Muslim community in Damascus shared the site with the Christian community, who worshiped in a Byzantine church enclosed inside a walled compound. But by 705, the Muslim community had grown so large that radical steps had to be taken to accommodate it. The Byzantine church was torn down, leaving a large courtyard, and the compound walls were transformed into the walls of the mosque. A large prayer hall was constructed against the *qibla* wall and decorated with an elaborate facade that faced into the courtyard, while the street side of the mosque was left relatively plain.

The Great Mosque of Damascus was the work of the Umayyad [oo-MAH-yahd] caliphs, a Meccan family who were relatives of the Prophet. The first of the Umayyad family to come to power was Ali, the Prophet's cousin, son-in-law, and first convert to Islam. In 661, a rival faction that opposed Ali's rise to power based solely on his familial connections assassinated him. The leader of the *Umma*, they argued, should simply be the best Muslim, whomever that might be. (This division exists to this day. Those who believe that only descendants of Ali should rule are known as Shiites, and they live largely in Iran and Iraq. A more moderate group, known as Sunnis, who today represent the vast majority of Muslims, believe that religious leaders should be chosen by the faithful. These two groups continue to vie for power in modern-day Islam, especially in Iraq. A more conservative group, the Kharijites [KHA-ree-jytes], who originally supported the assassination of Ali on grounds of his moral weakness, still survives in Oman and North Africa.)

After Ali's assassination, the Umayyad family briefly fell from power until Abd al-Malik [ubd al MAH-luk] (r. 685–705) subdued the family's adversaries in 692. His son, al-Walid [al wah-LEED] (r. 705–715), was responsible for the construction and decoration of the Great Mosque in Damascus. One large section of the original interior decoration survives—a glass mosaic landscape in the covered walkway surrounding the courtyard. The mosaics were probably the work of Christian Byzantine artisans brought to Damascus by al-Walid. Rising in improbable scale above the walkway is an expanse of colonnaded pavilions, towering trees, and arched

Fig. 9.8 Courtyard of the Great Mosque of Damascus, Syria. 706–15. Muslim builders may have considered the site of this mosque to possess mystical powers. The Byzantine church that had stood here was dedicated to John the Baptist. It had supplanted a Roman temple of Jupiter, which had earlier supplanted a temple dedicated to Haddad, the ancient Ammonite storm god.

bridges (Fig. **9.9**). It has been suggested that this is the Paradise promised by the Prophet in *Surah* 76:14 of the Qur'an (see Reading 9.1a, page 288), but it may be, instead, that this landscape was designed as simply an attractive decorative addition.

Images in Muslim Art

It is worth noting that human figures are notably absent in the Great Mosque's mosaic decoration. Neither are there any animals. In fact, Muslim religious architecture is so notably free of figurative decoration that many people, even some Muslims, assume that representations of "living beings" are forbidden in Islam. As we saw in Chapter 8, the Byzantine emperor Leo III attributed the successes of the Muslim armies to their ban on human figures in their mosques. The following admonition from the Qur'an (5:92) is often cited by Muslims who worry about the role of image-making in Muslim art and decoration: "O believers, wine and arrow-shuffling idols and divining arrows are an abomination, / some of Satan's work; then avoid it." But, it can be argued, "idols" here refers to pagan idols of the kind the Prophet eliminated from the Kaaba in Mecca. Also, at the time, Muhammad had allowed a painting of Mary and the infant Jesus to remain in the building. The hadiths, however, also supported those who opposed image-making. There the Prophet is reported to have warned, "An angel will not enter a house where there is a dog or a painting." Likewise, the Prophet claimed that "those who make these pictures will be punished on the Day of Judgment by being told: Make alive what you have created."

Some religious scholars believed that the ban on representation applied only to "living" things. Thus, the depiction of Paradise, as on the walls of the Great Mosque of Damascus, was acceptable, because Paradise is "beyond the living." Such thinking would also lead the Muslim owner of a Persian miniature representing a prince feasting in the countryside to erase the heads of all those depicted (Fig. **9.10**). Such an act is closely related to Byzantine iconoclasm, as no one could presume to think that figures without heads could possibly be "alive." In fact, as we will see, Muslim artists in Persia took great delight in illustrating literary texts, creating scene after scene depicting people in various forms of action, including lovemaking. Their freedom to do so is partly explained by their distance from more conservative brands of Arabian Islam, but also by their belief that they were not illustrating "living beings" so much as fictive characters.

Whatever an individual Muslim's feelings about image-making might be, all Muslims recognized that it posed a problem. The practical solution to the problem was to decorate without images, and this was especially true for the decoration of both the Qur'an and religious architecture.

Fig. 9.9 Detail of mosaic decoration, Great Mosque of Damascus. 715. The decorative scheme of such panels reflects Byzantine influence, as well as the Roman love of landscape mosaic.

At the heart of Islamic culture was the word, in the form of the recitations that make up the Qur'an. In fact, those who transcribed the Qur'an enjoyed a status higher than that of artists and architects and at least equal to that of poets, whose largely oral works had, from pre-Islamic times, been considered the highest form of art. It is also important to remember that the Qur'an is itself a work of oral poetry.

ISLAM IN AFRICA AND SPAIN

Scholars once believed that the rapid expansion of Islam was entirely due to the determination of the faithful to convert new followers to the faith, but overpopulation of the Arabian peninsula probably also played a role. If faith offered the excuse, the practical result of Islamic expansion was the acquisition of new territories and the wealth they brought with them.

After gaining control of virtually all of the Middle East, the Arabic Muslim armies moved into North Africa in 639. After gaining control of the port of Alexandria, they launched a navy that seized Cyprus and Rhodes and began attacking Italy and Sicily. They moved across North Africa and took Carthage in 698, defeating the native Berber tribes. In 711, Muslim armies, under the command of a freed Berber slave, Tariq [TAH-ruk], crossed into Spain at the Strait of Gibraltar (*Gibraltar* is a corruption of the Arabic words

Fig. 9.10 Page from a copy of Nezami's *Khamseh* (the "Quintet"), illustrating a princely country feast, from Persia (modern Iran). 1574–75. Illuminated manuscript, 9³/₄" × 6". India Office, London. Nezami's poem, written in the twelfth century, consists of five romantic epics in 30,000 couplets. It became one of the most widely illustrated poems in Persian literature.

Muslim armies had conquered most of North Africa, Muslim traders, following the trade routes created by the Saharan Berber peoples, began trading for salt, copper, dates, and especially gold with the sub-Saharan peoples of the Niger [NY-jur] River drainage. Gradually they came to dominate the trans-Saharan trade routes (Map **9.3**), and Islam became the dominant faith of West Africa. By the ninth century, a number of African states existed in the broad savanna south of the Sahara Desert known as the Sudan [soo-DAN] (which literally means "land of the blacks"). These states seemed to have formed in response to the prospects of trade with the Muslim and Arab world. Ghana [GAHN-uh], which means "war chief," is an early example, and its name suggests that a single chieftain, and later his family, exerted control over the material goods of the region, including gold, salt, ivory, iron, and particularly slaves. Muhammad accepted slavery as the just spoils of war, although no Muslim was ever to enslave another Muslim. Between the ninth and twelfth centuries, the slave trade grew from 300,000 to over a million, and it was so lucrative that the peoples of the Sudan, all eager to enslave each other for profit, fought each other. (There is some reason to believe that many African converts to Islam were initially attracted to the religion as a way to avoid becoming slaves, since the faithful were exempt from servitude.) Finally, the empire of the Mali [MAH-lee] people subsumed Ghana under the leadership of the warrior-king Sunjata [soon-JAH-tuh] (r. 1230–55) and gained control of the great trade routes north out of the savanna, through Timbuktu, the leading trading center of the era.

In 1312, Mansa Moussa [MAHN-sah MOO-sah] (*mansa* is the equivalent of the term "emperor") came to the Malian throne. A devout Muslim, he built magnificent mosques throughout his empire, including the Djingareyber [jin-gah-REY-bur] Mosque in Timbuktu [tim-BUK-too]

meaning "Rock of Tariq") and moved quickly northward, deep into France. They were finally defeated in 732 at the Battle of Poitiers, also known as the Battle of Tours, by the king of the Franks, Charles Martel, and pushed back south of the Pyrenees. In the succeeding centuries, most of Europe became increasingly united in its opposition to Islam. This resulted in a series of military crusades to free the Holy Land, and Jerusalem in particular, of Muslim influence (discussed in Chapter 10). However, the Arabs maintained a dominant presence in Spain, particularly in the southern region of Andalusia [an-duh-LOO-zhee-uh] (*al-Andalus* [al AN-da-loos], in Arabic). There Muslim culture flourished until Christian armies finally expelled the Muslims in 1492, the same year that Columbus set sail for America.

Islamic Africa

The Muslim impact on the culture of North Africa cannot be overstated. Beginning in about 750, not long after

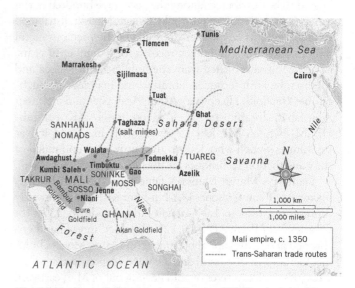

Map 9.3 The Trans-Saharan trade routes. ca. 1350. The shaded portion indicates the empire of Mali in the fourteenth century. The dashed lines trace the main trans-Saharan routes of the period.

Fig. 9.11 Djingareyber Mosque, Timbuktu, Mali. ca. 1312. Today the mosque—and the entire city of Timbuktu—is in danger of becoming a desert, as the sands from the Sahara overtake what once was the Mali savanna.

(Fig. **9.11**). Still standing today and made of burnt brick and mud, it dominates the city. Under Moussa's patronage, Timbuktu grew in wealth and prestige and became a cultural focal point for the finest poets, scholars, and artists of Africa and the Middle East. To draw further attention to Timbuktu, and to attract more scholars and poets to it, Mansa Moussa embarked on a pilgrimage to Mecca in 1334. He arrived in Cairo at the head of a huge caravan of 60,000 people, including 12,000 servants, with 80 camels carrying more than two tons of gold to be distributed among the poor. Five hundred of the servants carried staffs of pure gold. In fact, Moussa distributed so much gold in Egypt that the value of the precious metal fell dramatically and did not recover for a number of years. When Moussa returned from the holy cities of Mecca and Medina, he built mosques, libraries, and madrasas throughout his kingdom. He convinced the Arab poet and architect Abu-Ishaq Ibrahim-es-Saheli [aboo iss-HAAK eeb-rah-HEEM es-SAA-heh-lee] to return with him, and it was Ibrahim-es-Saheli who devised the burnt brick and much of the construction techniques for the Djingareyber Mosque.

Such was Mansa Moussa's fame that the Jewish mapmaker Abraham Cresques [AY-bru-hum KREK] prominently represented him in his *Catalan Atlas*, made in 1375 for Charles V of France (Fig. **9.12**). Crowned in gold and enthroned above his capital of Timbuktu, Mansa Moussa holds a golden orb in one hand and a golden scepter in the other. Cresques depicts a river of gold flowing out of Mali eastward to Cairo and Alexandria. The caption to the king's right reads, "So abundant is the gold which is found in his country that he is the richest and most noble king in the land."

Islamic traditions meanwhile continued to exist alongside indigenous African art and music. For instance, the military exploits of the first Malian *mansa*, Sunjata, still survive in an epic poem, the *Sunjata*. The poem was passed down through the generations, much in the way that the Homeric epics must have been passed down in prehistoric Greece. Its transmitters were Malian **griots** [gree-YOH], professional poet/storytellers who chant or sing traditional narratives from memory, generally accompanying themselves on a harp, either a three- or four-stringed **bolon** [boh-LON], or a 21-stringed *kora* [KOH-rah]. The *Sunjata* was not transcribed until the twentieth century. The poem opens with the griot identifying himself (**Reading 9.3a**):

READING 9.3a

from the *Sunjata*, 12th century

I am a griot. . . . We are vessels of speech, we are the repositories which harbor secrets many centuries old. The art of eloquence has no secrets for us; without us the names of kings would vanish into oblivion, we are the memory of mankind; by the spoken word we bring to life the deeds and exploits of kings for younger generations. . . . Listen to my word, you who want to know; by my mouth you will learn the history of Mali.

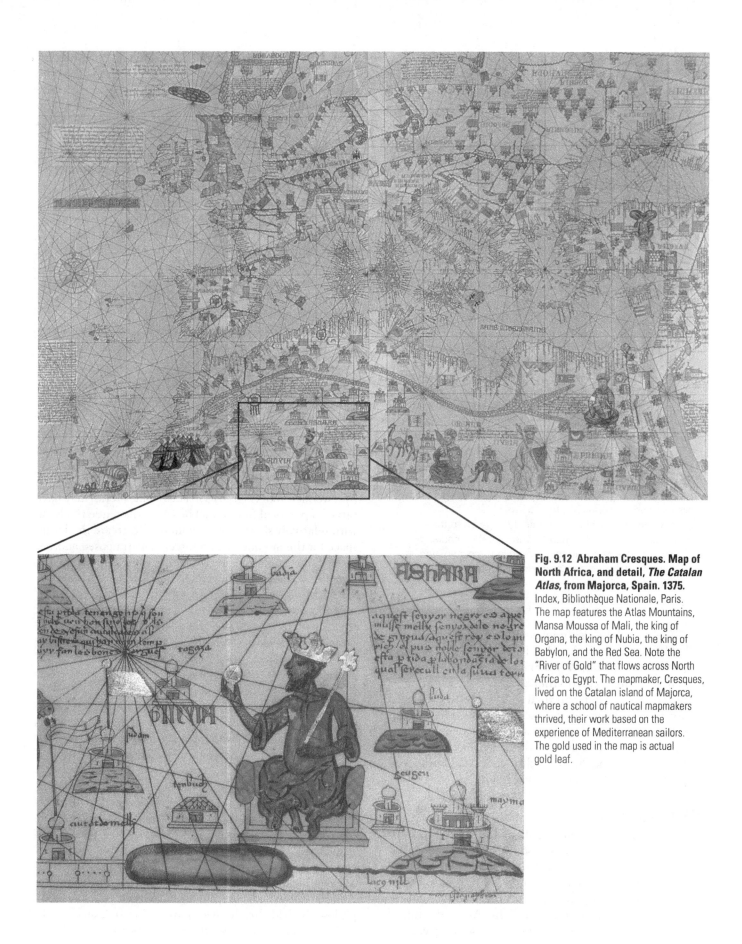

Fig. 9.12 Abraham Cresques. Map of North Africa, and detail, *The Catalan Atlas*, from Majorca, Spain. 1375. Index, Bibliothèque Nationale, Paris. The map features the Atlas Mountains, Mansa Moussa of Mali, the king of Organa, the king of Nubia, the king of Babylon, and the Red Sea. Note the "River of Gold" that flows across North Africa to Egypt. The mapmaker, Cresques, lived on the Catalan island of Majorca, where a school of nautical mapmakers thrived, their work based on the experience of Mediterranean sailors. The gold used in the map is actual gold leaf.

Later in the poem, Sunjata oversees a festival in celebration of his military exploits, a description that creates a vivid picture of Malian tradition (**Reading 9.3b**):

HEAR MORE at www.myartslab.com To this day, griots in West Africa perform the _Sunjata_ (track **9.1**). The performance features many of the characteristics common to West African music. These include polyrhythmic percussion, featuring as many as five to ten different rhythms simultaneously played on a variety of instruments (such as drums, rattles, and, here, bows and spears knocking together), communal performance, responsive chants, and what in another context might be considered "noise"—shrill cries, for instance—adding to the tonal richness of the whole.

Islamic Spain

Like Islamic Africa, Islamic Spain maintained its own indigenous traditions while it absorbed Muslim ones, thus creating a distinctive cultural and political life. In 750, the Abbasids [AB-ass-eed], a large family that claimed descent from Abbas [AB-bass], an uncle of Muhammad, overthrew the Umayyad caliphs. The Abbasids shifted the center of Islamic power from Damascus, where the Umayyads had centered their power, to a magnificent new capital in Iraq popularly known as Baghdad. In the middle of the ninth century, they moved again, to the complex at Samarra (see Fig. 9.5), 60 miles farther up the Tigris, probably in an attempt to seek more space to build palaces and mosques. Meanwhile, Spain remained under Umayyad control, initially under the leadership of Abd ar-Rahman (r. 756–88) [abd ur rahh-MAN], who had escaped the Abbasid massacre of Umayyads in Syria in 750, arriving in Córdoba [KOR-doh-buh] in 756. For over three centuries, the Spain he encountered had been controlled politically by a Germanic tribe from the north, the Visigoths, who had become Christian. But some 45 years earlier, in about 711 or 712, these Christian Visigoths had been defeated in southern Spain by a force of invading Muslim Arabs and Berbers. Gradually, Abd ar-Rahman solidified Muslim control of the region, first in Córdoba, then in Seville, Toledo (the former Visigothic capital), and Granada.

The Great Mosque of Córdoba In the last years of his reign, secure in his position, Abd ar-Rahman built a magnificent new mosque in Córdoba, tearing down an existing Visigothic church and building his new mosque in its place, for which the Christian church was handsomely reimbursed. Abd ar-Rahman's original design included a double-tiered system of reused Roman and Visigothic columns and capitals supporting horseshoe shaped double arches, all topped by a wooden roof (Fig. **9.13**). The double arches may have served a practical function. The Visigoths tended to build with relatively short, stubby columns. To create the loftier space for the mosque, the architects superimposed another set of columns on top, creating the double tier. But the design also echoes the same double-tiered design found at the Great Mosque at Damascus, which also reuses Roman columns, and the architects may have simply copied the Damascus model. The arches also employ a distinctive design of alternating stone and red brick voussoirs, the wedge-shaped stones used to build an arch (see _Materials & Techniques_, page 196). The use of two different materials is functional as well, combining the flexibility of brick with the strength of stone. The hypostyle plan of the mosque was infinitely expandable, and subsequent Umayyad caliphs enlarged the mosque in 852, 950, 961–76, and 987, until it was more than four times the size of Abd ar-Rahman's original and incorporated 1,200 columns.

Under the Umayyad caliphs, Muslim Spain thrived intellectually. Religious tolerance was extended to all. (It is worth noting that Muslims were exempt from taxes, while Christians and Jews were not—a practice that encouraged conversion.) Spanish Jews, who had been persecuted under the Visigoths, welcomed the Muslim invasion and served as scientists, scholars, and even administrators in the caliphate [KAY-lih-fate]. Classical Greek literature and philosophy had already been translated into Arabic in Abbasid Baghdad. The new School of Translation established

Fig. 9.13 Great Mosque of Córdoba. Begun 785, extensions 852, 950, 961–76, and 987. The caliphs of Spain intended their mosque to rival those in Jerusalem, Damascus, and Iraq. The forestlike expanse of the interior is a result of these aspirations. Even though only 80 of the original 1,200 columns survive, the space appears infinite, like some giant hall of mirrors.

LEARN MORE View an architectural simulation of Islamic arches at **www.myartslab.com**

by the Umayyads in Toledo [toh-LEH-doh] soon was responsible for spreading the nearly forgotten texts throughout the West. Muslim mathematicians in Spain invented algebra and introduced the concept of zero to the West, and soon their Arabic numerals replaced the unwieldy Roman system. By the time of Abd ar-Rahman III (r. 912–61), Córdoba was renowned for its medicine, science, literature, and commercial wealth, and it became the most important center of learning in Europe. The elegance of Abd ar-Rahman III's court was unmatched, and his tolerance and benevolence extended to all, as Muslim students from across the Mediterranean soon found their way to the mosque-affiliated madrasa that he founded—the

earliest example of an institution of higher learning in the Western world.

Outside of Córdoba, Abd ar-Rahman III built a huge palace complex, Madinat al-Zahra, to honor his wife. (Its extensive remains are still being excavated.) Its staff included 13,750 male servants along with another 3,500 pages, slaves, and eunuchs. Its roof required the support of 4,300 columns, and elaborate gardens surrounded the site. As many as 1,200 loaves of bread were required daily just to feed the fish in the garden ponds.

The decorative arts of the era are equally impressive. A famous example is a **pyxis**, a small, cylindrical box with a lid, made for Prince al-Mughira, Abd ar-Rahman III's son (Fig. **9.14**) in 968. Carved in ivory by artisans at Madinat al-Zahra, perhaps to hold the prince's jewelry or toiletries, each of its four sides is decorated with a medallion linked to the others by borders of delicately pierced foliage of an oriental palm. In one of these medallions, a lutist stands between two cross-legged figures, one holding a fan, the other a bottle of a kind associated particularly with the Umayyad caliph. Above them to the right two falconers stand back-to-back—the falcon being the traditional symbol of the Umayyad dynasty. Almost every element in the design has symbolic meaning, especially the oriental palm tree, which symbolizes the exile of the dynasty, banished to the distant land of Spain by the Abbasids.

The city of Córdoba reflected the splendor of its palace. Writers at the time, visiting the caliphate, testify that its population was about 500,000 (compared to 40,000 in Paris at about the same time). There were 1,600 mosques, 900 public baths, and more than 80,000 shops. About half the population had running water and lavatories in their homes. And the main city streets were lighted by torchlight at night.

Fig. 9.14 Royal workshop of Madinat al-Zahra, Pyxis of al-Mughira. ca. 968. Elephant ivory, carved and engraved decoration, trace of black inlay, possibly jade, height 6″. Musée du Louvre, former Riano Collection, purchased 1898. OA 4068. The Arabic inscription around the base of the lid reads: "God's blessing, favors, joy, beatitude to al-Mughira son of the Commander of the faithful, may God have mercy upon him, in the year 357 [of the Hegira]."

Jews in Muslim Spain Jews had settled in Spain as early as 586 BCE, when Nebuchadnezzar [neh-boo-kad-NEZ-zur] II conquered Jerusalem and destroyed the First Temple in Jerusalem. The Hebrew word for Spain was *Sepharad* [SEF-ar-ud], and the Spanish Jews were thus known as Sephardim [suh-FAR-deem]. Under Umayyad rule, the Jewish population flourished to such an extent that some scholars refer to the period as the Golden Age of Jewish Culture. Jews served at the highest levels of government and participated in the social and intellectual fervor that marked the Umayyad court. They dedicated themselves to the study of science and medicine. In fact, Abd ar-Rahman III's court physician was the Jewish Hasdai ibn Shaprut [huz-DAH-ee ubun shap-ROOT] (ca. 915–ca. 990). Jewish scholars also devoted themselves, under Hasdai ibn Shaprut's patronage, to the art of poetry and the study of Hebrew grammar. He was also instrumental in making Córdoba the new center of Jewish theological studies.

The Umayyad caliphate in Spain ultimately collapsed in the eleventh century, when internal politics caused it to break up into small competing states called *taifas*. Taifa Spain was far less tolerant of Judaism than the Umayyads, and persecutions began. The first one was on December 30, 1066, when the Jews were expelled from Granada and 1,500 families who refused to leave were killed. Nevertheless, Jewish culture still thrived, especially in Toledo and

Córdoba. It was in Córdoba that Moses Maimonides (1138–1204), one of the greatest Jewish scholars, was born, although he and his family were driven out of the country in 1148 by the Almoravids, a Muslim Berber dynasty that had been called into Spain in 1085 from its capital in Marrakesh, in present-day Morocco, in order help the *taifas* drive Christian armies from northern Spain. Maimonides is renowned for being the first person to write a systematic summary of Jewish law, the *Mishneh Torah*. He also produced one of the great philosophical works of Judaism, *Guide to the Perplexed*, a work about the nature of God in general that would influence later Christian thinkers such as Thomas Aquinas (see Chapter 12).

One of the great Jewish poets of the era is Judah Halevi [YOO-dah hah-LEH-fee] (ca. 1075–1141). In Córdoba, he wrote one of the best-known books of the era, *The Book of Argument and Proof in Defense of the Despised Faith*, later known as *The Book of the Kuzari*. This dialogue between a Jewish scholar and the pagan king of the Khazars [khah-ZARS], a seminomadic Turkish people, is considered by many to be one of the most important works of Jewish philosophy. The book argues, among other things, that the Hebrew language is itself divine, that the Torah is supernatural—not just a "gift from God" but the very "presence of God"—and that the special function of the Jewish people in God's plan is to bring about the redemption of the world.

Halevi was a poet of both secular and religious verse, including love songs, drinking songs, and autobiographical lyric poems concerning his faith. One of the most moving of the latter is "My Heart Is in the East." It embodies feelings shared by all Jews of the Diaspora (**Reading 9.4**):

READING 9.4

Judah Halevi, "My Heart Is in the East"

My heart is in the East, and I live at the edge of the West.
I eat. I taste nothing. How can I enjoy it?
How can I fulfill my word to leave
While Zion is locked up in red Edom [EH-dum][1]
and I stand in the ropes of Arabia?
Easily I could give up
all the good wonders of Spain.
Glory would be to see the dust of the Temple,
our ravaged shrine.

[1]**Edom:** a Hebrew word meaning "red" but referring to Esau in the Hebrew Scriptures as well as to the nation tracing its ancestry to him.

Before the end of his life, Halevi did leave his native Spain for Zion, perhaps driven out by the Berbers. He reached Alexandria, where he continued to write, but died six months later.

The Alhambra The collapse of the Umayyad caliphate and the subsequent rise and fall of the various Islamic dynasties was the inspiration for a pioneering work of sociology, the *Muqaddimah* [moo-QAD-dee-ma] (literally "Introduction") of Ibn Khaldun [ubun khal-DOON] (1332–1406), the first volume of a universal history that comprises six books. Originally conceived by its Tunisian-born author as a history of the North African Berber dynasties that rose to power in Spain after the Almoravid arrival in 1085, the work is based on Ibn Khaldun's central concept of *asabiyah* [ah-sa-BEE-ah], or "group feeling." *Asabiyah* is the source of cohesion within a community, and although it occurs almost naturally in small groups, such as families or tribes, religion can greatly expand its effects. Khaldun analyzes how *asabiyah* can carry groups to power, but he also demonstrates how, over time, the power of *asabiyah* dissipates in a group, causing its downfall and its eventual replacement by a new group with a more vital or contemporary sense of itself as a coherent power.

Of all the Berber dynasties in Spain, the Nasrid [nahs-REED] dynasty (r. 1230–1492) represented this new, stronger power, and their architecture embodied their sense of *asabiyah*. On a hill above Granada they erected a magnificent palace and fortress, which flourished as a center for the arts. Named the Alhambra [ahl-HAHM-bra]—from the Arabic word for "red citadel"—after the reddish tone of its walls, it gives us some sense of what the Abd ar-Rahman III's palace complex in Córdoba must have been like.

Within the walls of the Alhambra are palaces, mosques, gardens, quarters for artisans, baths, and tombs. The Palace of the Myrtles served as the official chambers for receiving and hosting visitors. Named after the shrubs planted in its courtyard, it was based on the plan of an urban dwelling in the Arab heartland, where life centered around a sheltered outdoor patio surrounded by doorways leading to the bedrooms, sitting rooms, and storage areas. The Palace of the Lions, named after the fountain in its courtyard surrounded by 12 stone lions, served as a private residence (Fig. **9.15**). The various rooms of the palaces opened into their central courtyards. Poetic texts adorn the palaces, carved into the capitals of their colonnades and inscribed on their walls and **miradors** [MEE-rah-dohrs], projecting rooms with windows on three sides. On a mirador overlooking the gardens of one palace are the words "I am a garden adorned with beauty. Gaze upon my loveliness and you will know this to be true." On another is the poignant phrase "I believe that the full moon has its home here." On the walls beneath the decorated ceilings of the Palace of the Lions, the fourteenth-century court poet Ibn Zamrak [ubun ZAM-rak] outlined the spiritual essence of the architectural traceries and grilles of the palace's arches and domes:

> And how many arches rise up in its vault supported by columns which at night are embellished by light!
>
> You would think that they are heavenly spheres whose orbits revolve, overshadowing the pillar of dawn when it barely begins to appear after having passed through the night.

The play of light and shadow, and the airy lightness of the stone- and plasterwork that adorn the Alhambra, symbolize the celestial heavens. The ceiling of the Hall of the Abencerrajes [ah-ven-ser-RAKH-ess] is decorated with **muqarnas** [moo-QARR-nass], small nichelike components unique to Islamic architecture that are combined in successive layers to enclose a space and produce surfaces rich

Fig. 9.15 Courtyard of the Palace of the Lions, Alhambra, Granada, Spain. 1354–91. The 12 stone lions supporting the fountain were salvaged from an earlier complex that stood on the Alhambra hill overlooking Granada.

Fig. 9.16 *Muqarnas* dome (plaster ceiling), Hall of the Abencerrajes, Palace of the Lions, Alhambra, Granada. 1354–91. The Hall of the Abencerrajes may have been used as a music room, the elaborate ceiling contributing to its nearly perfect acoustics.

in three-dimensional geometric compositions (Fig. **9.16**). Here they are used to catch the changing light as it moves from window to window across the top of the dome drum. The inescapable conclusion is that the Alhambra was meant to be something akin to heaven on earth, or paradise (from the Persian word for an enclosed park, *faradis* [faa-raa-DEES]), the literal embodiment of what, in the Great Mosque of Damascus, could only be imaged in mosaic (see Fig. 9.9).

The visitor to the Alhambra is struck by one other inescapable reality—there is water everywhere, in gardens, courtyards, and patios. Inscribed on the wall of one courtyard are the words, "The water in the basin in my center is like the soul of a believer who rests in the remembrance of God." But the water in the Alhambra is not merely passive. It flows, gurgles, and bubbles. Everywhere there is the *sound* of water, the essential *melody* of nature.

THE ARTS OF THE ISLAMIC WORLD

Between the eighth and thirteenth centuries, the Islamic world, from Baghdad in the east to Córdoba in the west, developed artistic traditions and practices compared to which the arts in Western Europe simply paled. With the same technical virtuosity that the architects at the Alhambra employed, Islam's musicians, bookmakers, illustrators, and poets crafted beautiful works of complex abstract design.

Music in the Islamic World

Music was central to Islamic culture. Though Muhammad and his followers initially viewed music with some skepticism, believing that it distracted the faithful from their true purpose, within a century of his death, Muslim worship had become a highly musical event. In the call to prayer, each of the call's seven phrases is sung, with a long pause between each phrase and each phrase becoming more melodic than the last. In the daily prayer service and on holy days, verses from the Qur'an are chanted and special songs are sung.

Traditional Arabic music is based on intonations and rhythms closely related to the inflections of words. It uses many more pitch intervals than Western music, breaking what we think of as a given pitch into fractions of semitones and microtones. In addition, Arabic song is "voiced" through the nose as well as the mouth, resulting in a range of distinctly nasal pitches, as in the Andalusian song from the "Nuba 'al'istihlal'" [na-ba aal-iss-teehh-LAAL], "Songs to be sung after sunset" (track **9.2**). These songs were often accompanied, at least outside the mosque, by a range of instruments, including drums, tambourine, flute, oboe, and lute—or oud [ood], from the Arabic for "wood"—a bent-necked, pear-shaped string instrument. As Islam spread, the *oud* became known, throughout North Africa, as the *qitara* [qee-TAH-rah]—the guitar—which achieved its modern form in Islamic Spain. Like Arabic music in general, the *qitara* was believed to be closely connected to nature. Its four strings variously represented the four seasons, the four phases of the moon, the four alchemical elements (hotness, coldness, dryness, and moistness), or the four bodily humors (in the medieval world, the four elemental fluids of the body—blood, phlegm, choler or yellow bile, and melancholy or black bile).

During the Abbasid era (750–1258), only an accomplished musician could be considered a truly educated person. Al-Kindi [al-KIN-dee] (790–874) studied the effects of music on people's feelings and behavior and developed a system of modes, or scales, corresponding to the emotions that the music was meant to evoke. In effect, the Arabs were the first to put into writing the concepts of scale that would become second nature in European theory. (Their notation, like European chant, lacked rhythmic notation until the twelfth to thirteenth centuries.) Many theorize that the new instruments were introduced into Europe from the Middle East, and may have been accompanied by the theoretical ideas behind them. By the ninth century, the renowned musician Ziryab [zeer-YAB] (789–857) arrived in Córdoba from Baghdad and founded the first conservatory of music in Spain. Here, musicians began to experiment with ensemble compositions divided into five or more movements performed by string, wind, and percussion instruments, and often accompanied by a vocal chorus. New instruments were invented—trumpets, viols, and kettledrums. In essence, the elements of the Western orchestra were now in place.

The Art of the Book

Sometime in the eighth century, the art of papermaking was introduced into the Arabic world from China. The process involved extracting cellulose pulp from any of a number of plants, suspending the pulp in water, catching it on a fine screen, and then drying it into sheets. By the first years of the ninth century, most official documents in Baghdad were executed on paper, and soon afterward books, which were more affordable than parchment manuscripts, began to increase in number. Calligraphers and artists created not only scholarly treatises but also romances, epics, and lyric poetry, and most Abbasid cities soon boasted special booksellers' markets. As Jonathan M. Bloom notes in his history of papermaking in the Islamic world, *Paper Before Print*, "Paper . . . became the prime medium of memory." Bloom suggests that although scholars have long recognized "the major achievements of intellectual life under the Abbasids . . . these achievements were not accidental. Rather, they were tied to the introduction of paper: they were a product of both increased intellectual curiosity—itself fostered by the growth of learning made possible by the explosion of books—and attempts to exploit the potential applications of paper." It is likely that the West did not produce paper in any sufficient quantity for another 500 years—until the invention of the printing press—because of its comparative lack of interest in the written word. The richest library in the West by the mid-fourteenth century, for instance, was the college library of the Sorbonne in Paris, which boasted some 2,000 volumes. By contrast, a single tenth-century Andalusian scholar, Ibn Hani al-Andalusi [ubun HAA-nee al an-DA-loo-see], reputedly owned a private library of some 400,000 volumes. Muslim culture, in turn, was slow to adopt the printing press because it so valued the art of calligraphy.

As a result of its book production, Abbasid Baghdad at the height of its influence, from the ninth to the twelfth centuries, was the center of world culture. Trade flourished as silk and porcelain from China, horses from Arabia, cotton from Egypt, and minerals from throughout Europe overflowed its markets. As one late ninth-century visitor remarked, "Goods are brought from India, Sind [i.e., Pakistan], China, Tibet, the lands of the Turks . . . the Ethiopians, and others to such an extent that [the goods] are more plentiful in Baghdad than in the countries from which they come. They can be procured so readily and so certainly that it is as if all the good things of the world are sent there, all the treasures of the earth assembled there, and all the blessings of creation perfected there." There are, he commented further, "none more learned than their scholars, better informed than their tra-

ditionists, more cogent than their theologians . . . more literate than their scribes, more lucid than their logicians . . . more eloquent than their preachers, more poetic than their poets." The book made this cultural eloquence manifest and transportable. Islamic learning—and with it, Islamic faith—spread throughout the world.

Nezami's Haft Paykar One of the most widely illustrated poems of the Middle Ages is the Haft Paykar [pay-KAR] ("Seven Beauties"). It is one of five romantic epics in 30,000 couplets that make up Khamseh [KHAM-sa] (Quintet) by the Persian poet considered to be the master of the genre, Nezami [nee-ZAH-mee] (ca. 1141–1203 or 1217), whose full name is Elyas Yusof Nezami Ganjavi [eel-YAS YOO-suf nee-ZAH-mee gan-YAH-vee]. A romantic epic is a poem that celebrates love between a man and woman as a cosmic force for harmony and justice. Thus, the love stories that form the epic's core narrative are also vehicles for treating broader philosophical issues such as just rule, human perfection, and spiritual growth. The Haft Paykar, Nezami's masterpiece, narrates how, one day, the legendary Persian prince Bahram Gur [BAH-ram GOOR] discovers a mysterious pavilion with portraits of seven beautiful princesses decorating its walls (Fig. **9.17**). He falls in love

Fig. 9.17 *Prince Bahram Gur Introduced into the Hall of Seven Images,* from a copy of Nezami's poem *Haft Paykar* ("Seven Beauties"), from *Nezami's Khamseh,* in the *Anthology* of Iskandar Sultan. From Shiraz, Iran. 1410. Illuminated manuscript, 9½″ × 5⅞″. Calouste Gulbenkian Foundation Museum, Lisbon. Another illustration of Nezami's poem is reproduced in Fig. 9.10, but defaced by its owner.

with all of them, marries them, sets up each princess in a separate pavilion of her own, and visits them one by one. Each princess tells him a story—each of about 1,000 couplets, two-line rhymed stanzas—that is meant to instruct him in the art of love and the love of beauty. **Reading 9.5** includes the first 29 couplets of "The Tale of the Black Princess."

READING 9.5

from Nezami, *Haft Paykar*, "The Tale of the Black Princess," 1197

When Bahram pleasure sought, he set
his eyes on those seven fair portraits;
On Saturday, from Shammasi [SHA-ma-see] temple[1] went
in Abbasid black[2] to pitch his tent,
Entered the musk-hued dome, and gave
his greetings to the Indian maid.
Til night he there made merry sport,
burnt aloes-wood,[3] and scattered scent.
When Night in kingly fashion spilled
black grains of musk on whitest silk,
The king from that Kashmiri spring[4]
sought perfume like the dawn breeze brings:
That she might loose some women's words,
sweet stories from her store of pearls,
Those tales for which all hearers long,
and soothe to sleep the drunken man.
That Turk-eyed, Hindu-born gazelle
loosed fragrant musk, her tale to tell.
She said, "May the king's fanfare play
above the moon's high throne; and may
He live as long as turns the world;
may all heads at his threshold bow.
May he gain all his wishes; may
his fortune never flag." This prayer
Concluded, she bowed low, and loosed
from sugared lips sweet aloes-wood.
She told (her eyes cast down in shame)
a tale unmatched by anyone. . . .

[1]**Shammasi temple:** the temple of fire, served by white-robed priests.
[2]**Abbasid black:** the color of the Abbasid caliphs.
[3]**aloes-wood:** incense made of aloe.
[4]**Kashmiri spring:** a reference to the "black princess," who is from India.

The story of Bahram and his seven wives is a narrative device known as a **framing tale**. This form allows the poet to unite different tales—in this case seven—under an overarching narrative umbrella. The Western reader is probably most familiar with the framing tale in *The Thousand and One Nights*, also known as *The Arabian Nights*.

The Thousand and One Nights The Thousand and One Nights is a compilation of prose tales from various sources—Persian, Arabic, and Indian—that were united into a single narrative between the eighth and tenth centuries in Baghdad. It is likely that Nezami knew it well. The framing tale derives from the Indian story of Scheherazade [shuh-hera-ZAAD] (Shahrasad [SHAHH-raa-zaad] in Persian),

who chooses to marry King Shahryar [shahh-ra-YAHR], who so fears the prospect of female infidelity that he kills each new wife on the morning after their wedding night. In a conscious defense of womankind, Scheherazade knows that if she can tell a story each night and carefully construct it so as to reach its climax just after dawn, the king must let her live until the next evening in order to hear the tale's ending. After a thousand nights—and some 250 tales—the king comes to appreciate Scheherazade's beauty, wit, and civilizing power, and so spares her the fate of all his previous wives.

Both the *Haft Paykar* and *The Thousand and One Nights* show the centrality of love and sexuality in Islamic culture. In Islam, erotic sensory satisfaction, love, luxury, sensuality, and enjoyment were manifestations of divine grace. And although both framing tales portray women in almost total subservience to the ruler/husband, the women in each tale assert a certain real authority. In the *Haft Paykar*, women bring the prince Braham Gur to a state of wisdom and spiritual wholeness. In *The Thousand and One Nights*, women's intelligence, wit, and reason at least equal and sometimes surpass that of their male counterparts.

The Thousand and One Nights was extremely popular in the West from the eighteenth century onward, and it exercised a considerable influence on the development of the novel in Western literature. It contains a wealth of stories popular to the present day—the adventures of Sinbad the Sailor, Ali Baba, and Aladdin, to name just a few—but its eroticism and ribald humor have often been sanitized in Western retellings. The stories wind in and out of one another in a seemingly endless pattern of repetition. The famous "Tale of the Fisherman and the Genie" (see **Reading 9.6**, pages 311–313) is a sequence of stories within stories that mirrors the framing technique of the whole, the fisherman telling tales to outwit an angry genie just as Scheherazade tells her tales to outwit the king. The sequence is repeatedly interrupted as dawn approaches and Scheherazade's stories must end for the night.

The Thousand and One Nights embodies a tension that pervades Islamic culture to this day and, it is fair to say, Western culture as a whole. That tension is between the exercise of authoritarian power over women in patriarchal society and the need for women to free themselves of that power—in Scheherazade's case, in order to survive. Related to this is the tendency of patriarchal society to reduce women to sexual objects even as it recognizes their great intellectual capacity. Scheherazade's tales must be understood in this context: They allow her to resist the king whom she entertains nightly, a man who is empowered by the *shari'a* (shah-REE-a) or a like set of laws, who feels no compunction about executing wife after wife, day after day.

The Sufi Tradition

After the 1258 fall of Baghdad to Mongol invaders—the conquering Mongols would themselves become Muslim—the art of bookmaking shifted to Iran, where a thriving literary culture, exemplified by the poetry of Nezami, already existed. Particularly at the provincial capitals of Shiraz and

Fig. 9.18 *Dervishes Dancing,* from a copy of *Sessions of the Lovers,* **from Turkey. Sixteenth century.** Illuminated manuscript, approx. 9″ × 6″. Bodleian Library, Oxford. The Sufi's goal was to achieve direct contact with God through mystical trance, and the ecstatic whirling dance could, the Sufis believed, induce such a trance. In this miniature, the dervishes dance to the accompaniment of flutes and tambourines.

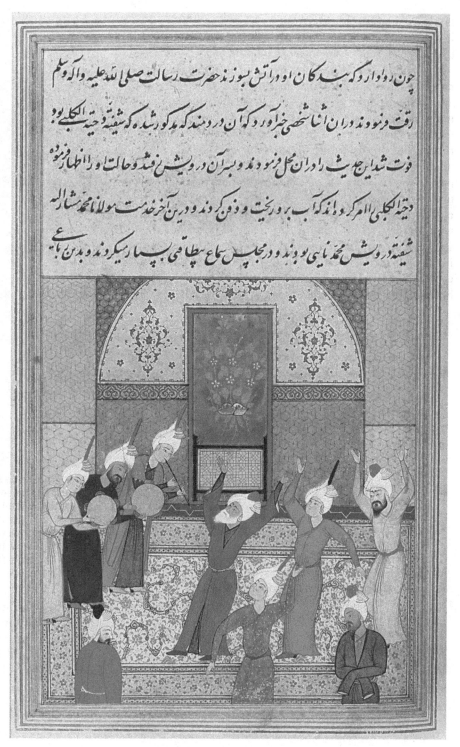

Herat, home to a number of important Persian poets and painters, the art of the book became associated with the mystical practices of the Sufi [SOO-fee] orders. Sufism (from the Arabic word for "wool," *suf,* a reference to the coarse woolen garments worn by Sufi practitioners) embraces a wide range of mystical practices. All of them share a belief in attaining visionary experience and divine inspiration by means of trances achieved in the intense experience of music, poetry, and dance. Thus, the ecstasy of the wild, whirling dervish dance (the Persian word for a Sufi or Muslim mystic is *darvish*) represents the path of the soul as it moves closer to God (Fig. **9.18**). The great Sufi poets—Sa'di [SAA-adi] (ca. 1213–92), Rumi [ROO-mee] (ca. 1207–73), and Jami [JAH-mee] (1414–92) among them—emphasize the pursuit of the beautiful, often in the form of a beautiful woman or, in the case of Rumi, a beautiful man. However, such a pursuit is an allegory for, or figurative representation of, the pursuit of the beauty that is God.

For instance, Jami's version of the "Seduction of Yusuf [YOO-suf] and Zulaykha [zoo-LAY-kuh]" (**Readings 9.7a** and **9.7b**), a story celebrated by several Sufi writers, retells, in elaborate fashion, the story of Joseph and the wife of Potiphar [POT-uh-fur], Zuleika [zoo-LAY-kuh], which appears in both the Bible and Qur'an. Yusuf protests that his love is not sexual but divinely inspired:

READING 9.7a

from Jami, "Seduction of Yusuf and Zulaykha," 1483

I would not passion's victim be,
And turned from sin—but not from thee.
My love was pure, no plant of earth
From my rapt being sprung to birth:
I loved as angels might adore. . . .

His pure adoration leads Yusuf to understand "the great lesson"—"That vice and bliss are wide apart." His love for his lady leads him to the love of God.

In Jami's poem, Zulaykha builds a palace with seven rooms, each decorated with an erotic painting of herself and Yusuf, in order to seduce the beautiful youth. As she leads the unsuspecting Yusuf from room to room, she locks each door behind her. When they reach the last room, she throws herself on Yusuf, who flees as each of the seven doors miraculously opens before him. In Jami's poem, the palace and its decorations stand for the temptations of the material world with its seven climes, the habitable climatic regions of the earth (Fig. **9.19**). Yusuf's beauty, which Zulaykha mistakenly sees as physical rather than spiritual, is comparable to the beauty of God, and his faith in the all-seeing God unlocks the doors to allow his escape. Recalling Yusuf's power over her, Zulaykha then bemoans her loss:

READING 9.7b

from Jami, "Seduction of Yusuf and Zulaykha" (before 1492)

Let me look back to that dark hour
That bound my spirit to thy power—
Thy grateful words, thy glance recall,
My hopes, my love—and curse them all;
Let me thy tender looks retrace,
The glories of thy heavenly face;
Thy brow, where Aden's[1] splendor lies,
And the mild luster of thine eyes:
Yet let my heart no weakness prove,
But hate thee as I once could love.
What fearful eloquence was thine,
What awful anger—just—divine!
Shuddering, I saw my heart displayed
And knew all this I should have said!
'Twas mine to shrink, withstand, in time,
For, while I sinned, I knew my crime.
O wretched, wavering heart!—as vain
Thy wild resentment as thy pain:
One thought alone expels the rest,
One sole regret distracts my breast,
O'ermastering and subduing all—
More than my crime, more than my fall:
Are not shame, fear, remorse, forgot,
In that one thought—he loves me not?

[1]**Aden:** the Garden of Eden.

As we will see in the following chapters, Zulaykha's point of view, and, more powerfully, Yusuf's understanding of love itself, would soon make its way to Europe, particularly in the tradition of "courtly love" championed by the troubadour poets.

Rumi's poetry, especially the *Mathnavi* [MAT-nuh-vee] (Rhymed Discourses), an epic-length verse collection of mystical stories composed of some 27,000 verse couplets, is

Fig. 9.19 Bihzad. *The Seduction of Yusuf*, from a copy of Sadi's *Bustan* ("Orchard"), prepared for Sultan Husayn Mirza at Herat, Persia (modern Afghanistan). 1488. Ink and color on paper, 11⅞" × 8⅔". National Library, Cairo. Bihzad is one of the most renowned illustrators of the fifteenth century. In illustrating this manuscript, he worked together with Sultan Ali Mashhadi, who was himself the greatest calligrapher of the day. The text of Sadi's version of the Yusuf story is in the cream-colored panels in the top, middle, and bottom of the page.

considered the masterwork of the Sufi tradition—"the Qur'an in Persian," Jami called it. The stories, which invariably end happily, illustrate God's limitless mercy toward humankind, and Rumi invokes the Qur'an's message of hope repeatedly. Indeed, for him hope is virtually synonymous with faith. The stories continually cite the Qur'an and interpret it in terms of human potential for mystical union with God, a potential hinted at in physical union with a lover. This hinted potential is the subject of Rumi's collection of about 30,000 verses entitled *The Divan of Shams of Tabriz*. Rumi thought of Shams (meaning "Sun") of Tabriz [tah-BREEZ] as the "Divine Beloved," the physical incarnation of spiritual love. Rumi met him in 1244, and when Shams disappeared 15 months later, Rumi wrote poems describing the loss of his lover in terms of abandonment by God. Poems like "Love's Body," "Caring for My Lover," and "The Clear Bead at the Center" (see **Reading 9.8**, page 313) are at once carnal and spiritual, erotic and mystical, and they speak of the rebirth of the human spirit through love.

The Islamic Heritage

slam is often considered outside the Western tradition, but it is a fundamental part of the Western heritage. As we have seen, Western music—indeed, the Western orchestra—originates in Muslim musical traditions. The spiritual depth of the love poem, as it comes to fruition in the work of the medieval troubadour poets and the poets of the Renaissance, is first developed in the Muslim world. Many of the decorative effects achieved in medieval architecture and design reflect the interlace and arabesques that inform Islamic architecture. See, for example, the portal of Saint Michel d'Aiguilhe, in Le-Puy-en-Venay, France (Fig. **9.20**), the first stop on a Christian pilgrimage route to Santiago de Compostela, where the body of the apostle Saint James the Greater lay at rest, a pilgrimage itself modeled in many ways on the Muslim **hajj** to Mecca. The portal incorporates the colored stonework and double arches of the mosque at Córdoba and the intricate design of a mihrab niche.

Fig. 9.20 Portal of Saint Michel d'Aiguilhe, Le-Puy-en-Venay, France. ca. 1162–80. Charles Martel stopped the Arab invasion of France at Poitiers in 792, but decorative work such as this underscores the lasting Islamic influence in Europe (see Chapter 13).

But in its insistence that Jesus was a "mere" prophet and not the son of God, and in its belief that the Qur'an superseded both the Hebrew and Christian Scriptures, Islam inevitably came into conflict with the Christian West. By the time that Pope Urban II (papacy 1088–99) launched the First Crusade in 1095, gathering over 100,000 people to march on Jerusalem, Islam represented the forces of darkness to European Christians. Their determination to liberate the Holy Land from Muslim domination became a key factor in the history of the late Middle Ages.

A notable symbol of this determination is an Islamic bronze griffin that, from 1100 to 1828, sat atop Pisa Cathedral, itself built to celebrate the victory in 1063 of this Italian city-state over Muslim forces in the western Mediterranean (Fig. **9.21**). Decorated with incised feathers, its back designed to suggest silk drapery, the griffin symbolized to Muslims eaglelike vigilance, lionlike courage, and, perhaps most of all, the rich history of Mesopotamia and Persia. But the Catholic Church appropriated this bronze griffon to different ends and transformed its meaning. From its perch atop Pisa Cathedral it symbolized the dual nature of Christ, his divinity (the eagle) and his humanity (the lion). The composite creature was, in the Church's mind, the image of the Christian victory over Islam. ■

Fig. 9.21 Griffin, from the Islamic Mediterranean, probably Fatimid Egypt. Eleventh century. Bronze, height 3′ 6 ⅛″. Museo dell'Opera del Duomo, Pisa. The griffin was moved into the museum in 1828 to protect it from the elements.

What was the message of the Prophet Muhammad?

According to tradition, beginning in 610 the Muslim prophet Muhammad began to recite messages from God, which he dictated to scribes who collected them to form the scriptures of Islam, the Qur'an. At the core of the Qur'an is the concept of "submission" or "surrender" to Allah, the all-merciful, all-seeing, all-powerful God. Other than the Qur'an, what other work forms the basis of Islamic faith? How is the idea of community reflected in the mosque and its attendant rituals? How is it reflected in the idea of the jihad? What are the "lesser" and "greater" forms of the jihad? What is the *shari'a*, and how would you describe traditional relations between men and women as outlined in the *shari'a*?

Why did Islam spread so rapidly?

Islam spread rapidly throughout the Middle East. It was appealing both as a religion that welcomed all converts and as a form of social organization that drew no distinction between clergy and congregation. As the center of the religious community, the mosque serves as meetinghouse, courthouse, and administrative center. What role do the madrasas, or teaching colleges, built at mosques, play?

How did Islam come to Africa and Spain?

In the eighth and ninth centuries, Muslims came to dominate the trans-Saharan trade routes, and Islam became the dominant faith of North and West Africa. Muslims especially traded in salt, gold, and slaves (Muhammad had expressly authorized the practice of enslaving conquered peoples). By 1312, the Malian ruler Mansa Moussa, a devout Muslim, had built the Djingareyber Mosque in Timbuktu and led a pilgrimage to Mecca. The epic of *Sunjata*, detailing the exploits of the first Malian king, reflects this world and is still sung by Malian griots, or professional poets, to this day.

In Spain, the Umayyad caliph Abd ar-Rahman built a magnificent new mosque in Córdoba, and by the middle of the tenth century, under the leadership of Abd ar-Rahman III, Córdoba was the most important center of learning in Europe. How did the Jewish population of Spain fit into this culture? What cultural priorities are reflected in such Spanish Muslim works as the Alhambra in Granada?

What place do the arts hold in the Islamic world?

Many faithful believed that Muhammad had opposed image-making in the hadith. As a result, the art of calligraphy assumed a central place in Islamic visual culture, especially the bismallah, consisting of the phrase "In the name of Allah, the Beneficent, Ever-Merciful," with which every pious Muslim begins any statement or activity. How does iconoclasm manifest itself in Islam? Traditional Arabic music is based on intonations and rhythms closely related to the inflections of words, and it uses many more pitch intervals than Western music, but how does it contribute to the development of Western music?

The art of papermaking transformed Islamic culture, as the book became the prime medium of memory and Baghdad became a major publishing center. One of the most widely illustrated poems of the Middle Ages is Nezami's *Haft Paykar* (*Seven Beauties*), a romantic epic. What is the primary narrative device that it employs? How is this device central to *The Thousand and One Nights*, a prose compilation of Persian, Arabic, and Indian stories told by Scheherazade? After the fall of Baghdad to invading Mongols in 1258, book publishing moved to Iran, where we find the mystical poetry of Sufi poets such as Jami and Rumi. What is the central theme of their work?

PRACTICE MORE Get flashcards for images and terms and review chapter material with quizzes at **www.myartslab.com**

GLOSSARY

bismillah A sacred invocation of the name of Allah.

bolon A three- or four-stringed harp.

caliph A successor of Muhammad.

calligraphy The art of producing artistic, stylized handwriting.

chador A covering worn by Muslim women that covers the wearer from head to toe and most or all of the face.

couplet A two-line rhymed stanza.

framing tale A narrative device that allows a writer to unite different tales under an overarching narrative umbrella.

griot A West African poet/storyteller who chants or sings traditional narratives from memory, generally accompanied by a harp.

hadith The collection of the sayings of Muhammad and anecdotes about his life, accepted as a source of Islamic doctrine.

hajib The Islamic practice of dressing modestly; specifically, the requirement that women be covered or veiled.

hajj A pilgrimage to Mecca made as a religious duty for Muslims.

hijra The flight of Muhammad from Mecca in 622.

hypostyle A vast space filled with columns supporting a roof.

jihad The impassioned religious struggle undertaken by Muslims as a religious duty. The jihad may take one of two forms: the lesser is a holy war; the greater is self-control over the baser human appetites.

mihrab A niche in the wall of a mosque commemorating the spot at Medina where Muhammad planted his lance to indicate the direction in which people should pray.

minbar The stepped pulpit for the preacher on the *qibla* wall of a mosque.

mirador A projecting room with windows on three sides.

mode A series of different scales.

mosque A building used for worship by Muslims.

muqarnas A small, nichelike component unique to Islamic architecture and used in multiple rows to enclose a space.

pyxis A small, cylindrical box with a lid.

qibla The wall of a mosque indicating the direction of Mecca.

Qur'an The sacred text of Islam composed of the revelations of Allah to Muhammad.

romantic epic A poem that celebrates love between a man and woman as a cosmic force for harmony and justice.

Umma The community of all Muslims.

READINGS

READING 9.1

from the Qur'an, *Surah* 47

The Qur'an consists of the revelations said to have been made to Muhammad and preserved in oral traditions by his followers, who used them in ritual prayers. The core of Islamic faith, they were written down and gathered into a single book in 651–52 at the order of Uthman [oot-MAN], the third caliph, or successor to the Prophet. Divided into 114 chapters, or surahs ("units of revelation"), the Qur'an is, very often, a book of remarkable beauty, but in the surah reproduced here, it reveals itself to be less than tolerant of those who do not accept the Muslim faith.

SURAH 47 MUHAMMAD

In the name of Allah, most benevolent, ever-merciful.

1. (As for) those who disbelieve and turn away from Allah's way, He shall render their works ineffective.

2. And (as for) those who believe and do good, and believe in what has been revealed to Muhammad, and it is the very truth from their Lord, He will remove their evil from them and improve their condition.

3. That is because those who disbelieve follow falsehood, and those who believe follow the truth from their Lord; thus does Allah set forth to men their examples.

4. So when you meet in battle those who disbelieve, then 10 smite the necks until when you have overcome them, then make (them) prisoners, and afterwards either set them free as a favor or let them ransom (themselves) until the war terminates. That (shall be so); and if Allah had been pleased He would certainly have exacted what is due from them, but that He may try some of you by means of others; and (as for) those who are slain in the way of Allah, He will by no means allow their deeds to perish.

5. He will guide them and improve their condition.

6. And cause them to enter the garden which He has made 20 known to them.

7. O you who believe if you help (the cause of) Allah, He will help you and make firm your feet.

8. And (as for) those who disbelieve, for them is destruction, and He has made their deeds ineffective.

9. That is because they hated what Allah revealed, so He rendered their deeds null.

10. Have they not then journeyed in the land and seen how was the end of those before them: Allah brought down destruction upon them, and the unbelievers shall have the like of it. 30

11. That is because Allah is the Protector of those who believe, and because the unbelievers shall have no protector for them.

READING CRITICALLY

Despite their apparent intolerance for non-Muslims, this *surah* also contains many passages that could be called compassionate and caring. How are the two opposing sentiments reconciled?

READING 9.6

"Tale of the Fisherman and the Genie" from *The Thousand and One Nights* (ca. 800–1300)

The Thousand and One Nights was assembled sometime between the eighth and tenth centuries from stories of Persian, Arabic, and Indian origin that had circulated orally for hundreds of years. The work itself, consisting of some 250 tales, exists in many versions—often sanitized in English translation, reducing this adult masterpiece to a collection of children's stories. It is a framed tale in which Scheherazade, a woman of great wit and beauty, tells a story each night to her king and husband. He is a man so obsessed with the possibility of female adultery that, until he marries Scheherazade, he has killed each of his new brides the morning after their wedding night. To forestall her own death, Scheherazade cleverly stops her stories each morning before they reach their conclusion. "The Tale of the Fisherman and the Genie," the opening of which is excerpted here, is itself a sequence of tales within a tale, mirroring the structure of the whole, as the fisherman tells his stories in order to forestall the anger of a Genie.

I have heard, Oh worthy King, that there was once a poor, old Fisherman who had a wife and three children to support. Each day, it was his custom to cast his fishing-net into the ocean exactly four times, and no more. One day, at about noon, he went towards the seashore, where he set his basket down in the sand. Tucking up his shirt and plunging into the water, he cast his net and waited until it settled to the bottom of the sea. Then, he gathered the cords of the net together, and tried to haul it away. But its heaviness overpowered him, and no matter how hard he tried, he could not pull it up. So he carried the ends of the cords to the shore, 10 drove a stake into the sand, and bound the cords tightly to the stake. Then he stripped his clothes from his body and dove into the water, working hard until he finally raised the net from the sea.

Rejoicing, he put his clothes back on and went to examine the net and found a dead jackass inside of it, which had torn all the net's meshes. As he saw this, the Fisherman sadly exclaimed, "There is no majesty, and there is no might except Allah the glorious, the great! But, well, this is a strange sort of daily bread." He paused, considering, and then murmured to himself, "Well, up and at it! I'll finish my fishing now, for I'm very sure of Allah's 20 goodness."

So the Fisherman gazed at the dead ass for a moment, and then pulled it free from the netting. He wrung out the net, and spread it over the sand. Calling out "In Allah's name!" he plunged back into the sea. He cast the net a second time. . . .

[*He casts his net three times, pulling a large earthen pitcher out of the sea the second time, and shards of pottery and glass the third, blessing Allah each time although he catches no fish. On the fourth cast he pulls out . . .*] a cucumber-shaped copper jar, brimming with something mysterious. The mouth of the jar 30 was sealed with lead, and stamped with the seal of our Lord Solomon, David's son, Allah praise them! Seeing this the Fisherman rejoiced and said, "If I sell this in the brass bazaar, I could get ten golden dinars for it!" He shook the jar, and finding it heavy, murmured, "I wish I knew what was in it. I feel as if I must find out—so I'll open it and look inside, and then I'll store it in my bag, to sell at the brass market. Taking out a knife, he pried the lead until he had loosened it from the jar. He set the seal on the ground, and turned the vase upside-down, shaking it and trying to pour out whatever could be inside. Surprisingly, 40 nothing emerged, and the fisherman stood in wonder.

But suddenly, a spiral of smoke burst from the jar, rising toward the heavens. The fisherman marvelled as it was drawn into the air, ascending far above him. As it reached its full height, the thick, vaporous smoke condensed and formed a Genie, so huge that his head brushed the sky, and his feet touched the ground. The Genie's head curved as large as a dome; his hands dangled, big as pitchforks. His legs were long as masts, his mouth as wide as a cave, his teeth like large stones, and his nostril flared like pitchers' spouts. His eyes shone like two 50 lamps, and his face proved fierce and threatening.

Now, when the Fisherman saw the Genie, his muscles quivered, his teeth chattered, and his throat grew too dry to swallow. Paralyzed, clenched with fear, he could do nothing.

The Genie looked at him and cried, "There is no god but *the* God, and Solomon is the prophet of God." He added, "Oh Apostle of Allah, do not slay me. Never again will I oppose you or sin against you."

The Fisherman replied, "Oh Genie, did you say, 'Solomon the Apostle of Allah?' Solomon has been dead for nearly eighteen 60 hundred years, and now we're in the last days of the world! Where have you come from? What's happened to you? Why have you been in that jar?"

When the Evil Spirit heard the Fisherman's words, he answered, "There is no god but *the* God. Be happy, Fisherman!"

"Why should I be happy?" asked the Fisherman.

"Because," replied the Genie, "you must die a terrible death this very hour."

"You deserve heaven's abandonment for your good tidings!" cried the Fisherman. "For what reason should you kill me? 70 What have I done to deserve death? I, who freed you from the jar, dragged you from the depths of the sea, and brought you up to dry land?"

"Ask me only in which way you will die, how I will slaughter you," said the Genie.

"What's my crime?" the Fisherman persisted. "Why such retribution?"

"Hear my story, Oh Fisherman!" cried the Genie.

The Fisherman swiftly answered, "Tell it, but tell it briefly. My heart is in my mouth." 80

And so, the Genie began his tale. "I am one of the heretical Genie," he explained. "I, along with the famous Sakhr al Jinni, sinned against Solomon, David's son. After this, the Prophet Solomon sent his minister, Asaf son of Barkhiya, to seize me. This minister bound me and took me against my will, bringing me to stand before the Prophet Solomon like a supplicant. When Solomon saw me, he appealed to Allah, and demanded that I embrace the True Faith and obey Allah's commands. I refused; and so he sent for this jar and imprisoned me in it, sealing it with lead and stamping it with the Most High Name. He ordered an- 90 other spirit to carry me off, and cast me into the center of the ocean. I lived there for a hundred years, and during this time I said in my heart, 'I'll forever reward whoever releases me with the greatest of riches.' But an entire century passed, and when no one set me free, I began the second century saying, 'I'll reveal the secret treasures of the earth to whoever will release me.' Still, no one set me free, and soon four hundred years passed. Then I said, 'I'll grant three wishes to whoever will release me.' Yet again, no one set me free. Then I became angry, so furious, I said to myself, 'From now on, I'll kill whoever re- 100 leases me, and I'll let him choose what type of death he will die.' And now, as you're the one who's released me, I give you the choice of your death."

The Fisherman, hearing the words of the Genie; exclaimed, "Oh Allah! How could it be that I didn't come to free him before this? Spare my life, Genie, and Allah will spare yours; don't kill me, and Allah will never send anyone to kill you!"

"There is no help for you. You must die," the Genie obstinately explained. . . .

As the Genie spoke, the Fisherman said to himself, "This is 110 a Genie, but I'm a man to whom Allah has given a cunning wit. So now, as he uses his malice to destroy me, I'll use my intelligence and cunning to stop *him*." He turned to the Genie and said, "Have you really resolved to kill me?"

"Of course."

"Even so," exclaimed the Fisherman, "if I ask you a question about a certain matter, will you swear by the Most Great Name, engraved on the seal-ring of Solomon, Son of David, that you'll answer it truthfully?"

The Genie trembled as he heard the Fisherman mention the 120 Most Great Name. "Yes," he promised the Fisherman, though his mind grew troubled. "Yes, ask, but be brief."

The Fisherman said, "How did you fit into this bottle, which doesn't even look big enough to hold your hand, or even your foot? How could it have been big enough to contain all of you?"

"What!" replied the Genie. "You don't believe my whole body was in there?"

"No!" cried the Fisherman. "I'll never believe it until I see all of you inside of it, with my own eyes." 130

And then Scheherazade saw that dawn crept over the edge of the horizon, and so she stopped telling her story. But the next day, when the fourth night came, her sister said to her, "Please finish the story. None of us are sleepy." And so, Scheherazade resumed her storytelling . . . .

READING CRITICALLY

In what way does the Genie mirror the king in both action and attitude?

---

from Rumi, *The Divan of Shams of Tabriz* (ca. 1250)

Jalal ad-Din Rumi [jaa-LAAL udd-een ROO-mee] was born in the Persian province of Khorasan [KHOR-uh-sahn] in 1207. After the Mongol invasion of central and western Asia, he settled in Anatolia, a region of Asia Minor known as Rum (Rome in Turkish). Jalal ad-Din means, literally, "Glory of Religion." His entire name means, then, "Roman Glory of Religion." Rumi became a leader of the Sufi community, named sheik, or elder, and received the title "Mevlana," [meh-woo-LAH-nuh] meaning "our master." He is still known by that name throughout the Middle East and India. The four poems below are from a collection of lyrics entitled The Divan of Shams of Tabriz, which contains about 30,000 verses celebrating the poet's physical love for Shams ad-din [SHAM-ss add-EEN] of Tabriz, who represented for him the physical incarnation on earth of the spiritual love of God.

LOVE'S BODY

The moon and a batallion of stars came
and the sun, a lonely horseman, dissolved.
The moon lives beyond the night, beyond the day.
What eye can see him?
The sightless eye is a minaret.
How can it make out the bird on the minaret?
Sometimes the cloud in our heart is tight
because we love the moon.
Sometimes it falls away.
When you began to love your passion died 10
and though you had a thousand things to do,
you did nothing,
but since one day granite becomes a ruby,
it isn't lazy.
If in the market of love you see decapitated heads
hanging from butcher hooks,
don't run off. Come in. Look closely.
The dead are alive again.

CARING FOR MY LOVER

Friends, last night I carefully watched my love
sleeping by a spring circled with eglantine.[1]

The houris[2] of paradise stood around him,
   their hands cupped together
between a tulip field and jasmines.
Wind tugged softly in his hair.
His curls smelled of musk and ambergris.[3]
Wind turned mad and tore the hair right off
   his face
like a flaming oil lamp in a gale. 10
From the beginning of this dream I told myself
   go slowly, wait
for the break into consciousness. Don't breathe.

THE CLEAR BEAD AT THE CENTER

The clear bead at the center changes everything.
There are no edges to my loving now.
I've heard it said there's a window that opens
from one mind to another,
but if there's no wall, there's no need
for fitting the window, or the latch.

READING CRITICALLY

Explain, in your own words, the argument of "The Clear Bead at the Center."

---

[1]**eglantine:** sweetbrier, a fragrant pink climbing rose.
[2]**houris:** beautiful virgins provided in paradise to faithful Muslims.

[3]**musk and ambergris:** perfumes.

11 Centers of Culture
Court and City in the Larger World

THINKING AHEAD

How did poetry, art, and architecture of the Tang and Song dynasties reflect the values of the Chinese state?

What religions shaped Indian and Southeast Asian civilization?

Why did the Japanese capital move to Asuka, Nara, Heian-kyo, and Kamakura?

What shapes did civilization take in Africa?

Where did culture thrive in Mesoamerica?

Who were the Moche and the Inca?

Buddhism lies at the heart of culture in Asia during the period that in the West we call the Middle Ages. Between the first and third centuries CE, Buddhist missionaries from India had carried the religion over the Silk Road (see *Continuity & Change*, page 235, Chapter 7) into Southeast Asia and north into China and Korea. By 600 CE, Buddhism had reached all the way to Japan (Map **11.1**).

The first Chinese Buddhist monk to set out on the Silk Road in search of Buddhist scripture to translate into Chinese was Zhu Shixing [joo shih-hsing] of Hunan province. His journey dates from about 260 CE. At the same time, far away on the Silk Road, a resident of Dunhuang [doon-hwahng] began his life's work as a translator of Buddhist texts. One of the most telling manifestations of the religion's spread is the appearance everywhere of images of Buddha (Fig. **11.1**). In early Buddhist art, the Buddha was never shown in figural form. It was believed to be impossible to represent the Buddha, since he had already passed to nirvana. Instead, his presence was symbolized by such things as his footprints, the banyan tree (see Chapter 7), the wheel (representing *dharma*, or the Wheel of Law), or elephants (see Fig. 7.19).

By the fourth century, during the reign of the Gupta rulers in India, the Buddha was commonly represented in human form. Typically his head is oval, framed by a halo. Atop his head is a mound, symbolizing his spiritual wisdom, and on his forehead is a "third eye," symbolizing his spiritual vision. His demeanor is gentle, reposed, and meditative. His elongated ears refer to his royal origins, and his hands are set in one of several symbolic gestures, called **mudra**. At Bamiyan, on the Silk Road in present-day Afghanistan, two massive Buddhas, 175 and 120 feet tall, were carved into a cliff face in the third century CE. These figures were completely destroyed by the fundamentalist Islamic Taliban in 2001. However, many surviving replicas from the Silk Road era suggest that the hands of these Buddhas, which succumbed to natural forces long ago, were held up in the *Dharmachakra* mudra [dahr-mah-chahk-rah mood-rah], the teaching pose. This mudra symbolizes intellectual debate and is often associated with Buddhist centers of learning. Painted gold and studded with jewels, and surrounded by caves decorated with Buddhist wall paintings, these enormous images reflect the magnitude of Buddha's eternal form, at which the earthly body can barely hint.

◄ **Fig. 11.1 Colossal Buddha, Bamiyan, Afghanistan. ca. third century CE.** Stone, height 175′. This sculpture thus embodies the spread of ideas across Asia during the period of the European Middle Ages. Buddhism would spread, through China, to Japan by 600 CE. Indian Hinduism would, in turn, spread across Southeast Asia. This and another colossal sculpture of Buddha nearby were destroyed in February 2001 by the fundamentalist Islamic Taliban, who evidently felt that as false idols they were an affront to Mohammed.

HEAR MORE Listen to an audio file of your chapter at **www.myartslab.com**

Fig. 11.2 *Large Seated Buddha with Standing Bodhisattva,* **from cave 20, Ungang, Shaanxi, China, Northern Wei dynasty. ca. 460–70 CE.** Stone, height 44′. By the last half of the fifth century, when this sculpture was carved, the Chinese Wei rulers, who lived near the eastern end of the Silk Road, had become acquainted with the Indian Buddhist religion.

A seated Buddha from another cave, in Ungang, Shaanxi, China (Fig. **11.2**) exhibits the *Dhyana* mudra [duh-YAH-nuh mood-rah], a gesture of meditation and balance. The lower hand represents the physical world of illusion, the upper, nirvana. Together they symbolize the path to enlightenment. The bodhisattva—a person of near total enlightenment who has vowed to help others achieve it—standing next to him is exhibiting the *Abhaya* mudra [uh-BAH-yah mood-rah], a gesture of reassurance, blessing, and protection.

This chapter traces the development of five great centers of culture during the period that coincides with Europe's Middle Ages: China, India, Japan, Africa, and the Americas. It was a period of great cross-fertilization in Asia, as the example of Buddhism demonstrates. Chinese technological innovation was unrivaled in the world, and Chinese art and literature flourished as well. In India, Buddhists, threatened by invading Muslims from Persia, retreated into the Himalayan Mountains, even as the Hindu religion regained prominence and spread across Southeast Asia. In Japan, a feudal, military society vied with Buddhist teaching for pre-eminence. Across the African continent, sophisticated peoples rose to dominate their regions. Similarly, in the Americas, cultures in Mesoamerica and Peru achieved similar levels of complexity and sophistication without the kind of contact with other great cultures that marked

development in Asia. This chapter's overview of these cultures puts the Western Middle Ages in a broader perspective. During these years, the growing globalization of culture was just beginning to assert itself on the Silk Road. As we will see, the world's centers of culture were never again to be isolated from each other.

DEVELOPMENTS IN CHINA

After the fall of the Han dynasty in 220 CE (see Chapter 7), China entered an uneasy period. Warring factions vied for control of greater or lesser territories, governments rose to power and fell again, civil wars erupted, and tribes from Central Asia continuously invaded. During this time, Buddhism began to spread through the culture. The Confucian ethical system (see Chapter 7) seemed to have resulted in civil and cultural dysfunction. In contrast, Buddhism offered an ethical system based less on social and civic duty and more on each person's responsibility for his or her actions. Especially in its emphasis on meditation and enlightenment, Buddhism was compatible with Daoism (also discussed in Chapter 7). By the seventh century CE, Chinese leaders had learned to take the best from all three—Confucianism, Buddhism, and Daoism—and the culture was once again unified.

Map 11.1 The spread of
Buddhism, 500 BCE–
eleventh century CE.

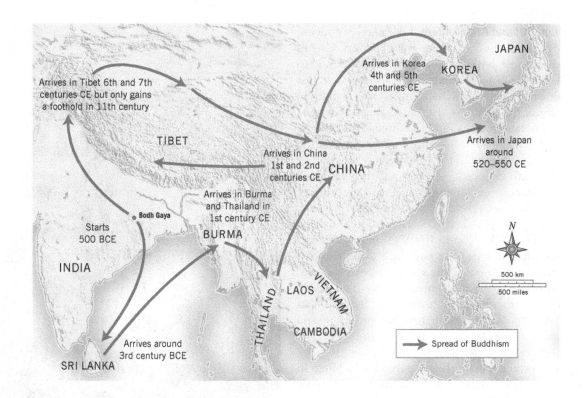

The Tang Dynasty in Chang'an, "The City of Enduring Peace" (618–907 CE)

In 618, the Tang dynasty reestablished a period of peace and prosperity in China that, except for a brief period of turmoil in the tenth century, would last for 660 years. The Tang dynasty the product of the largest and most organized government in the world in the last half of the first millennium. Its capital was the eastern end of the Silk Road, Chang'an, "City of Enduring Peace" (present-day Xi'an, which is about one-seventh the size of the Tang capital). The city had served as the capital of the Han dynasty as well, but as the Tang restored trade along the Silk Road, they created elaborate plans to restore the city, too. By the eighth century, its population was well over 1 million, living inside a walled perimeter nearly 26 miles in length and enclosing almost 42 square miles. Outside the walls lived perhaps as many as another million people. Among its inhabitants were Korean, Japanese, Jewish, and Christian populations, and its emperors maintained diplomatic relations with Persia.

Chang'an was the largest city in the world, laid out in a carefully conceived grid that dramatized the Tang commitment to social order and mirrored, they believed, the order of the cosmos (Fig. **11.3**). Each of the city's 108 blocks was itself a miniature walled city, with its own interior streets and gates that locked at night. Astronomers laid out the streets by aligning them with the shadow of the sun at noon and the position of the North Star at night, thereby orienting the city to the four cardinal directions. The imperial palace was located at the north end, facing south, thus symbolizing the emperor looking out over his city and,

by extension, his empire. Traditionally, Chinese emperors turned their backs to the north, from where, it was believed, evil spirits (not to mention Huns) came. Government buildings occupied the space in front of the imperial palace. A 500-foot-wide avenue led from these directly to the southern gate.

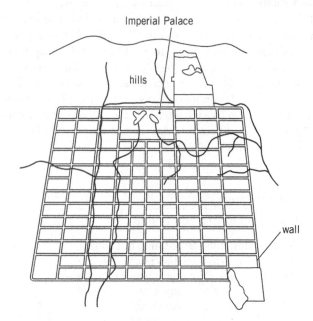

Fig. 11.3 Plan of the Tang capital of Chang'an, China. ca. 600. The location of the capital had been determined in Han times by the practice of *feng shui*, literally "wind and water," which assesses the primal energy that flows through a particular landscape. In this case, the hills to the north of the city and the streams running through it were understood to protect the precinct. *Feng shui* is still practiced to this day.

Tang Art and Architecture Like all great Chinese dynasties, the Tang were great builders. One of their most important accomplishments was to build the Grand Canal on the Yellow River, just downstream from Chang'an, to the Hangzhou Bay, at the mouth of the Yangzi River, thus uniting northern and southern China. The Chinese had developed iron- and steel-casting during the Han dynasty in the third century BCE, and by the sixth or seventh century CE, the technique had become commonplace, used to construct not only suspension bridges but also **pagodas**. (Equally sophisticated iron- and steel-casting would not develop in the West until the eighteenth century.) The pagoda is a multistoried structure of successively smaller, repeated stories, with projecting roofs at each story. The design derives from Han watchtowers and Indian stupas (see Fig. 7.17), which had become more and more towerlike in the sixth century CE. The pagoda was understood to offer the temple a certain protection. Of the few surviving buildings in China that predate 1400, the Great Wild Goose Pagoda at Ci'en [tseh-ehn] Temple in Chang'an is one of the most magnificent (Fig. **11.4**). It was built—entirely of masonry, not iron or steel—in 645 for the monk Xuanzang [shoo-ehn-tsahng], who taught and translated the materials he brought back with him from a 16-year pilgrimage to India. In its simplicity and symmetry, it represents the essence of Tang architecture.

Tang Poetry The Tang valued education above all. The imperial college at Chang'an trained all civil servants (women were excluded), and intellectual achievement was held in high esteem. Confucian and Daoist philosophy dominated the arts, particularly poetry, where two Tang poets, the Daoist Li Bai (701–62) and the Confucian Du Fu (712–70), achieved special prominence. Both relied for inspiration on *The Book of Songs* (see Chapter 7) but extended its range considerably. Their different temperaments are expressed in two short poems (**Reading 11.1a**):

Fig. 11.4 Great Wild Goose Pagoda at Ci'en Temple, Xi'an, Shanxi. Tang dynasty, first erected 645 CE. The Temple was rebuilt in the eighth century, when two stories were added to the original five.

Li Bai is famous for the self-examination in his poems, his colloquial speech, and his frank celebration of his own sensuality. We see these characteristics, too, in his poem, "Drinking Alone by Midnight," addressed to the moon (see **Reading 11.1** on page 397).

The poems of Du Fu are sometimes full of pathos. He wrote "Dreaming of Li Bai" when his friend was in exile in the south. The two belonged to a group called the Eight Immortals of the Wine Cup, famous for gathering in a garden of peach and plum trees on moonlit spring nights, where they drank wine to unleash their poetic temperaments. Like all the Immortals of the Wine Cup, Li Bai and Du Fu were equally expert in poetry, calligraphy, and painting—as well as statesmanship and philosophy. They present a model of what 500 years later the West would come to call the "Renaissance Man," the perfectly rounded individual, at home in any arena. They also embody the complex characteristics of Tang culture—at once strong and vigorous as well as passionate and sympathetic, simultaneously realistic and idealistic, intensely personal even while dedicated to public service.

READING 11.1a

Poems by Li Bai and Du Fu

"Summer Day in the Mountains" by Li Bai
Lazy today, I wave my white feather fan.
Then I strip naked in the green forest,
untie my hatband and hang it on a stone wall.
Pine wind sprinkles my bare head.

"Broken Lines" by Du Fu
River so blue the birds seem to whiten.
Flowers almost flame on the green mountainside.
Spring is dying yet again.
Will I ever go home?

The Song Dynasty and Hangzhou, "The City of Heaven" (960–1279 CE)

"The most splendid city in the world"—so the Venetian explorer Marco Polo (1254–1324) described Hangzhou, the capital of China's Southern Song dynasty (1127–1279) when Polo first visited it in 1274. Although Hangzhou was now the world's largest city—home to about 2 million people—no other Westerner had ever seen it. Marco Polo's father and uncle had a successful trading business with the East, and Polo lived with them in China for 17 years.

He wrote at length about his journey to Hangzhou in his *Travels*, first published in 1299. He claimed that he first visited the city as the ambassador of Kublai Khan. Northern Song China was already in Kublai Khan's hands, conquered in 1271, but he would not conquer the Southern Song on the Yangzi River until 1279. So when Polo first saw Hangzhou, it was still a Song city. Its lakes and parks were so beautiful, filled with floating teahouses from which passengers could view the palaces, pagodas, and temples that dotted the shore, that the city was known as Kinsai [KEEN-sa-hee], or the "City of Heaven." The entire city, some 200 square miles, was protected by a 30-foot-high wall, with even higher watchtowers rising above it. Inside the walls, a system of canals, which must have reminded Polo of his native Venice, was crisscrossed by some 12,000 bridges. These canals were fed by the most famous and probably most beautiful lake in China, the so-called West Lake, a popular resort. Beautiful women and pleasure-seekers gathered on houseboats on its waters, and writers and artists congregated in the tranquil libraries and monasteries on its shores.

"In this city," Polo would write, "there are 12 guilds of different crafts, and each guild has 12,000 houses in the occupation of its workmen. Each of these houses contains at least 12 men, while some contain 20 and some 40, including the apprentices who work under the masters. All these craftsmen had full employment since many other cities of the kingdom are supplied by this city." In fact, each guild was formed around people from the same province. In Hangzhou, tea and cloth merchants hailed from the eastern province of Anhwui, carpenters and cabinetmakers from the city of Ningbo, and so on. All came together to enjoy the benefits of trade and commerce in the capital. Foodstuffs, silks, spices, flowers, and books filled the markets (Reading 11.2):

READING 11.2

from Marco Polo, *Travels*

Those markets make a daily display of every kind of vegetable and fruit; and among the latter there are in particular certain pears of enormous size, weighing as much as ten pounds apiece, and pulp of which is white and fragrant like a confection, besides peaches in their season both yellow and white, of every delicate flavor. . . .

From the Ocean Sea also come daily supplies of fish in great quantity, brought 25 miles up river, and there is also great store of fish from the lake, which is the constant resort of fishermen, who have no other business. Their fish is of sundry kinds, changing with the season; and it is remarkably fat and tasty. Anyone who should see the supply of fish in the market would suppose it impossible that such a quantity could ever be sold; and yet in a few hours the whole shall be cleared away; so great is the number of inhabitants who are accustomed to delicate living.

These citizens "accustomed to delicate living" apparently lived remarkably well: "The houses of the citizens are well built and elaborately finished," Polo claims, "and the delight they take in decoration, in painting and in architecture, leads them to spend in this way sums of money that would astonish you." In other words, Hangzhou was a center of Asian culture that no one in the West, save Marco Polo, could even dream existed, in many ways exceeding anything the West had realized.

The Song dynasty enjoyed tremendous prosperity. It was the world's greatest producer of iron, and its flourishing merchant class traded not only along the Silk Road (see Chapter 7) but also throughout the Southeast Asian seas by boat. The government was increasingly controlled by this wealthy merchant class. Crucial to their rise was the development of movable type, which allowed the Song to begin printing books on paper. The printing press revolutionized the transmission of knowledge in China. (Gutenberg's movable-type printing press, which, in the West, we commonly credit with revolutionizing the transmission of knowledge, was 400 years in the future.) The children of the thriving merchant class attended public, private, and religious schools, where they could study the newly printed books—including *The Book of Songs*, required reading for all Chinese civil servants, and various encyclopedias—as they prepared for government examinations. This new class of highly educated government officials restored Confucianism to dominance and strengthened it with relevant additions from Daoism and Buddhism. Buddhism was officially rejected as foreign, but its explanation of the universe provided an invaluable metaphysical element to Confucianism. As a result, these new officials brought to government a deep belief, based on neo-Confucian teaching, that the well-run society mirrored the unchanging moral order of the cosmos.

Chan Buddhism Especially important to artists and literati in the Song era was the development of Chan Buddhism. "Chan" (better known in the West as "Zen," as it is pronounced in Japanese) derives from the Sanskrit word *dhyana*, meaning "meditation." Like Daoism, Chan Buddhism teaches that one can find happiness by achieving harmony with nature. By using yoga techniques and sitting meditation, the Chan Buddhist strives for oneness with the Dao ("the Way") and the Confucian *li*, the principle or inner structure of nature. The Chan Buddhists thought that the traditional scriptures, rituals, and monastic rules of classical Buddhism were essentially beside the point, because Buddha's spirit was innate in everyone, waiting to be discovered through meditation. Thus, the poets and artists who practiced Chan Buddhism considered themselves instruments through which the spirit of nature expressed itself.

Song Painting This essential "rightness" of the Song world is manifested especially in Chinese painting of the Song era, when landscape painting became the principal and most esteemed means of personal and philosophic expression in the arts. The landscape was believed to embody the underlying principle behind all things, made manifest in the world through its material presence. Closely akin to the spiritual quest of the Dao, the task of the artist was to reveal the unifying principle of the natural world, the eternal essence of mountain, waterfall, pine tree, rock, reeds, clouds, and sky. Human figures are dwarfed by the landscape, insignificant in the face of nature. Over and over again, the paintings of the period rise from foreground valleys to high mountaintops, the eye following paths, cascading waterfalls, rocky crags, and tall pines pointing ever higher in imitation of "the Way," the path by which one leaves behind the human world and attains the great unifying principle (see *Closer Look*, pages 366–367).

The Yuan Dynasty (1279–1368)

Throughout the period known as the medieval era in the West, China was threatened from the north by nomadic tribes. The Northern Song capital of Bianjing [beehn-geeng] had fallen to tribes from Manchuria in 1126, forcing the Song to retreat south to Hangzhou. Finally, the Song dynasty succumbed to the Mongol leader Kublai Khan in 1279. Kublai Khan ruled from a new capital at present-day Beijing, transforming it into a walled city constructed on a grid plan and extending the Grand Canal to provision the city.

Calling themselves the Yuan dynasty, the Mongols under Kublai Khan and his descendants controlled the highest posts in the government, but they depended on Chinese officials to collect taxes and maintain order. The Chinese understood the need to cooperate with the Mongols, but they viewed the Mongols as foreigners occupying their homeland. (Remember, foreigners were banned from entering the Forbidden City.)

Not long after Marco Polo's arrival in China, the scholar-painters of the Chinese court, unwilling to serve under foreign domination, were retreating from public life. But while in exile, they created an art symbolic of their resistance. Paintings of bamboo, for instance, abound, because bamboo is a plant that might bend, like the Chinese themselves, but never break. Painted in 1306, Cheng Sixiao's [chehng-sih-she-how] *Ink Orchids* (Fig. **11.5**),

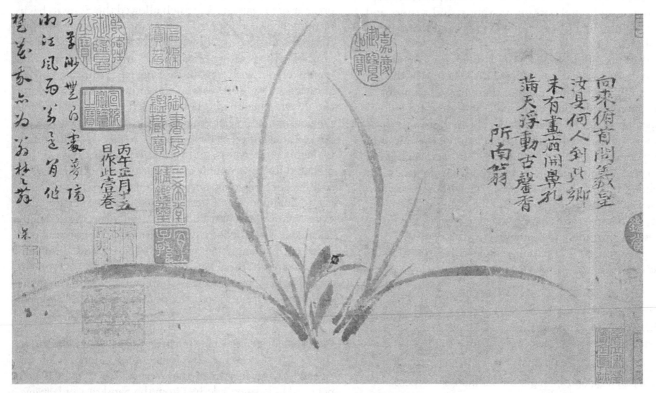

Fig. 11.5 Cheng Sixiao, *Ink Orchids*. Yuan dynasty, 1306. Ink on paper, 10 1/8" × 16 3/4". Municipal Museum of Fine Art, Osaka, Japan. Artists of the Yuan dynasty such as Cheng Sixiao painted for their fellow artists and friends, not for the public. Thus, Cheng Sixiao could feel comfortable describing his political intentions in the text accompanying this painting.

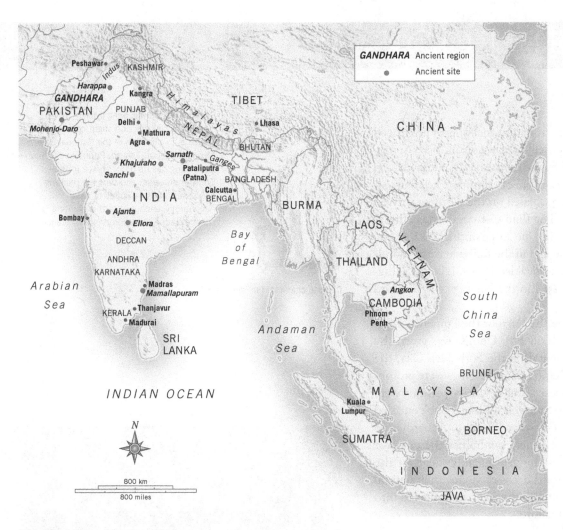

Map 11.2 India and Southeast Asia.

according to its inscription, is meant to protest the "theft of Chinese soil by the invaders." Orchids, in fact, can live without soil, in rocks or in trees, sustained by the moisture in the air around them, even as Sixiao the painter thrives. The Mongols were finally overthrown in 1368, when Zhu Yuanzhang (r. 1368–98) drove the last Yuan emperor north into the Gobi desert and declared himself first emperor of the new Ming dynasty. China was once again ruled by the Chinese.

INDIAN AND SOUTHEAST ASIAN CIVILIZATIONS

By 1200, Indian civilization was among the world's oldest, and it asserted broad influence over all of Southeast Asia (Map **11.2**). Its history during the centuries before and after 1200 was largely determined by competing religious forces, especially Buddhism, Islam, and Hinduism. Buddhism,

which flourished in India from about 100 to 600 CE, had steadily waned in influence. It was further diminished when Muslim invaders entered northern India in the eleventh and twelfth centuries, destroying centers of worship in their path. Many of the Buddhist monks fled north into Nepal and across the Himalayas into Tibet or eastward into present-day Myanmar (formerly Burma). The Muslim invaders, who established their capital at Delhi, brought with them new forms of art and architecture rooted in Persian court traditions. Meanwhile, Hinduism became increasingly popular, and it gradually asserted itself as the dominant Indian religion. Well into the fifteenth and sixteenth centuries, India was ruled by Hindu dynasties, especially in the south, where the culture was relatively isolated from the influence of the Delhi sultans. Hinduism spread throughout Southeast Asia, where Cambodian monarchs constructed magnificent temples inspired by Indian prototypes.

CLOSER LOOK

The human presence in nature goes almost unnoticed in Guo Xi's [gwoh hsee] hanging scroll, *Early Spring*. Nature, embodied by the mountain, is all-embracing, a powerful and imposing symbol of eternity. The composition of Guo Xi's painting is based on the Chinese written character for mountain. The fluid gestures of the calligrapher's hand are mirrored in Guo Xi's painting, both in the organization of the whole and in the individual brush-and-ink strokes that render this ideal landscape. Like the calligrapher, Guo Xi is interested in the balance, rhythm, and movement of his line.

A court painter during the reign of the Emperor Shenzong [shehn-tsohng] (r. 1068–85), Guo Xi was given the task of painting all the murals in the Forbidden City, the imperial compound in Beijing that foreigners were prohibited from entering. His ideas about landscape painting were recorded by his son, Guo Si [gwoh seh], in a book entitled *The Lofty Message of the Forests and Streams*. According to this book, the central peak here symbolizes the emperor himself and its tall pines the gentlemanly ideals of the court. Around the emperor the masses assume their natural place, as around this mountain the trees and hills fall into the order and rhythms of nature.

Guo Xi, *Early Spring*. Song dynasty, 1072. Hanging scroll, ink and slight color on silk, length 5′. Collection of the National Palace Museum, Taipei, Taiwan, Republic of China. Everything has its proper place in the Chinese universe, and thus the painting possesses multiple points of view. Accordingly, each part of this painting is constructed at the appropriate "distance."

Chinese character for "mountain."

Something to Think About . . .

In the West, landscape painting did not become a popular genre until the eighteenth century. What differences in attitude between East and West during the Middle Ages might account for this?

Barely noticeable, two figures get out of their boat at the bottom left, and another figure stands on the shoreline at the right. Two waterfalls cascade down the hillside behind this second figure, and a small village can be seen nestled on the mountainside above the falls.

**SEE MORE** For a Closer Look at Guo Xi's *Early Spring*, go to **www.myartslab.com**

Guo Xi's *Early Spring*

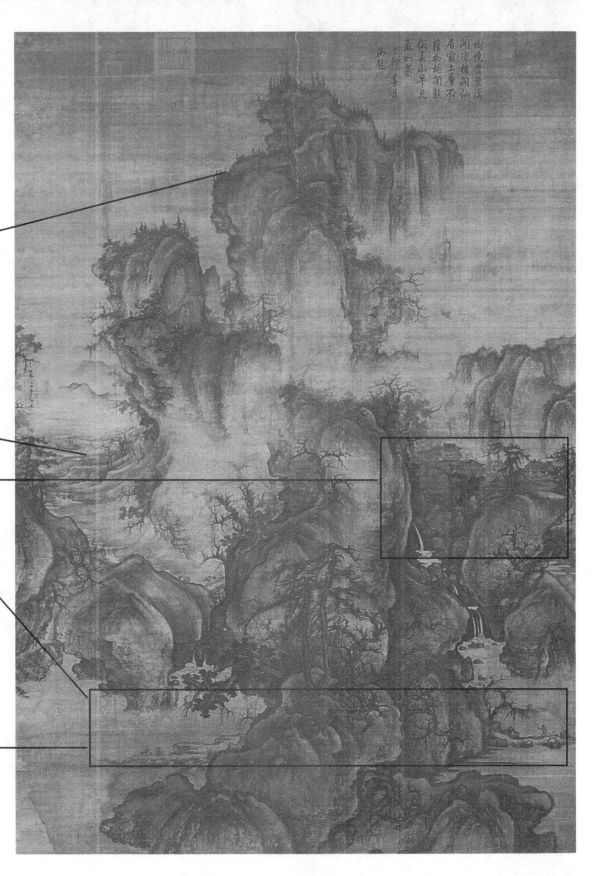

The central mountain is painted so that we gaze up to it in the "high distance," as we would gaze up at the emperor.

On the left side of the painting, we gaze far off into a "level distance," creating a sense of limitless, eternal space.

In the humbling "deep distance" of the foreground, far below our point of view, we see images that reflect our own insignificance in nature.

Fig. 11.6 *Manjushri, thangka* **from Central Tibet. Thirteenth century.** Gouache on cotton, height 22″.
Private collection. At the base of the *thangka* are three images of Manjushri wielding swords with four arms,
representing his ability to cut through ignorance.

Fig. 11.7 Jungle filled with ancient temples and pagodas, Bagan, Myanmar (formerly Burma).
1057–1287. The temple complex at Bagan covers an area of approximately 16 square miles. © Keren Su/Corbis. All Rights Reserved.

Buddhist Art and Architecture

High in the isolated valleys of the Himalayas in Nepal and Tibet, Buddhist monks adapted Buddhism to the native Tibetan mystical religion known as Bon [bohn]. The local religious leaders, known as *lamas* (meaning "none superior"), considered themselves the reincarnation of earlier deceased lamas and Buddhist bodhisattvas. The chief lama, the Dalai (meaning "ocean"), was believed to be the reincarnation of the bodhisattva Avalokiteshvara [avah-lo-kee-TESH-varah], the embodiment of compassion in this new form of Buddhism. Enlightenment, not simply nirvana, is the goal of this version of Buddhism, generally known as Mahayana, and the vow of every bodhisattva is to help others achieve enlightenment before they themselves cross over into paradise.

Among the artistic expressions of this faith were rolled-up cloth paintings, known as *thangkas* [TAHN-kas]. As monks traveled from one monastery to another, they would unroll *thangkas* as aids to instruction. Painted on the *thangkas* were images representing Buddhist figures of authority, including lamas, bodhisattvas, and the Buddha himself, which, the Tibetans believed, were manifest in their images. The *thangka* reproduced here (Fig. **11.6**) represents Manjushri [MAHN-joo-shree], a bodhisattva associated with a great historical teacher, thus symbolizing wisdom.

In Myanmar, Anawratha [eh-nuh-YAH-thah], the first king of the Bagan Empire (r. 1044–1077), was a devout Buddhist. His capital at Bagan became a center of Buddhist learning, attracting monks from across Southeast Asia, especially from India, as Muslims gained control of the subcontinent. There he built the Shwesandaw Paya, or "Sunset Temple," in 1057 (visible at the top left of Fig. **11.7**), a five-terraced structure topped by a circular stupa that, legend has it, contains the hairs of Buddha. For the next two centuries, until Bagan was overrun by the army of Kublai Khan in 1287, Anawratha's heirs built more than 13,000 temples, pagodas, and other religious structures, of which some 2,200 temples remain standing.

Hindu Art and Architecture

As we saw in Chapter 7, Hindu religion and art are infused with a deep respect for sexuality, evident even in the architecture. The Kandarya [KAHN-dahr-yah] Mahadeva temple (Fig. **11.8**) at Khajuraho, the capital of the Chandella [chan-deh-lah] dynasty, represents the epitome of northern Indian Hindu architecture. Its rising towers are meant to suggest the peaks of the Himalayas, home of the Hindu gods, and this analogy would have been even clearer when the temple was painted in its original white gesso. The plan (Fig. **11.9**) is a double cross, with arms extending north and south from the east–west axis. At the first crossing is the *mandapa* [MAHN-dah-pah], the columned assembly hall. At the second crossing is the *garbhagriha* [GARB-hah-gree-hah], or "womb chamber," the symbolic sacred cavern at the heart of the sacred mountain/temple. Here rests the cult image of the Brahman, in this case the *lingam*, or symbol of male sexuality, of Shiva, the first, or formless emanation of the Brahman. (Recall from Chapter 7 that the Brahman is the creator and the universal soul.) Although it is actually almost completely dark, the *garbhagriha* is considered by Hindu worshippers to be filled with the pure light of the Brahman. The towers of the temple rise from east to west, as if gathering around the central tower, known as the *shikara* [SHEE-kah-rah], that rises to a height of over 100 feet above the *garbhagriha*. As the height increases, the temple seems to gather the energy of the Hindu religion to a single rising point, soaring with the spirit of the worshipper.

By the twelfth century, Hinduism had spread from India southeast into present-day Cambodia, where Hindu art achieved a monumental imperial grandeur. In Cambodia, the Khmer monarchy established its capital at Angkor, about 150 miles northwest of present-day Phnom Penh. Covering about 70 square miles, the city was crossed by broad avenues and canals and filled with royal palaces and temples. The largest of these temples, Angkor Wat (Fig. **11.10**), was created by Suryavarman [suhr-YAH-vahr-mahn] II (r. 1113–ca. 1150). Five central towers, representing the five peaks of Mount Meru, the center of the Hindu cosmos, rise above a moat surrounding the complex. The approach to the galleries at the towers' base is from the west, crossing a long bridge

Fig. 11.8 Kandarya Mahadeva temple, Khajuraho, Madhya Pradesh, India. Chandella dynasty, ca. 1025–50. The temple's formal design, like that of all Hindu temples, was prescribed in the *shastras*, a body of ancient Hindu writing that sets out the principles of poetry, music, dance, and the other arts. By the second millennium, most temples followed the *shastras* only loosely, freely elaborating on the basic plan.

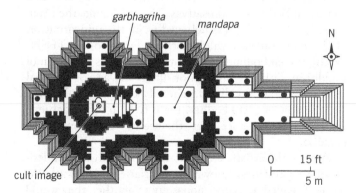

Fig. 11.9 Plan of Kandarya Mahadeva temple, Khajurabo, India. ca. 1025–50. The temple's main features are the *garbhagriha*, the cult image, and the *mandapa*.

Fig. 11.10 Angkor Wat, Cambodia. Early twelfth century. The entire complex was constructed in the short span of about 30 years.

over the moat, which symbolizes the oceans surrounding the known world. On June 21, the summer solstice and the beginning of the Cambodian solar year, a visitor to the temple arriving through the western gate would see the sun rise directly over the central tower. In this way, the symbolic evocation of the cosmos, so fundamental to Hindu temple architecture, is further elaborated in astronomical terms.

There are literally miles of relief sculptures decorating the walls of Angkor Wat, including images of the *apsaras*, mythological goddesses whose dances were used by the gods to seduce mortals, and *devatas*, guardian spirits who stand individually or in groups with an air of refined elegance (Fig. **11.11**). They are uniformly bare-breasted and wear both a crown and a pleated *sampot* (a wrapped skirt), rolled at the top below the belly to open like a flower. The ubiquity of such figures underscores the important role of goddess worship in Hindu culture (see Chapter 7).

Hindu artists also mastered the art of bronze-casting. In the Tamil Nadu [TA-mul NAH-doo] region of southern India, artists began making large bronze editions of Shiva in his manifestation as Shiva Nataraja [nah-tuh-RAH-juh], Lord of the Dance, as early as the tenth and eleventh centuries. Such images were commissioned as icons for the region's many temples. Since Shiva embodies the rhythms of the universe, he is also a great dancer. All the gods were present when Shiva first danced, and they begged him to dance again. Shiva promised to do so in the hearts of his devotees as well as in a sacred grove in Tamil Nadu itself.

Fig. 11.11 *Devata*, Angkor Wat, Cambodia. Early twelfth century. There are over 2,000 devatas at Angkor Wat.

Fig. 11.12 *Shiva Nataraja, Lord of the Dance,* from Southern India. Eleventh century CE. Copper, height 43 ¹/₈″. © The Cleveland Museum of Art. Purchase from the J. H. Wade Fund, 1930.331. In his back left hand, Shiva carries fire, representing the destructive energy of his dance at the end of each cosmic age, which cleanses sins and removes illusion from the world. In his back right hand, he holds an hourglass-shaped drum, which represents the rhythmic sound of his dance as he ceaselessly re-creates the universe.

As he dances, he is framed in a circle of fire, symbolic of both creation and destruction, the endless cycle of birth, death, and reincarnation (Fig. **11.12**).

The Rise of Court Life in Japan

Although Buddhism may have been known in Japan earlier, it is commonly believed that it arrived in the Yamato period (see Chapter 1) from Korea and China. According to the *Chronicles of Japan*, a statue of Buddha and a collection of sacred Buddhist texts were given to Japanese rulers by the king of the Baekje region of Korea in 552. Chinese calligraphy was already the basis of the Japanese written language, and to some, Buddhism seemed equally amenable to Japanese adaptation. But Buddhism was by no means welcomed by all. Of the three rival clans then most powerful in Yamato Japan—the Soga, Mononobe, and Nakatomi, each tied to the imperial family through marriage to the emperor—both the Mononobe, who were in charge of the emperor's military, and the Nakatomi, in charge of Shinto ritual, opposed the introduction of Buddhism into the country. But the Soga, managers of imperial estates who were in constant contact with the Koreans and Chinese, were deeply attracted to the religion, and the Yamato emperor allowed them to practiced it within their own clan. As the Soga gained more and more power over the last decades of the sixth century, they eventually defeated the Mononobe and Nakatomi in a civil war, and the head of the Soga clan, Umako, installed his 39-year-old daughter, Suiko, as empress and declared her 29-year-old nephew, Shotoku [SHOH-toh-koo] (r. 593–622), her regent and crown prince. The capital was moved inland from Osaka on the coast to the Soga homeland in the Asuka valley in the central Yamato plain.

Shotoku, whose name means "Wise and Virtuous," emphasized the importance of the Chinese model of civil administration, and introduced Confucianism to the court. When he built a new palace at Ikaruga [ee-KAH-roo-gah], in the central Asuka plain, he constructed a Buddhist temple next to it. Others were built during his administration, and over 1,300 Buddhist monks and nuns were ordained. But Buddhism was in fact practiced only by a small number of aristocracy around the Asuka capital.

The Coming of the Fujiwara

In 645, the Nakatomi, who had been forced to tolerate Buddhism even as they continued to maintain Shinto ritual at court, rebelled, executing the Soga clan. Anyone else who showed resistance to their rule was executed as well. Nakatomi no Kamatari (614–669) was awarded the surname of Fujiwara by Emperor Tenji for his part in crushing the Soga and placing Tenji on the throne. The Fujiwara clan, thus directly descended from the Nakatomi, would become the greatest noble clan of classical Japan, ruling it for 500 years.

In 708, the Fujiwara oversaw the construction of a new capital at Hojeikyo, commonly called Nara after its location in the Nara plain, some 15 miles to the northwest of Asuka (see Map **11.3**). It was laid out according to the principles of Chinese city planning as a walled city on the model of Chang-an (see Fig. 11.3), 2.7 miles from east to west and about 3.1 miles from north to south, with a broad avenue running north and south in its center culminating at the Heijo Palace. And although the Nakatomi/Fujiwara clan had despised the Buddhist-leaning Soga the century before, at Nara, they officially accepted Buddhism as the state religion. Magnificent temples and monasteries were constructed, including what would remain, for a thousand years, the largest wooden structure in the world, the Todaiji temple (Fig. **11.13**). It houses a giant bronze, known as the Great Buddha, over 49 feet high and weighing approximately 380 tons. According to ancient records, as many as 2.6 million people were required to aid in its construction, although that number represents approximately half of Japan's population at the time and is probably a

Map 11.3 Japan. Isolated from the Asian mainland, Japan was both slow to develop and susceptible to the influence of the more advanced cultures once it became aware of them.

gross exaggeration. The original temple was twice destroyed by warring factions, in 1180 and again in 1567. The current Buddha is in fact a 1691 reconstruction of the original, and the Todaiji temple is itself a reconstruction of 1709. The restored temple is considerably smaller than the original, approximately two-thirds its size, and now stands 188 feet in width and 156 feet in height.

Fig. 11.13 Todaiji Temple, Nara, Japan. 752. The temple's sweeping horned roof is typical of Japanese architecture

The Heian Period: Courtly Refinement

The acceptance of Buddhism by the Fujiwara clan at Nara suggests that the conflict between the clans in the earlier Yamato period was probably as much about power as it was religion. But it is also true that by the seventh century Buddhist doctrine and Shinto had begun to influence each other. The Great Buddha at Nara became identified with the Shinto goddess Amaterasu (see Chapter 1), and Buddhist ceremonies were incorporated into Shinto court ritual. But between 784 and 794, the capital of Japan was moved to Heian-kyo—modern-day Kyoto—which quickly became the most densely populated city in the world. According to records, the move occurred because the secular court needed to distance itself from the religious influence of the Buddhist monks at Nara. Indeed, one of these monks had risen to power as the lover of the Empress Koken (r. 749–59, 765–70).

Like Nara, Heian-kyo was modeled on Chang'an, the capital of the Tang dynasty, and, also as at Nara, the ordered grid of its streets was a conscious bow to Chinese philosophy and its reflection in the workings of government. Between the late eleventh and the middle of the twelfth century at Heian-kyo, scholars estimate that the royal family regularly dedicated new Shinto shrines and new Buddhist temples.

Life of the Nobility At Heian-kyo, the arts flourished in an atmosphere of elegance and refinement. The nobility numbered around 100,000, and they lived in residential complexes that extended across several acres with multiple single-story pavilions and secondary halls tied together by covered walkways. The entire complex usually encircled a garden with a pond and small streams crossed by bridges, the whole surrounded by an earthen wall (Fig. 11.14). As in traditional Shinto shrines, the roofs of the complex were made of cypress-bark shingles. This style of architecture is known as *shinden-zukuri* [SHEEN-dehn SOO-koo-ree], after its main hall, or *shinden*, and *zukuri*, "style." Following Chinese tradition, it was oriented to the south. It was large enough to accommodate the nobleman's several wives—limited polygamy was practiced by the high aristocracy, permitting a nobleman to have one or two lesser wives who could bear him fully recognized children. Theoretically at least, these lesser wives enjoyed less prestige in the court. Behind the *shinden*, in a separate hall to the north, lived the main wife, known as the *kita no kata*, "the person to the north." Secondary wives lived in pavilions to the east and west. Each hall could open into the gardens by means of latticed shutters that could be raised to take advantage of good weather.

Life in the Heian court was determined by gender. Men lived public lives: women much more private ones. In fact, women were rarely visible. An aristocratic woman might make a public excursion to a Buddhist temple, but she would remain out of public view. She might receive a male visitor, but the two would converse through a portable set of curtain panels. Women were, however, highly educated, and they were expected to contribute to the aesthetic of the Heian court. They were judged on their looks—although it is striking to note that there are almost no detailed descriptions of a woman's face or body in Heian writing—on the arrangement of their many layers of silk robes, on their perfumes, on the beauty of their calligraphy, and on their ability to compose poetry at a moment's notice. As opposed to a man's identity, which was regularly displayed in public settings, a woman's identity was defined particularly by her speech, her correspondence, and her poetry and other writings.

Literature and Calligraphy Although many court gatherings took place for the purpose of poetry competitions, in which both men and women participated, poems were generally composed for a single recipient—a friend or lover—and a reply was expected. In her *Diaries*—or *Nikki* in Japanese—

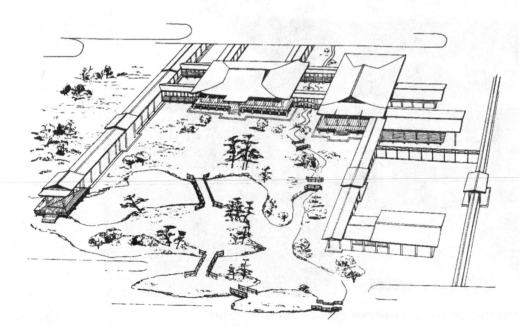

Fig. 11.14 Reconstruction drawing of a *shinden-zukuri* mansion. No original mansions of the nobility survive in present-day Kyoto. Drawings such as this one are based on the ample literary description of these elaborate residences, as well as their representation in illustrated scrolls.

Murasaki Shikibu (973/8–aft. 1014), one of the most accomplished women of the Heian court, a lady-in-waiting to the Empress Shoshi [SHOH-shee] (988–1074), describes just such an exchange (**Reading 11.3**):

READING 11.3

from Murasaki Shikibu, _Diaries_

I can see the garden from my room beside the entrance to the gallery. The air is misty, the dew is still on the leaves. The Lord Prime Minister is walking there; he orders his men to cleanse the brook. He breaks off a stalk of omenaishi[1] [oh-MEH-nah-ee-shee], which is in full bloom by the south end of the bridge. He peeps in over my screen! His noble appearance embarrasses us, and I am ashamed of my morning face.[2] He says, "Your poem on this! If you delay so much the fun is gone!" and I seize the chance to run away to the writing-box, hiding my face:

> Flower-maiden in bloom—
> Even more beautiful for the bright dew,
> Which is partial, and never favors me.

"So prompt!" said he, smiling, and ordered a writing-box to be brought [for himself].
His answer:

> The silver dew is never partial.
> From her heart
> The flower-maiden's beauty.

[1]**omenaishi:** a flowering plant.
[2]**morning face:** a face without powder or makeup.

Something of the flavor of court life is captured in this brief passage, in the private space of the gentlewoman's world, her relation to the gentlemen of the court, the attention of the two poets to natural beauty, and the expression of that beauty as a means of capturing personal feeling.

Diaries, or _nikki_, comprised an important literary form that tell us much about court life in the Heian period. Murasaki's poems—indeed her entire text—are written in a new, purely Japanese writing system, known as **_hiragana_** [HEER-ah-gah-nah]. Beginning in the early ninth century, _hiragana_ gradually replaced the use of Chinese characters and enabled writers to spell out the Japanese language phonetically. The university curriculum remained based on Chinese classics and history, and the formal workings of state and government still required the use of Chinese. Chinese was the language of the world of men. Since the Heian court strongly discouraged displays of education in Chinese by women, they were taught the _hiragana_ script, even though many court women actually knew Chinese quite well.

The popularity of _hiragana_, even among men, who recognized its convenience, encouraged the development of new Japanese forms of poetry, especially the **_waka_** [WAH-kah] (literally the "poetry of Wa," or Japan). A _waka_ consists of 31 syllables in 5 lines on a theme drawn from nature and the changing of seasons. Here is a _waka_ by one of the great poets of the Heian period, Ki no Tomonori [KEE noh TOH-moh-noh-ree] (act. 850–904) (**Reading 11.4**):

READING 11.4

Ki no Tomonori, "This Perfectly Still"

This perfectly still
Spring day bathed in the soft light
From the spread-out sky.
Why do the cherry blossoms
So restlessly scatter down?

The tension here, between the calm of the day and the restlessness of the cherry blossoms, is meant to mirror a similar tension in the poet's mind, suggesting a certain sense of anticipation or premonition. _Waka_ serves as a model for other Japanese poetic forms, particularly the famous **haiku**, the 3-line, 17-syllable form that developed out of the first three lines of the _waka_.

Sei Shonagon's _Pillow Book_ Aside from poetry and diaries, the women of the Japanese court also created a new literary form, the _zuihitsu_ [ZU-EE-heet-soo] (literally, "by the line of the brush"), random notes or occasional writings. The first of these was the _Pillow Book_ by Sei Shonagon [SAY SHOH-nah-gohn] (ca. 965–aft. 1000), lady-in-waiting to the imperial consort Teishi [TAY-shee] (970–1001) and head of a literary salon that openly competed against that of Murasaki Shikibu, a rivalry that helped to inspire the literary innovation of the period. The clarity of Sei Shonagon's observation in the _Pillow Book_ is captured in her short list of "Elegant Things" (**Reading 11.5a**):

READING 11.5a

from Sei Shonagon, _Pillow Book_, "Elegant Things"

A white coat worn over a violet waistcoat.
Duck eggs.
Shaved-ice mixed with liana syrup[1] and put in a new
 silver bowl.
A rosary[2] of rock crystal.
Wisteria blossoms. Plum blossoms covered with snow.
A pretty child eating strawberries.

[1]**liana [LEE-ah-nah] syrup:** a light, sweet syrup made from fruit of a climbing vine.
[2]**rosary:** not the series of prayers practiced by Roman Catholics, but rather a miniature sculpture of a rose garden made of rock crystal.

Another, longer list, entitled "Hateful Things" (see **Reading 11.5** on pages 398–399), gives the reader a remarkable overview of daily life in the Heian court. Sei Shonagon looks at the entirety of her world, from its insects to the palace dog.

The First Novel: *The Tale of Genji* Murasaki Shikibu, whose *Diaries* we discussed previously, is more famous as the author of a long book of prose and poetry (over 1,000 pages in English translation), including many exchanges of poetry of the type recorded in her *Diaries*. Many consider it the world's first novel—certainly no fiction in the Western world matches its scope until the eighteenth century. Called *The Tale of Genji*, it tells the story of Genji, an imperial prince, born to the favorite wife of the emperor, though she is too low in rank for her son to be an heir to the throne. Much of the action takes place in the homes and gardens of Heian-kyo, and besides being a moving romantic story covering 75 years of the hero's life, from his birth to his death, the novel presents us with a vivid picture of life in Japanese society at the turn of the millennium. As opposed to the *Diaries*, the stories related in *The Tale of the Genji* are, of course, fiction, but, as Genji says at one point in the *Tale*: "Among these lies there certainly are some plausible touching scenes, convincingly told; and yes, we know they are fictions, but even so we are moved."

Soon after it was written, *The Tale of Genji* was illustrated in a handscroll that was an ensemble of more than 100 excerpts from the *Tale*, written in elegant calligraphy on decorative paper probably at court. The paintings, of which only 20 of the original 100 survive, have been attributed to Takayoshi (Fig. **11.15**). Most are focused on intimate episodes of high narrative tension, and of the 20 paintings that survive, 17 depict events happening either in the outer corridor or on the veranda or outer corridor of a *shinden*.

As the scroll was unwound, the viewer would have first seen the right side of Fig. 11.15, the courtyard (now brown but originally silver), and then, at a sharp angle, the veranda and curtain wall of a house in which a deeply moving scene is unfolding in the outer corridor. As a young man, Genji had fallen in love with his father's youngest wife, Fujitsubo [foo-JEE-tsoo-boh], and fathered a son by her. Genji's own father, the emperor, acknowledged the child as his own, and the boy eventually became emperor himself. Genji came to understand the human consequences of his youthful actions only when his own youngest wife bore a son by another man and Genji was forced to acknowledge the child as his own, just as his father had accepted Genji's son. Depicted here is the moment of Genji's acceptance of his wife's son.

The scene is depicted from an aerial perspective just above the roof, which has been "blown off" (a technique known as *fukinaki yatai*) in order to provide a view of the interior. The result is a highly chaotic composition in which geometrical lines of the architecture play off against the figures and their clothing. Genji holds the child in his arms. Beside him to the right, half hidden by the curtains, bowls of food are placed for the ritual celebration. Ladies-in-waiting, one dressed in black, sit below, and at the extreme upper left, the child's mother is indicated by a heap of fabric. Genji knows that the attendants understand that he is not the child's father, and yet he fully understands his duty.

Although Genji is the hero of the book, Murasaki Shikibu gives the women of the Heian court full treatment, chief among them the tellingly named Murasaki, whose own life, from childhood to death, is fully narrated. She is Genji's greatest love, and she receives his lavish attentions. And yet, given the polygamous nature of Japanese society, she suffers much. She is unable to bear Genji a child, and Genji must turn elsewhere for an heir. Likewise, her social status is not high enough to qualify her as his principal wife. Thus, despite her wit and intelligence, her beauty and charm, she is condemned to second-class status.

Fig. 11.15 Attributed to Takayoshi. Illustration to the Azumaya chapter of *The Tale of Genji* by Murasaki Shikibu. Late Heian period, twelfth century. Handscroll, ink and color on paper, height 8 ¹/₂″. Tokugawa Art Museum, Nagoya, Japan. Of the original illustrations of *The Tale of Genji*, only 20 pictures survive.

Yamato-e and Omna-e Painting The *Genji* scroll has often been described as an example of *yamato-e* [yah-MAH-toh ay] painting, a term coined during the Heian period to distinguish between Japanese and Chinese (*kara-e*) [KAH-rah ay] painting styles. This distinction announces a movement away from traditional Chinese styles to one characterized by Japanese literary themes, native subject matter, and landscapes evocative of traditional poetry. But recently scholars have suggested that *yamato-e* refers more specifically to large-scale landscape paintings generally executed on walls, sliding doors, and folding screens, and that the *Genji* illustrations are, rather, examples of *omna-e* paintings, "women's pictures." *Omna-e* pictures are not necessarily works done exclusively by women, but are rather pictures appropriate to the space of women's lives at court. By the time of the Genji scrolls, *omna-e* paintings were executed by professional artisans at court.

The Kamakura Period (ca. 1185–1392): Samurai and Shogunate

During the Heian period, the emperors had increasingly relied on regional warrior clans—**samurai** (literally, "those who serve")—to exercise military control, especially in the countryside. Over time these clans became more and more powerful, until, by 1100, they had begun to emerge as a major force in Japanese military and political life, inaugurating the Kamakura Period, which takes its name from the capital city of the most prominent of these clans, the Minamoto. Their newfound power in many ways represented a resurgence of the familial clan-based system of authority that had been deeply engrained in Japanese society since at least the time of the Yamato emperors, but almost inevitably, their rise also resulted, as it had among the Yamato clans, in intense rivalry and, eventually, warfare.

Pure Land Buddhist Art As war spread across the country, many Japanese felt that it announced the coming of *Mappo*, the so-called Third Age of Buddha, often translated as the "Age of Dharma Decline." Prophesied to begin 2,000 years after the death of Sakyamuni Buddha, it would last, so it was believed, for 10,000 years. During this period no one would be able to attain enlightenment and society would descend into a condition of degeneracy and corruption. Pure Land Buddhism seemed to offer a way out. Pure Land Buddhism had originated in the late sixth century in China as a particular form of Mahayana Buddhism. The Mahayana Buddhists believed the compassion for all beings is the foundation of faith and that not nirvana but buddhahood is one's ultimate goal. They recognized Buddhas other than Sakyamuni, among them Amitabha Buddha, the Buddha of Infinite Light and Life who dwells in a paradise known as the Western Pure Land. This Pure Land Buddhism had been introduced to Japan as early as the seventh century, the Chinese Amitabha Buddha becoming Buddha Amida. Particularly attractive to the Japanese was the Pure Land belief that by chanting *Namu Amida Butsu* [nah-moo ah-MEE-dah boots(u)] ("Hail to the Buddha Amida"), the faithful would be reborn into the Western Pure Land paradise, where the enlightenment impossible to achieve in the world might finally be attained.

One of the early practitioners of the Pure Land chant was the monk Kuya [koo-yah] (903–972), who traveled on foot around the countryside chanting and doing charitable deeds. His enduring popularity is underscored by the fact that more than 200 years after his death, his likeness would be represented in a sculpture by the Kamakura artist Kosho [koh-shoh] (Fig. **11.16**). His staff is topped by deer horns, symbolic of his slaying of a deer, the violence of whose death converted him to Buddhism. The most remarkable feature of the sculpture, however, is Kosho's representation of the chant. It consists of six small buddhas, emanating from Kuya's mouth. Each buddha represents one syllable of the *Namu Amida Butsu* chant (the final "u" of which is silent).

Fig. 11.16 Kosho. *Kuya Preaching.* **Kamakura period, before 1207.** Painted wood with crystal inlaid eyes, height 46 ¹/₂″. Rokuhara Mitsu-ji, Kyoto. Kuya wears a gong held to his chest by a yoke over his shoulders. The gong would have accompanied him as he danced while chanting.

The Arts of Military Culture The Kamakura period actually began when the Minamoto clan defeated its chief rival, the Taira, in 1185, but the contest for power between the two dominated the last years of the Heian period. The complex relationship between the Fujiwara of the Heian era and the samurai clans of the Kamakura is embodied in a long handscroll narration of an important battle of 1160, from the *Scrolls of Events of the Heiji Period*, painted by an unknown artist in the thirteenth century perhaps 100 years after the events themselves (Fig. **11.17**). In 1156, Go Shirakawa [goh sheer-ah-kah-wah] (1127–1192; r. 1156–1158) ascended to the throne, with the Fujiwara to serve in what had become their traditional role as regent to the emperor, the highest position in the government. But Go Shirakawa resisted the Fujiwara attempt to take control of the government, and in 1157, they recruited one of the two most powerful samurai clans, the Minamoto, to help them stage a coup and imprison the emperor. *Night Attack on the Sanjo Palace* depicts the moment troops led by Fujiwara Nobuyori attacked the emperor's palace in the middle of the night, taking him prisoner and burning his palace to the ground. The chaos and violence of the events are captured by the sweeping linear ribbons of flame and smoke rising to the upper right and the confusion of horsemen, warriors, fleeing ladies, the dead, and the dying in the foreground, all framed by an architecture that falls at a steep diagonal to the bottom left. The samurai warriors, dressed in elaborate iron armor, were master horsemen and archers. In this scene, many hold their bows, the lower portions of which are smaller than the top in order that they might pass over a horse's neck. As it turned out, this was a brief moment of triumph for the Minamoto. The rebellion was quickly quashed by the second of the powerful clans, the Taira, and for the next 20 years, the Taira managed to control the Japanese imperial court with the abdicated emperor Go Shirakawa's blessing. But in 1185, the Minamoto samurai army, led by Minamoto Yoshitsune (1159–1189), defeated the Taira, killing virtually all male members of the Taira clan and large numbers of their wives and children.

Yoshitsune's brother, Yoritomo (1147–1199), had sat out the war in Kamakura, and as soon as the war was ended, he quickly disposed of all samurai rivals in the region, including his own brother, whom he hunted down, but who managed to commit suicide rather than be captured. Yoritomo demanded that all other samurai lords pledge allegiance to him or risk the fate of his brother, and he soon

Fig. 11.17 *Night Attack on the Sanjo Palace*, detail, from the *Scrolls of Events of the Heiji Period.* **Kamakura period, late thirteenth century.** Handscroll, ink and colors on paper, 16 1/4" × 275 1/2". Courtesy, Museum of Fine Arts, Boston. Reproduced with permission. © 2006 Museum of Fine Arts, Boston. All Rights Reserved. Fenollosa-Weld Collection (11.4000). This is the central scene of the scroll, which begins with the army moving toward the palace from the right and ends with it leaving in triumph to the left.

controlled most of the Japanese archipelago. He established his rule at Kamakura, and thus removed Japanese government from the influence of both the aristocratic court at Heiankyo and the Buddhist stronghold at Nara. Interestingly, Yoritomo never tried to assume the imperial throne, and neither did any of the subsequent samurai rulers. Instead, he considered himself the emperor's servant, much as the Fujiwara had served the Heian emperors. But, in 1192, the imperial court granted him the title of Seiitai Shogun, literally "Barbarian-subduing General," and as **shogun**—that is, general-in-chief of the samurais—his military form of government, known as the shogunate, ruled the country for 150 years.

Yoritomo's shogunate was, in many ways, defined by land reforms that he immediately instituted. In essence, he granted the country estates that had belonged formerly to his enemies as gifts to his followers. These new landholders came to be officially known as *daimyo*, literally "great name," by the fifteenth century. They defined themselves first by the absolute allegiance to the shogun, and then by their devotion to military arts and their concern for their "great name"—by extension, their honor, their fame, and their pride in their family or clan. Eventually, when Japan

enjoyed an extended period of peace, from 1600 until the mid-nineteenth century, these values were codified and expanded upon by a *daimyo* class—whose militarism seemed increasingly irrelevant—into a well-defined code of conduct, **bushido**, "the way of the warrior," which continues to influence many aspects of Japanese society to this day.

THE CULTURES OF AFRICA

Just as in Europe and Asia, all over Africa, powerful kingdoms arose during this period. Several large kingdoms dominated the western African region known as the Sahel, the grasslands that serve as a transition between the Sahara desert and the more temperate zones to the west and south. Among the most important is the kingdom of Mali, discussed in Chapter 9, which shows the great influence Islam had come to have on much of northern Africa long before the end of the first millennium CE. Farther south, along the western coast of central Africa, were the powerful Yoruba state of Ife [EE-fay] and the kingdom of Benin [buh-NEEN]. On the eastern side of Africa, the Zagwe dynasty continued long Christian traditions in the Horn of Africa, while the Arab Swahili culture thrived along the central

east coast. Farther south, near the southeastern tip of Africa, the ancient Shona civilization produced urban centers represented today by the ruins of "Great Zimbabwe" (Map **11.4**).

Ife Culture

The Ife culture is one of the oldest in West Africa. It developed beginning around the eighth century along the Niger River, in what is now Nigeria. It was centered in the city of Ife. By 1100, it was producing highly naturalistic, sculptural, commemorative portraits in clay and stone, probably depicting its rulers, and not long after, elegant brass sculptures as well.

An example of Ife brasswork is the *Head of a King* (or *Oni* [OH-nee]) (Fig. **11.18**). The parallel lines that run down

the face represent decorative effects made by scarring— **scarification**. A hole in the lower neck suggests that the head may have been attached to a wooden mannequin, and in memorial services, the mannequin may have worn the royal robes of the Ife court. Small holes along the scalp line suggest that hair, or perhaps a veil of some sort, also adorned the head. But the head itself was, for the Ife, of supreme importance. It was the home of the spirit, the symbol of the king's capacity to organize the world and to prosper. Ife culture depended on its kings' heads for its own welfare. Since the Ife did not leave a written record of their cultural beliefs, we can best understand their ancient culture by looking at their contemporary descendants.

Yoruba Origin Myths The Yoruba people, whose population today is about 11 million, trace their ancestry directly to Ife

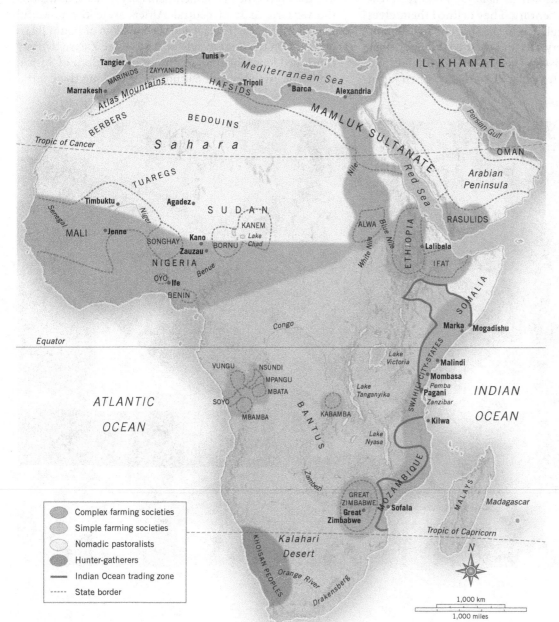

Map 11.4 Africa. ca. 1350, including predominant forms of economic activity.

Complex farming societies
Simple farming societies
Nomadic pastoralists
Hunter-gatherers
Indian Ocean trading zone
State border

culture. The Yoruba cosmos consists of the world of the living (*aye* [aye-yeah]) and the realm of the gods (*orun* [oh-ROON]). The gods are themselves called *orisha* and among them are the primordial deities, who created the world, as well as forces of nature, such as thunder and lightning, and ancestral heroes who have risen to immortality. Linking these two worlds is the king, who serves as the representative in this world of those existing in *orun*. The king's head is thus sacred, and his crown, or *ade* [ah-DEH] (Fig. **11.19**), rising high above his head, symbolizes his majesty and authority. Rows of beads fall over his face to shield viewers from the power of his gaze. Imagery on the crown varies, but often refers to Ife myths of origin, similar to myths of origin found throughout the world (see Chapter 1). The first Yoruba king, Oduduwa [oh-DOO-doo-wah], from whom all subsequent kings descend, is frequently represented. According to leg-

end, Oduduwa was ordered to create a land mass out of the watery reaches of Earth so that it might be populated by people. Oduduwa lowered himself down onto the waters, the legend continues, and emptied Earth from a small snail shell onto the water. He then placed a chicken on the sand to spread it and make land. Finally he planted some palm kernels. It was at Ife that he did this, and Ife remains the most sacred of Yoruba sites.

Fig. 11.18 Head of an *Oni* (King). Ife culture, Nigeria. ca. thirteenth century. Brass, height, 11 ⁷⁄₁₆". Museum of Ife Antiquities, Ife, Nigeria. The metal used to cast this head is an alloy of copper and zinc, and therefore not technically bronze, but brass.

Fig. 11.19 *Ade*, or beaded crown, Yoruba culture, Nigeria. Late twentieth century. Beadwork, height, 6'1 ¼". © The Trustees of the British Museum/Art Resource, NY. Today, approximately 50 Yoruba rulers wear beaded crowns and claim descent from Oduduwa.

Benin Culture

Sometime around 1170, the city-state of Benin, some 150 miles southeast of Ife, also in the Niger basin, asked the *oni* of Ife to provide a new ruler for their territory, which was, legend has it, plagued by misrule and disorder. The *oni* sent Prince Oranmiyan [oh-RHAN-mee-yan], who founded a new dynasty. Oranmiyan was apparently so vexed by the conditions he found that he named his new state *ibini*, "land of vexation," from which the name Benin derives. After some years, Oranmiyan returned home, but not until after he had impregnated the Benin princess. Their son Eweka [eh-WEE-kah] would become the first king, or *oba*, as the Benin culture called their ruler, ruling from 1180 to 1246.

Already in place at the capital, Benin City, were the beginnings of a massive system of walls and moats that would become, by the fifteenth century, the world's largest human-built earthwork. According to archeologist Phillip Darling, who has studied the wall and moat system for several decades, they total some 10,000 miles in length, or some four to five times the length of the main Great Wall of China. These earthworks consist of moats, the dirt from which was piled alongside them to make walls up to 60 feet high. They were probably first dug over a thousand years ago to protect settlements and their farmlands from the nocturnal raids of the forest elephant. But as Benin grew, linear earth boundaries demarcated clan or family territories and symbolically signified the boundary between the real physical world and the spirit world. When the British arrived in the late nineteenth century, the walls were still largely intact (Fig. **11.20**), but they were soon destroyed by British forces, and what remains of them have been increasingly consumed by modern urbanization.

Like the Ife to the north, the Benin rulers also created life-like images of their ancestor rulers. In the first half of the twentieth century, recognizing that many of the oral traditions of Benin culture were in danger of being lost, the Benin court historian, Chief Jacob Egharevba (1893–1981), recorded as many traditional tales and historical narratives as he could find and published them in his *Short History of Benin*. This is his account of the origins of brass-casting (see *Materials & Techniques*, page 40 in Chapter 2) of *oba* heads in Benin culture (**Reading 11.6**):

READING 11.6

from Jacob Egharevba, *A Short History of Benin*

Oba Oguola [r. 1274–1287] wished to introduce brass casting into Benin so as to produce works of art similar to those sent him from Ife. He therefore sent to the Oni of Ife for a brass-smith and Iguegha was sent to him. Iguegha was very clever and left many designs to his successors, and was in consequence deified, and is worshipped to this day by brass-smiths. The practice of making brass-castings for the preservation of the records of events was originated during the reign of Oguola.

The artists, members of the royal casters' guild, lived in their own quarters just outside the palace in Benin, where they are located to this day. Only the *oba* could order brass-work from them. These commissions were usually memorial heads, commemorating the king's royal ancestors in royal costume (Fig. **11.21**). (The head shown in Figure 11.21 was made in the mid-sixteenth century, but heads like it were made in the earliest years of bronze production in the culture.) As in Ife culture, the *oba*'s head was the home of the spirit and the symbol of the *oba*'s capacity to organize the world and to prosper.

This power could be described and commemorated in an oral form known as a **praise poem**. Praise poems are a major part of West African culture. By praising something—a

Fig. 11.20 Drawing of Benin City as it appeared to an unknown British officer in 1891. The network of walls and moats visible in this drawing covers an area of over 2,500 square miles.

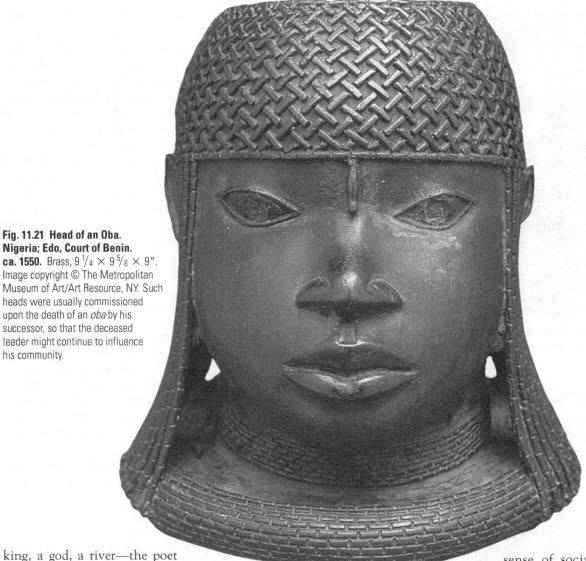

Fig. 11.21 Head of an Oba. Nigeria; Edo, Court of Benin. ca. 1550. Brass, 9 ¼ × 9 ⅝ × 9". Image copyright © The Metropolitan Museum of Art/Art Resource, NY. Such heads were usually commissioned upon the death of an *oba* by his successor, so that the deceased leader might continue to influence his community.

king, a god, a river—the poet was believed to gain influence over it. Almost everyone in West African culture has praise poems associated with them. These poems often use a poetic device known as **anaphora** [un-NAF-uh-ruh], a repetition of words and phrases at the beginning of successive sentences that, owing to the particularities of the West African languages, is almost impossible to duplicate in translation. But the poems are intended to create a powerful and insistent rhythm that rises to a crescendo.

West African Music

The rhythm-driven crescendo of the Benin praise poem shares much with African music as a whole. In fact, the poem may have been accompanied by music. African music is part of the fabric of everyday life, accompanying work, poetry, ceremony, and dance, and often evoked by visual art. The Western idea that music can be isolated from everyday experience is almost incomprehensible to the African sensibility. Typically consisting of a single line of melody without harmony, African music is generally communal in nature, encouraging a sense of social cohesion by promoting group activity. As a result, one of the most universal musical forms throughout Africa is **call-and-response** music, in which a caller, or soloist, raises the song, and the community chorus responds to it.

Call-and-response music is by no means simple. The Yoruba language, for instance, is tone-based; any Yoruba syllable has three possible tones and this tone determines its meaning. The Yoruba reproduce their speech in the method of musical signaling known as **talking drums** (track 11.1), performed with three types of batá drums, which imitate the three tones of the language. In ritual drumming, the drums are played for the Yoruba gods and are essentially praise poems to those gods. Characteristic of this music is its polyrhythmic structure. Here as many as five to ten different "voices" of interpenetrating rhythms and tones, often repeated over and over again in a call-and-response form, play off against one another. This method of playing against or "off" the main beat is typical of West African music and exists to this day in the "off-beat" practices of Western jazz.

HEAR MORE at www.myartslab.com

Fig. 11.22 Beta Ghiorghis (House of Saint George), Lalibela, Ethiopia. Thirteenth century. Saint George Church is one of more than 1,500 stone carved churches that can still be seen in Ethiopia.

East Africa: The Zagwe Dynasty

Ironically, one of the dynasties of greatest cultural importance in medieval East Africa was also one of the shortest lived and least revered. In the region of today's Ethiopia, the Zagwe dynasty reigned for approximately 150 years, from the early twelfth century (when the declining Aksumite Empire fell), to 1270, when the last Zagwe ruler was deposed. The new ruling family claimed descent from King Solomon, and in order to give the impression that their family had a dazzling and unbroken chain of legitimate power reaching back into biblical times, they embarked on a campaign to discredit the Zagwe dynasty as usurpers and their reign as a disgrace. Nevertheless, the Zagwe rulers had already ensured their survival as a respected part of Ethiopian history by the rock churches they left behind.

The most famous of these was commissioned by the emperor Lalibela. In the town now known by his name, he ordered the construction of a series of churches. Unlike most buildings, instead of being built up from the ground, the churches at Lalibela were carved downward through the soft rocks at the site (Fig. **11.22**). Engineers had to conceive of the completed building in advance, including decorative details, because subtractive techniques such as carving do not allow for repair of mistakes. Once the shell of the building was carved, the interior was hollowed out into rooms for use in Christian worship and study.

Fig. 11.23 The Great Mosque at Kilwa, interior, Tanzania. Built and remodeled over the centuries, it was completed with barrel vaulting and domes by the mid-fifteenth century.

The Swahili Coast

In the medieval era, Christian places of worship were rare in Africa. In the trading centers of the north and west, Islam was the dominant nonindigenous religion. East Africans had traded with Arab sailors since before the beginning of the common era, from trade depots along a narrow coastal strip ranging from today's Somalia through Mozambique (see Map 11.4). When these traders embraced Islam, the people the Arabs called Swahili, from the Arabic word for "shore," were quick to follow. From Mogadishu in the north to Sofala in the south, a region known as the Swahili Coast, Arabs and Africans blended their customs to create one of the most vibrant cultures in Africa. They also created a new language—Swahili, an African language with many borrowings from Arabic.

Looking directly out onto the Indian Ocean, Swahili ports played a key role in trade with all of Asia from the medieval era onward. The great Chinese explorer Zheng He (see Chapter 18) reached the Swahili coast, trading Chinese porcelain and other goods for African products such as spices and wild animals to take back to the Chinese emperor.

The Swahili were renowned for their architecture. Using local materials such as fossilized coral limestone, they built mosques and other buildings, carving trims and decorations directly into the stone in floral designs, arabesques, and other patterns like those in the Qur'an (see Chapter 9). So beautiful were these works that, upon visiting Kilwa, medieval explorer Ibn Battuta pronounced it "the most beautiful of cities." The mosque at Kilwa (Fig. 11.23) would have been where Ibn Battuta stopped to pray. Constructed of pieces of fossilized coral bound together by cement made from sand, the pillars, arches, and walls of the mosque were coated in a glossy plaster also made from coral, into which patterns were excised.

Great Zimbabwe

In embracing Islam, the people of the Swahili Coast transformed their society, but the influence of the new faith did not spread far inland. West of Sofala, at a port at the southern end of the Swahili Coast, the Shona people built an entirely indigenous African civilization in the region of today's Zimbabwe. The Shona people, who still occupy the region today, are thought to have first come to the region by 1100 CE. At first the Shona relied on their advanced skills at mining, animal husbandry, and agriculture to sustain their communities in the rocky grasslands of the region, but as the Swahili Coast became more and more lucrative as a center of trade, the Shona positioned themselves as an inland hub of trade to which coastal traders could travel to procure goods for export. From surrounding regions, they mined or imported copper and gold, and in return received exotic goods such as porcelain and glass from Asia and the Middle East.

Between the thirteenth and fifteenth centuries, the Shona erected the massive stone buildings and walls of a city known today as Great Zimbabwe. (The word *zimbabwe* is thought to refer to "palaces of stone.") A huge city for its time, the ruins cover one square mile and are believed to have housed a population of somewhere between 10,000 and 20,000. Great Zimbabwe has several distinct areas. The oldest of these, a hilltop enclosure known as the Hill Ruin, probably served as a lookout, but may also have been set apart for religious ceremonies or initiation rites. Built around 1250, it has a perimeter wall of smooth stone blocks that follows the contours of the hilltop. Inside this wall are several smaller enclosures with floors of clay that were hardened and polished to a shine. The enclosures also had ceremonial platforms decorated with carved geometric patterns and tall rock monoliths topped by carved birds, possibly representing messengers from the spirit world (Fig. 11.24).

Below the Hill Ruin stands the Great Enclosure, a group of structures also encircled by a tall stone wall (Fig. 11.25). This part of Great Zimbabwe was built approximately a century later, using a different style for the perimeter wall. Here, Shona craftsmen built a double wall with a space between the two walls only wide enough to allow single-file

Fig. 11.24 Bird carved from soapstone, Great Zimbabwe, Zimbabwe. ca. 1200–1400 CE. Height 14.5″, atop a stone monolith (total height: 64″). Great Zimbabwe Site Museum, Zimbabwe. One of eight such decorative monoliths at Great Zimbabwe, the bird is not a recognizable species and includes certain human features such as toes instead of talons. This has led to speculation that the figure may represent deceased Shona rulers who were believed to have the power to move between the spirit and human worlds. A crocodile, possibly another symbol of royalty, climbs up the front of the monolith.

Fig. 11.25 Double perimeter wall and remains of two towers that resemble Shona granaries in the Great Enclosure, Great Zimbabwe. ca. 1200–1400 CE. The skill of the craftsmen who built these structures was extraordinary. They used no mortar, but instead fit the stones together so tightly that the walls reached 30 feet in height and were so sturdy that most of them are intact today. Only the clay smoothed over the walls, and the wooden roofs over some of the structures, have eroded away in the last eight centuries.

passage. They tapered the walls inward from a 17-foot-thick base for greater strength and stability, and topped the exterior wall with an alternating diagonal pattern of dark and light-colored rocks. This decoration may have been meant to represent lightning, or perhaps the zebra, an animal frequently depicted in Shona art. These decorative stripes are echoed inside the courtyard of the enclosure, where a large platform similar to those in the Hill Ruin was constructed. One other notable feature of the Great Enclosure is two conical structures that interrupt passage around the perimeter wall. These are likely to have been ancient granaries, for the Shona people today still use similar structures.

The remainder of Great Zimbabwe consists of clusters of smaller buildings known as the Valley Ruin. Historians and archeologists presume from this that most of the population lived in the valley and that the Great Enclosure was probably a royal residence. One intriguing mystery, how-ever, is the reason for the massive walls of the Great Enclosure and Hill Ruin. Despite the turrets and lookout spots, the walls do not appear to have been meant for defense, and from this, scholars have surmised that the walls may have existed primarily to serve as a buffer between royalty and the common people, and as a constant reminder of their power and status.

THE CULTURES OF MESOAMERICA IN THE CLASSIC ERA

The cultures of pre-Columbian Mesoamerica, comprising modern-day Nicaragua, Honduras, Guatemala, Belize, and southern Mexico, possessed a great sense of their own history. They were fully aware that cultures at least as great as themselves—the Olmec in particular (see Chapter 1)—

Map 11.5 The Americas. The two chief centers of cultural development in pre-Columbian times in the Americas were Mesoamerica, the semicircular land mass extending from central Mexico south and east through Guatemala and the Yucatan peninsula, and the central Andes of South America in modern-day Peru.

had preceded them. But during a period of about a thousand years, roughly 250 BCE to 900 CE, which archeologists call the Classic Era, the cultures of Mesoamerica flourished. "Pre-Columbian" refers to the era before Columbus arrived in the Americas in 1492, and the title "Classic Era," borrowed from Greco-Roman culture, designates what historians consider to be the high point of pre-Columbian culture in the Americas. Three great cultures thrived in Mesoamerica during the Classic Era: the Zapotec culture in the state of Oaxaca; the somewhat mysterious but enormously influential civilization centered at Teotihuacán, just north of Tenochtitlán (present-day Mexico City); and to the south, the Maya culture in the states of Yucatan, and Chiapas, and the countries of Belize, and Guatemala

(Map 11.5). These cultures were at once highly developed and, from a Western point of view, seemingly backward, astronomically sophisticated, with two separate but extraordinarily accurate calendars, yet lacking both a domesticated beast of burden capable of carrying an adult. Even more astonishing, they lacked one of the most fundamental tools of civilization—the wheel. Although they used wheels on children's toys, they never enlarged them for use on wagons or carts. These civilizations never discovered how to process bronze or iron, yet they moved and cut stones weighing in excess of 100 tons and built enormous temples, the centerpieces of cities rivaling any in Europe or Asia. But what they lacked, they probably did not need, and what they developed was extraordinary.

Monte Albán and Zapotec Culture

Zapotec culture, which occupied the territory later controlled by the Mixtec, was centered at Monte Albán in Oaxaca. The Zapotecs had themselves been closely tied to the Olmecs (see Chapter 1), but instead of living in the alluvial lowlands of the Gulf coast, they built their capital atop a mountain overlooking the three major valleys of central Oaxaca. It seems likely that they were the first Mesoamerican people to use the 260-day calendar, and they possessed a writing system, although, with the exception of names, dates, and places, it remains largely undeciphered. Like the Olmec before them, they valued jade above all other precious stones or metal—more than gold and silver. Jade would remain the most treasured material through the entire history of the cultures of Mesoamerica, from the Olmecs to the Aztecs. The translucent green color of jade symbolized water, fertility, and vegetation—in short, the life force. Large stones were very rare, and specimen pieces were passed down from generation to generation. A particularly fine example is a bat god from Monte Albán, discovered in the grave of an early Zapotec king (Fig. **11.26**). Worn as the symbol of his power, its eyes, made of shell, stare fiercely out at any who would have approached him.

Teotihuacán

Teotihuacán thrived from about 50 to 750 CE. By the fourth century CE, it was a center of culture comparable to Constantinople in the Old World. In contrast to the later Mayan cities, many of which were quickly forgotten and overgrown in the jungle, Teotihuacán remained, for the Maya, the Aztecs, and other Mesoamerican civilizations, a holy site, the manifestation on Earth of Tollan, the Mesoamerican mythic place of origin. Even a thousand years after it flourished, the most important Aztec rulers made pilgrimages to it.

The city is laid out in a grid system, the basic unit of which is 614 square feet, and every detail is subjected to this scheme, conveying a sense of power and mastery. A great, broad avenue, known as the Avenue of the Dead, runs through the city (Figs. **11.27** and **11.28**). It links two great pyramids, the Pyramids of the Moon and the Sun, both surrounded by about 600 smaller pyramids, workshops and numerous plazas, and a giant market area. There are some 2,000 known apartment complexes—more are likely to be excavated—nearly all adorned with complex murals related to ritual life. Their size, location (nearer or farther from the center), and their quality of construction is indicative of the social status of the inhabitant. The Pyramid of the Sun is oriented to mark the passage of the sun from east to west and the rising of the stellar constellation, the Pleiades, on the days of the equinox. Each of its two staircases contains 182 steps, which, when the platform at its apex is added, together total 365. The pyramid is thus an image of time. This representation of the solar calendar is

Fig. 11.26 Jade pendant, Zapotec, Monte Albán, State of Oaxaca, Mexico. Late pre-Classic (200 BCE–100 CE). Jade with shell inlays, 11′ × 6 ³/₄″. National Museum of Anthropology, Mexico. Though found at Monte Albán, where it was discovered in a tomb, this piece may well have been passed down from the Olmecs. It represents a bat god.

echoed in another pyramid at Teotihuacán, the Temple of the Plumed (or Feathered) Serpent, which is decorated with 364 serpent fangs.

At its height, in about 500 CE, about 200,000 people lived in Teotihuacán, making it one of the largest cities in the world. Scholars believe that a female deity, associated with the moon, as well as cave and mountain rituals, played an important role in Teotihuacán culture. The placement of the Pyramid of the Moon, in front of the dead volcano Cerro Gordo (see Fig. **11.28**), supports this theory. It is as if the mountain, seen from a vantage point looking north up the Avenue of the Dead, embraces the pyramid in its flanks. And the pyramid, in turn, seems to channel the forces of nature—the abundant water on the mountain in particular—into the heart of the city.

Fig. 11.27 Teotihuacán, Mexico, as seen from the Pyramid of the Moon, looking south down the Avenue of the Dead, the Pyramid of the Sun at the left. ca. 350–650 CE. One of the largest cities in the world by the middle of the first millennium, Teotihuacán covered an area of nearly 9 square miles.

LEARN MORE View an architectural simulation of Teotihuacán at **www.myartslab.com**

Fig. 11.28 The Pyramid of the Moon, looking north up the Avenue of the Dead. Beginning at the southern end of the city, and culminating at the Pyramid of the Moon, the Avenue of the Dead is 2 $^1/_2$ miles long.

Fig. 11.29 Madrid Codex, leaves 13–16. ca. 1400. Amatl paper, 56 leaves, painted on both sides and screenfolded. Museo de América, Madrid. Diviners would have used this text to predict events such as flood, drought, or an abundant harvest.

Mayan Culture

To the south, another culture, that of the Maya, both pre-dated and post-dated that of Teotihuacán. The Maya occupied several regions: the highlands of Chiapas and Guatemala; the Southern lowlands of Guatemala, Honduras, El Salvador, Belize, and the Northern lowlands in the states of Yucatan, Campeche, and Quintano Roo. They were never unified into a single political entity, but rather consisted of many small kingdoms that engaged in warfare with one another over land and resources.

An elaborate calendar system enabled them to keep track of their history—and, evidence suggests, predict the future. It consisted of two interlocking ways of recording time, a 260-day calendar and a 365-day calendar. The 260-day calendar probably derives from the length of human gestation, from a pregnant woman's first missed menstrual period to birth. When both calendars were synchronized, it took exactly 52 years of 365 days for a given day to repeat itself—the so-called calendar round—and the end of each cycle was widely celebrated.

The Mayan calendar was put to many uses. An example is the Madrid Codex (Fig. **11.29**), one of the four surviving Mayan codices. It consists of 56 stucco-coated bark-paper leaves, painted, with the exception of one page, on both sides. Over 250 separate "almanacs" that place events of

both a sacred and secular nature within the 260-day Mesoamerican ritual calendar fill its pages. It records events concerning particularly the activities of daily life (planting, tending crops, the harvest, weaving, and hunting), rituals, astronomic events, offerings, and deities associated with them. The four horizontal rows in the lower half of each panel are composed of the glyphs of the 20 named days recycling 13 times. Sky serpents who send the rain and speak in thunder are shown weaving around the rows of glyphs. In the shorter top two leaves, standard numerology can be seen. The Mayans wrote numbers in two ways, as a system of dots and bars, seen here, and in a set of pictorial variants. Twenty was expressed with a glyph of the moon, and zero with a shell glyph, a number, incidentally, used widely in Mesoamerica many centuries before Hindu mathematicians "discovered" it in India.

The City of Palenque Among the most important Mayan cities is Palenque, one of the best-preserved of all Mayan sites. Lost in the jungle for centuries following its decline, which occurred around the year 850, Palenque was rediscovered in 1746 by a Spanish priest who had heard rumors of its existence. The Temple of Inscriptions, facing into the main courtyard of the so-called Palace, which may have been an administrative center rather than a royal residence, rises in nine steps, representing the nine levels of the Mayan Underworld (Fig. **11.30**). It is inscribed with the history of the Palenque kings, who were associated with the jaguar. The first recorded king is K'uk B'alam [k'oohk-b'ahl-um—the apostrophes indicate glottal stops], "Quetzal Jaguar," who, so the inscriptions say, founded the city on March 11, 431. Palenque's most powerful king was K'inich Janaab' Pakal I (Great Sun Shield), known as Pakal [pah-CAL] (603–83), who ruled for 67 years, and the Temple of Inscriptions was erected over his grave.

In 1952, Alberto Ruz, a Mexican archeologist, discovered the entrance to the tomb of Lord Pakal, under the pyramid. It was hidden under large stone slabs in the floor of the temple at the top of the pyramid. Ruz had to clear the passage down to Pakal's tomb, at the very base of the structure, which had been back-filled with stone debris. When he reached the tomb, he found that Pakal's face was covered with a jade death mask. A small tube connected the tomb with the upper level, thus providing the dead king with an eternal source of fresh air. It also functioned as a form of communication between the living and the ancestor. Pakal was buried in a large uterus-shaped stone sarcophagus weighing over five tons and covered with jade and cinnabar.

The *Popol Vuh* The *Popol Vuh* [po-pole voo] is a Mayan book of creation. It was written in Quiché, a surviving Mayan dialect still spoken in the Guatemalan highlands, and produced between 1554 and 1558 by a Guatemalan Indian. Despite its late date, it probably represents Mayan belief systems that date back over a thousand years. Sometime in about 1700, a Dominican priest, Francisco Ximénez [hee-may-nez] copied the manuscript, adding a Spanish translation in a column paralleling the Quiché original. The original has since disappeared. Over a hundred years later, the Ximenez copy was found in the archives of San Carlos University in Guatemala City by Brasseur de Bourbourg, who brought it to Paris and published a version of it in 1858. It was subsequently sold to the Newberry Library in Chicago, along with other documents from the Brasseur collection, where it remained uncatalogued and unknown until 1941. The *Popol Vuh* is in four parts, beginning with the deeds of Mayan gods in the darkness of a primeval sea (**Reading 11.7**):

READING 11.7

from *Popol Vuh: The Great Mythological Book of the Ancient Maya*

Before the world was created, Calm and Silence were the great kings that ruled. Nothing existed, there was nothing. Things had not yet been drawn together, the face of the earth was unseen. There was only motionless sea, and a great emptiness of sky. There were no men anywhere, or animals, no birds or fish, no crabs. Trees, stones, caves, grass, forests, none of these existed yet. There was nothing that could roar or run, nothing that could tremble or cry in the air. Flatness and emptiness, only the sea, alone and breathless. It was night; silence stood in the dark.

In this darkness the Creators waited, the Maker, Tepeu, Gucumatz, the Forefathers. They were there in this emptiness, hidden under green and blue feathers, alone and surrounded with light. They are the same as wisdom. They are the ones who can conceive and bring forth a child from nothingness. And the time had come. The Creators were bent deep around talk in the darkness. They argued, worried, sighed over what was to be. They planned the growth of the thickets, how things would crawl and jump, the birth of man. They planned the whole creation, arguing each point until their words and thoughts crystallized and became the

Fig. 11.30 "Palace" (foreground) and Temple of Inscriptions (tomb pyramid of Lord Pakal), Palenque, Mexico. Maya culture. 600–900 CE. These two buildings, along with two other temples not seen in this view, formed the central complex of Palenque. Another complex to the north is composed of five temples and a ball court, and a third group of temples lies to the south. Palenque was the center of a territory that may have been populated by as many as 100,000 people.

LEARN MORE Gain insight from an extended primary source from *Popol Vuh* at **www.myartslab.com**

same thing. Heart of Heaven was there, and in the darkness the creation was planned.

Then let the emptiness fill! they said. Let the water weave its way downward so the earth can show its face! Let the light break on the ridges, let the sky fill up with the yellow light of dawn! Let our glory be a man walking on a path through the trees! "Earth!" the Creators called. They called only once, and it was there, from a mist, from a cloud of dust, the mountains appeared instantly. . . .

The gods try three times to create mankind, once out of animals, a second time out of mud, and a third time out of wood. Wood proves most successful, though the wooden men are killed off as well, and their descendants become monkeys. The rest of Part 1 and all of Part 2 deal with two sets of twins—the Hero Twins, Hunhapu [hoon-AH-poo] and Xbalanque [shibah- LEN-kay]; and their half-brothers, the Monkey Twins, Hun Batz´ [hoon-bahts] and Hun Chouen [hoon-choo-en]. Both sets of twins are ballplayers. Summoned to Xibalba [shibahl-bah] (the Underworld), Hunhapu and Xbalanque undergo a series of tests, transformations, and resurrections.

The connection of the traditional Mesoamerican ballgame to forces of life and death, evidenced so substantially in the *Popul Vuh*, underscores its significance to the culture. Almost all major sites had ball courts (Fig. 11.31). Players directed a heavy, solid rubber ball with their heads, thighs, or knees, padded to absorb the impact, through the opponent's ring high on the wall on each side of an I-shaped court. The game was closely associated with Mayan myths of origin and had deep religious significance. The ball represented the sun, and the duty of the players was to keep it from falling to earth as it passed through day and night (the games often lasted for several days). The sharply angled walls of the court itself were associated with the crack in the top of Creation Mountain described in the *Popul Vuh*

(the Mayan word for crevice, *hom* [hahm], is also the word for ball court), and play was intimately tied to the gods themselves. The losing team was believed to have betrayed both the sun and the gods. Evidence suggests that the post-Classic Maya decapitated the losing team and displayed their heads on poles surrounding the ball court, and later on wooden scaffolds or stone monuments called "skull racks."

By 900 CE, Mayan culture had collapsed as a result of a wide variety of events, including overpopulation and accompanying ecological degradation, political competition, and war. Its peoples, who survive in large numbers to this day, returned to simple farming around the ruins of their once-great cities.

The Post-Classic Era: Toltecs and Aztecs

In the north, after the decline of Teotihuacán, the Toltec culture rose to power. Centered in Tula in the modern state of Hidalgo, in terms of architecture, symbols, planning, and narrative programs, the Toltecs were a bridge between Teotihuacán and the Aztecs. When, in the twelfth century, Tula was burned and its inhabitants scattered, one of these surviving groups was the Mexica. Later known as the Aztecs, they wandered into the Valley of Mexico in about 1325 and built a village on the shores of Lake Texcoco. There they saw an eagle perching on a prickly pear cactus (*tenochtli*) [teh-nok-tlee], a sign that their wandering was over. They dug canals and drained the shallow areas of the lake, converting them into fertile fields, and there, as well, they built the city of Tenochtitlán on an island in the lake's center.

Blood sacrifice was central to Aztec culture, merging perfectly with the warrior traditions inherited from the Toltecs. The Aztecs believed that the sun, moon, and earth all depended upon human blood for their sustenance. Their chief activity, as a result, was war, and the chief goal of war was to capture sacrificial victims, as well as acquire territory and exact tribute to buttress the life of the elites, including quetzal feathers, copal resin for incense, and cotton for warrior uniforms. At puberty, boys were placed under jurisdiction of a local warrior house and trained for war, where they learned that success in life equaled the number of enemies captured alive for later ritual killing. Death itself, when realized in the pursuit of such honor, was the greatest honor an Aztec male could achieve.

Centered at Tenochtitlán, Aztec culture would survive until the arrival of the Spanish in 1519. In only a few years it was almost totally destroyed, its vast quantities of magnificent goldwork looted and returned to Europe to be melted down to support the warring ways of the European kings (see Chapter 18).

Fig. 11.31 Ball court at Copán, Honduras, Maya Culture. ca. 711-736 CE. This is the second-largest ball court in Mesoamerica. The largest is at Chichen Itza.

THE CULTURES OF SOUTH AMERICA

As in Mesoamerica, complex cultures developed in South America during the period corresponding to the Middle Ages in Europe, particularly in the area of present-day Peru (see Map 11.5). The region is one of dramatic contrast. The snow-capped peaks and high grasslands of the Andes mountains capture rainfall from the Pacific Ocean, creating rivers that drop quickly to the sea across one of the most arid deserts in the world.

The Moche

In these river valleys, which are essentially oases in the coastal desert, Moche culture flourished for a thousand years, from about 200 BCE to 800 CE. The Moche built large mound temples made entirely of **adobe** bricks, sun-baked blocks of clay mixed with straw. The largest, located in the Moche Valley, from which the culture takes its name, is the so-called Pyramid of the Sun. It is over 1,000 feet long and 500 feet wide and rises to a height of 59 feet. In these pyramids, people buried their dead, accompanied by gold earrings, pendants, necklaces, and other ornaments, as well as elaborately decorated ceramic bowls, pots, and bottles.

The most distinctive bottles depict scenes representative of Moche culture as a whole, usually on bottles with distinctive stirrup spouts that curve elegantly away from the body of the vessel (Fig. **11.32**). The list of the subjects depicted is almost endless—animals of all kinds, from seals to owls, warriors, plants, musicians, homes, children at play, women weaving, couples engaged in sex, a man washing his hair—as if the culture was intent on representing every facet of its daily life. Recent research suggests, however, that every one of these scenes has a ritual or symbolic function. This figure, for instance, may well represent the Warrior priest who presided over Moche sacrifice ceremonies, in which prisoners captured in battle were sacrificed and their blood drunk by elaborately dressed warriors.

The Inca

In about 800 CE, the Moche suddenly vanished, many believe as a result of floods brought about by a series of weather events related to El Niño. This major temperature fluctuation of the waters of the Eastern Pacific Ocean results in substantial changes in rainfall levels both regionally and worldwide. The resulting political vacuum lasted for over 400 years until, around 1300, Inca culture emerged. One of many farming cultures in the southern Peruvian highlands, the Inca took advantage of the Andean camelids—llamas, alpacas, vicuñas, and guanacos, beasts of burden unknown to the cultures of Mesoamerica—to forge trading networks that eventually united the southern highlands and northern coastal lowlands under their rule. Large irrigation projects transformed both the river valleys and the desert between them into rich agricultural regions.

Fig. 11.32 *Moche Lord with a Feline*, from Moche Valley, Peru. Moche culture. ca. 100 BCE–500 CE. Painted ceramic, height 7 1/2″. Buckingham Fund. 1955-2281. Photograph © 2006, The Art Institute of Chicago. All Rights Reserved. Vessels of this kind, depicting almost every aspect of Moche life, were buried in large quantities with Moche rulers.

The Inca were, above all, masterful masons. Working with stone tools and without mortar, they crafted adjoining granite blocks that fit so snugly together that their walls have, for centuries, withstood earthquakes that have destroyed many later structures. Few of the blocks are the same size, and some have as many as 30 faces. Still, the joints are so tight that even the thinnest knife blade cannot be forced between the stones. Cuzco (meaning "navel of the earth"), the capital of the Inca Empire, was laid out to resemble a giant puma, and its masonry, much of which still survives, is unmatched anywhere in the world. At Machu Picchu (Fig. **11.33**, on page 394), stone buildings, whose thatched and gabled roofs have long since collapsed, are set on stone terraces in a setting that was designed, recent research has shown, as a royal retreat for the Inca ruler, Pachacuti Inka Yupanqui [pah-chah-coo-tee ink-ah yoo-pahn-kee], who built the complex between 1460 and 1470 to get away from the noise and congestion of the capital.

About 1,200 people lived in Machu Picchu's approximately 170 residences, most of them women, children, and priests. The Inca also created an extraordinary network of roads, ranging from as wide as 50 feet to as narrow as 3 feet, and extending from desert to Andes peaks for some 15,000 miles. Nearly a thousand lodgings were built along the routes, and relay runners could carry news across the region in less than a week.

The Inca were especially attracted to textiles, which apparently they valued even more than gold or other minerals, at least in part because of the extremely high, and cold, elevations at which they lived. The exact meaning of the design of an Inca weaving that survives from the time of the Spanish conquest is unclear, but scholars believe it is largely

Fig. 11.33 Machu Picchu, Inca culture, Peru. ca. 1450. Machu Picchu survived destruction by the Spanish when they invaded in 1532, partly because of its remote location, high in the Andes, and partly because, compared to the Inca capital of Cuzco, it probably seemed small and comparatively insignificant. Nevertheless, by about 1537 it was abandoned as Inca civilization collapsed, victim not only of the Spanish conquistadores, but also of disease, especially smallpox.

symbolic (Fig. **11.34**). Most Inca tunics include only a few examples of the small square units, called *t'oqapu*, that cover this one entirely. In fact, no other known tunic incorporates such a large number and wide variety. Each of these *t'oqapu* may have held special meaning or significance, referring to specific peoples, places, or things. It seems likely that this particular tunic was worn by the ruler himself, its large number of *t'oqapu* conveying the message that he controlled an enormously diverse culture.

Llamas were the source of wool for the Inca. One was sacrificed in Cuzco each morning and evening, and a white llama was kept at Cuzco as a symbol for the Inca as a whole. According to Spanish commentators, the Cuzco llama was paraded through the streets of the city during celebrations of the coming planting season each April, dressed in a red tunic and wearing gold jewelry. These processions also included life-size gold and silver images of llamas, people, and various Inca gods.

Melted for currency by the Spanish throne, none of these large objects survive. Small objects of gold and silver, which symbolized to the Inca the sun and the moon, were once scattered through the central plaza of Cuzco. The plaza—in Incan times twice as large as it is today—was excavated to a depth of between 6 and 12 inches, its sacred soil carried away to each of the four quadrants of Tahuantinsuyu [ta-WAHN-tin-SOO-yah], as the Inca called their homeland, "Land of the Four Quadrants." The plaza was then refilled with sand brought from the ocean, in which offerings of gold and silver llamas and human figures were distributed. The plaza thus symbolized a great body of water, at once the Pacific Ocean and Lake Titicaca, from which the Inca creator deity, Ticsivirachocha [TIC-see-VEER-ah-COH-cha], had emerged after the great flood to repopulate the world. It was thus, for the Inca before the arrival of the Spanish, the very center of the world.

Fig. 11.34 Tapestry–weave Inca tunic, south coast of Peru. ca. 1440–1540. Camelid fiber and cotton, 35 1/8″ × 30″. Dunbarton Oaks Research Library and Collections, Washington, D.C. Each square represents a specific group, or an individual's identity, and functions much like a heraldic device or a logo.

The Spanish and the Fate of the Inca and Aztec Capitals

One of the most elaborately decorated of all Inca sites was Cuzco's Coricancha [KORE-eh- KAHN-cha] (literally, "the corral of gold"), the Inca Temple of the Sun facing the plaza (Fig. 11.35). Dedicated to Inti [in-tee], the sun god, the original temple was decorated with 700 sheets of gold studded with emeralds and turquoise and designed to reflect the sunlight admitted through its windows. Its courtyard was filled with golden statuary—"stalks of corn that were of gold—stalks, leaves and ears," the Spanish chronicler Pedro de Cieza de León reported in the mid-sixteenth century. "Aside from this," he continued, there were "more than twenty sheep [llamas] of gold with their lambs and the shepherds who guarded them, all of this metal."

After their conquest of Peru, the Spanish quickly adapted the foundations of the Inca temple to their own purposes, constructing a Dominican church and monastery on the original Inca foundations. The Inca traditionally gathered to worship at the curved, circular wall of the Coricancha, and thus the apse of Santo Domingo was purposefully constructed above it to emphasize Christian control of the native site. This story—of European control over former native sites and resources—would be all too common in the continuing history of the Western hemisphere, as we will discover in Chapter 18.

But where the Spanish in Peru incorporated Inca stone masonry into their own colonial architecture—the streets

Fig. 11.36 Serpent heads in the archeological zone of the Templo Mayor, Mexico City, Mexico. Aztec culture.

of Cuzco are lined to this day with original stone walls—in Mexico, they would obliterate the Aztec capital of Tenochtitlán altogether. Even the giant temple in the heart of the city, the Templo Mayor, was brought to ruin, the Spanish building the capital of what they called New Spain atop its rubble (see Chapter 23). Not until 1978, when workers digging for the electric company excavated a huge disk over 10 feet in diameter and weighing 8.5 tons (see Fig. 18.2), did researchers determine where the temple originally stood, just to the northeast of the Zócalo, the main square of modern Mexico City. In order to accommodate excavation, 13 buildings had to be demolished, four dating from the nineteenth century, the others from the 1930s. The pyramid was composed of four sloped stairways, one on each side, topped by a great platform upon which stood two shrines, one dedicated to Tlaloc, the god of rain and agriculture, and one to Huitzilopochtli, god of war. Each stairway was defined by railings that flanked the stairs terminating, at the base, in menacing serpent heads (Fig. 11.36). Today the Museum of the Templo Mayor supervises continuing archeological work at the site and houses the more than 7,000 artifacts discovered there. ■

Fig. 11.35 Original Inca stone wall of the Coricancha with a Dominican monastery rising above it, Inca culture, Cuzco, Peru.

How did poetry, art, and architecture of the Tang and Song dynasties reflect the values of the Chinese state?

Between the first and third centuries CE, Buddhism spread from India north into China, and with it came images of the Buddha. During the Tang dynasty, trade on the Silk Road flourished. As reflected in the plan of their capital Chang'an, the Tang were committed to social order. The Tang valued the arts—they were especially gifted ceramic artists—and education. Confucian, Buddhist, and Daoist philosophy informed government affairs. How did these philosophies inform the poetry of writers like Li Bai and Du Fu as well? When Marco Polo visited Hangzhou in 1274, it was still the capital city of the Southern Song dynasty. It enjoyed tremendous prosperity, controlled in no small part by a thriving merchant class whose sons had benefited from the invention of the printing press at schools that prepared them for government examinations. What did these students learn from studying the Chinese classics? Many poets and artists of the period practiced the neo-Confucian Chan Buddhism. How were these beliefs reflected in their work? In 1279, the Song fell to the Mongol leader Kublai Khan, who ruled China from Beijing as founder of the Yuan dynasty. The scholar-painters of the Chinese court, unwilling to serve under foreign domination, retreated into exile. How did their artworks reflect their resistance?

What religions shaped Indian and Southeast Asian civilization?

During the era known as the Middle Ages in the West, the history and art of India and Southeast Asia were dominated by the interaction of Buddhism, Islam, and Hinduism. Forced out of northern India by invading Muslims, the Buddhists retreated north into Nepal and across the Himalayas into Tibet or eastward into presentday Myanmar (formerly Burma). In Tibet, a new brand of Buddhism developed under the local religious leaders—the lamas, and the chief lama—the Dahlai. How would you describe Tibetan Buddhism? Meanwhile Hinduism continued to thrive especially in southern India and Cambodia. Distinct Hindu temple styles developed, the chief example of which is the Kandarya Mahadeva temple at Khajurabo which mirrored the Hindu cosmos. As Hinduism spread into Cambodia, enormous temple complexes were constructed, especially at Angkor Wat. What does the sculpture program at Angkor Wat suggest about the Hindu religion?

Why did the Japanese capital move to Asuka, Nara, Heiankyo, and Kamakura?

The end of the Yamato period in Japan was marked by strife between the imperial Sago clan, who were deeply attracted to Buddhism, and the Mononobe, who were in charge of the emperor's military, and the Nakatomi, in charge of Shinto ritual, both of whom opposed the introduction of Buddhism into the country. Prince Shotoku moved the capital to Asuka and introduced Confucian principles into court affairs, but his descendants were executed. Factions continued to fight even after the imperial capital was moved again to nearby Nara and then Heian-kyo (modern Kyoto). During the more stable Heian period, conflicts continued. Nevertheless, the Heian court was one of the greatest elegance and refinement. Noble women lived in extreme seclusion, but could distinguish themselves through their correspondence and verse. Instead of writing in the official Chinese writing style, these women wrote in a new, distinctly Japanese writing system, *hiragana*. Among the most important writers at the Heian court were the Lady Ise, the earliest female master; Sei Shonagon, author of *The Pillow Book*; and Murasaki Shikibu, whose *Diaries* are surpassed only by her monumental fictional narrative, *The Tale of Genji*. How would you describe the style of the scroll illustrations of *The Tale of Genji*? When, again, conflicts among various clans led to the downfall of the Heian dynasty, warriors known as samurai took over the country. The most powerful samurai, Minamoto Yoritomo, took the title of shogun and inaugurated the first shogunate, the Kamakura dynasty. He isolated his government from both the imperial court at Heian-kyo and the Buddhist monks at Nara. But both the court and Buddhism still thrived. What form of Buddhism became increasingly popular? Why?

What shapes did civilization take in Africa?

By 1100, the Yoruba civilization, centered in the west African city of Ife, was producing highly naturalistic commemorative portraits in clay and stone, probably depicting their rulers, and not long after, elegant brass sculptures as well. In Benin, a huge complex of moats and walls developed at the capital. The art of lost-wax casting was perfected there as well. What was the purpose of these sculptures? How are these same purposes reflected in praise poems? In East Africa, Ethiopia was developing monumental architecture in the form of carved rock Christian churches, while farther down the coast the Swahili culture, a hybrid of indigenous African and Arab Muslim customs and languages, fostered cosmopolitan port cities.

Who were the Moche and the Inca?

Moche culture arose in the river valleys of the coastal plains of Peru in about 200 BCE. It produced elaborate ceramic stirrup-spouted bottles that depicted every aspect of Moche life. How might we account for the disappearance of the Moche around 800 CE? Over four hundred years later, the Inca emerged, with their capital at Cuzco in the high Andes, but their influence extended to the coastal plains as well. They were extraordinary masons, and they were especially attracted to textiles. The llama, from which they derived the wool to make their textile wares, was sacred to them. They decorated their temples freely with gold. What did gold represent to them? What about silver? How did all their artworks in precious metals disappear?

PRACTICE MORE Get flashcards for images and terms and review chapter material with quizzes at **www.myartslab.com**

GLOSSARY

adobe A sun-baked block of clay mixed with straw.

anaphora A repetition of words and phrases at the beginning of successive sentences intended to create a powerful and insistent rhythm that rises to a crescendo.

bushido The somewhat mythologized code of conduct practiced by the samurai.

call-and-response A form of music in which a caller, or soloist, raises the song, and the community chorus responds to it.

daimyo The head of a *samurai* clan and landholder.

haiku A form of Japanese poetry consisting of three lines containing usually five, seven, and five syllables.

hiragana A purely Japanese writing system that developed in the early ninth century.

mudra A symbolic gesture.

negative space The space around or between the main objects in a composition.

pagoda A multistoried structure of successively smaller, repeated stories, with projecting roofs at each story.

praise poem A poem in praise of something designed to gain influence over it.

samurai The regional warrior clans of Japan.

scarification Decorative effects made on the face or body by means of intentional scarring.

shogun The general-in-chief of the samurai.

talking drums In Africa, a form of musical signaling.

waka A form of Japanese poetry consisting of 31 syllables in 5 lines on a theme drawn from nature and the changing of seasons.

READINGS

READING 11.1

Poems by Li Bai and Du Fu

Li Bai and Du Fu are generally considered the greatest poets of the Tang dynasty. The two became close friends after Li Bai was summoned to the capital at Chang'an by the Emperor Xuanzong [shoo-ehn-tsahng] in 742. They wrote many poems to one another, a good example of which is the second of the two poems below, while the first poem below underscores his sense of isolation and loneliness after he was expelled from court in 762. After the collapse of the Tang court in the mid-750s, Du Fu wandered down the Yangtze River, finding patrons and dreaming of his return to Chang'an, until his death in 770.

LI BAI, "DRINKING ALONE BY MOONLIGHT"

A pot of wine in the flower garden,
but no friends to drink with me.
So I raise my cup to the bright moon
and to my shadow, which makes us three,
but the moon won't drink
and my shadow just creeps about my heels.
Yet in your company, moon and shadow,
I have a wild time till spring dies out.
I sing and the moon shudders.
My shadow staggers when I dance.   10

We have our fun while I can stand
then drift apart when I fall asleep.
Let's share this empty journey often
and meet again in the milky river of stars.

DU FU, "DREAMING OF LI BAI"

I've swallowed sobs from the lost dead,
but this live separation is chronic grief.
From the malarial south of the river
no news comes of the exiled traveler,

but you visit my dream, old friend,
knowing I ache for you.
Are you a ghost?
No way to tell with the long road between us.
Your spirit comes through the green maple woods
slips home past darkening border fortresses.   20
You are caught in the law's net,
so how can your spirit have wings?
The sinking moon pours onto the rafters
and your face glows in my mind.

The water is deep, the waves are wide.
Don't let the dragons snatch you!

READING CRITICALLY

Both poems develop the image of moonlight. Traditionally, in China, the full moon is a symbol of good luck, harmony, and abundance. How does this symbol inform these two poems?

READING 11.5

from Sei Shonagon, *The Pillow Book*, "Hateful Things"

We know almost nothing about Sei Shonagon except what she writes about herself in The Pillow Book. *"Hateful Things" is one of 164 such lists in Sei Shonagon's* Pillow Book. *Others include "People Who Look Pleased with Themselves," "Insects," "Things without Merit," and so on. But lists are not her only subject. She continually turns her attention to minute observations of court life, in entries such as "The Cat Who Lived in the Palace" or "The Women's Apartments along the Gallery."*

One is in a hurry to leave, but one's visitor keeps chattering away. If it is someone of no importance, one can get rid of him by saying, 'You must tell me all about it next time'; but, should it be the sort of visitor whose presence commands one's best behaviour, the situation is hateful indeed.

One finds that a hair has got caught in the stone on which one is rubbing one's inkstick, or again that gravel is lodged in the inkstick, making a nasty, grating sound.

Someone has suddenly fallen ill and one summons the exorcist. Since he is not at home, one has to send messengers to   10
look for him. After one has had a long fretful wait, the exorcist finally arrives, and with a sigh of relief one asks him to start his incantations. But perhaps he has been exorcizing too many evil spirits recently; for hardly has he installed himself and begun praying when his voice becomes drowsy. Oh, how hateful!

A man who has nothing in particular to recommend him discusses all sorts of subjects at random as though he knew everything.

An elderly person warms the palms of his hands over a brazier and stretches out the wrinkles. No young man would   20
dream of behaving in such a fashion; old people can really be quite shameless. I have seen some dreary old creatures actually resting their feet on the brazier and rubbing them against the edge while they speak. These are the kind of people who in visiting someone's house first use their fans to wipe away the dust from the mat and, when they finally sit on it, cannot stay still but are forever spreading out the front of their hunting costume[1] or even tucking it up under their knees. One might suppose that such behaviour was restricted to people of humble station; but I have observed it in quite well-bred people,   30
including a Senior Secretary of the Fifth Rank in the Ministry of Ceremonial and a former Governor of Suruga.

I hate the sight of men in their cups who shout, poke their fingers in their mouths, stroke their beards, and pass on the wine to their neighbours with great cries of 'Have some more! Drink up!' They tremble, shake their heads, twist their faces, and gesticulate like children who are singing, 'We're off to see the Governor.' I have seen really well-bred people behave like this and I find it most distasteful.

To envy others and to complain about one's own lot; to   40
speak badly about people; to be inquisitive about the most trivial matters and to resent and abuse people for not telling one, or, if one does manage to worm out some facts, to inform everyone in the most detailed fashion as if one had known all from the beginning—oh, how hateful!

One is just about to be told some interesting piece of news when a baby starts crying.

A flight of crows circle about with loud caws.

An admirer has come on a clandestine visit, but a dog catches sight of him and starts barking. One feels like killing the   50
beast.

One has been foolish enough to invite a man to spend the night in an unsuitable place—and then he starts snoring.

A gentleman has visited one secretly. Though he is wearing a tall, lacquered hat[2], he nevertheless wants no one to see him. He is so flurried, in fact, that upon leaving he bangs into something with his hat. Most hateful! It is annoying too when he lifts up the lyo blind[3] that hangs at the entrance of the room, then lets it fall with a great rattle. If it is a head-blind, things are still worse, for being more solid it makes a terrible noise when it is dropped. There is no excuse for such carelessness. Even a head-blind does   60
not make any noise if one lifts it up gently on entering and leaving the room; the same applies to sliding-doors. If one's movements are rough, even a paper door will bend and resonate when opened; but, if one lifts the door a little while pushing it, there need be no sound.

One has gone to bed and is about to doze off when a mosquito appears, announcing himself in a reedy voice. One can actually feel the wind made by his wings and, slight though it is, one finds it hateful in the extreme.

A carriage passes with a nasty, creaking noise. Annoying to   70
think that the passengers may not even be aware of this! If I am travelling in someone's carriage and I hear it creaking, I dislike not only the noise but also the owner of the carriage.

One is in the middle of a story when someone butts in and tries to show that he is the only clever person in the room. Such a person is hateful, and so, indeed, is anyone, child or adult, who tries to push himself forward.

One is telling a story about old times when someone breaks in with a little detail that he happens to know, implying that one's own version is inaccurate—disgusting behaviour!

Very hateful is a mouse that scurries all over the place. 80

Some children have called at one's house. One makes a great fuss of them and gives them toys to play with. The children become accustomed to this treatment and start to come regularly, forcing their way into one's inner rooms and scattering one's furnishings and possessions. Hateful!

A certain gentleman whom one does not want to see visits one at home or in the Palace, and one pretends to be asleep. But a maid comes to tell one and shakes one awake, with a look on her face that says, 'What a sleepyhead!' Very hateful.

A newcomer pushes ahead of the other members in a 90 group; with a knowing look, this person starts laying down the law and forcing advice upon everyone—most hateful.

A man with whom one is having an affair keeps singing the praises of some woman he used to know. Even if it is a thing of the past, this can be very annoying. How much more so if he is still seeing the woman! (Yet sometimes I find that it is not as unpleasant as all that.)

A good lover will behave as elegantly at dawn as at any other time. He drags himself out of bed with a look of dismay on his face. The lady urges him on: 'Come, my friend, it's getting light. 100

¹**Hunting costume:** men's informal outdoor costume, originally worn for hunting.
²**Eboshi (tall, lacquered hat):** black, lacquered head-dress worn by men on the top of the head and secured by a mauve silk cord that was fastened under the chin; two long black pendants hung down from the back of the hat. The *eboshi* was a most conspicuous form of headgear and hardly suited for a clandestine visit.

You don't want anyone to find you here.' He gives a deep sigh, as if to say that the night has not been nearly long enough and that it is agony to leave. Once up, he does not instantly pull on his trousers. Instead he comes close to the lady and whispers whatever was left unsaid during the night. Even when he is dressed, he still lingers, vaguely pretending to be fastening his sash.

Presently he raises the lattice, and the two lovers stand together by the side door while he tells her how he dreads the coming day, which will keep them apart; then he slips away. The lady watches him go, and this moment of parting will 110 remain among her most charming memories.

Indeed, one's attachment to a man depends largely on the elegance of his leave-taking. When he jumps out of bed, scurries about the room, tightly fastens his trouser-sash, rolls up the sleeves of his Court cloak, over-robe, or hunting costume, stuffs his belongings into the breast of his robe and then briskly secures the outer sash—one really begins to hate him.

READING CRITICALLY

During the Heian period, the finest writers of the day were by and large aristocratic women of middle rank like Sei Shonagon. How does "Hateful Things" reflect the prominence of women in court?

³**Iyo blind:** a rough type of reed blind manufactured in the province of Iyo on the Inland Sea.

BOOK THREE

The Renaissance
and the Age of Encounter
1400 TO 1600

Detail of Albrecht Altdorfer, *The Battle of Issus.* 1529 (see Fig. 17.1).

During the 200 years extending roughly from 1400 to 1600, Western European culture experienced a rebirth of classical learning and values. For this reason we call the period the Renaissance [REN-uh-sahnts], which means "rebirth" in French. By the middle of the fourteenth century, Dante Alighieri had picked the ancient Roman poet Virgil as his guide through his fictional Inferno and Purgatory, Petrarch was busy amassing his own classical library, and Boccaccio, who like Dante wrote in the vernacular Italian instead of Latin, was also learning Greek.

At the dawn of the Renaissance, then, the values of the classical past—simplicity, balance, and restraint in design, proportionality of parts, and purity of form—had already firmly established their place in Western culture. These values stimulated the emergence of humanism—the recovery, study, and spread of the art and literature of Greece and Rome, and the application of their principles to education, politics, social life, and the arts in general. In turn, humanism stimulated a new sense of the value of the individual. Each person has the capacity for self-determination in the search for truth and morality. Faith, sacred texts, or religious tradition were no longer the only guides.

After the Black Death, it seemed possible, even necessary, to begin again. In politics, feudal rule gave way to centralized forms of government. City-states flourished, strengthened by the influx of workers migrating from the countryside, as manufacture and trade supplanted agriculture as the basis of the European economy. The Church, which in medieval times had been the very foundation of Western culture, found itself challenged on all fronts. Politically, European monarchs questioned its authority. Philosophically, a growing class of intellectuals challenged its long-held doctrines. Morally, many of these same intellectuals denounced the behavior of its clergy and called for reform.

It was a time of invention and discovery. The printing press in Germany became a major instrument of change by making available to an ever-growing middle class works of literature, political tracts, and philosophical arguments that literally transformed their way of thinking. Even as the telescope revised human understanding of the cosmos and the world's place in it, previously unknown civilizations in the Americas, Africa, and the Far East changed the Western understanding of its world. The Age of Encounter, which began in the fifteenth century and ended in the seventeenth, resulted in the colonization of most of the non-Western world. The effect of Western colonization was the displacement, enslavement, and large-scale death of native peoples. Those cultures that the West did not come to dominate—China and Japan especially—were deeply affected by their encounters with the West.

By the start of the sixteenth century, the humanistic spirit had begun to generate new forms of art and literature. The use of the rules of scientific perspective allowed for the convincing representation of three-dimensional space on the two-dimensional surface of a panel or canvas. The introduction of oil painting as a medium contributed to this naturalism by enabling artists to render the natural world in more precise detail than did tempera and to imitate effects of light and shadow both in the atmosphere and on the surface of objects. In architecture, structural innovations permitted the construction of the largest spaces since antiquity. New literary forms—the English sonnet, the personal essay, and popular theater—responded to a growing secular taste. And in music, where the courts maintained their own rosters of musicians, vernacular song and dance became popular even as the Church sanctioned innovative forms of polyphonic music for its liturgy. In this atmosphere, individual composers began to be recognized across Europe, and their works were published and widely circulated. Following the lead of the early-fifteenth-century writer Christine de Pizan, women increasingly insisted on their own worth and dignity, assuming important roles as patrons, as artists in their own right, and, in England, as heads of state. All of these developments combined to bring Western culture to the threshold of modern life.

Early 1400s
Jan van Eyck painting

1404–1424
Chinese emperor Zhu Di sponsors naval expeditions to Indian Ocean and African coast

1420–1436
Filippo Brunelleschi, dome of Duomo at Florence

1435
Architect Leon Battista Alberti codifies optical perspective in *On Painting*

1435–1455
Johannes Gutenberg, Gutenberg Bible

1480–1550
Portuguese extend African slave trade to Europe, Brazil

ca. 1482
Botticelli, *Primavera*

1486
Pico della Mirandola writes *Oration on the Dignity of Man*, philosophical treatise

1492
Spanish King Ferdinand II and Queen Isabella finance Columbus's voyage to the New World

1495
Sesshu Tokyo, ink painting, Japan

1508
Michelangelo begins Sistine Chapel ceiling

1513
Machiavelli writes *The Prince*

1517
Martin Luther posts *Ninety-Five Theses* on church door at Wittenberg

1489–1576
Lifetime of Titian, *Venus of Urbino* (ca. 1538)

1519–1521
Hernán Cortés conquers Aztec Empire of Mexico

1525–1569
Lifetime of Pieter Bruegel the Elder, *Harvesters* (1565)

1536–1545
Council of Trent convened to plan Catholic Church reform; Pope Paul III initiates Inquisition

1564–1616
Lifetime of William Shakespeare, poet and playwright

LEARN MORE Explore an interactive timeline on **www.myartslab.com**

Encounter and Confrontation

The Impact of Increasing Global Interaction

What was Spain's primary motive in colonizing the Americas?

How did the Portuguese impact West African culture?

To what degree did contact with Europe affect Mogul India?

In what ways did Ming China make contact with the wider world?

Why did cultural refinement flourish in Muromachi and Azuchi-Momoyama Japan?

In 1519 to 1521, the Aztec empire of Mexico was conquered by the Spanish *conquistador* ("conqueror") Hernán Cortés [cor-TEZ] (1485–1547) and his army of 600 men through a combination of military technology (gunpowder, cannon, and muskets), disease inadvertently introduced by his troops, and a series of lies and violations of trust. The Aztecs possessed neither guns nor horses, nor much in the way of clothing or armor, all of which made them appear if not uncivilized, then completely vulnerable. They were also vulnerable because other native populations in Mexico deeply resented the fact that the Aztecs regularly raided their villages to obtain victims for blood sacrifice. According to Aztec legend, at the time of their exile from Tula, the supreme spiritual leadership of the culture was assumed by the bloodthirsty Huitzilopochtli [wee-tsee-loh-POCH-tlee], the god of war, who had emerged fully grown from the womb of his mother Coatlicue [coh-ah-TLEE-coo-eh], the earth goddess, wielding his weapon, the Fire Serpent, Xiuhcoatl [SHEE-oo-koh-ahtl]. A sculpture depicting Coatlicue may have originally stood in the temple to Huitzilopochtli at Tenochtitlán atop the Templo Mayor

(Fig. **18.1**; and see Fig. 11.36). Her head is composed of two fanged serpents, symbolizing two rivers of blood flowing from her decapitated head. She wears a necklace of human ears, severed hands, and, at the bottom, a human skull. The connection of blood to fertility is made clear in the snake that descends between her legs, which suggests both menstruation and the phallus.

Huitzilopochtli was born full-grown out of Coatlicue of necessity. Coatlicue was also mother of Coyolxauhqui [coh-yohl-SHAU-kee], the Moon, and one day, while she was sweeping her temple on top of Coatepec hill, symbolically represented in Tenochtitlán by the Templo Mayor, she had been miraculously impregnated with Huitzilopochtli by a ball of feathers that floated down from the sky. Coyolxauhqui viewed the pregnancy of her mother as an affront, and she conspired to kill her mother. At that moment, Huitzilopochtli was born. He decapitated his treacherous sister, and cast her down from the top of Coatepec hill. At each tumble of her fall, she was further dismembered. This is the Aztec explanation for the phases of the moon. As the moon wanes each month, more and more of its disappears.

◀ **Fig. 18.1 Coatlicue, Aztec. Fifteenth century.** Basalt, height, 8′ 3″. National Museum of Anthropology, Mexico City. Coatlicue is represented as headless because, as legend has it, she was decapitated at the beginning of the present creation.

HEAR MORE Listen to an audio file of your chapter at **www.myartslab.com**

Fig. 18.2 *The Moon Goddess Coyolxauhqui*, **Aztec, from the Sacred Precinct, Templo Mayor, Tenochtitlán. ca. 1469.** Stone, diameter 10′ 10″. Museo Templo Mayor, Mexico City. The sculpture was found lying at the base of the Templo Mayor, as if cast down by Huitzilopochtli.

A giant disk, over 10 feet across, found at the base of the Templo Mayor, depicts the goddess (Fig. **18.2**), decapitated, arms and legs dismembered. She is adorned with a two-headed serpent belt bearing a skull, as does her mother Coatlicue in Fig. 18.1. Her torso, with flaccid breasts, is shown frontally. Issuing from her mouth is what appears to be her last breath. Thus victorious over the moon, Huitzilopochtli ordered the Aztec priests to search for a cactus with a great eagle perched upon it and there establish a city in his name. They soon found the place on the shores of Lake Texcoco. The cactus bore red fruit in the shape of the hearts that Huitzilopochtli devoured, and the eagle was the symbol of the god himself. The Aztecs proceeded to build their great city, Tenochtitlán, "the place of the prickly pear cactus."

Anthropological evidence suggests that just before Cortés's arrival, in about 1450, the Aztecs, in their thirst for blood sacrifice, had wiped out the entire population of Casas Grandes, near present-day Chihuahua in northern Mexico, a trading center containing over 2,000 pueblo apartments. Given such Aztec behavior, other tribes were willing to cooperate with Cortés. Cortés quickly realized he could exploit these vulnerabilities to great military advantage. One of the most important documents of the Spanish conquest, the 1581 *History of the Indies of New Spain*, by Diego de Durán, depicts this technological superiority (Fig. **18.3**). Durán was a Dominican priest fluent in Nahuatl, the Aztec language. His *History* is the product of extensive interviews and conversations with the Aztecs themselves. It represents a concerted effort to preserve Aztec culture, recounting Aztec history from its creation story through the Spanish conquest. In this illustration, a well-armed army led by Pedro de Alvarado, one of Cortés's generals,

confronts the Aztec military orders of the Eagle and the Jaguar. The Spanish wear armor and fight with crossbows and firearms, while the Aztecs have only spears.

Despite their technological superiority, Alvarado's men were in some jeopardy. Alvarado was besieged by Aztecs angry at the slaughter of hundreds of Aztecs during the Fiesta of Toxcatl, staged to impress their Spanish visitors. The massacre by the Spaniards is illustrated in Durán's *History* (Fig. **18.4**). The infamy of the Spaniards' attack and the Aztec retaliation are also described by a Franciscan missionary, Bernardino de Sahagún. Like Durán, Sahagún was fluent in Nahuatl, and he based his *History of the Things of New Spain* on interviews with surviving Aztecs (see **Reading 18.1**, pages 619–620, for his full account).

Throughout these events, the Aztec king Motecuhzoma (formerly spelled Montezuma) had remained a prisoner of the Spanish forces. Cortés had pledged his friendship, but once he had been admitted into Tenochtitlán itself, he imprisoned Motecuhzoma. The Spanish conquistador had learned of an Aztec myth concerning Quetzalcóatl, the Feathered Serpent, who was widely worshiped throughout Mexico. In this myth, Quetzalcóatl was dethroned by his evil brother, Tezcatlipoca, god of war, and fled to the Gulf of Mexico, where he burst into flames and ascended to the heavens, becoming the Morning Star, Venus. In yet another

Figs. 18.3 and 18.4 (top) Aztecs confront the Spaniards; and (bottom) the Spanish massacre Aztec nobles in the temple courtyard. Both from Diego de Durán's *History of the Indies of New Spain.* **1581.** Biblioteca Nacional, Madrid, Spain. Durán's work was roundly criticized during his lifetime for helping the "heathen" Aztecs maintain their culture.

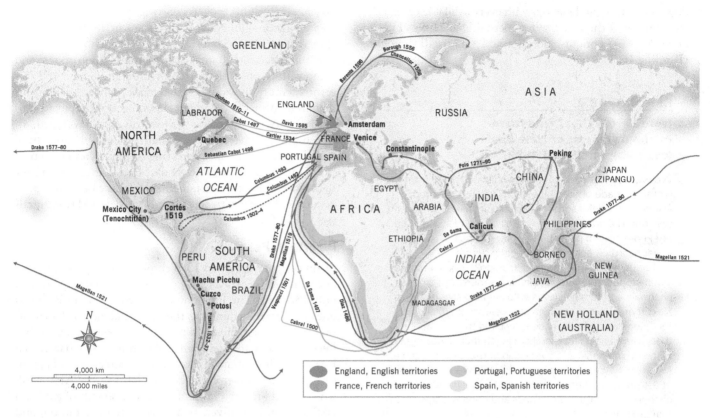

Map 18.1 World exploration. 1486–1611. Note Marco Polo's overland route to China in 1271 to 1295, which anticipated the great sea explorations by 200 years.

version, he sailed away across the sea on a raft of serpents, promising one day to return. It was reputed that Quetzal-cóatl was fair-skinned and bearded. Evidently, Motecuh-zoma believed that Cortés was the returning Quetzalcóatl and welcomed him without resistance. Within two years, Cortés's army had crushed Motecuhzoma's people in the name of Spain. Of the 20 to 25 million inhabitants of Mexico at that time, only about 2 million survived—the remainder were wiped out by war and disease.

This chapter surveys the cultures of the Americas, Africa, India, China, and Japan in this period, and considers how Europe transformed these cultures as it explored the world (see Map **18.1**) and was itself transformed by contact with them. But European contact was not the only interaction these cultures experienced in the era. They also impacted one another. From a Western perspective, these cultures represented a wider world with Europe at its center. But from the point of view of these cultures, Europe represented the periphery, a cultural force invading their own centers of culture from the outside.

THE SPANISH IN THE AMERICAS

When Cortés entered the Aztec island capital of Tenochtitlán (Fig. **18.5**), more than 200,000 people lived there. Gold-laden temples towered above the city. Gardens rich in

Fig. 18.5 Plan of Tenochtitlán, from Cortés's first letter to the king of Spain. 1521. Bernal Díaz, one of Cortés's conquistadors, compared the plan of Tenochtitlán to Venice. Set in the middle of Lake Texcoco, it was crisscrossed by canals. In the center of the island is the Templo Mayor.

flowers and fruit, and markets with every available commodity dominated the city itself as Bernal Díaz (1492–1584), one of Cortés's conquistadores, would later recall the sight (**Reading 18.2**):

READING 18.2

from Bernal Diaz, *True History* of the Conquest of New Spain (ca. 1568; published 1632)

We were astounded. . . . These buildings rising from the water, all made of stone, seemed like an enchanted vision. . . . Indeed some of our soldiers asked whether it was not all a dream. . . . It was all so wonderful that I do not know how to describe this first glimpse of things never heard of, seen, or dreamed of before. . . .

Let us begin with the dealers in gold, silver, and precious stones, feathers, cloaks, and embroidered goods, and male and female slaves who are also sold there. . . . Next there were those who sold coarser cloth, and cotton goods and fabrics made of twisted threads, and there were chocolate merchants with their chocolate. In this way you could see every kind of merchandise to be found anywhere in New Spain. . . . We were astounded at the great number of people and the quantities of merchandise, and at the orderliness and good arrangements that prevailed.

What most astonished Cortés himself, as it had Diaz, was that Aztec civilization was as sophisticated as his own and unlike the civilization Columbus had encountered, with its naked, seemingly innocent natives. "So as not to tire Your Highness with the description of things of this city," Cortés wrote Queen Isabella of Spain, "I will say only that these people live almost like those in Spain, and in as much harmony and order as there, and considering that they are barbarous and so far from the knowledge of God and cut off from all civilized nations, it is truly remarkable to see what they have achieved in all things." This inclination to see a thriving civilization as uncivilized because it is unlike one's own is typical of the attitude of Westerners toward the peoples with whom they came into contact in the Age of Encounter. Other peoples were exactly that—the "Other"—a separate category of being that freed Western colonizers from any obligation to identify these peoples as equal, or even similar, to themselves (see *Context*, page 596).

It seemed paramount to the Spanish crown to begin to raise the native population from its "barbarous" condition by bringing it, as Columbus had put it from the beginning, to "the knowledge of God." The Spanish essentially obliterated the traditions of the Native American cultures they encountered, burning all their books, destroying almost every record of their history that they could lay their hands on, and crippling for all time our ability to adequately piece together a full picture of their culture. Churches were quickly built in Mexico City. And as the Church sought to convert native populations to the Catholic faith, the musical liturgy became a powerful tool. As early as 1523, Spanish monks created a school for Native Americans in Texcoco, Mexico (just east of Mexico City), and began teaching music, including Gregorian chant, the principles of polyphony, and composition, on an imported organ. Throughout the sixteenth century, missionaries used music, dance, and religious dramas to attract and convert the indigenous population to Christianity. A syncretic culture quickly developed, in which European styles were Indianized, and Indian culture was Christianized. An interesting example can be seen in the paintings depicting festival days in the seventeenth century, where Christian sacraments—in this case, marriage—occur side by side with traditional Aztec and Mayan rituals (see *Closer Look*, pages 594–595).

Pizarro in Peru

Spain conquered Peru in 1533 through the exploits of Francisco Pizarro [pee-ZAH-roh] (1474–1541) with an army of only 180 men. The Inca Empire Pizarro found in Peru was one of the largest empires in the world and included, in addition to Peru itself, most of what is now modern Ecuador, Bolivia, northern Chile, and part of Argentina (see Chapter 11). Pizarro's military strategy was aided by simple deceit. He captured the Inca emperor, Atahuallpa [ah-tah-HWAHL-pah], who offered Pizarro a ransom of 13,420 pounds of gold and 26,000 pounds of silver. Pizarro accepted the ransom and then executed the unsuspecting emperor. He next proceeded to plunder Peru of the gold and silver artifacts that were part of its religious worship of the sun (gold) and moon (silver).

No work better may exemplify the impact of Spanish colonization on the native Inca of Peru than a portrait of Atahuallpa painted in Cuzco [KOOZ-koh], the traditional capital of the Inca Empire, in the mid-eighteenth century (Fig. **18.6**). It is one of a series of 14 portraits of the Inca kings, most of which are based on an engraving by Antonio de Herrera in *General History of the Deeds of the Castilians*, first published in 1615, some 80 years after Pizarro's betrayal of Atahuallpa. Representations of the Inca kings were very popular in Peru in the seventeenth and eighteenth centuries, especially in the Cuzco households of the Peruvian *caciques*—Indian nobility who proudly traced their heritage back to the royal Inca families. Although painted by Cuzco Indians, the framing device and the portrait conventions are entirely European. Even more remarkable is the text around the frame identifying Atahuallpa. It labels him the "Bastard Tyrant," suggesting that this particular series of portraits may have been destined for a Spanish colonial household. After a series of rebellions throughout Peru in the late eighteenth century, however, Spanish rulers banned portraits of the Inca kings and destroyed many of them. At the same time, they banned native costumes, especially the elaborate costumes of the nobility that adorn Atahuallpa in this work.

Gold and Silver: The Monetary Motive

The acquisition of gold, silver, and other treasure was a strong motivation for European colonization of the Americas. Great masses of treasure were sent home from the New

Fig. 18.6 *Atahuallpa*, from Peru. Mid-eighteenth century. Oil on canvas, 23 3/4″ × 21 5/8″. The Brooklyn Museum. 45.128.189. Note Atahuallpa's scepter, with its golden sun. Gold, for the Inca, was the "sweat of the sun." Each year, as the winter solstice approached and the sun seemed to disappear more each day, a priest would hold a ceremony at a large stone column called the *intihuatana*, meaning "for tying the sun," in order to prevent the sun from disappearing altogether. The Spanish destroyed the *intihuatanas*, but one survives at Machu Picchu.

the grasp of the conquistadores under royal order who followed in Pizarro's footsteps in Peru, often with unhappy results. The treasures of gold and silver that were brought back would be melted down for currency, far more important than their artistic value to the warring Spanish monarchy. In fact, almost no gold or silver objects survive from the conquest.

Throughout the first half of the sixteenth century, the Spanish purchased thousands of slaves from the Portuguese and set them to work panning gold in the mountains of the Americas. But in 1555, the process for isolating silver from waste by combining it with mercury was developed, and silver began to be mined at an extraordinary rate. The largest silver mine in the Americas was at Potosí [poh-toh-SEE], Bolivia, 13,000 feet high in the Andes. From 1580 to 1650, the mines at Potosí never produced less than 7.6 million pesos annually, minted into coins near the mines. The city's population in 1547 was about 14,000. By 1650, Potosí had become the largest city in the Americas, with a population of nearly 160,000.

The Spanish conscripted Indians from their traditional agricultural chores to work the mines at Potosí. (African slaves worked almost all other mines in the Americas, but they were unable to adjust to the extremely high elevation of Potosí.) Spain instituted the *repartimiento*—called the *mita* by the Indians—requiring adult male Indians to devote a certain number of days each year to working for Spanish economic interests. At Potosí, 13,300 Indians were conscripted annually under the *mita*, one-third of them working at any one time. Literally thousands upon thousands of Indians rotated through the mine in the 70 years of its maximum output, and many thousands of them died in its inferno-like conditions. Under the *mita*, the Indians received minimum wages and had to buy supplies from the mine owners. This created a system of *debt patronage* that lasted into the early twentieth century across South America and Mesoamerica.

The wealth generated by the Potosí mine was arguably responsible for the ascendancy of Spain as an empire during the sixteenth century. But the exploitation of the people and natural resources of the Americas that the Potosí mine represents thrusts the dark side of the Age of Encounter into astonishing relief. The Dominican monk Francisco de la Cruz [crooz] was one Spaniard who recognized this: "One of the reasons God will punish Spain is because it has not given due succour and salvation to the Indians. . . . The time will come when Peru will be ruled independent of Spain." The Inquisition burned Cruz at the stake in Lima on April 13, 1578, for such progressive thinking.

World. When the first Royal Fifth (that is, one-fifth of the treasures collected by Cortés and earmarked by contract for the king) arrived in Brussels, the German artist Albrecht Dürer was present:

> I saw the things which were brought to the King from the New Golden Land: a sun entirely of gold, a whole fathom [six feet] broad; likewise, a moon, entirely of silver, just as big; likewise, sundry curiosities from their weapons, armor, and missiles; very odd clothing, bedding, and all sorts of strange articles for human use, all of which is fairer to see than marvels. These things were all so precious that they were valued at a hundred thousand guilders. But I have never seen in all my days that which so rejoiced my heart, as these things. For I saw among them amazing artistic objects, and I marveled over the subtle ingenuity of the men in these distant lands. Indeed I cannot say enough about the things which were there before me.

Accounts like this helped give rise to the belief in an entire city of gold, El Dorado, which continued to elude

CLOSER LOOK

This monumental *biombo* (folding screen) is a work exceptional for its depiction of the syncretism of Christian and Native traditions in seventeenth-century Mexico. The Spanish and Portuguese word *biombo* was derived from the Japanese word for folding screen, *byobu* (literally, "protection from the wind"). *Biombos* were first introduced to New Spain (Mexico) from Japan through the legendary Manila galleons that traded across the Pacific at the end of the sixteenth century. By the seventeenth century, they had become a standard and fashionable decoration in elite households. This *biombo* depicts festivities taking place in a village situated near canals—probably Santa Anita Ixtacalco, a famous site in the environs of Mexico City.

Something to Think About . . .

What does this *biombo* have in common with the casta painting tradition (see Fig. 18.12)?

Here an Indian lies on the ground and juggles a log with his feet; the surrounding crowd includes Spaniards, recognizable by their seventeenth-century capes and collars.

The foreground is filled with Indians, many of them in native costume.

Folding Screen with Indian Wedding and Flying Pole

A *palo volador,* or flying pole, from which men called *voladores* swing to the ground on ropes. It represents a long-standing tradition preserved from pre-Hispanic times. Archeologist Demetrio Sodi has described *El Volador,* the original dance as performed by the Maya: "Five men are chosen to perform the dance. In the past, the dancers dressed as eagles or other birds. [Here all pretence of costume has been forsaken, suggesting that its purpose is more entertainment than ritual.] One is the captain and four take the roles of birdmen. A tall, strong, straight tree is stripped of its branches and bark and set upright in the main square of the town. A wooden cylinder is attached to the top of the trunk, with a frame from which hang the four ropes to which the birdmen are tied. The captain stands on top of the cylinder, playing a drum and flute, and dances, turning to the four corners of the universe. [This figure is likewise missing in the painting.] Then the four birdmen, tied by their ankles and hanging head down, slowly descend. The number of circles they turn before touching the earth varies, but in pre-Hispanic times, and even now on certain occasions, they circled thirteen times. The number of turns multiplied by the four birdmen equals the number of years of the pre-Hispanic calendar: fifty two, divided by four, thirteen year periods. *El Volador* undoubtedly has an intimate relation to worship of the sun. The captain who turns toward the cardinal points and the birdmen dressed as eagles (birds of the sun), make this clear."

The landscape is completely imaginary, based on the Flemish landscape tradition or the Italian landscapes of Annibile Carracci.

Here nine Indians perform a *tecontin,* or Dance of Motecuhzoma. At the left, a sumptuously dressed figure plays the part of Motecuhzoma. An attendant holds a *mosqueador,* a large feather fan, over his head. The eight other dancers imitate the dance performed by the Aztec king, accompanied by a harpist and guitarist.

Indian newlyweds leave the church. Contemporary accounts tell us that at the dance's conclusion, the Motecuhzoma figure would lead all present in celebrating the Christian sacrament of marriage.

Folding Screen with Indian Wedding and Flying Pole (Biombo con desposorio indígena y palo volador). **circa 1690.** Oil on canvas, 66" × 120". Los Angeles County Museum of Art. Purchased with funds provided by the Bernard and Edith Lewin Collection of Mexican Art Deaccession Fund. M.2005.54.

The "Other" in Western Consciousness

Any history of Western civilization must account for the relation of Western cultures to the other cultures with which they came into contact. The Age of Encounter, which began in the fifteenth century and ended in the seventeenth, resulted in the colonization of most of the non-Western world. Only the vast interior of Asia escaped Western domination. The effect of Western colonization was the displacement, enslavement, and large-scale death of native peoples. This last effect was at least partly unintentional, as Europeans introduced into the uncharted territories of their conquest common European diseases that the immune systems of native populations could not successfully fight. From the Western perspective, it hardly mattered. Europeans thought of these peoples as being in a state of cultural childhood, and because childhood mortality was extremely high in the Renaissance and something Europeans accepted as natural, they could absorb the deaths of these New World "children" with composure. Above all, these "innocents" were "primitive"—that is, they knew nothing of the Christian God and Western culture. At the very least, they required "civilizing."

Homi Bhaba [ho-mee bah-bah], a great student of contemporary global culture, has reminded us of the "artifactual" consequences of Western colonization in an essay exploring the connection between contemporary culture and its colonial heritage. "The great remains of the Inca or Aztec world are the debris . . . of the Culture of Discovery," he writes. "Their presence in the museum should reflect the devastation that has turned them from being signs in a powerful cultural system to becoming the symbols of a destroyed culture." The headdress of Motecuhzoma, presented to the Holy Roman Emperor Charles V by Cortés and now in the Museum of Ethnology in Vienna, is a case in point. Consisting of 450 green tail feathers of the quetzal bird, blue feathers from the cotinga bird, beads, and gold, it is a treasure of extraordinary beauty and can be appreciated in purely aesthetic terms, as the museum presents it. Yet as Homi Bhaba points out, "It seems appropriate . . . [to make] present in the display of art what is so often rendered unrepresentable or left unrepresented—violence, trauma, dispossession." In other words, Bhaba believes that the headdress's history, the tale of Cortés and his betrayal of Motecuhzoma, should enter into the museum display.

Bhaba is critiquing museum practice, but his admonition applies as well to this text. Many of the images in Chapter 23 are symbols of destroyed cultures. They were once signs of power. They were quickly consigned, in Western consciousness, to the category of the "Other." Those classified as "Other" were thought to be incapable of utilizing their own natural resources for themselves. The West considered those whom they colonized to be weak (because unsophisticated in the uses of Western technology), uneducated (though highly trained in their own traditions), and morally bankrupt (because "bloodthirsty," "naked," and "uninhibited"). Remember, the Greeks called all peoples who did not speak Greek "barbarians" (see Chapter 5). And just as the Romans tried to "Romanize" their provincial holdings, so too did Western colonizers from the era of the great explorers try to "civilize" the peoples they encountered.

Quetzal feather headdress, Aztec. ca. 1520. Museum für Völkerkunde, Vienna. There is speculation but no proof that this headdress was worn by the Aztec emperor Motecuhzoma.

WEST AFRICAN CULTURE AND THE PORTUGUESE

Portugal was as active as Spain in seeking trading opportunities through navigation, but focused on Africa and the East instead of the Americas. In 1488, Bartholomeu Dias [DEE-az] (ca. 1450–1500), investigating the coast of West Africa (Map **18.2**), was blown far south by a sudden storm, and turning northeast, found that he had rounded what would later be called the Cape of Good Hope and entered the Indian Ocean. Following Dias, Vasco da Gama [VAHZ-koh da GAH-mah] (ca. 1460–1524) sailed around the cape with four ships in 1497 and reached Calicut, India, 10 months 14 days after leaving Lisbon. Then, in 1500, Pedro Cabral [kah-BRAHL] (ca. 1467–ca. 1520), seeking to repeat da Gama's voyage to India, set out from the bulge of Africa.

Sailing too far westward, he landed in what is now Brazil, where he claimed the territory for Portugal.

After Bartholomeu Dias's exploration of the west coast of Africa, it did not take long for European and African traders to extend existing practices of human exploitation that were common on both continents. This trade in human labor would eventually take on a scope and dimension not previously seen. The Portuguese exploitation of African labor was financed principally by a Florentine banker together with a group of other financiers from Genoa. Over the course of four centuries, the Portuguese transported millions of Africans across the Atlantic (Map **18.3**) on the **Middle Passage**, so named because it formed the base of a triangular trade system: Europe to Africa, Africa to the Americas (the Middle Passage), and the Americas to Europe. No one can say with certainty just how many slaves made the crossing, although estimates range between 15 and 20 million. Part of the problem is the unknown numbers who died of disease and harsh conditions during the voyage. For instance, in 1717, a ship reached Buenos Aires with only 98 survivors of an original 594 slaves. Such figures were probably not unusual.

For a while, at least, the Portuguese enjoyed a certain status as divine visitors from the watery world, the realm of Olokun [OH-loh-koon], god of the sea. They were considered to be the equivalent of the mudfish, because they could both "swim" (in their boats) and walk on land. The mudfish was sacred to the people of Benin [bay-NEEN], who saw it as a symbol of both transformation and power. (It lies dormant all summer on dry mudflats until fall when

Map 18.2 Sub-Saharan West Africa. 1200–1700. While Muslim traders had extensive knowledge of North Africa, little was known of sub-Saharan Africa before the Portuguese explorations of the fifteenth and sixteenth centuries.

the rains come and it is "reborn.") (The fish is a symbol of power because it can deliver strong electric shocks and possesses fatal spines.) Likewise, the Portuguese seemed to be born of the sea and possessed fatal "spines" of their own—rifles and musketry.

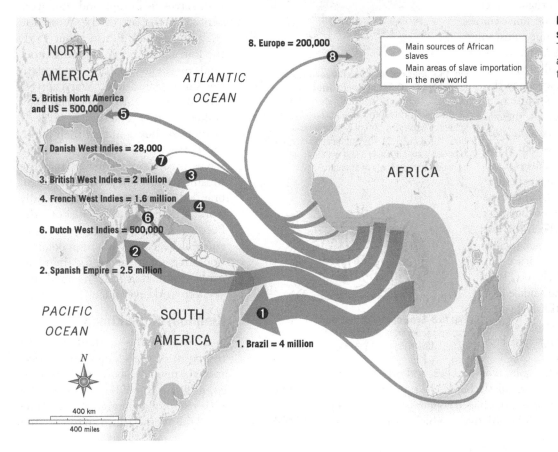

Map 18.3 Transatlantic slave trade. 1450–1870. These numbers are approximate, and subject to much scholarly debate.

8. Europe = 200,000

NORTH AMERICA

ATLANTIC OCEAN

5. British North America and US = 500,000

7. Danish West Indies = 28,000

3. British West Indies = 2 million

4. French West Indies = 1.6 million

6. Dutch West Indies = 500,000

2. Spanish Empire = 2.5 million

PACIFIC OCEAN

SOUTH AMERICA

1. Brazil = 4 million

AFRICA

Main sources of African slaves
Main areas of slave importation in the new world

An example of this association of the mudfish with the Portuguese is a decorative design that forms the tiara of an ivory mask worn as a hip pendant by the *oba* Esigie [OH-bah ay-SEE-gee-yay] (r. 1504–1550) (Figs. **18.7** and **18.8**). (An *oba* is the supreme traditional head of a Yoruba town.) The pendant probably depicts the queen mother (that is, the *oba*'s mother), or *iyoba* [ee-YOH-bah]. Esigie's mother was named Idia [ih-dee-YAH], and she is the first woman to hold officially the position of *iyoba*. Apparently, when the neighboring Igala [ee-GAH-lah] people of lower Niger threatened to conquer the Benin, Idia raised an army and by using magical powers helped Esigie defeat the Igala army. Part of her magic may have been the enlistment of Portuguese help. In acknowledgment of the Portuguese aid, the *iyoba*'s collar bears decorative images of bearded Portuguese sailors and alternating sailors and mudfish at the top of her tiara.

The impact of the Portuguese merchants, and of the Catholic missionaries who followed them, was not transforming, though it was undeniable and at times devastating. The Benin culture has remained more or less intact since the time of encounter. Today, for instance, during rituals and ceremonies, the *oba* wears at his waist five or six replicas of masks such as the *iyoba*'s, as well as the traditional coral-bead headdress. Oral traditions, like the praise poem (see Chapter 11), remain in place, despite attempts by Western priests to suppress them. If anything, it has been the last 50 years that have most dramatically transformed the cultures of Africa. But it was the institution of slavery, long practiced in Africa and the Middle East and by the Yoruba of Ife [EE-fay] (their founding city) and the Benin peoples, that most dramatically impacted Portuguese and Western culture.

At first Benin had traded gold, ivory, rubber, and other forest products for beads and, particularly, brass. The standard medium of exchange was a horseshoe-shaped copper or brass object called a *manilla* [mah-NEE-yah], five of which appear

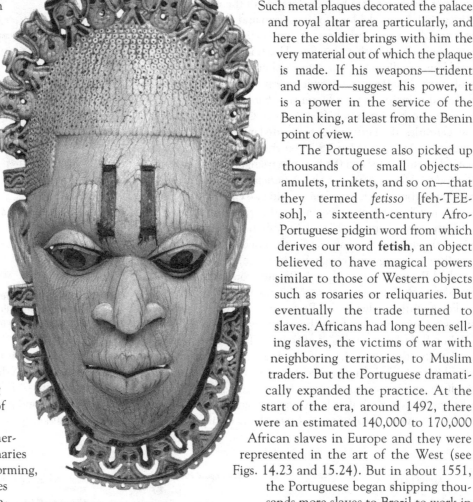

Fig. 18.7 Mask of an *iyoba* (queen mother), probably Idia, Court of Benin, Nigeria. ca. 1550. Ivory, iron, and copper, height 9 3/8″. The Metropolitan Museum of Art, New York. The Michael C. Rockefeller Memorial Collection, Gift of Nelson A. Rockefeller, 1972. (1978.412.323). The scarification lines on the forehead were originally inlaid with iron, and so were its pupils, both symbols of strength.

Fig. 18.8 Symbol of a coiled mudfish. Found throughout the art of Benin and in the tiara worn by the *iyoba* in Fig. 18.7.

in an early sixteenth-century Benin plaque portraying a Portuguese warrior (Fig. **18.9**). Such metal plaques decorated the palace and royal altar area particularly, and here the soldier brings with him the very material out of which the plaque is made. If his weapons—trident and sword—suggest his power, it is a power in the service of the Benin king, at least from the Benin point of view.

The Portuguese also picked up thousands of small objects—amulets, trinkets, and so on—that they termed *fetisso* [feh-TEE-soh], a sixteenth-century Afro-Portuguese pidgin word from which derives our word **fetish**, an object believed to have magical powers similar to those of Western objects such as rosaries or reliquaries. But eventually the trade turned to slaves. Africans had long been selling slaves, the victims of war with neighboring territories, to Muslim traders. But the Portuguese dramatically expanded the practice. At the start of the era, around 1492, there were an estimated 140,000 to 170,000 African slaves in Europe and they were represented in the art of the West (see Figs. 14.23 and 15.24). But in about 1551, the Portuguese began shipping thousands more slaves to Brazil to work in the sugar plantations. War captives proved an insufficient source of bodies, and the Portuguese took whomever they could get their hands on. Furthermore, they treated these slaves much more harshly than the Muslims had. They chained them, branded them, and often literally worked them to death. In short, the Portuguese inaugurated a practice of **cultural hegemony** (cultural domination) that set the stage for the racist exploitation that has haunted the Western world ever since.

Kingdom of the Kongo

A thousand miles south of Benin, in the basin of the Congo River, comprising parts of present-day Angola, Gabon, the Democratic Republic of Congo, and the Republic of Congo, the kingdom of the Kongo rose to prominence sometime around 1400. Like many of the West African cultures to the

Fig. 18.9 *Portuguese Warrior Surrounded by Manillas,* Court of Benin, Nigeria. Sixteenth century. Bronze. Kunsthistorisches Museum, Vienna, Austria. Notice the background of the bronze incised with jungle floral images.

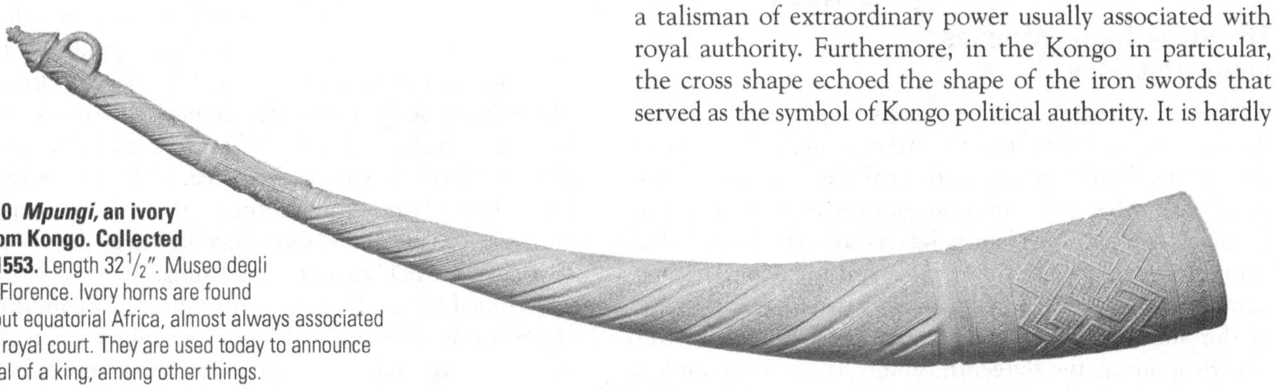

Fig. 18.10 *Mpungi,* an ivory horn, from Kongo. Collected before 1553. Length 32 1/2″. Museo degli Argenti, Florence. Ivory horns are found throughout equatorial Africa, almost always associated with the royal court. They are used today to announce the arrival of a king, among other things.

north, its resources derived from the equatorial forest. Its capital city, Mbanza Kongo [um-BAHN-zah KON-go], was home to from two to three million people. *Mbanza* means "residence of the king," and its king lived in a royal residence on the top of a hill overlooking the Lulunda River.

One of the king's titles was *Matombola* [mah-tom-BOH-lah], "the one who summons spirits from the land of the dead." This land, the Kongolese believed, lay across the sea, beneath the waters of the earth. Thus, when the Portuguese arrived by sea, they were believed to be visitors from that other world, and it was assumed that their king was the Kongo ruler's counterpart among the dead. As a result, one of the first gifts that the Kongolese king sent to the king of Portugal was an ivory horn carved from an elephant tusk (Fig. **18.10**), associated in the Kongolese mind with all royalty. The gift served to establish, at least from the point of view of the Kongolese king, the equality of the two rulers. An account of a visit to Mbanza Kongo by Portuguese missionaries in 1491 describes how horn players painted in white in memory of their ancestors met them. They played their song 12 times, a deep resonating melody that the missionaries found wholly melancholy. In fact, the Kongolese believed that the dead understood these notes, and that at their sound the ancestors of the royal line rose up to aid the ruler in governing his people.

The Kongolese were attracted to Christianity. As early as 1491, the Kongo King Nzinga aNkuwa [un-ZING-ah ah-un-KOO-ah] converted and was baptized as Joao I. Not long after, his son and heir ordered that Christianity become the state religion. The interest shown by the African peoples in the message of the Christian missionaries (as well as earlier, in the sub-Sahara, to Islamic missionaries) can be explained by the fact that they, too, traditionally accepted the duality of the universe and the existence of an afterlife. And yet the Africans showed an amazing capacity to adapt the outward forms of Christianity to their own cultural practices. For instance, across almost all of West Africa, the cross traditionally stood for the order of the cosmos, and was a talisman of extraordinary power usually associated with royal authority. Furthermore, in the Kongo in particular, the cross shape echoed the shape of the iron swords that served as the symbol of Kongo political authority. It is hardly surprising, then, that Christian crosses were soon adapted to the traditional ritual practices of the Kongo royal court. They could help the ruler in his role as healer, judge, or even rainmaker—any time it might be necessary to make contact with ancestral spirits.

Such Africanization of the postmedieval Christian practice is especially apparent in an ivory Crucifixion plaque from the Vili [VEE-lee] culture (a subset of the Kongo kingdom) on the Atlantic coast north of the Congo River (Fig. 18.11). The Vili artist depicted Christ with African facial features, as well as the beard (symbol of wisdom) and hairstyle of the Kongo nobility. Attendants kneel beside Christ in the traditional posture of respect, touching his loincloth, which he wears in the Vili royal manner, in admiration for the material itself. It is not so clear, in other words, whether the Vili artist who made this plaque was representing Christian doctrine or adapting it to African tradition by equating Christ with Kongolese royalty—in much the same way that Europeans rulers, especially the pope, identified themselves and their governments with the Church. What this and other images like it demonstrate is the complex exchange between cultures that the Age of Encounter inaugurated. We must read these images, simultaneously, as emblems of the forcible transformation of other cultures into the likeness of the West and as adaptive strategies for cultural survival.

Fig. 18.11 Crucifixion Plaque, from Loango area of Pointe Noire (Democratic Republic of the Congo), Vili culture. Collected in 1874. Ivory, 3 1/4" × 2 1/4". Museum für Völkerkunde, Berlin. The Portuguese claimed to have converted the Kingdom of the Kongo to Christianity as early as the 1490s.

The Slave Trade: Africans in the Americas

Adaptive strategies were especially important to those Africans transported across the Atlantic in the Portuguese slave trade. Torn from their native cultures, and often resituated with other Africans from cultures utterly unfamiliar to them, their cultural identity was severely challenged. But before long, across South America and Mexico, Africans outnumbered white Spaniards roughly two to one. Because of the almost total absence of European women in the Americas during the sixteenth century, the Spanish turned to other women for sexual partners. Very soon there were large numbers of people of variously mixed race, called *castas* [KAS-tas] or castes. The most common *castas* were *mestizo* [mes-TEE-zoh] (Spanish-Indian), *mulatto* [moo-LAH-toh] (Spanish-black), *zambo* [ZAM-boh] (black-Indian), and then later, in the seventeenth century, *castizo* [kas-TEE-zoh] (a light-skinned mestizo) and *morisco* (a light-skinned mulatto). By the eighteenth century, as growing numbers of Philippinos and other Asian populations arrived in Mexico (generally as slaves), and as the various castes themselves intermingled, a new term came into the language to indicate racial indeterminacy, *tente en el aire* [TEN-tay en el AY-ray], "hold yourself in the air." By the end of the century, fully one-quarter of the population was of mixed race.

Indeed, by the early years of the eighteenth century, a distinct genre of painting even developed, so-called **casta painting** (Fig. 18.12). By and large, casta paintings exist in sets of sixteen recording the process of race-mixing in the Americas. Each portrays a man and a woman of different races with one or two of their children, and each is titled with a sort of equation, as in the image illustrated here, a Spaniard plus a black equals a mulatto. These casta paintings are generally arranged hierarchically, with pure-blooded Spanish or *criollo* [kree-OH-yo] (descendents of pure-blooded Spanish born in Mexico) parents producing equally pure-blooded offspring in the first position. The offspring of black parents were at the bottom, and Indians variously in the middle. The painting reproduced here is positioned, as inscribed at the top left, in sixth place in the hierarchical scale (so high, despite the black mother, because of the Spanish father). The Spaniard's African wife is making hot chocolate at the stove, while his mulatto son brings him a brazier to light his cigarette. The social difference between father and son is highlighted by the distinct difference in the richness of their clothing.

While it is clear that the casta paintings are indicative of the Spanish obsession with racial genealogy and a genuine interest in dynamics of racial intermixing—never before so readily apparent—that obsession was at least partly based on

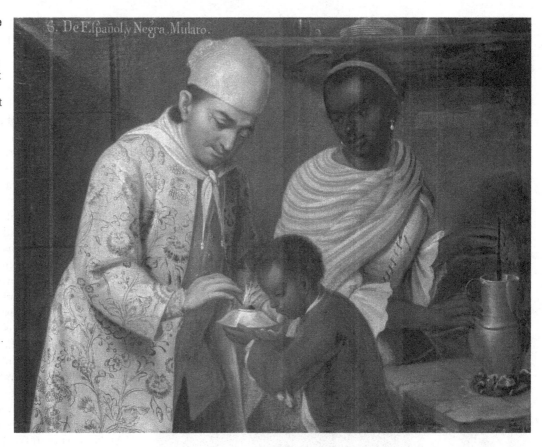

Fig. 18.12 Attributed to José de Alcíbar, *From Spaniard and Black, Mulatto (De español y negra, mulatto)*. ca. 1760. Oil on canvas, 31″ × 38¹⁄₄″. Denver Art Museum, Collection of Jan and Frederick R. Mayer. The man's coat underscores the cultural complexity of the scene. It is chintz, imported from India.

the Spanish nobility's insistence on affirming its own position at the top of the ladder. That said, the Franciscan priest Fray Juan de Torquemada, one of the first great historians of New Spain, could see in the great diversity of skin color that abounded in Mexico, the manifestation of divine purpose (**Reading 18.3**):

> ## READING 18.3
>
> ### from Fray Juan de Torquemada, *Indian Monarchies* (1615)
>
> There is no other reason for this [variation in human complexion] than God's wish to display his marvels through the variety of colors. Like the colors of the flowers in a field, he wished for them to preserve that given to them by Nature. In this way, just as God is praised in the many shades of the flowers, so too is the Almighty blessed and praised in the different and varied colors of mankind. It is through his artifices and paintings that he chose to show the boundlessness of his wisdom.

The full title of Torquemada's book is *The Twenty-One Ritual Books and Indian Monarchy with the Origin and Wars of the West Indians, of Their Populations, Discoveries, Conquest, Conversion and Other Marvelous Things of the Same Land,* and this passage is taken from Ilona Katzew's groundbreaking study of 2004, *Casta Painting,* easily the most extensive survey of the genre ever compiled. Katzew argues that in

the sense of heterogeneity established both in the writings of Torquemada and others and in casta paintings themselves, New Spain established an identity distinct from the Old World—and, it is worth pointing out, distinct from that of its neighbors to the north as well.

The cultures of New Spain and Peru comprised a diverse and pluralistic society like none before it in the world. Black Africans from widely divergent cultures in the Gulf of Guinea, the Congo River basin, and what is now Angola, introduced new words into the Spanish-Mexican language and new musical instruments (notably the marimba) and rhythms into popular music. As we saw, the religions of their native Africa had accepted a division of existence into a dual system roughly approximating the Christian division of body and soul, and they accepted the idea of an afterlife. So black Africans in the Americas readily accepted Christianity, to which they brought their own African practices, many of which have survived.

INDIA AND EUROPE: CROSS-CULTURAL CONNECTIONS

The synthesis of cultures so evident in the pluralistic society that developed in New Spain is also apparent in the art of India during roughly the same period. But in India, the synthesis was far less fraught with tension. The reason has much to do with the tolerance shown by India's leaders in the seventeenth and eighteenth centuries toward forces from the outside, which, in fact, they welcomed.

Islamic India: The Taste for Western Art

India's leaders in the seventeenth and eighteenth centuries were Muslim. Islamic groups had moved into India through the northern passes of the Hindu Kush by 1000 and had established a foothold for themselves in Delhi by 1200. In the early sixteenth century, a group of Turko-Mongol Sunni Muslims known as *Moguls* (a variation on the word *Mongol*) established a strong empire in northern India, with capitals at Agra and Delhi, although the Hindus temporarily expelled them from India between 1540 and 1555.

Their exile, in Tabriz, Persia, proved critical. Shah Tamasp Safavi [SAH-fah-vee] (r. 1524–1576), a great patron of the arts who especially supported miniature painting,

received them into his court. The Moguls reconquered India with the aid of the shah in 1556. The young new Mogul ruler, Akbar [AK-bar] (r. 1556–1605), was just 14 years of age when he took the throne, but he had been raised in Tabriz and he valued its arts. He soon established a school of painting in India, open to both Hindu and Islamic artists, taught by Persian masters brought from Tabriz. He also urged his artists to study the Western paintings and prints that Portuguese traders began to bring into the country in the 1570s. By the end of Akbar's reign, a state studio of more than 1,000 artists had created a library of over 24,000 illuminated manuscripts.

Akbar ruled over a court of thousands of bureaucrats, courtiers, servants, wives, and concubines. Fully aware that the population was largely Hindu, Akbar practiced an official policy of religious toleration. He believed that a synthesis of the world's faiths would surpass the teachings of any one of them. Thus he invited Christians, Jews, Hindus, Buddhists, and others to his court to debate with Muslim scholars. Despite taxing the peasantry heavily to support the luxurious lifestyle that he enjoyed, he also instituted a number of reforms, particularly banning the practice of immolating surviving wives on the funeral pyres of their husbands.

Under the rule of Akbar's son, Jahangir [juh-HAHN-geer] (r. 1605–1627), the English taste for portraiture (see Chapter 24) found favor in India. The painting *Jahangir in Darbar* is a good example (Fig. **18.13**). It shows Jahangir, whose name means "World Seizer," seated between the two pillars at the top of the painting, holding an audience, or *darbar*, at court. His son, the future emperor Shah Jahan [shah juh-HAHN], stands just behind him. The figures in the street are a medley of portraits, composed in all likelihood from albums of portraits kept by court artists. Among them is a Jesuit priest from Europe dressed in his black robes (although nothing in the painting shows a familiarity with Western scientific perspective). The stiff formality of the figures, depicted in profile facing left and right toward a central axis, makes a sharp contrast to the variety of faces with different racial and ethnic features that fills the scene.

The force behind this growing interest in portraiture was the British East India Company, founded by a group of enterprising and influential London

Fig. 18.13 Attributed to Manohar, *Jahangir in Darbar*, Indian. Mughal period. About 1620. Northern India. Opaque watercolor and gold on paper, 13 3/4″ × 7 7/8″. Francis Bartlett Donation of 1912 and Picture Fund 14.654. Courtesy, Museum of Fine Arts, Boston. Nothing underscores the Mogul lack of interest in Western perspective more than the way in which the figure in the middle of the street seems to stand on the head of the figure below him.

Fig. 18.14 Bichitr. *Jahangir Seated on an Allegorical Throne,* from the *Leningrad Album of Bichitr.* **ca. 1625.** Opaque watercolor, gold, and ink on paper, 10″ × 7 ⅛″. Freer Gallery of Art, Smithsonian Institution, Washington, D.C. (42.15V). Behind the shah is a giant halo or nimbus consisting of the sun and a crescent moon. It recalls those behind earlier images of Buddha.

businessmen in 1599. King James I awarded the Company exclusive trading rights in the East Indies. A few years later, James sent a representative to Jahangir to arrange a commercial treaty that would give the East India Company exclusive rights to reside and build factories in India. In return, the Company offered to provide the emperor with goods and rarities for his palace from the European market.

Jahangir's interest in all things English is visible in a miniature, *Jahangir Seated on an Allegorical Throne,* by an artist named Bichitr (Fig. **18.14**). The miniaturist depicts Jahangir on an hourglass throne, a reference to the brevity of life. The shah hands a book to a Sufi teacher, evidently preferring the mystic's company to that of the two kings who stand below, an Ottoman [OT-tuh-mun] Turkish ruler who had been conquered by Jahangir's ancient ancestor Tamerlane and, interestingly, King James I of England. The English monarch's pose is a three-quarter view, typical of Western portraiture but in clear contrast to the preferred profile pose of the Mogul court, which Jahangir assumes. The figure holding a picture at the bottom left-hand corner of the composition may be the artist Bichitr himself. Two Western-style putti [POO-tee] (cherubs) fly across the top of the composition: The one at the left is a Cupid figure, about to shoot an arrow, suggesting the importance of worldly love. The one at the right apparently laments the impermanence of worldly power (as the inscription above reads). At the bottom of the hourglass, two Western-style angels inscribe the base of the throne with the prayer, "Oh Shah, may the span of your life be a thousand years." The throne itself is depicted in terms of scientific perspective, but the carpet it rests upon is not. Framing the entire image is a border of Western-style flowers, which stand in marked contrast to the Turkish design of the interior frame. All told, the image is a remarkable blend of stylistic and cultural traditions, bridging the gap between East and West on a single page.

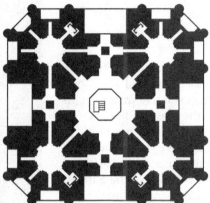

Fig. 18.15 Taj Mahal, Agra, India. Mogul period. ca. 1632–1648. Originally Shah Jahan planned to build his own tomb across the river, a matching structure in black marble, connected to the Taj Mahal by a bridge. The Shah's tomb was never built, and he is buried, with his beloved wife, in a crypt in the mausoleum's central chamber.

Fig. 18.16 Plan of the Taj Mahal, Agra. ca. 1632–1648.

Mogul Architecture: The Taj Mahal

Addicted to wine laced with opium, Shah Jahangir died in 1628, not long after the completion of the miniature wishing him a life of a thousand years. While his son Shah Jahan (r. 1628–1658) did not encourage painting to the degree his father and grandfather had, he was a great patron of architecture. His most important contribution to Indian architecture—and arguably one of the most beautiful buildings in the world—is the Taj Mahal [tazh muh-HAHL] ("Crown of the Palace"), constructed as a mausoleum for Jahan's favorite wife, Mumtaz-i-Mahal (the name means "Light of the Palace"), who died giving birth to the couple's fourteenth child (Fig. **18.15**).

Sited on the banks of the Jumna [JUM-nuh] River at Agra in northern India, the Taj Mahal is surrounded by gardens meant to evoke a vision of paradise as imagined in the Qu'ran (compare the mural in the Mosque of Damascus, Fig. 9.9). Measuring 1,000 by 1,900 feet, the garden is interspersed with broad pathways, reflecting pools, and fountains that were originally lined by fruit trees and cypresses, symbols, respectively, of life and death. To the west of the building, in the corner of the property, is a red sandstone mosque, used for worship. Rising above the garden, and reflected in its pools, is the delicate yet monumental mausoleum of Taj Mahal itself.

The white marble tomb is set on a broad marble platform with minarets at each corner, their three main sections corresponding to the three levels of the mausoleum proper, thus uniting them with the main structure. At the top of these minarets are *chattri* [CHAT-tree], or small pavilions that are traditional embellishments of Indian palaces, from which muezzins can call the faithful to worship at the property's mosque. The main structure, the Taj Mahal proper, is basically square, although each corner is sliced off in order to create a subtle octagon. Each facade is identical: a central *iwan* (a traditional Islamic architectural feature consisting of a vaulted opening with an arched portal), flanked by two stories of smaller *iwans*. These voids in the facade contribute to the sense of weightlessness the building seems to possess. Four octagonal *chattris* positioned at each corner of the roof provide a transition to the central onion dome, which rises on its drum in a graceful swelling curve. The facades are inlaid with inscriptions and arabesques of semiprecious stones—carnelian, agate, coral, turquoise, garnet, lapis, and jasper—but so delicate and lacelike that they emphasize the whiteness of the whole rather than call attention to themselves.

Inside the Taj Mahal, the sequence of rooms is set out according to the favorite pattern of the Mogul period: an interpenetrating square and cross. There are eight small rooms on each of the two stories: one in each corner and one behind each *iwan*. The largest chamber is the octagonal central area, which rises two stories to a domed ceiling beneath the outer dome (Fig. **18.16**). An intricately carved openwork marble screen surrounds this central area.

With the Taj Mahal, Shah Jahan brought the Mogul style of architecture to its peak of beauty and splendor. Yet, in its placement among expanses of water and gardens, the Taj Mahal is similar to other buildings of the time, such as the Red Fort, the nickname for the palace which was constructed by Shah Jahan across the Jumna River from the Taj Mahal in Delhi. He fully intended it to be the most magnificent palace on the face of the earth. At its center, surrounded by gardens, pavilions, and baths, was the Peacock Throne Room (Fig. **18.17**). There, the shah sat upon an enormous solid gold throne (subsequently destroyed and looted by Persian warriors in 1732), set upon a 6-by-4-foot platform. The platform throne itself supported 12 pillars covered with emeralds, over which was an enameled canopy inlaid with diamonds, emeralds, rubies, and garnets. It was flanked on each side by jeweled peacocks. The marble walls of the room were themselves inlaid with precious and semiprecious stones in a mosaic technique the Moguls had learned from the Italians, called *pietra dura* (Italian for "hard stone"), also employed at the Taj Mahal. Around the ceiling of the room, the shah had these words inscribed: "If there is a paradise on the face of the earth, It is this, oh! it is this, oh! it is this." Such architectural splendor served one purpose—to glorify the worldly power of the ruler.

In 1658, Shah Jahan became very ill, and his four sons battled each other for power. The conservative, Aurangzeb (r. 1658–1707), eventually triumphed and confined his father to the Red Fort. Aurangzeb reinstituted traditional forms of Islamic law and worship, ending the pluralism that had defined the Mogul court under his father and grandfather even as he began to reinstate traditional Muslim prohibitions against figural art. But from his rooms in the Red Fort, the shah could look out over the Jumna River to the Taj Mahal and re-create in poetry the paradise where he believed he would come to rest with his wife (**Reading 18.4**):

Fig. 18.17 The Peacock Throne Room, Red Fort (Shahjahanabad), Delhi. Mogul period, after 1638. The design of the Peacock Throne itself has been attributed to one Austin de Bordeaux, whom the French physician François Bernier (1625–1688) described, in his *Travels in the Mogul Empire* (1670), as "a Frenchman by birth, who after defrauding several of the Princes of Europe, by means of false gems, which he fabricated with peculiar skill, sought refuge in the great Mogul's court, where he made his fortune."

READING 18.4

Shah Jahan, inscription on the Taj Mahal (ca. 1658)

Like a garden of heaven a brilliant spot,
Full of fragrance like paradise fraught with ambergris.
In the breadth of its court perfumes from the nose-gay
    of sweet-hearts rise.

Shah Jahan's tomb is, in fact, next to his wife's in the crypt below the central chamber of the Taj Mahal. Above both tombs are their marble cenotaphs, beautifully inlaid in *pietra dura* by the artisans of northern India.

CHINA: THE MING DYNASTY (1368–1644)

The **cultural syncretism**, or intermingling of cultural traditions, that marks the Americas, was largely resisted by Chinese populations when Europeans arrived on its shores. The reasons are many, but of great importance was the inherent belief of these cultures in their own superiority. For cen-

turies, the Chinese had resisted Mongolian influence, for instance, and at the same time had come to prefer isolation from foreign influence.

This is not to say that the Chinese totally removed themselves from the world stage. Some 92 years before the Portuguese explorer Vasco da Gama landed in Calicut, India, inaugurating Portuguese sea trade in the eastern oceans, a massive Chinese fleet had sailed into that port to inaugurate a sea trade of its own. It was the brainchild of the emperor Zhu Di [joo dee] (r. 1402–1424). His father Zhu Yuanzhang [joo wan-jang] (r. 1368–1398), had driven the Mongols out of China in 1368, restored Chinese rule in the land, and established the dynasty called Ming ("bright" or "brilliant") at Nanjing. Confucian scholars, who under the Mongolian rule of Kublai Khan had found themselves utterly neglected (see Chapter 11), were once again welcomed at court.

The Ming emperors were consumed by fear of Mongol reinvasion and in defense created what was arguably the most despotic government in Chinese history. Zhu Yuanzhang enlisted thousands of workers to reinforce the Great Wall of China (see Fig. 7.1) against invasion from the north, and untold numbers of them perished in the process. He equipped huge armies and assembled a navy to defend against invasion from the sea. Artists whose freedoms had been severely restricted under the Mongols (see Chapter 11) were even less free under the Ming. But in a bow to scholarship and the arts, Zhu Di commissioned the compilation of an authoritative 11,095-volume encyclopedia of Chinese learning. He also undertook the

Fig. 18.18 The Forbidden City, now the Palace Museum, Beijing. Mostly Ming dynasty (1368–1644).
View from the southwest.

LEARN MORE View an architectural simulation of The Forbidden City at **www.myartslab.com**

construction of an Imperial Palace compound in Beijing on the site of Kublai Khan's ruined capital (Figs. **18.18** and **18.19**). The palace complex, known as the Forbidden City, was, among other things, the architectural symbol of his rule.

The name refers to the fact that only those on official imperial business could enter its gates. Although largely rebuilt in the eighteenth century during the Qing [ching] dynasty (1644–1900), the general plan is Ming but based on Mongol precedents. In fact, the Mongols had reserved the entire northern side of Beijing for themselves, and the resident Chinese had lived only in the southern third of the city. Ming emperors preserved this division, allowing ministers and officials to live in the northern or Inner City and commoners in the southern or Outer City.

The Forbidden City itself was in the middle of the Inner City. Like the Tang capital of Chang'an (see Chapter 11), Beijing is laid out on a grid, and the Forbidden City is laid out on a grid within the grid along a north–south axis according to the principles of *feng shui* [fung shway] ("wind and water"). In Daoist belief, certain "dragon lines" of energy, or *qi*, flow through the earth, along mountains and ridges, down streams and rivers, influencing the lives of people near them. Evil forces were believed to come from the north and so the city opened to the south. Since emperors were considered divine and closely connected to the forces of the cosmos, the practice of *feng shui* was especially crucial in constructing royal compounds.

Following traditional practice, the Forbidden City covers about 240 acres and is walled by 15 miles of fortifica-tions. It is composed of 9,999 buildings and rooms, each constructed with nails, nine nails per row. The number nine in Chinese sounds like the word for "everlasting," and because nine was believed to be the extreme of positive numbers, the maximum of the singular, it was thus reserved for use only by the emperor. The buildings in the complex follow traditional patterns of post-and-lintel construction that date back to the Shang and Zhou periods.

The emperors and their families rarely left the Forbidden City's confines. Visitors entered through a monumental U-shaped Meridian Gate and then crossed the Golden Water River, spanned by five arched marble bridges. Across the courtyard stands the Gate of Supreme Harmony, on the other side of which is another giant courtyard leading to the Hall of Supreme Harmony. Here, on the most important state occasions, the emperor sat on his throne, facing south, his back to the evil forces of the north. Behind the Hall of Supreme Harmony are increasingly private spaces, devoted to day-to-day routine and living quarters. The balance and symmetry of the compound were believed to mirror the harmony of the universe. Situated, as it was believed, in the middle of the world, the Forbidden City was the architectural symbol of the emperor's rule and of his duty as the Son of Heaven to maintain order, balance, and harmony in his land.

The Treasure Fleet: Extending China's Influence

Zhu Di called himself the Yongle [yohng-leh] emperor, meaning "lasting joy," a propagandistic name designed to deflect attention from the tyranny of his court. His massive

Fig. 18.19 The Hall of Supreme Harmony. As seen from across the square beyond the Gate of Supreme Harmony. Height 115′. Elevated on three tiers of marble platforms, the hall is the largest building in the complex. No other building, anywhere in the empire, was allowed to be higher. It houses the main throne of the emperor, from which he presided over ceremonies celebrating the winter solstice, the new year, and his own birthday. Along the stairs rising to the hall are 18 *dings*—bronze food vessels (see Chapter 7)—that represent the 18 provinces of Ming China. On the terrace stand a bronze crane and a bronze tortoise, symbols of everlasting rule and longevity. Red and gold lacquered brackets resting on the lintels support flaring upswept eaves, which disguise the enormous weight of the tiled roof. These brackets are carved in a variety of calligraphic designs, many of which also appear on Shang and Zhou bronzes. The red walls contrast dramatically with the roof tiles lacquered in a glowing yellow, a color reserved for imperial structures.

construction projects served to establish the grandeur of his authority. Among the largest of these was his "treasure fleet" of 317 ships, crewed by 27,000 men and headed by a ship that was 440 feet long, one of the largest wooden ships ever built. Unlike the European ocean expeditions undertaken a century later, these voyages were not primarily motivated by trade and exploration, but rather by the desire of the Yongle emperor to extract tribute from states throughout the Indian Ocean and the Southeast Asia. Still, trade was the result. Under the command of Zheng He [jehng heh] (1371–1435), a Muslim eunuch who had served Zhu Di since childhood,

the fleet sailed in seven expeditions between 1404 and 1435 throughout the oceans of Southeast Asia to India, Saudi Arabia, and down the African coast (see Map 18.4).

China, like many cultures, saw itself through ethnocentric eyes. It viewed itself as the great Middle Kingdom, believed to be at the center of the four seas and at the heart of the four cardinal directions. Zhu Di conceived of the treasure fleet as his chief means to extend Chinese influence throughout the "four corners" of the world. To that end, all the provinces of China had to provide goods for the fleet to trade—from Suzhou [soo-joh] and Hangzhou [hahng joh], fine silks and

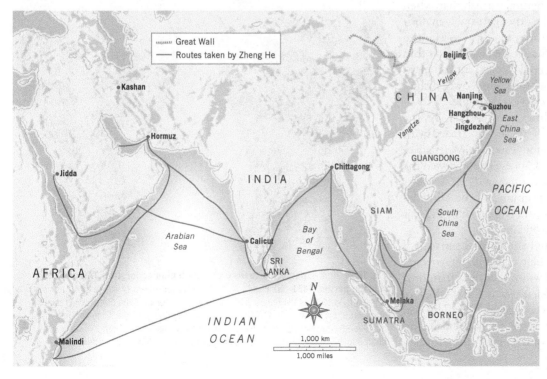

Map 18.4 Ming China. 1368–1644. This map also shows the routes taken by Zheng He and the Chinese Treasure Fleet. In 30 years, Zheng He traveled more than 186,000 miles, the equivalent of 7½ circumnavigations of the world.

brocades; from the imperial porcelain works at Jingdezhen, fine white porcelain; from Jiaxing [ja-hseeng], lacquerware; and from Guangdong [gwah-dohng], iron, required not only for trade but for construction of the fleet itself.

Zheng He's first voyage was to Calicut, the center of the spice trade. Here he obtained cardamom, cinnamon, ginger, turmeric, and, above all, pepper, literally worth its weight in gold. (The small cargo of pepper that Vasco da Gama eventually brought back from Calicut paid for his voyage several times over.) Calicut became a regular port of call for the fleet, as did Malacca, on the Malay peninsula, where cloves, nutmeg, sambal oelek [SAM-bal OH-lek] (a red hot pepper), and other Indonesian spices were available. He also acquired precious tree resins, such as camphor and frankincense, used for making incense. In Siam (now Thailand), he discovered mahogany, a hard wood, excellent for making ship rudders, and he paid the Siamese in gold for the trees. But the Middle East and Africa yielded some of the most precious treasures. Hormuz [HOR-muz], on the Persian Gulf, was famous for its pearls from the banks off what is now Bahrain, but it was also a center of trade in precious stones. In return for porcelains and silks, Zheng He acquired sapphires, rubies, topaz, and amber, as well as Middle Eastern woolens and carpets.

Luxury Arts

The lavish lifestyle of the Ming court ensured the production of vast quantities of decorative luxury goods. In addition, as trade flourished, many Chinese merchants became increasingly wealthy and began to collect paintings, antiques, finely made furniture, and other quality objects for themselves. **Lacquerware** was extremely popular. Made from the sap of the Chinese *Rhus vernicifera* [roos ver-ni-SI-fer-ah] tree (a variety of sumac), lacquer is a clear, natural varnish that, when applied to wood, textiles, or other perishable materials, makes them airtight, waterproof, and resistant to both heat and acid. A surface coated with many thin layers of lacquer can be carved through into all manner of designs. Lacquerware furniture, bowls, dishes, and other small articles were very desirable.

One of the commodities most prized by the Chinese themselves and by those who traded with China was **porcelain** ceramic ware (see *Materials & Techniques*, page 609). The Chinese had invented the process for making porcelain around 1004 CE at Jingdezhen, which by the beginning of the Ming dynasty boasted 20 kilns. At Zhu Di's death in 1424, it had almost tripled in size to 58 kilns.

Ming painters decorated the unfired surfaces of their porcelain ware with blue cobalt glazes, covered everything with a layer of white glaze, and then fired their works. During the reign of Zhu Di, the look of Chinese porcelain improved dramatically. This was due largely to the fact that Zheng He had traded Chinese produce for a cobalt ore, probably from Kashan

[kah-SHAHN], Persia, high in iron and low in manganese (just the opposite of Chinese ore), which allowed for a new richness of color. Among the Ming artists' favorite motifs were fish, waves, and sea monsters, but particularly dragons, because they symbolized the emperor. His veins were said to flow with the dragon's blood (Fig. **18.20**). The dragon was everywhere on Ming art, from textiles to lacquerware and jade carvings. Note that the two vases in Fig. 18.20 are mirror images, the finely outlined forms of the dragons seemingly mimicking each other's flight. Their gestures, in fact, suggest the graceful movements of **T'ai Chi Ch'uan** [ty chee chwahn], the Chinese martial art that includes solo forms, or routines, and two-person forms, known as "pushing hands." These two dragons, their bony claws reaching toward one another, particularly evoke the "pushing hands" form. The two vases create a sense of balance, like the balance of *yin* and *yang* (see Fig. 7.5), the symbol for which is, in fact, the symbol for t'ai chi itself.

Painting and Poetry: Competing Schools

The imperial court and the newly rich merchant class also acquired paintings, considered luxury goods in their own right. As in the Tang dynasty (see Chapter 11), a class of highly educated **literati**, or literary intelligentsia—artists equally expert in poetry, calligraphy, and painting—executed the works. Many paintings combine image and poem, the latter written in a calligraphy distinctly the artist's own.

Late in the Ming dynasty, an artist, calligrapher, theorist, and high official in the government bureaucracy

Fig. 18.20 Pair of porcelain vases with cobalt blue underglaze. Ming dynasty, Xuande period (1426–35). Height 21³/₄″. The Nelson-Atkins Museum of Art, Kansas City, Missouri. As early as the Bronze Age, the Chinese associated the dragon with sudden manifestations of nature, such as wind, rain, and lightning. By the Song and Tang dynasties (fifth–tenth centuries), painting pictures of dragons was a method of praying for rain. For Chan Buddhists (see Chapter 11), the dragon symbolized sudden enlightenment.

Porcelain

Porcelain is a ceramic ware that is made by combining clays rich in kaolin, a highly refined mineral found in abundance near Jingdezhen, with the mineral feldspar and sometimes quartz. Porcelain requires extremely high firing temperatures, and it seems likely that the Chinese developed the techniques for firing porcelain while casting bronze vessels. When fired at 1800°F to 2400°F (1000°C to 1300°C), the minerals in the kaolin clay fuse into a translucent, glasslike, and extremely strong ceramic ware. In fact, the ceramic contains a high percentage of actual body glass. As a result, porcelains tend to transmit light and make a clear, ringing sound when struck. Imperial porcelain was traditionally thought to be "as white as jade, as bright as a mirror, as thin as paper, with a sound as clear as a bell." Europeans tried desperately to match Chinese quality but did not succeed until kaolin was discovered in Saxony in the early 1700s, leading to the creation of the great Meissen [MY-sen] porcelain factory in Germany.

named Dong Qichang [dahng chee-chang] (1555–1636) wrote an essay that has affected the way we have looked at the history of Chinese painting ever since, although many scholars, even in Dong Qichang's time, viewed it as oversimplified. He divided the history of Chinese painting into two schools, Northern and Southern, although geography had little to do with it. It was not place but the spirit in which the artist approached the painting that determined its school. A painter was Southern if unorthodox, radical, and inventive, like the Southern brand of Chan (Zen) Buddhism; a painter was Northern if conservative and traditional in approach, like the Northern brand of Chan Buddhism.

Northern School *Hundreds of Birds Admiring the Peacocks* by Yin Hong, a court artist active in the late fifteenth and early sixteenth centuries, is an example of the Northern style (Fig. **18.21**). It has a highly refined decorative style, which emphasizes the technical skill of the painter. It also has a rich use of color and reliance on traditional Chinese painting, in this case the birds-and-flowers genre that had been extremely popular in the Song dynasty, which flourished contemporaneously with the Early Middle Ages in the West. Like Guo Xi's Song dynasty painting *Early Spring* (see *Closer Look*, Chapter 11, pages 366–367), the Yin Hong painting also has a symbolic meaning that refers directly to the emperor. Just as the central peak in *Early Spring* symbolizes the emperor himself, with the lower peaks and trees subservient to him, here a peacock symbolizes the emperor, and around it "hundreds of birds"—that is, the court officials—gather in respect and submission.

Southern School The Southern style is much more understated than the Northern

school, preferring ink to color and free brushwork (emphasizing the abstract nature of painting) to meticulously detailed linear representation. For the Southern artist, reality rested in the mind, not the physical world, and so

Fig. 18.21 Yin Hong, *Hundreds of Birds Admiring the Peacocks.* Ming dynasty, ca. late fifteenth century–early sixteenth century. Hanging scroll, ink and color on silk, 7'10½" × 6'5". © The Cleveland Museum of Art. Purchase from the J. H. Wade Fund, 74.31. The Chinese traded in the Middle East for peacocks, considered the most supreme of all ornamental birds, in exchange for silk.

Fig. 18.22 Shen Zhou. *Poet on a Mountaintop,* **leaf from an album of landscapes; painting mounted as part of a handscroll. Ming dynasty, ca. 1500.** Ink and color on paper, 15 1/4″ × 23 3/4″. The Nelson-Atkins Museum of Art, Kansas City, Missouri. Shen Zhou places himself at the center of this composition in a relaxed and casual manner that reflects Chan Buddhism, which is more intuitive than intellectual. Note the informal simplicity of his brushwork and calligraphy.

LEARN MORE Gain insight from a primary source document from Shen Zhou at **www.myartslab.com**

self-expression is the ultimate aim. Furthermore, in the Southern school, the work of art more systematically synthesized the three areas of endeavor that any member of the literati should have mastered: poetry, calligraphy, and painting.

So, a Southern-school painting like *Poet on a Mountaintop* by Shen Zhou [joh] (1427–1509) radicalizes traditional Chinese landscape (Fig. **18.22**). In the earlier Song dynasty landscapes, the unifying embrace of the natural world dwarfs human figures (see *Closer Look*, pages 366–367). But in Shen Zhou's Ming-dynasty painting, the poet is the central figure. He faces out over an airy void in which hangs the very image of his mind, the following poem:

> White clouds like a belt encircle the mountain's
>   waist
> A stone ledge flying in space and the far thin road.
> I lean alone on my bramble staff and gazing
>   contented into space
> Wish the sounding torrent would answer to your
>   flute.

An artist capable of putting himself at the center of both painting and poem would have had no desire to enter the government bureaucracy. Shen Zhou lived out his life in the district of Suzhou, far from court. But, interestingly, it was Shen Zhou's style of work, and the style of other literati painters in the Southern school, that the Ming theorist Dong Qichang most preferred and that would become the dominant, orthodox style of painting in the Qing dynasty to follow.

JAPAN: COURT PATRONAGE AND SPIRITUAL PRACTICE

Long before Ming rulers finally overthrew the Mongol Yuan dynasty in China in 1368, the Japanese rulers of the Kamakura period (see Chapter 11) had repelled the Mongol Kublai Khan's attempts to conquer their island country in both 1274 and 1281. The cost was high, and the islands were left impoverished. Conflict between competing lines of succession to the imperial throne destabilized the court. Gradually, in the provinces, localized village-level military leaders gained more and more authority until they controlled, after several generations, large regional areas of land. These lords, who would come to be known as *daimyo* [DY-mee-oh], or "great names," gained increasing strength, competing with the shogunate for power even as they began to war among themselves, seeking control of the entire nation. The power of the emperor was, however, rarely challenged, and the *daimyo* were important patrons of the imperial court, as well as major consumers of court-based arts and crafts. The principles and ethics of Zen Buddhism, the Japanese version of Chinese Chan Buddhism (see Chapter 11), also appealed to them. Throughout the twelfth and thirteenth centuries, Chan teachings gained an increasing foothold in Japan. The carefully ordered monastic lifestyle of Chan monks contrasted dramatically with the sometimes extravagant lifestyles of the Buddhist monasteries of the Heian period. And the Chan advocacy of the possibility of immediate enlightenment through meditation and self-denial presented, like Pure Land Buddhism (see Chapter 11), with which it competed for followers, an especially attractive spiritual practice.

The Muromachi Period (1392–1573): Cultural Patronage

By 1392, one shogun family, the Ashikaga [ah-she-KAH-gah], had begun to exercise increased authority over Japanese society. They had their headquarters in the Muromachi [MOO-roh-mah-chee] district of Kyoto (hence the alternative names for the period in which they ruled.) It was a period of often brutal civil war as the *daimyo* vied for power. Although Kyoto remained in a state of near-total devastation—starvation was not uncommon—the Ashikaga shoguns built elaborate palaces around Kyoto as refuges from the chaos outside their walls. One of the most elaborate of these, now known as Kinkakuji [KIN-kah-koo-jee], the Golden Pavilion (Fig. **18.23**), was built as a setting for the retirement of the Ashikaga shogun Yoshimitsu [yoh-shi-MEE-tsoo] (1358–1408). Begun in 1399, its central pavilion is modeled on Chinese precedents. Its first floor was intended for relaxation and contemplation of the lake and gardens. A wide veranda for viewing the moon, a popular pastime, fronted its second floor. And the top floor was designed as a small Pure Land Buddhist temple, containing a sculpture of Amida Buddha, the Buddha of Infinite Light and Life who dwells in the paradise of the Western Pure Land, along with 25 bodhisattvas. The gardens surrounding

the pavilions at Kinkakuji provided the casual stroller with an ever-changing variety of views, thus creating a tension between the multiplicity of scenes and the unity of the whole. As a matter of policy, Yoshimitsu associated himself with the arts in order to lend his shogunate authority and legitimacy. Therefore, he and later Ashikaga shoguns encouraged some of the most important artistic developments of the era in painting and garden design. They also championed important new forms of expression, including the tea ceremony and Noh drama.

Painting in the New Zen Manner The question of the extent of the influence of Zen on Japanese art is a problematic one. As has often been pointed out, the features normally associated with Zen (Chan) Buddhism in the arts—simplicity of design, suggestion rather than description, and controlling balance through irregularity and asymmetry—are also characteristic of indigenous Japanese taste. Still, a number of Japanese artists, usually Zen monks themselves, turned to China and its Chan traditions for inspiration. In order to acquaint himself more fully with Chinese traditions, for instance, Sesshu Toyo [ses-shoo toh-yoh] (1420–1506), a Zen priest-painter, traveled to China in 1468–69, copying the Song dynasty masters and becoming adept at the more abstract forms of representation practiced by the Chan Buddhist literati. Like other painters of his era inspired by the Chinese, Sesshu worked in multiple pictorial modes—depictions of Buddhist scenes, portraits, flower and bird painting, and, most famously, landscapes. *Haboku Landscape for Soen* is an example of the latter, painted in the new

Fig. 18.23 Kinkakuji (Temple of the Golden Pavilion), Rokuonji, Kyoto. Rebuilt in 1964 after the original of the 1390s. The original Kinkakuji was set ablaze and completely destroyed in 1950 by a young monk protesting the commercialization of Buddhism after World War II. The restoration closely approximates its original appearance.

Zen Buddhist manner known as *Haboku* [HAH-boh-koo] (Fig. **18.24**). *Haboku* means "broken ink," the application of one layer of ink over another, "breaking" the initial surface or description. No mark on this painting could actually be thought of as representational. Rather, the denser ink suggests trees and rocks, while the softer washes evoke tall mountains in the distance, water, and mist. And instead of the panoramic landscapes of the Chinese Song dynasty that Sesshu studied in China, with its deep space, symmetrical balance, and vast array of richly detailed elements (compare Guo Xi's *Early Spring*, *Closer Look*, Chapter 11), Sesshu's landscape is startlingly simple, almost impressionistic in its mistiness, and asymmetrical in its composition. Sesshu executed the work as a farewell gift for his pupil, Josui Soen [JOH-soo-ee soh-ehn] (active 1495–99), a monk painter who subsequently took the painting to Kyoto. It was so admired there that six leading Zen Buddhist monks added expressions of praise for the work above Sesshu's own inscription. Perhaps a phrase from Sesshu's inscription most fully captures the spirit of the piece: "My eyes are misty," he writes, "and my spirit exhausted"—the very essence of a heartfelt farewell.

Zen Gardens Perhaps inspired by the gardens surrounding shogun palaces such as Kinkakuji, designers made gardens a regular feature of Muromachi Zen temples, especially the *karesansui* [kay-ray-SAHN-soo-ee], or "withered or **dry landscape**" garden. Japanese gardeners had long featured water as an important, even primary element, but around Kyoto, with its limited number of springs and mountain streams, gardeners turned their attention away from the streams and ponds that characterize the Golden Pavilion at Kinkakuji and increasingly focused their attention on rocks and a few carefully groomed plantings as the primary feature of garden design.

An especially remarkable example is a garden in the precinct of Daisen-in [DAH-ee-sehn-in], a subtemple of the Daitokuji [DAH-ee-toh-koo-jee] compound founded in 1509 in Kyoto by Kogaku Soko [koh-GAH-koo soh-koh] (1465–1548). Its design is usually attributed to the painter Soami [SOH-ah-mee] (d. 1525). The garden of the Daisen-in is actually a series of separate gardens arranged around Soko's residence, itself decorated with a variety of Soami's paintings. The garden that flanks two sides of the residence is a miniature landscape, the vertical rocks of which represent a mountain (Fig. **18.25**). A waterfall, suggested by a vein of white quartz, cascades down one rock, forming a river of white gravel across which a slab of stone has fallen like a natural bridge, connecting islands in the stream. Farther down, a boat-shaped rock sails in the wider expanse of the river. On the other side of the residence, the gravel stream flows into an expanse of carefully raked white gravel punctuated by two cones constructed of the same material. This wide expanse is meant to suggest the ocean, its raked lines waves rising to meet what may be two volcanic islands. (This last attribution remains a matter of speculation.) Taken as a whole, the flow of the pebble stream, from mountaintop to ocean, might best be viewed as a narrative, perhaps a metaphor for the passage of time, or even the passage of a Zen Buddhist philosopher

Fig. 18.24 Sesshu Toyo, ***Haboku Landscape for Soen*** **(detail). Muromachi period, 1495.** Hanging scroll, ink on two joined sheets of paper, total height 58 1/4". Tokyo National Museum. At the top of this painting is Sesshu's long inscription to Soen and the expressions of praise for the work later added by Zen monks in Kyoto.

from the relative complexity and confusion of early life to the expansive simplicity and enlightenment.

The Tea Ceremony *Matcha*, literally "finely powdered tea," was introduced into Japan from China during the early Kamakura period. By the end of the Kamakura period, tea contests to discern different teas and the regions in which they were grown had become popular. By the early

Note the similarity between the two tallest rocks in this garden and the two mist-covered mountains in the distance of Sesshu Toyo's *Haboku Landscape* (see Fig. 18.24). Both, it would seem, are realizations of the same aesthetic in different mediums, though it seems unlikely that either directly influenced the other.

Muromachi period, rules for the ways in which tea was to be drunk began to be codified, especially in Zen temples. By the sixteenth century, these rules would come to be known as the **Way of the Tea**, *chanoyu* [CHAH noh-yoo]. In small rooms specifically designed for the purpose and often decorated with calligraphy on hanging scrolls or screens, the guest was to leave the concerns of the daily world behind and enter a timeless world of ease, harmony, and mutual respect. The master of the ceremony would assemble a few examples of painting and calligraphy, usually *karamono* [kar-ah-MOH-noh], treasures imported from China, of which the Ashikaga shogun Yoshimasa (1430–1490), grandson of Yoshimitsu, had the finest collection.

Late in the fifteenth century, in a transformation traditionally attributed to Murata Shuko [SHOO-koh], a former Zen priest, the taste for displaying *karamono* in the tea ceremony was transplanted by a taste for things possessing the quality of **wabi** [wah-bee]—that is, things evidencing qualities of austerity and simplicity and showing the effects of time. These objects were thought to reflect a taste more Japanese than Chinese, a taste reflected in a comment attributed to Shuko: "The moon is not pleasing unless partially obscured by a cloud." The master of the ceremony would assemble a few examples of painting and calligraphy together with a variety of different objects and utensils for making tea—the kettle, the water pot, the whisk, the tea caddy, and above all the tea bowl, each prized for its aesthetic shape and texture. In a quiet, muted light, and on a floor covered with *tatami* [tah-TAH-mee], woven straw mats, the master and his guest would contemplate the tea, its preparation, and the objects accompanying the ensemble, which, it was understood, expressed the master's artistic sensibility. Together, guest and master would collaborate in a ritual of meditation to transform the drinking of tea into a work of highly refined art, known as the *wabicha*.

Interestingly, it was not at court where the *wabicha* developed into the classic tea ceremony, but among the rich merchant classes. Two merchants from Sakai, Takeno Joo (1502–1555) and Sen no Rikyu (1522–1591), are traditionally credited with inventing the ceremony proper. As Rikyu defined the ceremony:

> *Chanoyu* performed in a plain hut is above all an ascetic discipline, based on the Buddhist law, that is aimed at achieving spiritual deliverance. To be concerned about the quality of the dwelling in which you serve tea or the flavor of the food served with it is to emphasize the mundane. It is enough if the dwelling one uses does not leak water and the food served suffices to stave off hunger. This is in accordance with the teachings of Buddha and is the essence of the *chanoyu*. First, we fetch water and gather firewood. Then we boil the water and prepare tea. After offering some to the Buddha, we serve our guests. Finally, we serve ourselves.

The prominence of Rikyu and Joo in the development of the *chanoyu* presages a dramatic shift in Japanese culture, as the military class that had dominated Japanese society for centuries was beginning to give way to the interests of commerce and trade.

Noh Drama The Ashikaga shoguns, including Yoshimitsu and Yoshimasa, also enthusiastically supported the development of the important literary genre of Noh drama. The Noh drama was primarily the result of the efforts of Kan'ami Kiyotsugu [KAHN-ah-mee KEE-yoh-tsoo-goo] (1333–1384) and his son Zeami Motokiyo [SHE-ah-mee MOH-toh-kee-yoh] (1363–1443). They conceived of a theater incorporating music, chanting, dance, poetry, prose, mime, and masks to create a world of sublime beauty based on the ideal of *yugen* [YOO-gehn], which almost defies translation but refers to the suggestion of vague, spiritual profundity lying just below the surface of the Noh play's action (or, rather, the stillness of its inaction).

The word *noh* means "accomplishment," and it refers to the virtuoso performance of the drama's main character, whose inner conflicts must be resolved before his or her soul can find peace. There were five kinds of Noh plays, including "warrior plays" and "woman plays." The main characters of the warrior plays, which did not exist before Zeami, were historical personages of the samurai class derived from the same accounts as the Taira and Minamoto conflicts upon which the scroll painting *Night Attack on the Sanjo Palace* is based (see Fig. 11.17).

The Noh play *Semimaru* [she-MEE-mah-roo], written by Zeami in the early fifteenth century, belongs to the fourth, "miscellaneous" category of Noh plays, plays that treat, among other things, madness and vengeful ghosts. It recreates the medieval Japanese legend of Semimaru, a blind prince who lived as a beggar in a bamboo hut on Mount Osaka (see **Reading 18.5**, pages 620–621, for the first half of the play). His blindness was attributed to laxity in the performance of his religious duties in a former life, for which his emperor father exiled him from court, as Semimaru explains to his attendant, Kiyotsura [KEE-yoh-tsoo-rah], so that his ascetic lifestyle might "purge in this world my burden from the past, / And spare me suffering in the world to come." In the play, Semimaru meets up with his deranged sister, who was apparently similarly lacking in her performance of religious duties and is thus condemned to wander the countryside. She hears him playing the *biwa* [bee-wah], a short-necked lute. In fact, traditionally Semimaru was considered the greatest master of the biwa and flute, the music of which apparently brought his soul to a state of peace.

Noh is very different from Western drama. Semimaru wears a beautifully crafted mask with shut eyes that signify his blindness. He is accompanied by a chorus, which narrates events to the sound of wind instruments and drums, and by secondary characters, who help him accomplish his goals. The plot, which the audience would know quite well, is almost irrelevant—certainly it does not drive the action of the drama forward. The characters speak their lines in a stylized manner, and make no attempt at realistic tonal inflections. Three drums and a flute accompany their lines, their movements turn into dance, and the performance lasts for a much longer time than it takes simply to read it. In fact, although Noh plays often read well on the page, the total effect is lost without the nonverbal elements. Zeami's own explanation of the power of silence in Noh drama, from his essay "The One Mind Linking All Powers," gives a hint at what one would miss in reading (**Reading 18.6**):

READING 18.6
_____

from Zeami Motokiyo, "The One Mind Linking All Powers" (early fifteenth century)

Sometimes spectators of the Noh say that the moments of "no action" are the most enjoyable. This is one of the actor's secret arts. Dancing and singing, movements on the stage, and the different types of miming are all acts performed by the body. Moments of "no action" occur in between. When we examine why such moments without action are enjoyable, we find that it is due to the underlying spiritual strength of the actor, which unremittingly holds the attention.

The audience, in other words, is invited to see beyond everyday reality into the farther reaches of existence, into the aesthetic realm of the *yugen*.

The Azuchi-Momoyama Period (1573–1615): Foreign Influences

Even as Japanese culture flourished under the patronage of the Ashikaga shoguns, the country simultaneously endured many years of sometimes debilitating civil war. By the middle of the sixteenth century, the Ashikaga family had lost all semblance of power, and various *daimyo* controlled the provinces once again. Finally, one of their number, Oda Nobunaga [OH-dah NOH-boo-nah-gah] (1534–1582), son of a minor vassal, forged enough alliances to unify the country under a single administration. By 1573, Nobunaga had driven what remained of the Ashikaga out of Kyoto, inaugurating a period now known as the Azuchi-Momoyama, named for the location of Nobunaga's castle at Azuchi on Lake Biwa and that of his successor, Hideyoshi [hid-eh-YOH-shee] (1537–1598), at Momoyama, literally "Peach Hill," after an orchard of peach trees later planted on the ruins of the castle, south of Kyoto.

Nobunaga's victory was aided by the gunpowder and firearms introduced to Japan by Portuguese traders after they arrived in 1543. During the reign of Nobunaga, the West greatly expanded trade throughout Japan. In 1543, Portuguese traders first entered Japanese waters, and, from the Portuguese, the Japanese *daimyo* soon learned about Western firearms. Within 30 years, the civil conflict that Hideyoshi would bring to an end in 1590 was being fought with guns and cannon. Almost at the same time, in 1549, the priest Francis Xavier (1506–1552), one of the founders of the Jesuits, landed at Kagoshima dedicated to bringing Christianity to Japan. By the 1580s, the Church had converted as many as 150,000 Japanese to Catholicism.

The Momoyama Castle Although the arrival of gunpowder surely encouraged the Azuchi-Momoyama rulers to build much larger, more defensible castles than those of the earlier shogun, the primary purpose of the castles was more to

Fig. 18.26 Himeji Castle, Hyogo prefecture, near Osaka. Momoyama period, 1581, enlarged 1601–1609. The Tokugawa shoguns destroyed most of the Momoyama castles in the early seventeenth century because they believed the castles encouraged other *daimyo* to challenge their power.

impress upon the world the power and majesty of the *daimyo*. The Himeji [hee-MAY-jee] Castle near Osaka (Fig. **18.26**) is an example. Like most other castles of the era—roughly 40 were constructed across the country—it was built at the crest of a hill topped by a **tenshu** [TEHN-shoo], a defensible refuge of last resort much like the keep of an English castle (see Chapter 10). Lower down the hill's slope was a massive wall of stone.

The original *tenshu* was three stories high, but three more *tenshu* were added later. Two are three stories and one rises five stories above the hilltop. The resulting fortress is at once virtually impregnable and almost delicate in appearance, with its winglike white plaster rooflines and sharply pointed triangular tiled gables. In fact, because of the graceful, ascending rhythms of its forms, it has come to be known as White Heron Castle.

Namban and Kano-School Screen Painting The presence of foreign traders in Japan, principally Portuguese and Dutch, soon found its way into Japanese painting, particularly in a new genre of screen painting known as **namban** [NAHM-bahn]. *Namban* literally means "southern barbarian," referring to the "barbarian" Westerners who arrived from the south by ship. In the most popular theme of this genre, a foreign galleon arrives in Kyoto harbor (Fig. **18.27**). The ship's crew unloads goods, and the captain and his men proceed through the streets of the city to Nambanji, the Jesuit church in Kyoto. The priests themselves are Japanese converts to Christianity.

The uniqueness of these paintings is that they present a convergence of cultures, encouraged by the prospect of trade, not only with Europeans but with the peoples of other Asian countries, unparalleled in world history. The Portuguese, with the help of slave labor from Africa, had

Fig. 18.27 School of Kano. Namban six-panel screen. 1593–1600. Kobe City Museum of Namban Art, Japan. Across the bottom left of the screen, African slaves, dressed in Portuguese costume, carry goods. In the center panel, another holds an umbrella over the head of a figure dressed in red.

established a base in Macao, which they had been ceded by the Chinese in return for suppressing piracy on the Chinese coast, and they served as the conduit between China and Japan, exchanging Japanese silver for Chinese raw silk, which the Japanese processed into textiles, particularly kimonos, of remarkable quality. Only the cultural syncretism of New Spain even begins to compare.

The *namban* screens are only one example of the many types of screens commissioned by the Azuchi-Momoyama *daimyo* to decorate their palaces and castles. Traditional Japanese interiors consisted of mostly open rooms with little or no furniture. These angular spaces could be softened and subdivided by the placement of screens. They were often used as a backdrop behind an important person, or to create an eating area, a reception area, or a sleeping area. Themes depicted on the screens include cityscapes, mythological scenes, depictions of great battles, and images of dramatic performances, daily life in the court, and the common people working in the countryside. Perhaps the most famous screens of the Momoyama period are those produced by the Kano school. The many talented members of the Kano family first attracted the attention of the Ashikaga court in the late fifteenth century, but they reached their ascendancy in the Azuchi-Momoyama period in the work of Kano Eitoku [KAH-noh AY-toh-koo] (1543–1590), great-grandson of the school's founder.

The most important screens and door-panel paintings by Eitoku were destroyed when Nobunaga's castle at Azuchi was destroyed in 1582 after Nobunaga's assassination, but one door-panel painting attributed to him does survive, *Cypress Trees*, originally a set of panels for a paper-covered sliding door, over 5 ¹/₂ feet high (Fig. **18.28**). The twisted branch of a cypress extends from the right across the foreground of the composition. Behind it is a broad landscape of shoreline and cliffs, half-covered in gold-leafed clouds.

The panoramic sweep of such paintings is in keeping with the grandeur of the castles they most often decorated, and served to confirm the preeminent position of the Azuchi-Momoyama rulers and aristocracy who commissioned them.

The Closing of Japan

Nobunaga's successor, Hideyoshi, was deeply suspicious of Christianity. By 1587, he had prohibited the Japanese from practicing it and, in 1597, went so far as to execute 26 Spanish and Japanese Jesuits and Franciscans in Nagasaki. Succeeding rulers pursued an increasingly isolationist foreign policy. In 1603, Hideyoshi's successor, Tokugawa Ieyasu (1542–1616) instituted a shogunate based at his castle in Edo [EHH-doh] (present-day Tokyo) that was to last, in peace, for 250 years. Christianity, even as practiced by foreigners, was banned altogether in 1614. The new Tokugawa shoguns espoused a Confucianist philosophy based on the belief that every individual should be happy in their place if they understood and appreciated their role in a firmly structured society. While the emperor and his court were at the top of this structure, the Tokugawa shogun were its effective leaders, with 250 or so regional *daimyo* under the shogun exercising regional authority. The Tokugawa shogunate forbade the Japanese to travel abroad in 1635, and limited foreign trade in 1641 to the Dutch, whom they confined to a small area in Nagasaki harbor, and the Chinese, whom they confined to a quarter within the city of Nagasaki itself.

Japan would remain sealed from foreign influence until 1853, when the American commodore Matthew Perry sailed into Edo Bay with four warships and a letter from the President of the United States urging the Japanese to receive the American sailors. The following year, Japan formally reopened its ports to the world.

Fig. 18.28 Attributed to Kano Eitoku, *Cypress Trees*. Momoyama period, sixteenth century. Eight-fold screen (four shown), gold leaf, color, and ink on paper, height 67". Tokyo National Museum, Japan. The cypress is a traditional Japanese symbol of endurance.

The Influence of Zen Buddhism

Once Japan reopened its doors to world trade in 1853, the culture that it had developed over the 11 preceding centuries had an almost immediate impact on the West. Western artists of the nineteenth century, including Claude Monet [moh-NAY], Vincent van Gogh [go], and Mary Cassatt [kuh-SAHT], were fascinated by Japanese prints, which flooded European and New York markets in what amounted to an avalanche of images. Noh theater generated considerable excitement among Western writers. German playwright Bertolt Brecht and Irish poet William Butler Yeats would each write Noh plays of their own, and the American poet Ezra Pound freely adapted a number of traditional Noh plays. Especially appealing to Western sensibilities was Zen Buddhist philosophy, especially in forms more or less intentionally constructed to appeal to the modern Western mind.

The most influential disseminator of specifically modern version of Zen Buddhist philosophy in the West was the Japanese scholar D. T. Suzuki (1870–1966). In 1921, he and his wife began publishing *The Eastern Buddhist,* an English-language quarterly intended mostly for Westerners. His *Essays in Zen Buddhism,* published in London in 1927 and expanded upon in both 1933 and 1934, firmly established Suzuki's reputation. When, in April 1936, Suzuki was invited to London to speak at the World Congress of Faiths, he met the 20-year-old Alan Watts, who later the same year would publish his own very influential book, *The Spirit of Zen.*

After spending World War II in seclusion at Enkakuji [ehn-KAH-koo-jee], an important Zen temple in Kamakura, Suzuki moved to California in 1949, then to New York City, where from 1952 to 1957 he taught seminars on Zen at Columbia University. Composer John Cage attended these seminars for two years, and they deeply influenced his musical direction. A number of other twentieth-century Western intellectuals absorbed Suzuki's teachings as well, including psychoanalyst Carl Jung; poets Thomas Merton, Gary Snyder, and Allen Ginsberg; novelist Jack Kerouac; and potter Bernard Leach.

The many Asian members of the international Fluxus movement of artists, composers, and designers in the 1960s and 1970s, including Yoko Ono, popularized the Zen philosophical practice of posing riddles as a way to lead students to enlightenment. Ono's Fluxus compatriot,

Fig. 18.29 Nam June Paik, *TV Buddha*. 1974. Video installation with statue. Collection Stedelijk Museum, Amsterdam. Paik was deeply influenced by D. T. Suzuki through his close friendship with composer John Cage.

the Korean-born Nam June Paik [nahn joon pike] (1932–2006), one of the great innovators of video art, poses just such a riddle in his *TV Buddha* of 1974 (Fig. **18.29**). How, if he were alive today, would Buddha withdraw from the culture around him in order to meditate in pursuit of enlightenment? How, in meditating upon his own image reflected back to him on a TV screen, would he escape the charge of self-indulgent narcissism? Or would he escape it at all? What does it really mean to reflect upon oneself? These are the kind of questions that a Zen master might ask of Paik's work, just as they are the kind of questions a contemporary viewer might ask as well, which begins to suggest just how much Eastern philosophy has come to influence Western thought. ∎

What was Spain's primary motive in colonizing the Americas?

The arrival of Christopher Columbus in the Americas in 1492 inaugurated 125 years of nautical exploration of the globe by Europeans. Spain concentrated on the Americas. The Spanish did not come as families to settle a New World. Instead, Spanish men came in hopes of plundering America's legendary wealth of precious metals. The absence of Spanish women accelerated the intermingling of races in New Spain. How do you account for the inhuman treatment of native cultures by European explorers and colonial administrators?

How did the Portuguese impact West African culture?

The Portuguese slave trade transported many millions of Africans across the Atlantic on the Middle Passage, and the presence of the Portuguese is evident in much of the art produced in West Africa in the sixteenth century. How were the Portuguese first received in Africa? How is their presence reflected in West African art? How did the slave trade affect the population of New Spain?

To what degree did contact with Europe affect Mogul India?

Mogul leaders in India, particularly Akbar and Jahangir, not only introduced conventions of Islamic art to India but opened the doors of the country to English traders. The style of representation that resulted from this contact is a blend of stylistic and cultural traditions, East and West. The Taj Mahal, on the other hand, is a distinctly Mogul achievement. What aesthetic taste does it reflect?

In what ways did Ming China make contact with the wider world?

Nearly 100 years before the Portuguese sailed into the Indian Ocean, the Chinese emperor Zhu Di's Treasure Fleet, commanded by Zheng He, conducted trade expeditions throughout the area. What was the Chinese attitude toward the populations they encountered? One of the most important undertakings of Zhu Di's reign was the construction of the royal compound in Beijing, known as the Forbidden City. From what various cultural traditions does its design draw? In the Ming court, Dong Qichang wrote an essay dividing the history of Chinese painting into two schools, Northern and Southern. What are the characteristics of each? To what extent were these traditions related to painting elsewhere in the world?

Why did cultural refinement flourish in Muromachi and Azuchi-Momoyama Japan?

In Japan, political turmoil caused by war with the Mongols, instability at the imperial court, and, in the provinces, the increasing power of local military rulers, who would come to be known as *daimyo*, was finally mitigated by the ascendency of Ashikaga shoguns in the Muromachi period (1392–1573). In the midst of what often amounted to civil war, the Ashikaga shoguns were great cultural patrons. Why did they associate themselves with the arts? What was their attitude toward China and Chan (Zen) in particular? What elements of Japanese taste began to assert themselves in painting? In garden design? In the tea ceremony? What aesthetic feeling manifests itself particularly in Noh drama? How did trade with the Portuguese in the Azuchi-Momoyama period (1573–1615) influence Japanese culture? Screen painting became especially popular and depicted a wide variety of subjects. How does *namban* painting reflect Japan's increasing cultural syncretism? What aesthetic principles inform the large-scale landscapes of the Kano school?

PRACTICE MORE Get flashcards for images and terms and review chapter material with quizzes at **www.myartslab.com**

GLOSSARY

casta painting Paintings that depict the process of race-mixing in the Americas.

chattri Small pavilions that are traditional embellishments of Indian palaces.

cultural hegemony Cultural domination.

cultural syncretism The intermingling of cultural traditions.

daimyo Regional military leaders in Japan.

dry landscape A garden in a Japanese temple, distinguished by extreme simplicity and constructed largely from pebbles and rocks and a few carefully groomed plantings, that was conceived as an aid to meditation.

feng shui The practice of positioning objects according to certain principles that govern positive and negative effects.

fetish An object believed to have magical powers.

iwan A traditional Islamic architectural feature consisting of a vaulted opening with an arched portal.

lacquerware A type of decorative object made by coating it with several layers of lacquer and carving designs into the surface.

literati Literary intelligentsia.

Middle Passage The triangular trade route: Europe to Africa, Africa to the Americas, the Americas to Europe.

namban A genre of screen painting that emerged in Japan during the Momoyama period and whose imagery was influenced by the arrival by ship of Westerners.

Noh A type of Japanese dramatic play that includes music, chanting, dance, poetry, prose, mime, and elaborate masks and costumes, to create a total theatrical experience.

pietra dura A mosaic technique using precious and semiprecious stones.

porcelain A type of ceramic made by combining kaolin-rich clays with feldspar and sometimes quartz and fired at a high temperature.

T'ai Chi Ch'uan The Chinese martial art that includes both solo forms, or routines, and two-person forms known as "pushing hands."

tenshu A defensible refuge of last resort built as part of a Japanese castle.

wabi A Zen aesthetic of austerity, simplicity, and the appreciation of objects weathered by time.

Way of the Tea The Japanese tea ceremony—*chanoyu* in Japanese.

READINGS

READING 18.1

from Bernadino de Sahagún, *History of the Things of New Spain* (ca. 1585)

The History of the Things of New Spain *was written in the Nahuatl language under the supervision of the Benedictine monk Bernadino de Sahagún. First completed in about 1555, it relies on the memories of aging native Aztecs who had actually been alive during the conquest. The 1555 version has been lost. But in about 1585, Bernadino prepared a second version in Nahuatl. The description of Pedro de Alvarado's massacre of the Aztecs at the fiesta of Toxcatl, which follows, is from that later version and is particularly chilling.*

THE BEGINNING OF THE FIESTA

. . . All the young warriors were eager for the fiesta to begin. They had sworn to dance and sing with all their hearts, so that the Spaniards would marvel at the beauty of the rituals.

The procession began, and the celebrants filed into the temple patio to dance the Dance of the Serpent. When they were all together in the patio, the songs and the dance began. Those who had fasted for twenty days and those who had fasted for a year were in command of the others; they kept the dancers in file with their pine wands. (If anyone wished to urinate, he did not stop dancing, but simply opened his clothing at the hips and 10 separated his clusters of heron feathers.)

If anyone disobeyed the leaders or was not in his proper place they struck him on the hips and shoulders. Then they drove him out of the patio, beating him and shoving him from behind. They pushed him so hard that he sprawled to the ground, and they dragged him outside by the ears. No one dared to say a word about this punishment, for those who had fasted during the year were feared and venerated . . .

The great captains, the bravest warriors, danced at the head of the files to guide the others. The youths followed at a slight 20 distance. Some of the youths wore their hair gathered into large locks, a sign that they had never taken any captives. Others carried their headdresses on their shoulders; they had taken captives, but only with help.

Then came the recruits, who were called "the young warriors." They had each captured an enemy or two. The others called to them: "Come, comrades, show us how brave you are! Dance with all your hearts!"

THE SPANIARDS ATTACK THE CELEBRANTS

At this moment in the fiesta, when the dance was loveliest and when song was linked to song, the Spaniards were seized with 30 an urge to kill the celebrants. They all ran forward, armed as if for battle. They closed the entrances and passageways, all the gates of the patio: the Eagle Gate in the lesser palace, the Gate of the Canestalk and the Gate of the Serpent of Mirrors. They posted guards so that no one could escape, and then rushed into the Sacred Patio to slaughter the celebrants. They came on foot, carrying their swords and their wooden or metal shields.

They ran in among the dancers, forcing their way to the place where the drums were played. They attacked the man who was drumming and cut off his arms. Then they cut off his 40 head, and it rolled across the floor.

They attacked all the celebrants, stabbing them, spearing them, striking them with their swords. They attacked some of them from behind, and these fell instantly to the ground with their entrails hanging out. Others they beheaded: they cut off their heads, or split their heads to pieces.

They struck others in the shoulders, and their arms were torn from their bodies. They wounded some in the thigh and some in the calf. They slashed others in the abdomen, and their entrails all spilled to the ground. Some attempted to run away, 50 but their intestines dragged as they ran; they seemed to tangle their feet in their own entrails. No matter how they tried to save themselves, they could find no escape.

Some attempted to force their way out, but the Spaniards murdered them at the gates. Others climbed the walls, but they could not save themselves. Those who ran into the communal houses were safe there for a while; so were those who lay down among the victims and pretended to be dead. But if they stood up again, the Spaniards saw them and killed them. 60

The blood of the warriors flowed like water and gathered into pools. The pools widened, and the stench of blood and entrails filled the air. The Spaniards ran into the communal houses to kill those who were hiding. They ran everywhere and searched everywhere; they invaded every room, hunting and killing.

THE AZTECS RETALIATE

When the news of this massacre was heard outside the Sacred Patio, a great cry went up: "Mexicanos, come running! Bring your spears and shields! The strangers have murdered our warriors!"

This cry was answered with a roar of grief and anger: the peo- 70 ple shouted and wailed and beat their palms against their mouths. The captains assembled at once, as if the hour had been determined in advance. They all carried their spears and shields.

Then the battle began. The Aztecs attacked with javelins and arrows, even with the light spears that are used for hunting birds. They hurled their javelins with all their strength, and the cloud of missiles spread out over the Spaniards like a yellow cloak.

The Spaniards immediately took refuge in the palace. They began to shoot at the Mexicans with their iron arrows and to fire their cannons and arquebuses. And they shackled Motecuh- 80 zoma in chains.

READING CRITICALLY

When Columbus rescued Alvarado, the latter claimed that informants had told him the Aztecs planned to attack when the fiesta of Toxcatl was over in order to free Motecuhzoma. Does this claim alter your reaction to this Nahuatl version of events?

READING 18.5

Zeami Motokiyo, *Semimaru* (early fifteenth century)

Noh theater is very different from Western theater. It incorporates music, chanting, dance, poetry, prose, mime, and elaborate masks and costumes to create a total theatrical experience. It is perhaps closest to our musical form opera. But even opera cannot match the slow, ritualistic pace of Noh plays, which seek to create in their audience an ethereal sense of a transcendent, Zen Buddhist world. The following text, representing approximately the first half of the play, was written by one of the founders of the Noh tradition.

PERSONS

Prince Semimaru (tsure)
Kiyotsura, An Imperial Envoy (waki)
Two Palanquin Bearers (wakizure)
Hakuga No Sammi (Kyōgen)
Princess Sakagami, Semimaru's Sister (shite)

PLACE

Mt. Ōsaka in Ōmi Province

TIME

The Reign of Emperor Daigo: The Eighth Month

[The stage assistant places a representation of a hut at the waki-position. Semimaru enters, wearing the semimaru mask. He is flanked by two Palanquin Bearers who hold a canopy over him. Kiyotsura follows them.]

KIYOTSURA: The world is so unsure, unknowable;
    Who knows—our griefs may hold our greatest hopes,
    This nobleman is the Prince Semimaru   10
    Fourth child of the Emperor Daigo.

KIYOTSURA AND ATTENDANTS: Truly in this uncertain world
    All that befalls us comes our way
    As recompense for what we've done before.
    In his previous existence
    He observed intently the laws of Buddha
    And in this life was born a prince,
    Yet why was it—ever since he lay,
    An infant wrapped in swaddling clothes
    His eyes have both been blind. For him   20
    The sun and moon in heaven have no light;
    In the black of night his lamp is dark;
    The rain before the dawn never ends.

KIYOTSURA: His nights and days have been spent this way,
    But now what plan has the Emperor conceived?

    He ordered us to escort the Prince in secret,
    To abandon him on Mount Ōsaka
    And to shave his head in priestly tonsure.
    The Emperor's words, once spoken
    Are final—what immense pity I feel!   30
    Yet, such being the command, I am powerless.

KIYOTSURA AND ATTENDANTS: Like lame-wheeled carriages
    We creep forth reluctantly
    On the journey from the Capital;
    How hard it is to say farewell
    As dawn clouds streak the east!
    Today he first departs the Capital
    When again to return? His chances are as fragile
    As unraveled threads too thin to intertwine,
    Friendless, his destination is unknown.   40
    Even without an affliction
    Good fortune is elusive in this world,
    Like the floating log the turtle gropes for
    Once a century: The path is in darkness
    And he, a blind turtle, must follow it.[1]
    Now as the clouds of delusion rise
    We have reached Mount Ōsaka
    We have reached Mount Ōsaka.

[Semimaru sits on a stool before the Chorus. Kiyotsura kneels at the shite-pillar. The Bearers exit through the slit door.]   50

SEMIMARU: Kiyotsura!

KIYOTSURA: I am before you.

[From his kneeling position, he bows deeply.]

---

[1] In certain Buddhist texts, the rarity of meeting a Buddha is compared to the difficulty of a blind sea turtle's chances of bumping into a log to float on. The turtle emerges to the surface only once a century and tries to clutch the log, but it has a hole and eludes his grasp; this was a simile for the difficulty of obtaining good fortune.

SEMIMARU: Are you to leave me on this mountain?

KIYOTSURA: Yes, your highness, So the Emperor has commanded, and I have brought you this far,
But I wonder just where
I should leave you,
Since the days of the ancient sage kings
Our Emperors have ruled the country wisely,   60
Looking after its people with compassion—
But what can his Majesty have had in mind?
Nothing could have caught me so unprepared.

SEMIMARU: What a foolish thing to say, Kiyotsura, I was born
blind because I was lax in my religious duties in a former life,
That is why the Emperor, my father,
Ordered you to leave me in the wilderness,
Heartless this would seem, but it's his plan
To purge in this world my burden from the past,
And spare me suffering in the world to come,   70
This is a father's true kindness,
You should not bewail his decree.

KIYOTSURA: Now I shall shave your head,
His Majesty has so commanded.

SEMIMARU: What does this act signify?

KIYOTSURA: It means you have become a priest,
A most joyous event.

[Semimaru rises. The stage assistant removes his nobleman's outer robe and places a priest's hat on his head.]

SEMIMARU: Surely Seishi's poem described such a scene: 80
"I have cut my fragrant scented hair
My head is pillowed half on sandalwood."[2]

KIYOTSURA: Such splendid clothes will summon thieves, I fear.
Allow me to take your robe and give you instead
This cloak of straw they call a *mino*.

[Semimaru mimes receiving the mino.]

SEMIMARU: Is this the mino mentioned in the lines,
"I went to Tamino Island when it rained"?[3]

KIYOTSURA: And I give you this *kasa* rainhat
To protect you also from the rain and dew.   90

[He takes a kasa from the stage assistant and hands it to Semimaru.]

SEMIMARU: Then this must be the *kasa* of the poem
"Samurai—take a *kasa* for your lord."[4]

[Semimaru puts down the kasa.]

KIYOTSURA: And this staff will guide you on your way,
Please take it in your hands.

[He takes a staff from the stage assistant and hands it to Semimaru.]

SEMIMARU: Is this the staff about which Henjö wrote: 100
"Since my staff was fashioned by the gods
I can cross the mountain of a thousand years"?[5]

[Kiyotsura kneels at the shite-pillar.]

KIYOTSURA: His staff brought a thousand prosperous years,[6]

SEMIMARU: But here the place is Mount Ösaka,

KIYOTSURA: A straw-thatched hut by the barrier;

SEMIMARU: Bamboo pillars and staff, my sole support,

KIYOTSURA: By your father, the Emperor,

SEMIMARU: Abandoned,

CHORUS: I meet my unsure fate at Mount Ösaka.   110
You who know me, you who know me not[7]
Behold—this is how a prince, Daigo's son,
Has reached the last extremity of grief,

[He lowers his head to give a sad expression to his mask.]

Travelers and men on horses
Riding to and from the Capital,
Many people, dressed for their journeys,
Will drench their sleeves in sudden showers;
How hard it is to abandon him,
To leave him all alone;   120
How hard it is to abandon him,
To tear ourselves away.

[Kiyotsura bows to Semimaru.]

But even farewells must have an end;
By the light of the daybreak moon
Stifling tears that have no end, they depart.

[Weeping, Kiyotsura goes to the bridgeway.]

Semimaru, the Prince, left behind alone,
Takes in his arms his lute, his one possession,
Clutches his staff and falls down weeping.   130

[Semimaru picks up the staff and kasa, comes forward, and turns toward the departing Kiyotsura. Kiyotsura stops at the second pine and looks back at him, then exits. Semimaru retreats, kneels, drops his kasa and staff, and weeps. Hakuga no Sammi enters and stands at the naming-place.] . . .

READING CRITICALLY

One of the aims of Noh theater is to reveal the inner strength of a character even in the most tragic circumstances. How does this selection reflect Semimaru's inner strength?

[2]The poem referred to is by Li Ho and is actually a description of Hsi-shih (Seishi) rather than a poem by her. The meaning of the original verses was that Seishi's fragrant locks rivaled the perfume of cloves or sandalwood; however, the dramatist here misunderstood the Chinese and interpreted it as meaning she had cut her locks and now would have to rest her head on a hard pillow of sandalwood. (See commentary by Tanaka Makoto in Yōkyoku Shu, III, 205 [Nihon Koten Zensho series].)
[3]From the poem by Ki no Tsurayuki, no. 918 in the *Kosinshu*.
[4]From the anonymous poem, no. 1091 in the *Kosinshu*.

[5]From the poem by the priest Henjö, no. 348 in the *Kosinshu*.
[6]There is a pivot-word embedded here: *chitase no saka*, the slope of a thousand years; and *saka yuku tsue*, the staff that brings steady prosperity.
[7]An allusion to the poem, attributed to Semimaru himself, no. 1091 in the *Gasenshū*. The poem, about the Barrier of Osaka, originally had a meaning something like: "This is the Barrier where people come and go exchanging farewells; for friends and strangers alike this is Meeting Barrier."

INDEX

Temple, model of found in Sanctuary of Hera, Argos, *113*
Temple Mount, Jerusalem, 285
Temple of Athena Nike, Acropolis, Athens, 141, 144, *145*
Temple of Fortuna Virilis, 178–179, *179*, 258
Temple of Inscriptions, 390
Temple of Inscriptions, Palenque, Mexico, *391*
Temple of Mars the Avenger, 194
Temple of Portunus, 178–179, *179*
Temple of the Golden Pavilion, Japan, 611, *611*
Temple of the Plumed Serpent, 388
Temple of Venus, 194
Temple of Vesta, *194*
Temples
  Americas, 388, 390–391
  Athens, 141, 144–145
  Egypt, New Kingdom, 81–85
  Etruscan, *178*
  Greek, *109*, 113–114, 116, 178–179
  Japanese, 611
  Jerusalem, 285
  Roman, 194
Temples of Hera, Paestum, Italy, *109*, 113, *114*, 116
Templo Mayor, Mexico City, 395, *395*, 589, 590, *590*
The Temptation of Christ, from *Les Très Riches Heures du Duc du Berry* (Limbourg brothers), *420*
Ten Commandments, 50–51
Tenji, emperor, 373
Tenochtitlán, 395, *591*, 591–592
Tenshu, 615
Teotihuacán, 388–389, *389*
Tepidarium, 205
Teresa de Ávila, 668
Terra-cotta soldiers, *222–223*, 222–223
Terraferma, Venetian, 512–513, *513*
Tertullian, 205
Terza rima, 442
Terze rime (Franco), 522–523
Tetralogies, 153
Tetrarchy, 254
Tetzel, Johannes, 565
Textile production, 433
Textiles. See Tapestry
Textiles, Inca, 393–394, *394*
Thales of Miletus, 139, 148
Thamugadi, North Africa, 174–175, *175*
Thangkas, 369
That Jesus Christ Was Born a Jew (Luther), 570
Theater
  Aeschylus, 153
  Athenian, 151–156
  comedy, 152
  Euripides, 154–155
  performance space, 155–156
  Sophocles, 153–154
  tragedy, 152–155
Theater, Epidaurus, *155*
Thebes, 68–69, 79, 81
Theebes, Egypt, 79
Themistocles, 135
Theocracy, 67
Theodora, empress, 265, 272, 273–274
Theodoric, church building under, 270–271
Theodosius, 116, 265
Theogony (The Birth of the Gods) (Hesiod), 110
Theotokos and Child with Justinian and Constantine, Hagia Sophia, 276, 276

Theotokos and Child with Saint Theodore and Saint George, St. Catherine's Monastery, 274, *274*
Thera, 94–95, 96, *96*
Thermopylae, 135
Thespis, 152
Third Temple, Jerusalem, 245
The Third Tone of the Sacred Psalmody, ambulatory capital from the Abbey Church of Cluny, *342*
Thirty-Six Line Bible, 571
"This It Is Said of Ptah" (Memphis), 69
"This Perfectly Still" (Ki no Tomonori), 375
Tholos, *102*, 102
Tholos, Epidaurus, *115*
Thomas More (Holbein), 628–629, *629*
Thorn-Puller, 180, *180*, 464
The Thousand and One Nights, 306, 311–313
Three Towers Reliquary, Aachen Cathedral, Germany, *417*, 417
The Three Varieties of Music, 273
Through-composed, 524
Thucydides, *History of the Peloponnesian Wars*, 111, 138
Thutmose, 81
Thutmose II, 81
Thutmose III, 81
Tiberius, 180
Ticsivirachocha, 394
Tigris River, 32
Timbuktu, Mali, 297–298
Titian, 488
  The Rape of Europa, 659, 660
  Reclining Nude, *519*, 519
  Sacred and Profane Love, 518, 518–519, 525
  Self-Portrait, 527, *527*
  Venus of Urbino, *519*, 519
Titus, 165, 197
Titus Andronicus (Shakespeare), 641
"To Be a Woman" (Fu Xuan), 224
Toccata, 525
Todaiji temple, Nara, Japan, 373, *373*
Tokugawa Ieyasu, 616
Tolkien, J. R. R., *The Lord of the Rings*, 319
Toltecs, 392
Tomb of Guiliano de' Medici (Michelangelo), 508
Tombs
  Banqueting Scene, from the Tomb of the Diver, 151
  Chinese, 214
  Egypt, New Kingdom, 81–85
  Etruscan, 177
  of General Zhang, *221*
  mastaba, *72*, 73, 78
  of Qin Shihuangdi, 220, 222–223
  Shang Dynasty, China, 216–217
  Soldiers and horses, Emperor Shi-huangdi tomb, *222–223*, 222–223
  Sumerian, 35–37
  of Tutankhamun, 87–88
Toreador Fresco (Bull Leaping), Crete, 97, *97*
Torquemada, Fray Juan de, *Indian Monarchies*, 601
Tostig, Earl of Northumbria, 336
Tournai, Belgium, 537–539
Tower of London, 622–623
Town Hall, Bruges, Belgium, *419*, 419
Trackers (Sophocles), 152
Trade routes
  See also Silk Road
  African, 297
  medieval Europe, *432*
  Song dynasty, 363

Trans-Saharan, map of, *297*
  Venetian, 512
Tragedy, 152–155
The Tragedy of Hamlet, title page of, *642*
The Tragical History of Dr. Faustus (Marlowe), 640–641
Trajan, 197
Tranquility of Mind (Seneca), 189
Transept, 258
Transfiguration of Christ, St. Catherine's Monastery, 268, *269*
Travels (Polo), 235, 363
Travels in the Mogul Empire (Bernier), 605
Treasure fleet, 606–608, *607*
Treasury of Atreus, *102*, 102–103
The Tree of Jesse, Chartres Cathedral, 406, *406*, 408
Très Riches Heures du Duc de Berry, 420, *420*
Trial of Veronese, 666–667
The Tribute Money (Masaccio), *471*, 471
Triglyphs, 146
Trilithon, *14*, 17
Trinity (Masaccio), 470, *470*, 539
Triptych, 538, 545, 546
Triremes, 135
The Triumph of Death (Bruegel), *581*, 581
Triumph of Federigo and Battista da Montefeltro (Francesca), 481
Triumphal arches, 197, *197*
The Triumphs of Oriana (Morley), 638
Trivium, 414
Trobairitz, 346
The Trojan Horse, Chora, Mykonos, 106, *107*
Trojan War, 103, *104*, 105–106
The Trojan War (Euripides), 155
Trotula, *On the Diseases of Women*, 416
Troubadour poetry, 346, 346–349
Troubadours, 346
Troy, 103, *104*
True History of the Conquest of New Spain (Díaz), 592
Trumeau, 341
Trumpet, 177
Tudor, Owen, 629
Tudor England. *See* England, Tudor
Tudor genealogy, 629
Tumulus, 177
Tunstall, Cuthbert, 571
Tuscan order, *178*, 178, 476
Tutankhamun tomb, 64–65, *65*, 87–88, 88, *91*
Tutankhaten, 87
TV Buddha (Nam June Paik), 617, *617*
Tympanum, 339, *340*
Tyndale, William, 571
Typology, 251
Tzenuit, 293

U

Uban II, pope, 343
Ukraine, 7
Ulama, 295
Umako, 372
Umayyad caliphs, 295–296, 300–301, 302
Umma, 292
University, 414–417
University of Bologna, 414
University of Paris, 401, 414
Upanishads, 228
Upper Church, Basilica of San Francesco, Assisi, Italy, *423*, 423–424
Ur. *See* Sumerian Ur
Urban housing, 192

Urban II, pope, 309
Urbino, Italy, 480–481
Utopia (More), 628, 649
Utrecht Psalter, from Benedictine Abbey at Hautvilliers, France, *328*, 328

V

Valmiki, *Ramayana (Way of Rama)*, 229
Van der Weyden, Rogier, *Descent from the Cross*, 543–544, *544*
Van Eyck, Hubert, *Ghent Altarpiece*, 540–541, 540–541, 548, 578
Van Eyck, Jan, 536, 540–543
  The Adoration of the Lamb by All Saints, *541*, 541
  The Annunciation, 540, *540*
  Ghent Altarpiece, 540–541, *540–541*, 548, 578
  Giovanni Amolfini and His Wife Giovanna Cenami, 542–543, *543*
Van Gogh, Vincent, 617
Vanishing point, 470
Vantage point, 470
Vaphio Cup, Sparta, Greece, 100, *102*
Vasari, Giogio, 436, 437, 467, 484, 492–493, 518, 536, 664
Vatican Library, 496
Vatican Palace, 498
Vaults, 196
Vedas, 228
Vedic tradition, 228–231
Venantius Forunatus, 511
Venice. See Renaissance, in Venice
Venice, from *The Nuremberg Chronicle* (Schedel), *573*
Ventadour, Bernard de, 346–347
Venus, 112
Venus of Urbino (Titian), *519*, 519
Venus of Willendorf, 6
Verily, Verily I Say Unto You (Tallis), 638
Verism, 184
Verrocchio, 184
Vernacular, 444
  See also Language
  Bible, 562, 566–567, 570–577
  definition, 440
  literature, 424, 440–443
Veronese, *Feast in the House of Levi*, 666–667, 667
Verrocchio, Andrea del, 469
Verse anthem, 638
The Very Sumptuous Hours of the Duke of Berry, 420, *420*
Vespasian, 193
Vespasian Psalter, 324, *324*
Vespucci, Simonetta, 477
Vessel in the shape of an ostrich egg, Royal Cemetery at Ur, *31*
Vesta, 112
Via dei Fori Imperiali, 194
Victory (Michelangelo), 656, *656*
Viderunt Omnes (Pérotin), 413
View of Rome (Anonymous), 494–495
Vigils, 192
Vijd, Jodocus, 540
Vili culture, 600, *600*
Villa La Rotunda (Palladio), 526, *526*
The Village of Secotan (White), 644, 645
Village plan, Skara Brae, *10*
Villanella, 551
Virgil
  Aeneid, 165, 180–181, 189–190, 209–210
  in Dante's *Divine Comedy*, 440–442
  Georgics, 189–190
Virgin and Child, from the Abbey of Saint-Denis, 425, *425*

PHOTO CREDITS

Chapter 1

PO Werner Forman/Art Resource, NY; 1-1 Ministere de la Culture et de la Communication. Direction Regionale des affaires Culturelles de Rhone -Alpes. Service Regional de l'Archeologie;1-2 © Yvonne Vertut; 1-3 Erich Lessing/Art Resource, NY; 1-4 Dr. Semenov Yu, 2004. Courtesy Palaeontological Museum, National Museum of Natural History of NAS of Ukraine, Kiev, Ukraine.; 1-5 © Photo Atlante/Folco Quilici; 1-6 The Nicholson Museum, University of Sydney. NM57.03; 1-7 © David Lyons/Alamy; 1-9 Réunion des Musées Nationaux/Art Resource, NY; 1-10 © Judith Miller/Wallis and Wallis/Dorling Kindersley; 1-11 Réunion des Musées Nationaux/Art Resource, NY; 1-12 © Werner Forman/Art Resource, NY; 1-13 Yan Arthus-Bertrand/Altitude/ Photo Researchers, Inc.; 1-14 © Joe Cornish/Dorling Kindersley 1-15 © English Heritage.NMR Aerofilms Collection; 1-16 © Christopher and Sally Gable/ Dorling Kindersley; 1-17 John Deeks/Photo Researchers, Inc.; 1-19 Zuni, "Buffalo Kachina". c. 1875. Wood, cloth, hide, fur, shell, feathers, horse hair, and tin cones. © Millicent Rogers Museum; 1-20 © Kenneth Hamm/Photo Japan; 1-21 Suzanne Larronde Murphy; 1-22 © Tony Linck/SuperStock; 1-23 William Iseminger, "Reconstruction of Central Cahokia Mounds". c. 1150 CE. Courtesy of Cahokia Mounds State Historic Site;1-24 © Ministere de la Culture et des Communication; 1-25 Susan Rothenberg, "Untitled". 1978. Acrylic, Flashe, Pencil on Paper. 20″ × 20″. Collection Walker ARt Center, Minneapolis. Art Center Acquisition Fund, 1979. © 2008 Susan Rothenberg/Artist's Rights Society (ARS), NY; page 7, Musee des Antiquites Nationales, St. Germain-en-Laye, France/Giraudon/The Bridgeman Art Library.

Chapter 2

2-1 © Nik Wheeler/CORBIS; 2-2 Courtesy of the Penn Museum, film # 152071 Gold vessel in the shape of an ostrich egg; 2-3 The Oriental Institute Museum, Courtesy of the Oriental Institute of the University of Chicago; 2-4 Courtesy of the Oriental Institute of the University of Chicago; 2-5 © The Trustees of The British Museum/Art Resource, NY; 2-6 © The Trustees of the British Museum/Art Resource, NY; 2-7 Courtesy of the Penn Museum object # B17694, image #150848.Mythological figures, Detail of the sound box of "Sound Box of the Bull Lyre"; 2-8 © The Trustees of The British Museum/Art Resource, NY; 2-9 Scala/Art Resource, NY; 2-10 Réunion des Musées Nationaux/Art Resource, NY; 2-11 Réunion des Musées Nationaux/Art Resource, NY; 2-12 © The Trustees of The British Museum/Art Resource, NY; 2-13 SCALA/Art Resource, NY; 2-14 © The Trustees of the British Museum/Art Resource, NY; 2-15 Z. Radovan/www.BibleLandPictures.com; 2-16 Erich Lessing/Art Resource, NY; 2-17 Courtesy of the Oriental Institute of the University of Chicago; 2-18 Bildarchiv Preussischer Kulturbesitz/Art Resource, NY; 2-19 © Gérard Degeorge/CORBIS; 2-20 © Livius.Org; 2-21 Scala/Art Resource, NY; 2-22 © Joel Wintermantle /Alamy; page 39, SCALA/Art Resource, NY.

Chapter 3

3-1 Scala/Art Resource, NY; 3-2 Werner Forman/Art Resource, NY; 3-3 © Dorling Kindersley; 3-6 © Staffan Widstrand/naturepl.com; 3-8 Vanni/Art Resource, NY; 3-9 Araldo de Luca/The Egyptian Museum, Cairo/Index Ricerca Icongrafica; 3-10 King Menkaure (Mycerinus) and Queen. Egyptian, Old Kingdom, Dynasty 4, reign of Menkaure. About 2490-2472 BC. Findspot: Egypt, Giza, Menkaure Valley Temple. Greywacke. 142.2 × 57.1 × 55.2 cm (56 × 22 1/2 × 21 3/4 in.) Museum of Fine Arts, Boston. Harvard University-Boston Museum of Fine Arts, 11.1738. Photograph © 2008 Museum of Fine Arts, Boston; 3-11 Réunion des Musées Nationaux/Art Resource, NY; 3-12 The Art Archive/Egyptian Museum Cairo/Gianni Dagli Orti; 3-13 The Art Archive/Egyptian Museum Cairo/Alfredo Dagli Orti; 3-14 Scala/Art Resource, NY; 3-16 © The Metropolitan Museum of Art/Art Resource, NY. 3-17 © Peter A. Clayton; 3-18 © Yvonne Vertut; 3-20 akg-images/Andrea Jemolo; 3-21 © The Trustees of The British Museum/Art Resource, NY; 3-22 Bildarchiv Preussischer Kulturbesitz/Art Resource, NY; 3-23 Bildarchiv Preussischer Kulturbesitz/Art Resource, NY; 3-24 Scala/Art Resource, NY 3-25 © The Trustees of the British Museum/Art Resource, NY; 3-26 Scala/Art Resource, NY 3-27 © Erich Lessing/Art Resource, NY; 3-28 Scala/Art Resource, NY; 3-29 Courtesy of The Bodrum Museum of Underwater Archeology, Bodrum, Turkey; pages 70-71, Werner Forman/ Art Resource, NY; page 75, ©The Trustees of the British Museum/Art Museum, NY; page 84, © The Trustees of the British Museum.

Chapter 4

4-1 Nimatallah/Art Resource, NY; 4-2 Figure, Cyclades, ca. 2500 BCE, Marble, height: 15-3/4″ (40 cm). Museum of Cycladic Art. Nicholas P. Goulandris Foundation, no. 206; 4-3 Archeological Museum, Iraklion, Crete/Studio Kontos Photostock; 4-4 Erich Lessing/Art Resource, NY; 4-5 © Mauzy photo; 4-6 © Roger Wood/CORBIS; 4-7 National Archaeological Museum, © Hellenic Ministry of Culture, Archaeological Receipts Fund; 4-8 Studio Kontos Photostock; 4-9 National Archaeological Museum, Athens/Hirmer Fotoarchiv, Munich, Germany; 4-10 © Vanni Archive/CORBIS; 4-11 © Maltings Partnership/Dorling Kindersley; 4-12 Studio Kontos Photostock; 4-13 Museum of Fine Arts, Boston, Henry Lillie Pierce Fund. Photograph © 2008 Museum of Fine Arts, Boston; 4-14 Erich Lessing/Art Resource, NY; 4-15 Erich Lessing/Art Resource, NY; 4-16 © Marco Cristofori/Corbis; 4-17 © Marie Mauzy; 4-18 Nimatallah/Art Resource, NY; 4-19 Image copyright © The Metropolitan Museum of Art/Art Resource, NY; 4-20 Image copyright © The Metropolitan Museum of Art/Art Resource, NY; 4-21 Scala/Art Resource, NY; 4-22 Akropolis Museum, Athens/Studio Kontos Photostock; 4-23 The Art Archive/ Acropolis Museum Athens/Gianni Dagli Orti; 4-24 © The Trustees of The British Museum/Art Resource, NY; 4-25 The Dipylon Amphora, funerary urn in the geometric style from the Kerameikos Necropolis, Athens, c.750 BC (terracotta); 4-26 A. D. Painter, "Hydria (water jug)". Greek, Archaic Period, about 520 BCE. Greece, Attica, Athens. Ceramic, Black Figure. H: 53 cm (20 7/8″) D: 37 cm (14 9/16″). Courtesy, Museum of Fine Arts, Boston. Reproduced with permission. © 2005 Museum of Fine Arts, Boston. All Rights Reserved; 4-27 Scala/Ministero per i Beni e le Attività culturali/Art Resource, NY; 4-28 Scala/Art Resource, NY; 4-29 Scala/Art Resource, NY; 4-30 The Art Archive/Musée Archéologique Naples/Alfredo Dagli Orti; page 95, Nimatallah/Art Resource, NY; page 114, Canali Photobank, Milan, Italy; page 115 (top left), Nimatallah/Art Resource, NY; page 115 (top right), John Decopoulos; page 115 (bottom), Courtesy of the Library of Congress.

Chapter 5

5-1 © Marie Mauzy; 5-2 © Marie Mauzy; 5-3 Nimatallah/Art Resource, NY; 5-4 The Art Archive/ Musée Archéologique Naples/Alfredo Dagli Orti; 5-5 With permission of the Royal Ontario Museum © ROM; 5-6 Studio Kontos Photostock; 5-7 © Marie Mauzy; 5-8 With permission of the Royal Ontario Museum © ROM; 5-9 © The Trustees of The British Museum/Art Resource, NY; 5-10 © The Trustees of The British Museum/Art Resource, NY; 5-11 ©The Trustees of the British Museum/Art Resource, NY; 5-12 "Book VII of The Republic: The Allegory of the Cave", from THE GREAT DIALOGUES OF PLATO by Plato, translated by W.H.D. Rouse, copyright ©1956, renewed ©1984 by J.C.G. Rouse. Used by Permission of Dutton Signet, a division of Penguin Group (USA) Inc.; 5-13 Scala/Art Resource, NY; 5-14 Martin von Wagner Museum, University of Wurzburg, Wurzburg, Germany; 5-15 Bildarchiv Preussischer Kulturbesitz/Art Resource, NY; 5-16 © Ruggero Vanni/CORBIS; 5-18 Erich Lessing/Art Resource, NY; 5-19 Scala/Art Resource, NY; 5-20 P. Zigrossi/Vatican Museums, Rome, Italy; 5-21 Tourist Organization of Greece; 5-22 Vanni/Art Resource, NY; 5-23 Scala/Art Resource, NY; 5-24 Réunion des Musées Nationaux/Art Resource, NY; 5-25 © The Trustees of The British Museum /Art Resource, NY; 5-26 Scala/Art Resource, NY; page 143, Studio Kontos Photostock.

Chapter 6

6-1 Henri Stierlin; 6-2 © 1996 Harry N. Abrams, Inc.; 6-3 Ministero per i Beni e le Attivita Culturali/Roma; 6-5 Penelope Davies; 6-07 Canali Photobank, Milan, Italy; 6-9 Erich Lessing/Art Resource, NY; 6-10 Timothy McCarthy/Art Resource, NY; 6-11 © Araldo de Luca/CORBIS; 6-12 © The Metropolitan Museum of Art/Art Resource, NY; 6-13 Vatican Museums & Galleries, Vatican City/Superstock; 6-14 Foto Vasari/Index Ricerca Icongrafica; 6-15 Scala/Art Resource, NY; 6-16 Gemeinnutzige Stiftung Leonard von Matt, Buochs, Switzerland; 6-17 The Art Archive/ Musée Archéologique Naples/Gianni Dagli Orti; 6-18 Pubbli Aer Foto; 6-19 Canali Photobank, Milan, Italy; 6-20 Canali Photobank, Milan, Italy; 6-21 Werner Forman/Art Resource, NY; 6-22 Robert Frerck/Woodfin Camp & Associates, Inc.; 6-23 Scala/Art Resource, NY; 6-24 Canali Photobank, Milan, Italy; 6-26 Hemera Technolgies/Alamy; 6-27 Henri Stierlin; 6-28 Cambridge University Press. Reprinted with the permission of Cambridge University Press; 6-29 Canali Photobank, Milan, Italy; 6-30 © Alinari Archives/CORBIS; 6-31 Scala/Art Resource, NY; page 194 (top),

Italy/Giraudon/The Bridgeman Art Library; **12-18** Harl 4425 f.12v Garden scene, the lover and dame Oyseuse (Idleness) outside the garden walls, from the 'Roman de la Rose', Bruges, c.1490-1500 (vellum), Netherlandish School/ British Library, London, UK/© British Library Board. All Rights Reserved/The Bridgeman Art Library; **12-19** Erich Lessing/Art Resource, NY; **12-20** Giraudon/Art Resource, NY; **12-21** © Achim Bednorz, Koln; **12-22** Réunion des Musées Nationaux/Art Resource, NY; **12-23** © Achim Bednorz, Koln; **12-24** Scala/Art Resource, NY; **12-25** View of the church Santa Croce and its surroundings (photo)/Florence, Tuscany, Italy/© Sylvie Allouche/The Bridgeman Art Library; **12-26** Scala/Art Resource, NY; **12-27** Alinari/Art Resource, NY; **12-28** Scala/Art Resource, NY; **12-29** "St. Francis of Assisi Preparing the Christmas Crib at Grecchio, 1296-97 (fresco) by Giotto di Bondone (c.1266-1337)San Francesco, Upper Church, Assisi, Italy/Giraudon/The Bridgeman Art Library International"; **12-30** Réunion des Musées Nationaux/Art Resource, NY; **12-31** © National Gallery, London/Art Resource, NY; page 408 (left), Sonia Halliday Photographs; pages 408-409, Vanni/Art Resource, NY; page 409, © Dorling Kindersley.

Chapter 13

13-1 © Atlantide Phototravel/Corbis; **13-2** © Hideo Kurihara/Alamy; **13-3** Effects of Good Government in the Countryside, 1388-40 (fresco), Lorenzetti, Ambrogio (1285-c.1348)/Palazzo Pubblico, Siena, Italy/Alinari/The Bridgeman Art Library; **13-4** © Alinari/Art Resource, NY"; **13-5** Canali Photobank, Milan, Italy; **13-6** Scala/Art Resource, NY; **13-7** Cimabue (Cenni di Pepi)/Index Ricerca Iconografica; **13-8** Galleria degli Uffizi, Florence.; **13-9** The Art Archive/Duomo Florence/Alfredo Dagli Orti; **13-10** G. W. Scott-Giles;**13-11** G. W. Scott-Giles; **13-12** Image copyright © The Metropolitan Museum of Art/Art Resource, NY; **13-13** Erich Lessing/Art Resource, NY; **13-14** The Art Archive/Victoria and Albert Museum London/Eileen Tweedy; **13-15** Snark/Art Resource, NY; **13-16** Courtesy of the Library of Congress; page 438 (top), Alinari/Art Resource, NY; page 438 (bottom), Canali Photobank, Milan, Italy; page 439, Scala/Art Resource, NY.

Chapter 14

PO Erich Lessing/Art Resource, NY; **14-1** Scala/Art Resource, NY; **14-2** Erich Lessing/Art Resource, NY; **14-3** © Arte & Immagini srl/CORBIS; **14-4** Canali Photobank, Milan, Italy; **14-5** Erich Lessing/Art Resource, NY; **14-6** Scala/Art Resource, NY; **14-7** Scala/Art Resource, NY; **14-8** (left) © Achim Bednorz, Koln; **14-10** Canali Photobank, Milan, Italy; **14-11** Canali Photobank, Milan, Italy; **14-12** Scala/Art Resource, NY; **14-13** Canali Photobank, Milan, Italy; **14-14** Nimatallah/Art Resource, NY; **14-15** Scala/Art Resource, NY; **14-16** Scala/Art Resource, NY; **14-17** © Achim Bednorz, Koln; **14-18** Scala/Art Resource, NY; **14-19** Scala/Art Resource, NY; **14-20** Alinari/Art Resource, NY; **14-21** Scala/Art Resource, NY; **14-22** Italian Government Tourist Board; **14-23** Scala/Art Resource, NY; **14-24** HIP/Art Resource, NY; **14-25** Leonardo da Vinci (1452–1519), "The Last Supper". 1495-97/98. Mural (oil and tempera on plaster), 15′ 1 1/8″ × 28′ 10 1/2″. Refectory, Monastery of Santa Maria delle Grazie, Milan, Italy. IndexRicerca Iconografica. Photo: Ghigo Roli; **14-26** Quattrone/Courtesy of Embassy of Italy; **14-27** Erich Lessing/Art Resource, NY; **14-28** Réunion des Musées Nationaux/Art Resource, NY; **14-29** Scala/Art Resource, NY; **14-30** Scala/Ministero per i Beni e le Attività culturali/Art Resource, NY; **14-31**Hirmer Fotoarchiv, Munich, Germany; pages 468-469, © Dorling Kindersley; page 469 (bottom right), The Granger Collection, New York.

Chapter 15

15-1 Scala/Art Resource, NY; **15-2** Scala/Art Resource, NY; **15-3** Erich Lessing/Art Resource, NY; **15-4** Canali Photobank, Milan, Italy; **15-5** Cameraphoto Arte, Venice/Art Resource, NY; **15-6** akg-images/Pirozzi; **15-8** Zigrossi Bracchetti/Vatican Musei/IKONA; **15-9** Foto Musei Vaticani; **15-11** Canali Photobank, Milan, Italy; **15-12** Image copyright © The Metropolitan Museum of Art/Art Resource, NY; **15-13** A. Bracchetti/P. Zigrossi/IKONA; **15-14** Canali Photobank, Milan, Italy; **15-15** Scala/Ministero per i Beni e le Attività culturali/Art Resource, NY; **15-16** Scala/Art Resource, NY; **15-17** Scala/Art Resource, NY; **15-18** ONB, Picture Archive, Vienna: NB 6.673-C; **15-19** Cameraphoto Arte, Venice/Art Resource, NY; **15-20** Piero Codato/Cameraphoto Arte di Codato G.P. & C.snc; **15-21** ©Demetrio Carrasco/Dorling Kindersley; **15-23** Galleria Dell'Accademia, Venice/Cameraphoto Arte di Codato G.P. & C.snc; **15-24** Scala/Ministero per i Beni e le Attività culturali/Art Resource, NY; **15-25** Cameraphoto Arte, Venice/Art Resource, NY; **15-26** Scala/Ministero per i Beni e le Attività culturali/Art Resource, NY; **15-27** Scala/Ministero per i Beni e le Attività culturali/Art Resource, NY; **15-28** Erich Lessing/Art Resource, NY; **15-29** Digital Image © 2009 Museum Associates/LACMA/Art Resource, NY; **15-30** (left) Piero Codato/Cameraphoto Arte di Codato G.P. & C.snc; **15-31** Scala/Art Resource, NY; **15-32** Rembrandt van Rijn, "Self-Portrait". 1659. Oil on Canvas. .845 × .660 (33 1/4 × 26); framed: 1.229 × 1.041 ×.089 (48 3/8 × 41 × 3 1/2). Andrew W. Mellon Collection. Image © 2007 Board of Trustees, National Gallery of Art, Washington, D.C.; page 504, Vatican Museums, Rome, Italy; page 505, © The Gallery Collection/Corbis.

Chapter 16

16-1 Pieter Claeissens de Oude, "The Seven Wonders of Bruges (Septem admirationes civitatis Brugensis)". Penel 34 5/8″ × 48 3/4″. Monasterium de Wijngaard, Bruges, Belgium. Private Collection. LUKAS, Art in Flanders, Belgium; **16-2** Johannes Stradanus, "Jan va Eyck's Studio". Oil Painting. Stedelijke Museum, Bruges. LUKAS, Art in Flanders, Belgium; **16-3** Johannes Stradanus, "Jan va Eyck's Studio". Oil Painting. Stedelijke Museum, Bruges. LUKAS, Art in Flanders, Belgium; **16-4** Image copyright © The Metropolitan Museum of Art/Art Resource, NY; **16-5** Erich Lessing/Art Resource, NY; **16-6** Erich Lessing/Art Resource, NY; **16-7** © National Gallery, London/Art Resource, NY; **16-8** © Erich Lessing/Art Resource, NY; **16-9** Derechos reservados © Museo Nacional Del Prado – Madrid; **16-10** Scala/Art Resource, NY; **16-11** Adoration of the Magi, 15th-16th century (tapestry), Flemish School/Cathedral of St. Etienne, Sens, France/Flammarion Giraudon/The Bridgeman Art LibraryXIR 188856; **16-12** Munchner Stadtmuseum; **16-13** Matthias Grunewald, "Isenheim Altarpiece". First Opening. Left to Right: "Annunciation; Virgin and Child with Angels, Resurrection". c. 1510-15. Oil on panel. Center panel: 9′9 1/2″ × 10′ 9″ (2.97 × 3.28 cm). Musee d'Unterlinden, GLMAR.; **16-14** Matthias Grunewald, "Isenheim Altarpiece". Closed from the Community of Saint Anthony, Isenheim, Germany. Center Panels: "Crucifixion"; predella: "Lamentation" side panels. Musee D'Unterlinden.; **16-15** © The Trustees of the British Museum/Art Resource, NY; **16-16** Erich Lessing/Art Resource, NY; **16-17** Albrecht Duerer, German (1471-1528). Draftsman Drawing a Reclining Nude, c. 1520. Woodcut. Horatio Greenough Curtis Fund. Photograph © 2007 Museum of Fine Arts, Boston.; **16-18** Bildarchiv Preussischer Kulturbesitz/Art Resource, NY; **16-19** Foto Marburg/Art Resource, NY; page 548 (top left, bottom right), El Bosco (Bosch) (1450-1516), "Garden of Earthly Delights". El Jardin de Las Delicias-Triptico Tabla. 220 × 195. Photo Oronoz. Derechos reservados © Museo Nacional Del Prado–Madrid; page 548 (bottom left), The Garden of Earthly Delights: Allegory of Luxury, central panel of triptych, c.1500 (oil on panel) (see also 3425), Bosch, Hieronymus (c.1450-1516)/Prado, Madrid, Spain/The Bridgeman Art Library; pages 548-549, The Creation of the World, closed doors of the triptych 'The Garden of Earthly Delights', c.1500 (oil on panel) (see also 3425), Bosch, Hieronymus (c.1450-1516)/Prado, Madrid, Spain/The Bridgeman Art Library.

Chapter 17

17-1 Erich Lessing/Art Resource, NY; **17-2** Erich Lessing/Art Resource, NY; **17-3** Erich Lessing/Art Resource, NY; **17-4** Bettmann, Corbis/Bettmann;**17-5** © The Trustees of The British Museum/Art Resource, NY; **17-6** Bildarchiv Preussischer Kulturbesitz/Art Resource, NY; **17-7** Metropolitan Museum of Art, Rogers Fund, 1921, (21.36.145). Art Resource, NY; **17-8** © The Trustees of the British Museum; **17-9** The Last Supper, pub. 1523 (woodcut), Durer or Duerer, Albrecht (1471-1528)/Private Collection/The Bridgeman Art Library; **17-10** © Bayer&Mitko–ARTOTHEK; **17-11** Bildarchiv Preussischer Kulturbesitz/Art Resource, NY; **17-12** Image copyright © The Metropolitan Museum of Art/Art Resource, NY; **17-13** akg-images; **17-14** The Meat Stall, 1568 (oil on canvas), Aertsen, Pieter (Lange Pier) (1507/08-75)/Private Collection/Noortman Master Paintings, Amsterdam/The Bridgeman Art Library International; **17-15** German National Museum, Nuremberg, Germany; **17-16** Scala/Art Resource, NY; page 576 (bottom), Image copyright © The Metropolitan Museum of Art/Art Resource, NY; pages 576-577, Albrecht Durer, "Adam & Eve," First state, 1504. Engraving, 9 7/8 × 7 5/8 in. Albertina, Vienna;

Chapter 18

18-1 Werner Forman/Art Resource, NY; **18-2** "The Moon Goddess Coyoisauhqui" (She of the Golden Bells), from the Sacred Precinct, now the Museo Templo Mayer, Tenoctitlan. Aztec, 1469 (?). Stone. D: 10′10″ (3.33 m). Enrique Franco Torrijos, Mexico City/Embassy of Mexico; **18-3** Codex Duran: Pedro de Alvarado (c.1485-1541) companion-at-arms of Hernando Cortes (1485-1547) besieged by Aztec warriors (vellum), Duran, Diego (16th century)/Biblioteca Nacional, Madrid, Spain/The Bridgeman Art Library; **18-4** Massacre of the Mexicans (vellum), Duran, Diego (16th century)/Biblioteca Nacional, Madrid, Spain/The Bridgeman Art Library;**18-5** akg-images; **18-6** Artist Unknown, "Atahualpa". Fourteenth Inca, 1 of 14 Portraits of Inca Kings. Oil on canvas 23 5/8 × 21 3/4 in. (60 × 55.2 cm). Brooklyn Museum. 45.128.189. Dick S. Ramsay Fund, Mary Smith Dorward Fund, Marie Bernice Bitzer Fund, Frank L. Babbott Fund; Gift of The Roebling Society and the American Art Council; purchased with funds given by an anonymous donor, Maureen and Marshall Cogan, Karen B. Cohen, Georgia and Michael deHavenon, Harry Kahn, Alastair B. Martin, Ted and Connie Roosevelt, Frieda and Milton F. Rosenthal, Sol Schreiber in memory of Ann Schreiber, Joanne Witty and Eugene Keilin, Thomas L. Pulling, Roy J. Zuckerberg, Kitty and Herbert Glantz, Ellen and Leonard L. Milberg, Paul and Thérèse Bernbach, Emma and J. A. Lewis, Florence R. Kingdon.; **18-7** Image copyright © The Metropolitan Museum of Art/Art Resource, NY; **18-9** Kunsthistorisches Museum, Vienna, Austria; **18-10** Gabinetto Fotografico della Soprintendenza Per I Beni Artistici E Storici, Firenze; **18-11** Bildarchiv Preussischer Kulturbesitz/Art Resource, NY; **18-12** De Espanol y Negra, Mulato (From Spaniard and Black, Mulatto), Attributed to Jose de Alcibar, c. 1760, Oil on canvas. M1995.039 #6 Denver Art Museum: Collection of Frederick and Jan Mayer, Photo: © James O. Milmoe Denver

Art Museum; **18-13** Attributed to: Manohar, "Darbar of Jahangir". Indian. Mughal period. About 1620. Northern India. Opaque watercolor and gold on paper. 35 × 10 cm (13 3/4″ × 7 7/8″). Francis Bartlett Donation of 1912 and Picture Fund 14.654 Courtesy, Museum of Fine Arts, Boston. Reproduced with permission. © 2007 Museum of Fine Arts, Boston. All Rights Reserved.; **18-14** South Asian and Himalayan Art. Freer Gallery of Art and Arthur M. Sackler Gallery Archives Smithsonian Institution, Washington, D.C. F1942.15a;**18-15** Scala/Art Resource, NY; **18-17** ©Doranne Jacobson/International Images; **18-18** Wan-go H. C. Weng; **18-19** © Jon Arnold Images/DanitaDelimont.com; **18-20** Pair of "Vases", Xuande Period (1426-1435), Ming Dynasty (1368-1644). Porcelain with underglaze blue decoration, each: 21 3/4″ × 11 1/2″ (55.24 × 29.21 cm). The Nelson-Atkins Museum of Art, Kansas City, Missouri. Purchase: Nelson Trust, 4045.1,2. Photograph by Jamison Miller.; **18-21** Yin Hong (China, Ming dynasty, late 15th -early 16th century). "Hundred Birds Admiring the Peacocks". Hanging scroll, ink and color on silk; 240 × 195.5 cm. © The Cleveland Museum of Art, Purchase from the J.H. Wade Fund 1974.31; **18-22** Shen Zhou (Chinese 1427-1509), "Poet on a Mountain Top". Ming Dynasty (1368-1644). Album leaf mounted as a handscroll; ink and water color on paper; silk mount, image: 15 1/4″ × 23 3/4″ (38.73 × 60.32 cm). The Nelson-Atkins Museum of Art, Kansas City, Missouri. Purchase: Nelson Trust, 46-51/2. Photo: Robert Newcombe; **18-23** ©Demetrio Carrasco/Dorling Kindersley; **18-24** DNP Archives.Com Company, Ltd./Tokyo National Museum; **18-25** Paul Quayle; **18-26** Steve Vidler/SuperStock, Inc.; **18-27** Naizen Kano, "Nanban Byobu (Nanban six-panel screen)". Kobe City Museum, Kobe, Japan. 1593-600. Photo: Galileo Picture Services LLC, NY; **18-28** Cypress by Kano Eitoku, Muromanchi period (1368-1573) (from an eight-fold screen, colour on gold leafed paper), /Tokyo National Museum, Japan/The Bridgeman Art Library; **18-29** Collection Stedelijk Museum Amsterdam; pages 594-595, © Digital Image © 2009 Museum Associates/LACMA/Art Resource, NY; page 596, Erich Lessing/Art Resource, NY.

Chapter 19

19-1 © Angelo Hornak/CORBIS; **19-2** The Coronation Procession of King Edward VI (1537-53) 1547 (w/c on paper), English School, (16th century)/Society of Antiquaries of London, UK/The Bridgeman Art LibrarySOA 2916; **19-3** Canali Photobank, Milan, Italy; **19-4** HIP/ Art Resource, NY; **19-5** Scala/Art Resource, NY; **19-6** Erich Lessing/Art Resource, NY; **19-7** Elizabeth I, Armada portrait, c.1588 (oil on panel), English School, (16th century)/Private Collection/The Bridgeman Art Library;**19-8** Bildarchiv Preussischer Kulturbesitz/Art Resource, NY; **19-9** © Dorling Kindersley; **19-10** © The Trustees of the British Museum/Art Resource, NY; **19-11** Titlepage of 'Mr. William Shakespeares Comedies, Histories and Tragedies', engraved by Martin Droeshout (1601-50) 1623 (see also 54369), English School, (17th century)/ British Library, London, UK/Giraudon/The Bridgeman Art Library; **19-12** Courtesy of the Library of Congress; **19-13** The Art Archive/British Museum/Eileen Tweedy; **19-14** Private Collection/The Bridgeman Art Library International; **19-15** Jan Brueghel the Elder and Peter Paul Rubens, "Allegory of Sight", 1616, oil on wood. Derechos reservados © Museo Nacional Del Prado–Madrid; pages 632-633, © National Gallery, London/Art Resource, NY.

Chapter 20

20-1 © Adam Woolfitt/CORBIS All Rights Reserved; **20-2** Juan de Herrera (begun by Juan Bautista de Toledo). "Aerial View of the Escorial". Detail from anonymous 18th century painting, Madrid, Spain. 1563-84. 625″ × 520″ (191 × 160 m). Instituto Amatller de Arte Hispanico, Barcelona, Spain; **20-3** © Bettmann/CORBIS; **20-4** (left) Scala/Art Resource, NY; **20-4** (right) Scala/Art Resource, NY; **20-5** Foto Musei Vaticani; **20-6** Foto Musei Vaticani; **20-7** Kunsthistorisches Museum, Vienna, Austria; **20-8** Europa, 1559-62 (oil on canvas), Titian (Tiziano Vecellio) (c.1488-1576)/© Isabella Stewart Gardner Museum, Boston, MA, USA/The Bridgeman Art Library; **20-9** Galleria degli Uffizi, Florence.; **20-10** Foto Lensini Siena; **20-11** Lavinia Fontana, "Consecration of the Virgin. 1599. Oil on Canvas. 276.8 × 184.4 cm (9′ 2 1/4″ × 6′ 2 1/4″). Inv. 49. Photo: Jean Bernard. Marseille, Musée des Beaux-Arts; **20-12** Canali Photobank, Milan, Italy; **20-13** Scala/Art Resource, NY; **20-14** Kunsthistorisches Museum, Vienna, Austria; **20-15** Scala/Art Resource, NY; **20-16** Erich Lessing/Art Resource, NY; **20-17** © The Trustees of the British Museum/Art Resource, NY; **20-18** Artemisia Gentileschi (1593-1652/3), "Self-Portrait as La Pittura". The Royal Collection © 2010 Her Majesty Queen Elizabeth II. Photo by A. C. Cooper Ltd.; page 662, Hervé Champollion akg-images; page 663, © National Gallery, London/Art Resource, NY.

TEXT CREDITS

Chapter 2

Reading 2.1, page 42: From "The Law Code of Hammurabi" from LAW COLLECTIONS FROM MESOPOTAMIA AND ASIA MINOR, 2/e, 1997 by Martha T. Roth is reprinted by permission of the Society of Biblical Literature. **Reading 2.2,** page 45: "The Blessing of Inanna" from MESOPOTAMIA: WRITING, REASONING, AND THE GODS by Jean Bottero, trans. by Zainab Bahrani and Marc Van De Mieroop. Copyright © 1992 by the University of Chicago. Reprinted by permission of The University of Chicago Press. **Reading 2.3,** page 61: From THE EPIC OF GILGAMESH, with an Introduction and Notes, trans. by Maureen Gallery Kovacs. Copyright © 1989 by the Board of Trustees of the Leland Stanford Jr. University. All rights reserved. Used with the permission of Stanford University Press. www.sup.org. **Reading 2.3a-e,** pages 46-48: From THE EPIC OF GILGAMESH, with an Introduction and Notes, trans. by Maureen Gallery Kovacs. Copyright © 1989 by the Board of Trustees of the Leland Stanford Jr. University. All rights reserved. Used with the permission of Stanford University Press. www.sup.org. **Reading 2.4,** pages 61-63: From The Hebrew Bible Genesis 2-3, 6-7 from the NEW REVISED STANDARD VERSION OF THE BIBLE, copyright © 1989 by the National Council of the Churches of Christ in the U.S.A. Used by permission. All rights reserved. **Reading 2.4a,** page 51: From The Holy Bible Deuteronomy 6:6-9 from the NEW REVISED STANDARD VERSION OF THE BIBLE, copyright © 1989 by the National Council of the Churches of Christ in the U.S.A. Used by permission. All rights reserved. **Reading 2.4b,** page 52: From The Hebrew Bible Song of Solomon 4:1-6, 7:13-14 from THE SONG OF SONGS: A NEW TRANSLATION AND COMMENTARY by Ariel Bloch and Chana Bloch. Copyright © 1995 by Ariel Bloch and Chana Bloch. Reprinted by permission of Georges Borchardt, Inc., on behalf of Ariel Bloch and Chana Bloch. **Reading 2.5,** page 54: From the Hymn to Marduk From MESOPOTAMIA: WRITING, REASONING, AND THE GODS by Jean Bottero, trans. by Zainab Bahrani and Marc Van De Mieroop. Copyright © 1992 by the University of Chicago. Reprinted by permission of The University of Chicago Press.

Chapter 3

Reading 3.1, page 69: "This It Is said of Ptah" from ANCIENT EGYPTIAN LITERATURE: A BOOK OF READINGS, vol. 1, THE OLD AND MIDDLE KINGDOMS by Miriam Lichtheim. Copyright © 1973 by University of California Press. Reproduced with permission of University of California Press. **Reading 3.3,** page 86: From Akhenaten's Hymn to the Sun from ANCIENT EGYPTIAN LITERATURE: AN ANTHOLOGY, trans. by John L. Foster. Copyright © 2001. Used by permission of the University of Texas Press.

Chapter 4

Reading 4.1, page 128: From THE ILIAD by Homer, trans. by Robert Fagles, copyright © 1990 by Robert Fagles. Used by permission of Viking Penguin a division of Penguin Group (USA) Inc. **Reading 4.1a,** page 106: From THE ILIAD by Homer, trans. by Robert Fagles, copyright © 1990 by Robert Fagles. Used by permission of Viking Penguin a division of Penguin Group (USA) Inc. **Reading 4.2,** page 130: Excerpts from THE ODYSSEY by Homer, trans. by Robert Fitzgerald. Copyright © 1961, 1963 by Robert Fitzgerald. Copyright renewed 1989 by Benedict R.C. Fitzgerald, on behalf of the Fitzgerald children. Reprinted by permission of Farrar, Straus and

permission of Georges Borchardt, Inc., on behalf of the Estate of Ivan Morris. **Reading 11.5a,** page 375: "Elegant Things" from THE PILLOW BOOK OF SEI SHONAGON, tr. Ivan Morris. Copyright © 1991 by Columbia Univ. Press. Reprinted by permission of Columbia University Press and Oxford University Press (UK). Electronic rights for THE PILLOW BOOK OF SEI SHONAGON, tr. and ed. by Ivan Morris by permission of Georges Borchardt, Inc., on behalf of the Estate of Ivan Morris. **Reading 11.7,** page 391: Excerpt from POPUL VUH, trans. by Ralph Nelson. Copyright © 1974, 1976 by Ralph Nelson. Reprinted by permission of Houghton Mifflin Harcourt Publishing Company. All rights reserved.

Chapter 13

Reading 13.1, pages 454-455: From THE DIVINE COMEDY by Dante Alighieri, trans. by John Ciardi. Copyright © 1954, 1957, 1959, 1960, 1961, 1965, 1967, 1970 by the Ciardi Family Publishing Trust. Used by permission of W.W. Norton & Company, Inc. **Reading 13.2,** page 442: From THE DIVINE COMEDY by Dante Alighieri, trans. by John Ciardi. Copyright © 1954, 1957, 1959, 1960, 1961, 1965, 1967, 1970 by the Ciardi Family Publishing Trust. Used by permission of W.W. Norton & Company, Inc. **Reading 13.3,** page 443: From THE DIVINE COMEDY by Dante Alighieri, trans. by John Ciardi. Copyright © 1954, 1957, 1959, 1960, 1961, 1965, 1967, 1970 by the Ciardi Family Publishing Trust. Used by permission of W.W. Norton & Company, Inc. **Reading 13.4a,** page 445: From THE DECAMERON OF GIOVANNI BOCCACCIO, tr. Frances Winwar, copyright 1930 The Limited Editions Club, Inc.; renewed 1957. Used by permission. **Reading 13.6,** page 448: Excerpt from Sonnet 338; Sonnet 134 are from THE POETRY OF PETRARCH, trans. by David Young. Translation copyright © 2004 by David Young. Reprinted by permission of Farrar, Straus & Giroux, LLC **READING 13.7,** page 448: From "Prologue" from THE PORTABLE CHAUCER, ed. by Theodore Morrison, trans. by Theodore Morrison, copyright © 1949, © 1975, renewed © 1977 by Theodore Morrison. Used by permission of Viking Penguin, a division of Penguin Group (USA) Inc. **Reading 13.8,** page 457: From THE DECAMERON OF GIOVANNI BOCCACCIO, tr. Frances Winwar, copyright 1930 The Limited Editions Club, Inc.; renewed 1957. Used by permission.

Chapter 14

Reading 14.2, page 479: The poem "Triumph of Bacchus and Ariadne" from LORENZO DE MEDICI: SELECTED POEMS AND PROSE, tr. Jon Thiem. Copyright © 1992 by The Pennsylvania State University. Reproduced by permission of Pennsylvania State University Press. **Reading 14.3,** page 479: From the book ORATION ON THE DIGNITY OF MAN by Pico della Mirandola, trans. by A. Robert Caponigri. Copyright © 1956. Published by Regnery Publishing, Inc. All rights reserved. Reprinted by special permission of Regnery Publishing, Inc., Washington, D.C.

Chapter 15

Reading 15.1, page 503: "Sonnet to John of Pistoia on the Sistine Ceiling" from COMPLETE POEMS AND SELECTED LETTERS OF MICHELANGELO by Creighton Gilbert. Copyright © 1980 by Creighton Gilbert. Published by Princeton University Press. Reprinted by permission of Creighton Gilbert. **Reading 15.5,** pages 532-534: From THE NOBILITY AND EXCELLENCE OF WOMEN, AND THE DEFECTS AND VICES OF MEN by Lucrezia Marinella, ed. and trans. by Anne Dunhill. Copyright © 1999 by The University of Chicago. Reprinted by permission of the publisher. **Reading 15.5a,** page 522: From THE NOBILITY AND EXCELLENCE OF WOMEN, AND THE DEFECTS AND VICES OF MEN by Lucrezia Marinella, ed. and trans. by Anne Dunhill. Copyright © 1999 by The University of Chicago.

Reprinted by permission of the publisher. **Reading 15.6,** page 522: "Terze Rime, Capitolo 13" from POEMS AND SELECTED LETTERS BY VERONICA FRANCO, ed. and trans. by Ann Rosalind Jones and Margaret F. Rosenthal. Copyright © 1998 by The University of Chicago. Reprinted by permission of The University of Chicago Press.

Chapter 16

Reading 16.1, pages 558-559: From THE HEPTAMERON by Marguerite de Navarre, trans. with an introduction by P.A. Chilton (Penguin Classics, 1984). Reproduced by permission of Penguin Books Ltd.

Chapter 17

Reading 17.4, page 585: From THE REFORMATION WRITINGS OF MARTIN LUTHER, James Clarke & Co./The Lutterworth Press (2002). Reprinted by permission of the publisher. **Reading 17.6,** page 572: From Francois Rabelais, GARGANTUA AND PANTAGRUEL, Book 2, chapter 7 (1532–64), tr. Paul Brians from READING ABOUT THE WORLD, vol. 2, ed. by Paul Brians (Harcourt Custom Publishing, 1999). Reprinted by permission of Paul Brians. **Reading 17.7,** pages 586-587: From THE COMPLETE ESSAYS OF MONTAIGNE, trans. by Donald Frame. Copyright © 1957, 1958, 1976 by the Board of Trustees of the Leland Stanford Junior University, renewed 1971, 1976. All rights reserved. Used with permission of Stanford University Press. www.sup.org.

Chapter 18

Reading 18.1, pages 619-620: From FLORENTINE CODEX: GENERAL HISTORY OF THE THINGS OF NEW SPAIN by Bernardino de Sahagun, trans. by Arthur J.O. Anderson and Charles E. Dibble (1970). Reprinted by permission of the University of Utah Press. **Reading 18.5,** pages 620-621: From "Semimaru" by Zeami Motokiyo from TWENTY PLAYS OF THE NO THEATRE by Donald Keene, trans. by Royall Tyler. Copyright © 1970 by Columbia University Press. Reprinted with permission of the publisher. **Reading 18.6,** page 614: "The One Mind Linking All Powers" by Zeami Motokiyo from ANTHOLOGY OF JAPANESE LITERATURE, comp. and ed. by Donald Keene, copyright © 1955 by Grove Press, Inc. Used by permission of Grove/Atlantic, Inc.

Chapter 19

Reading 19.4, pages 635-636: "On Monsieur's Departure" from THE POEMS OF ELIZABETH 1, ed. by Leicester Bradner. Copyright © 1964 by Brown University. Reprinted by permission of University Press of New England, Lebanon, NH. Electronic rights by permission of Brown University Library.

Chapter 20

Reading 20.3, page 666: From "The Trial of Veronese" from LITERARY SOURCES OF ART HISTORY by Elizabeth Gilmore Holt. Copyright © 1947 Princeton University Press; 1975 renewed by Princeton University Press. Reprinted by permission of the publisher. **Reading 20.4,** pages 671-672: From THE COLLECTED WORKS OF ST. JOHN OF THE CROSS, tr. by Kieran Kavanaugh and Otilio Rodriguez. Copyright © 1964, 1979, 1991 by Washington Province of Discalced Carmeliees ICS Publications 2131 Lincoln Road, NE, Washington, DC 20002-1199 USA. www.icspublications.org. **Reading 20.5,** Pages 672-673:DON QUIXOTE DE LA MANCHA by Miguel de Cervantes Saavedra, trans. by Charles Jarvis, ed. by E.C. Riley (Oxford World's Classics, 1992). Reprinted by permission of the publisher.